AT EASTER ROAD THEY PLAY

AT EASTER ROAD THEY PLAY

A Post-War History of Hibs

Volume One

John Campbell

BIRLINN

First published in 2011 by
Birlinn Limited
West Newington House
10 Newington Road
Edinburgh
EH9 1QS

www.birlinn.co.uk

ISBN: 978 1 84158 989 3

British Library Cataloguing-in-Publication Data
A catalogue record for this book is available from the British Library

Typeset by Iolaire Typesetting, Newtonmore
Printed and bound by MPG Books Limited, Bodmin

To my son Kevin

To my niece Melissa who was cruelly taken from this world in
2007 but who will forever live on in the memory

CONTENTS

ACKNOWLEDGEMENTS

Over the period of time taken to write this book I have been helped and encouraged by many friends and I'd like to thank them all for giving me such tremendous backing. Though the list is long I'd like to single out Brian Johnson from the Programme Shop in Albion Road for access to and use of Hibs match programmes and yearbooks for the whole of the period covered as without them the task would have been so much harder; former director of the club Stephen Dunn and fellow Hibernian author Ted Brack both of whom were kind enough to read the whole manuscript and offer hugely appreciated advice and encouragement and to Ted and Lawrie Reilly for their fantastic forewords. Sincere thanks also to Peter Burns, Neville Moir and all at Birlinn publishers.

FOREWORD

Foreword from a Legend

It is a fortunate man who is able to play for the team which he loves. I was lucky enough to do exactly that, and not only did I play for Hibs, but my career coincided with the most successful spell in the club's history.

Before I signed on at Easter Road, I went with my dad to watch the Hibees play. After I stopped playing I went back to following the team from the stands. I go along to every home match to this day.

Like all football clubs, Hibs have had their ups and their downs. In all honesty, I would have to say that the current team isn't the most talented or exciting in Hibs history. That doesn't matter though. They wear the green and white of Hibernian and represent our beloved team. Like my grandfather and father before me and my son after me, I follow the Hibs through thick and thin.

John Campbell's meticulously researched and thoroughly readable record of Hibs from the mid-1940s to the mid-1960s covers my entire playing career and moves forward from there to the exploits of my hugely talented successor, Joe Baker.

Reading *At Easter Road They Play* brought back memories of giants of Scottish football whom I played with and against. It also recalled some great matches which I took part in or watched with a Hibs scarf around my neck. It recounts leagues won and cups oh so nearly won and great nights in Europe.

I hope younger Hibs fans don't think that we Hibees of a mature vintage are only interested in the past. We're proud of our careers and of our club's achievements but we also want nothing but success for the present Hibs team and those who follow them.

One thing is for sure: it's good to know your club's history and this book certainly tells the story of Hibernian Football Club in the twenty years which followed the Second World War in a most enjoyable way.

After a quiet period for books on Hibs, we are currently enjoying a rich vein of publications related to our favourite team. That can only be a good thing. *At Easter Road They Play* is an excellent Hibernian book and I wish John Campbell every success with it.

Lawrie Reilly

Foreword from a Fan

I first met John Campbell when he was editing the popular fanzine, *Hibs Monthly*, and I was writing for that same publication.

I was immediately impressed with John and wasted little time in coming to the conclusion that here was a man who loved Hibs and cared greatly about the club. It was apparent to me that not only was John concerned about the team's current fortunes, but that he also had a deep knowledge and understanding of Hibernian's illustrious past.

These twin interests in the present and past of the Hibees served John well as he involved himself in a number of Hibs-related projects. These included the fanzine itself, match commentary on Hibs games and providing historical material for the club's official website. All of these were carried out in an accomplished manner.

Now John has turned his hand to authorship and again he has succeeded. He has produced a fascinating and information-packed season-by-season account of Hibernian Football Club from the years after the end of the Second World War through to the middle of the Swinging Sixties.

If you want to know how Hibs were faring during the early part of Clement Attlee's premiership, to learn about the team's progress as floodlit football and European club competition got underway or check out where the boys in green and white were in the league table as the Beatles and the Rolling Stones fought it out for supremacy in the pop music charts, then this is the book for you.

It is certainly a book for me. Having been weaned by my Hibs-supporting uncle on tales of the Famous Five, I started attending games in the late '50s just as that great forward line was beginning to break up. I saw all of the Five in a Hibs jersey but I never saw them all play together.

As a primary schoolboy, I did see almost every game Joe Baker played for Hibs, though, and what a privilege it was to watch a world class performer (and in my opinion, that is exactly what he was) play for the team I supported.

I also saw the mesmeric maverick that was Willie Hamilton tease and tantalise opposition defences as I travelled through my teenage years. As if that wasn't enough, I was at Fir Park in 1963 when a slim youngster called Patrick Gordon Stanton made his first-team debut for Hibs and marked it with a goal.

I watched these great players, and many more besides, in that glorious emerald green and white Hibernian strip and urged them on with a passion for our club which still burns in me to this day.

Reading *At Easter Road They Play* has brought back a multitude of memories for me. I have been transported back to great games, peerless players and tremendous times.

I think I would have enjoyed this book just as much if I had been 16 rather than 63. This is a book for all true Hibees, written by one of their own. Whether you experienced the games or saw the players described in these pages at first hand or if you simply had tales of them passed down to you by friends and family, then John Campbell's chronicle provides you with records and recollections, dates and data, fun and facts.

John knows his Hibs history, of that there is no doubt. He also knows how to share it with others in a manner which is enjoyable and entertaining and at the same time interesting and informative. For me, *At Easter Road They Play* was a pleasure-filled literary journey. I hope that it will be exactly the same for everyone else who turns its pages.

I wish to congratulate John on a fine piece of work and I commend his book to the Hibernian faithful.

Ted Brack

Chapter One

1946/47

BACK IN THE GROOVE

In the close season of 1946 the footballing authorities in Scotland were at loggerheads with the UK Government over the admission prices to Scottish matches in comparison to those south of the border. In essence, part of the admission price to a football match related to entertainment tax and as the Government had cut the level of that tax it was insisting that the reduction be passed on to spectators. The Scottish Football League took a different view and at its AGM voted to maintain the 1s 6d admission from the previous season especially as costs had gone up – players' wages, for example, had risen by 25 per cent. Perhaps unsurprisingly, the Government was less than impressed by the stance of the SFL and when the relevant Finance Bill was being debated in the House of Commons the Chancellor of the Exchequer issued a stern warning: 'I shall be keeping a close eye on practices in the Scottish football field between the present time and the next budget.' He went on to warn that if the reduction in admission charges was not passed on voluntarily then the Government would take steps to enforce it.

A week later the SFL Management Committee met and decided to ratify its first decision and retain the admission charge at 1s 6d in direct contradiction of the Government's wishes. A letter would be sent to the Chancellor detailing the reasoning behind the decision and seeking an early meeting to resolve matters. At the same meeting the draw for the Scottish League Cup was made and Hibs found themselves in a section with Hamilton, Third Lanark and Celtic, the ties being scheduled to begin in mid-September.

League football got under way on 10 August 1946 and Hibs began their campaign with an Easter Road fixture against Queen of the South. The Dumfries side must have wondered what hit them as the home forwards ran riot and notched up a total of nine goals for the loss of just one. Jock Weir hit four, John 'Cubby' Cuthbertson two and there were singles from the other three forwards, Johnny Aitkenhead, Archie Buchanan and Gordon Smith, while Armstrong was on target for the visitors.

In the following midweek, Hibs travelled to Ibrox and were a goal down to Rangers inside two minutes after Davie Shaw was harshly adjudged to have handled in the box. Despite the protests of the Hibs players the referee held firm and Torry Gillick scored from the spot. The loss of that goal seemed to galvanise Hibs. They came roaring back, and on the half hour a great run and pass by Smith allowed Aitkenhead to equalise. The Rangers fans in the 60,000 crowd did not like what they were seeing as Hibs were by far the better outfit, and they proved that by scoring what would be the winning goal just a minute into the second-half when Weir headed home a cross by Aitkenhead. Try as they might the hosts could not draw level, thanks mainly to some stout defending and a great performance in goals from Jimmy Kerr.

Hampden Park beckoned for the early league leaders but it would be to play Queen's Park in the league rather than any cup match. A close-fought encounter was settled by a single goal, scored by Archie Buchanan, ensuring Hibs stayed top with six points out of six. Only Aberdeen and Partick Thistle could match that record. Somewhat surprisingly, Celtic found that they were rooted to the bottom with just one point.

It was back to Easter Road for the next outing and Clyde provided the opposition. This turned out to be one of those games where one side dominated throughout but were frustrated at almost every turn by a combination of poor finishing, good defending and top-class goalkeeping. In the end, Hibs had to settle for a 1–0 win after Smith's cross found Jock Weir in space and the little forward crashed home a low shot to beat Sweeney in the Clyde goal. Although not a convincing scoreline it was a convincing display by the green and whites and it kept them at the top of the league.

A second successive home game saw Hibs taking on Hamilton in what turned out to be a five-goal thriller with the home side edging it 3–2. A double by McFarlane of Hamilton might have won them the points on any other day but Cuthbertson matched that feat for Hibs and Buchanan struck the decisive goal. There was a sadness hanging over the stadium that afternoon, however, as it became known that Paddy Cannon had passed away, aged 90. Cannon had a long association with Hibs, having joined the club in 1896 as trainer/groundsman and he continued in that latter role well beyond his 70th birthday. A noted athlete, he had held many Scottish records and actually took part in the Powderhall Marathon at the age of 62. A real character, Paddy was at Easter Road almost every day until he died and he would be sorely missed.

The unbeaten start to the season finally came to an end when Hibs went down 2–1 at Pittodrie against Aberdeen. It was a cruel blow to Hibs, who lost Gordon Smith to injury after just eight minutes. Although the winger tried to return after treatment, his movement was so limited that he left the field for good before half-time. Leading by a Harris goal after 30 minutes, the Dons were pegged back early in the second-half when Cuthbertson equalised. Indeed, Hibs looked the more likely to go on and win, even with ten men, but fate dealt a cruel blow ten minutes from time when Hugh Howie sliced the ball into his own net when trying to clear a cross.

Three days later an injury-ravaged Hibs travelled to Fir Park to face a Motherwell side yet to win in the league. A valiant effort by the men from Edinburgh proved not to be enough as the Lanarkshire side took the points in a 2–1 win. The visitors actually opened the scoring early in the second-half when Willie Peat fired home a direct free kick from around 20 yards, but Motherwell equalised within minutes following an uncharacteristic error by Kerr in the Hibs goal. The keeper had punched clear a cross but was too slow getting back to his goal line and that allowed Humphries to equalise. In the dying minutes a corner from the right was clutched cleanly by Kerr but as he went to steady himself, Brown bundled both him and the ball over the line which was permissible in those days, and the referee allowed the goal to stand.

It was back to Easter Road for the next encounter and Kilmarnock provided the opposition. Hibs had some players back from injury and gave a start to young Lawrie Reilly, who marked the occasion with a fine goal – the first of so many to come in his Hibs career – which was added to by Weir and Aitkenhead, who got two each, and Arthur Milne to create a winning score of 6–0. The big Easter Road crowd was in good voice and thrilled that Reilly looked the part in stepping up to the first team.

The games were coming thick and fast and only three days later Hibs were at home again, this time for the first Edinburgh derby of the season. Having hit Kilmarnock for six there was an expectation that Hearts might suffer a similar fate, but it was not to be as the men from Gorgie had a solid outfit and a particularly strong defence. Early chances were passed up by Hibs and Hearts' keeper Brown had two great saves from Buchanan. At the other end, Jimmy Kerr was under increasing pressure as the match progressed until finally he was beaten after a Kelly cross was blasted high into the net by McCrae. Hibs tried everything to get level but found Brown and his defensive colleagues in top form, and so the bragging rights were bound for Gorgie along with the two points. One Hibs player who didn't feature that afternoon was Arthur Milne – he had been transferred to St Mirren after falling out of favour.

One of the surprise packages of the season so far had been Morton, and it was to Greenock that Hibs next travelled in the final league match before the League Cup kicked in. An outstanding performance by Kerr kept the free-scoring Morton forwards at bay while, at the other end, Aitkenhead and Weir scored the goals to win the game. Kerr's performance, including saving a penalty, had the Hibs fans in the crowd in raptures and Weir's goal was a real peach. It was no surprise, therefore, when Weir became the subject of a transfer bid by Swansea. Thankfully, the Hibs boss Willie McCartney was able to say a polite 'no' as he was more than happy to keep him at Easter Road.

The League Cup sectional matches began for Hibs with a home tie against an improving Celtic and so it was gratifying that the home side had enough in its armoury to see off the Parkhead side's challenge. Reilly, who played at outside right in place of the injured Smith, was the only Hibs forward not to find the net, but his two assists were vital in helping his team to a 4–2 win. Celtic's goals came from former Hibs man Tommy Bogan and Hughie Gallagher, the latter in the dying moments of the match, but by then Hibs had counted through Buchanan, Aitkenhead, Cuthbertson and Weir.

The good start in the section continued into the next match when Hibs travelled to Douglas Park and beat Hamilton 6–3. Buchanan and Weir each scored twice and Cuthbertson and Aitkenhead weighed in with a goal apiece. An uncharacteristically weak performance by the Hibs defence allowed McGuigan, Devine and Rothera to score for the hosts.

Game three of six in the section brought Third Lanark to Easter Road and the visitors cashed in on the continuing uncertainty in the Easter Road rearguard by scoring twice through McDonald and Carabine. Hibs managed only one goal through Buchanan and the loss of this match could cost them dear.

Next up was a visit to Parkhead. Hibs scored early through Weir but couldn't get a second and paid the price when McAloon grabbed a late equaliser.

In the close season just past, Hibs had toured Czechoslovakia and one of the teams they had met there were guests for a friendly at Easter Road on 16 October 1946. Sparta Prague drew a crowd of over 20,000 and their play was sparkling to say the least as Hibs struggled to contain them. Goals by Kokstein, Smatlik and Cejp helped the visitors to a 3–1 win, with Sammy Kean on target for the hosts.

The return of Gordon Smith to the starting line-up for the next League Cup match brought a 2–0 home win over Hamilton, the goals coming from Smith himself and the prolific Weir, but it was obvious the team were going through a rough patch as their passing game had deteriorated and their defending was decidedly suspect.

The final League Cup match, away to Third Lanark, saw Hibs needing a win to progress into the quarter-finals and the players did not let themselves or the fans down. The home side scored first through Venters but then conceded to Smith and Eddie Turnbull, who struck fine goals to win the match 2–1 for Hibs.

By sheer coincidence, Hibs' league campaign resumed with a home tie against Third Lanark and the green and whites looked to be getting back to their best form in a fine 4–1 win, with Eddie Turnbull getting a double. Archie Buchanan and Jock Weir were also on target and McCulloch hit the consolation for the visitors. The win put Hibs to the top of the table, albeit on goal difference over Rangers, but it was back down to earth with a bump just a week later when a vastly improved Celtic handed out a 4–1 thumping at Parkhead in a very physical encounter that saw the visitors suffer injuries to Buchanan, Kean and Kerr.

With the cold weather making for unpleasant playing and spectating conditions, Hibs next faced mid-table Falkirk at Easter Road and once again paid the penalty for defensive frailties. Two fine goals by Aitkenhead and Smith gained only a point as poor marking allowed Wardlaw to grab a double for the Bairns.

A second successive home game brought high-flying Partick Thistle to Easter Road but a truly inspired performance by Gordon Smith certainly clipped their wings. Although not on the scoresheet himself, Smith laid on four of the five goals scored by Hibs and was easily man of the match. A double from Jock Weir was impressive, but Turnbull outdid him by scoring an excellent hat-trick. The Jags counted only through a late Murphy volley.

One of the sides struggling near the foot of the table were St Mirren, and Hibs didn't help their cause when they went to Paisley and recorded a 1–0 win, thanks to a strike by Jock Weir. The Buddies had recently signed Arthur Milne from Hibs and though he played well against his former employers he could not open up the Hibs defence.

The season had now reached its midway point and Hibs started the second half of it with a visit to Palmerston Park to face Queen of the South. In their last meeting, Hibs had crashed nine goals past the Queens goalie and although they didn't emulate that feat this time around they did score enough to win the game 3–1. Willie Peat and Gordon Smith were on target for Hibs, as was new signing Willie Ormond who had joined from Stenhousemuir for a reported fee of £12,000. Queens managed a consolation through Dempsey.

With the festive period fast approaching, Hibs and Rangers served up a Christmas cracker of a game in front of 40,000 fans at Easter Road and although Duncanson struck first for the visitors, Ormond's late equaliser was no more than Hibs deserved for their part in a wonderful match. The sporting press praised the players for a good, clean contest – which, it must be said, was not always the case when these sides met.

On the Saturday before Christmas, Hibs visited a frosty Shawfield and found themselves two goals down going into the final 15 minutes of the game. At that point, Willie McCartney reshuffled his forward line and both Smith and Turnbull found the target to secure a hard-earned point for the visitors. It was a master stroke by McCartney and would become his trademark in the years ahead.

A friendly at Dens Park, Dundee, on Boxing Day didn't really offer up the best of entertainment and many of the fans in attendance were disappointed that Gordon Smith didn't play. However, they did at least witness two fine goals from Ormond and Cuthbertson that gave Hibs a 2–0 win. Amazingly, there was a crowd in excess of 10,000 at Easter Road that same day as Hibs and Hearts reserves met, with the home side winning 4–1.

The last game of 1946 gave Hibs the chance to extend their unbeaten run to eight games, including the Dundee friendly, but it would be a tough task because although they had home advantage they were meeting a very good-going Aberdeen. As expected, it was a tough game with Hibs ahead through Turnbull until the last five minutes when the Dons finally got their reward for hard work as Harris saved a point with an equaliser.

New Year's Day 1947 took Hibs to Tynecastle, where a fine match was witnessed by a large holiday crowd. *The Scotsman* match report for the game suggested that but for Brown in the Hearts goal, Hibs might have scored more than three. To the home side's credit, they stuck to the task and managed two goals in reply. Turnbull and Smith scored within a minute of each other towards the end of the first-half and then shortly after the interval Walker pulled one back. Hibs then scored again through Willie Finnegan before a late strike from Kelly made the game look closer than it really was.

Twenty-four hours later, at Easter Road, Hibs defeated the amateurs of Queen's Park 3–1, all the Hibs goals coming in the first-half. Turnbull got two and might have had a hat-trick had he not missed a penalty. Peat got the other, and Aitken scored for the visitors just past the hour mark.

A further 48 hours had elapsed when Hibs ran out at Easter Road to face Morton. It was a horrible day weather-wise, and the light was poor from low-lying cloud. The conditions underfoot were not great either, and the combination of all these things helped make it a dreary match that ended 1–1. It could all have been so different as once Ormond had given Hibs the lead the home side then won a penalty, but for the second game in a row Turnbull saw his effort saved. Henderson then equalised for Morton. Late in the game, Hibs were awarded a second penalty which Smith stepped forward to take, only to see Morton keeper McFeat make another brilliant save.

After that flurry of matches, the players had a well-earned rest as they were not in action again for another week. They then travelled to Douglas Park to face Hamilton and, unusually, failed to find the net at all. Thankfully, Hamilton suffered a similar fate and so only the one point was dropped. However, these missed opportunities against the weaker teams would end up costing Hibs the title. In the Hamilton game it seemed the players were hell-bent on finding Gordon Smith in every raid forward. While the winger tried his best, for once he could not conjure up a winner. Somewhat unfairly, Smith was pilloried in the west coast newspapers with suggestions that he was too greedy on the ball and often flattered to deceive. That sort of nonsense was soon put to bed as Hibs next took on Kilmarnock at Rugby Park and destroyed them in a 5–3 win, with Smith very much to the fore. The Hibs goals came from a Turnbull hat-trick, Ormond and Smith. So chastised were the men of the west of Scotland press, they devoted their entire match report to praising Hibs and even forgot to name the Killie scorers!

The last game in January had Hibs at Recreation Park in Alloa to compete in a Scottish Cup first-round tie. Any hopes of an upset were quickly dashed as Hibs raced into a first-half lead and the poor Alloa players must have been praying for the final whistle long before the end. The green and whites scored eight times without reply. Returning from injury, Weir got four and Turnbull and Ormond each grabbed a brace. Once again though, it was the wizardry of Gordon Smith that caught the eye.

The win at Alloa meant that Hibs had gone 14 matches without defeat, but such runs will always end sometime and this one did at Easter Road in February 1947. The opponents were Motherwell and their defenders were in fine form in repulsing the home attacks. Wave after wave broke down and it was probably inevitable that the visitors would capitalise. That's exactly what they did in scoring twice through Redpath and Robertson. Hibs did get a late consolation – an own-goal by Paton.

A three-week break due to severe weather conditions making pitches unplayable meant that Hibs' next outing was against Rangers at Ibrox in the Scottish Cup. On a treacherous surface, neither set of players could manufacture a goal so a replay would be required. That replay would have to wait, though, as Hibs were involved in a quarter-final League Cup match with Airdrie at Broomfield, and what a cracker it was. The first-half belonged totally to Hibs, with Smith grabbing two goals and Airdrie struggling to contain him. The half-time cup of tea must have worked miracles as the home side came out and scored three times, Flavell getting a double and Dalglish the other. Hibs then fought back and levelled, Smith securing his hat-trick but Airdrie struck again, with Flavell emulating Smith. Finnegan popped up with a late equaliser to force a replay.

That game took place at Easter Road in the following midweek and was watched by more than 23,000 spectators, many of whom must have been hoping for another goal glut. They would be disappointed because scoring chances were few and far between. At the end of the day, only one was scored, by Finnegan, taking Hibs into a semi-final clash with Rangers.

Just to confuse everyone, Hibs first faced Rangers at Easter Road in their Scottish Cup replay where a crowd in excess of 50,000 watched both sides slugging it out and looking like they'd need extra time. Late in the game, however, Gordon Smith went on a mazy run and exchanged passes with Cuthbertson before setting Finnegan free on the left. Finnegan delivered a low ball into the Rangers box for Ormond to fire home. The Hibs fans were still cheering when their heroes struck again just 60 seconds later. Once again, Smith was involved: his low shot may have been going in anyway, but Cuthbertson made contact to ensure that the ball entered the net. It was a truly fantastic 2–0 win that would take Hibs into a quarter-final home tie against Dumbarton.

A week had elapsed since Rangers were beaten in Leith and this time out it was 'B' Division Dumbarton who stood in the way of progress. A first-minute goal from Smith made things look ominous for the visitors, but they dug in and made life hard for Hibs. It was well into the second-half before Cuthbertson made the tie safe and carried Hibs into the semi, where they would meet Motherwell. Incidentally on the same day that Hibs had to work hard to beat Dumbarton, another 'B' Division side were causing a major upset when Arbroath defeated Hearts 2–1 at Gayfield.

On 22 March 1947 Hibs and Rangers clashed for the fifth time this season, with the Edinburgh side undefeated following two wins and two draws. This was the League Cup semi-final and the match was played at Hampden in front of 125,000 fans. A storming start by the Ibrox outfit saw Hibs all but blown away as the Gers struck three times before the half-time whistle. Although Hibs pulled one back after the break, the mountain was too hard to climb and Rangers had finally tamed the Leith outfit at the fifth attempt. Playing in that game were the Shaw brothers, both full backs, with Davie in the green and white of Hibernian and Jock in the blue of Rangers. Both had excellent games and both subsequently turned out for Scotland in an international match against England.

A week later Hibs were back at the national stadium for the Scottish Cup semi-final clash with Motherwell and what a marathon that match turned out to be. The rules for this semi were that the sides must play to a finish and that led to Hibs and Motherwell going into the record books: the winning goal was scored in the 142nd minute! Hibs had taken the lead away back in the 18th minute when Turnbull crashed a shot home from 25 yards but Motherwell equalised through Kilmarnock, who converted a penalty kick. Ninety minutes came and went, followed by the regulation 30 minutes of extra time and still the sides were deadlocked. A further 22 minutes elapsed before Hibs finally got the winner – and what a winner it was. Motherwell keeper Johnston cleared upfield and the ball fell to Hugh

Howie some 40 yards out. Instead of controlling and passing the ball, Howie simply booted it back towards the Motherwell goal and it sailed over the stranded keeper and into the net. The bizarre thing was that Howie had played in over 100 league matches for Hibs and never scored a goal, but you can bet he enjoyed getting that one!

Prior to the final, Hibs had some league matches to play and the first of those took place at Brockville where, after 75 goalless minutes, the match with Falkirk was abandoned when torrential rain made the playing surface dangerous for the players. In the following couple of days Hibs moved to strengthen their side by paying Clyde £10,000 for Leslie Johnstone, who made an immediate impact by scoring against Celtic at Easter Road on his debut. Lawrie Reilly also scored to help secure a confidence-boosting 2–0 win.

Willie McCartney put out an experimental eleven to face East Fife in a friendly and it is debatable whether his experiment worked as Hibs lost 4–2. East Fife scored twice through Davidson while Morris and Adams also found the net and Reilly and Johnstone repeated their feat of scoring against Celtic.

Five days later, thousands of Hibs fans made their way to Hampden to form part of the 82,000 watching the Scottish Cup final against Aberdeen. The Dons had never lifted the trophy and of course Hibs had not won it since 1902, so whichever group of fans were celebrating at the end it would be a very special day indeed. After just 30 seconds it was the Hibs fans who were celebrating as a mix-up between defender and goalkeeper in the Dons defence left Cuthbertson with a tap-in to put the green and whites a goal up. Many a side would have struggled to recover from such a blow, but not Aberdeen. They immediately went at Hibs and soon had the Edinburgh men on the back foot. After 35 minutes Hamilton equalised and before the break the South African centre forward Williams drew three defenders towards him before firing home what would be the winning goal from a tight angle. It was devastating for Hibs and their followers, but in truth Aberdeen won the match fairly and squarely.

A dejected Hibs side had to pick themselves up again as they still had four league games to play. The first of those brought a 1–0 home win over St Mirren, with Johnstone getting the goal. A week later, Hibs travelled to Firhill to face Partick Thistle and although the Edinburgh side could not now win the title there was a determination to finish second. Their cause was helped by a 2–0 win, thanks to second-half goals by Combe and Ormond. Leslie Johnstone wore number eight that day in order to accommodate one Robert Stirling, an ex-amateur signed by Willie McCartney from Dumbarton. Stirling would not be around long and made only a couple more appearances. He scored in both, the first coming in an away match against Third Lanark which Hibs won 2–0 with Bobby

Combe getting the other. A long and often entertaining season drew to a close when Hibs visited Brockville to replay the earlier abandoned match and won 3–2, Stirling among the Hibs scorers.

In between those two final league games, Hibs took on Hearts at Easter Road in the East of Scotland Shield final and dominated the game for the first hour but only had a Turnbull goal to show for their efforts. Inevitably, Hearts upped their game and Conn snatched an equaliser. Close to the end of the match a degree of uncertainty in the visiting defence allowed Willie Ormond to nip in and score the winner.

Interestingly, on the day Hibs lost 3–2 at home to Falkirk in the league the reserves were at Ibrox beating Rangers in the final of the Second XI Cup, no mean feat in itself but all the more remarkable because it meant they'd completed the treble, having earlier won the Second XI League Cup and league.

Chapter Two

1947/48

CHAMPIONS!

The close season of 1947 saw Willie McCartney active in the transfer market again as he swooped to sign Alex Linwood from Middlesbrough. At 27 years old, Linwood had moved south from St Mirren after scoring around 130 goals for the Paisley outfit and being capped for Scotland against England.

Having reached the semi-final of the League Cup the previous season, Hibs were anxious to go one better in 1947/48 but found themselves in a tough qualifying section alongside Hearts, Clyde and Airdrie. Indeed, their League Cup campaign started really badly with a 2–1 home defeat by Hearts as Willie Ormond's goal was cancelled out with interest by Archie Kelly and Johnny Urquhart in front of more than 43,000 fans.

Unlike the previous season, the League Cup would be interspersed with league matches and Hibs kicked off their campaign with a fine 2–0 win at Pittodrie with Turnbull and Smith the scorers.

In the following midweek it was back to League Cup duty and Hibs were in sparkling form when they demolished Clyde 5–1 at Easter Road. Leslie Johnstone was dropped in favour of Bobby Combe and the latter was instrumental in helping Smith grab three goals. Hibs were not so prolific in their next outing and had to settle for a 1–1 draw at Broomfield in a League Cup tie that saw Alex Linwood score his first for the club before the home side equalised in controversial fashion. It seemed that only referee Calder saw a Picken shot cross the line and despite the protests he would not change his mind.

That incident at Broomfield may well have caused Hibs to react in the best possible way as they met Airdrie again four days later at Easter Road in the league and thrashed them 7–1. Two goals each for Linwood and Ormond were slightly eclipsed by a Leslie Johnstone hat-trick. The Diamonds' counter came via a Peden penalty.

The next three fixtures would see the conclusion of the League Cup section and in the first Hibs travelled to Tynecastle intent on revenge for that earlier defeat. It was not to be as Laing and Kelly found the mark and only Johnstone could do so for the visitors.

Around this time the club held its AGM and declared a profit from the previous season of £16,636, the double cup run helping to create a profit when a loss had existed from the previous campaign. Hibs immediately invested some of that money to purchase five acres of ground and intended to use it to develop the stadium further.

The penultimate League Cup tie saw Clyde lose out to their visitors by the odd goal in seven at Shawfield. Dixon (2) and Riley found the net for the home side but a rampant Hibs won the day with Combe, Smith, Ormond and Johnstone finding the net. The watching Scotland selectors must surely have been impressed by the play of both Combe and Smith, who were outstanding throughout.

An ultimately unsuccessful League Cup campaign ended on a high note when Airdrie were once again thrashed at Easter Road, this time by a scoreline of 5–0. Despite the somewhat 'industrial' tactics employed by the visitors, Turnbull, Ormond, Combe and a double from Johnstone ensured that football won the day.

It was time to start concentrating fully on the league now and Hibs next visited Tynecastle. Having beaten their Edinburgh rivals twice in the League Cup section, Hearts made it a hat-trick of wins when they overcame their opponents 2–1 in front of 33,810 fans. Willie Ormond got the Hibs goal and the Hearts keeper George Paton was hailed as man of the match as he denied the green and whites on numerous occasions. Laing, from a penalty, and Urquhart beat Kerr in the Hibs goal.

A 2–1 home win over Clyde followed, with Bobby Combe and Eddie Turnbull on target, but the main talking point concerned a 'goal' scored by Gordon Smith, who rode a tackle, skipped into the Clyde penalty area and shot the ball home – only for the referee to call play back and award Hibs a free kick just outside the box. It was a curious decision and a number of Hibs players took the referee to task, but his mind was made up and thankfully the home side didn't need the goal to collect both points as only Riley had found the net for the visitors.

A week later, Hibs were at Hampden to face Queen's Park and had to fight all the way to secure the points. Aitken and Blyth found the net for Queens but Ormond, Johnstone and Turnbull scored to secure a 3–2 win.

Fulfilling a friendly in the Borders saw Hibs send a strong eleven to Selkirk and eleven also proved to be the number of goals they scored. Combe and Reilly each completing a hat-trick, Jimmy Cairns got two and there were singles for Smith, Ormond and Turnbull.

Queen of the South arrived next and the Doonhamers must have wished they hadn't bothered as they were thumped 6–0, the highlight of the game being a wonderful hat-trick from Lawrie Reilly, who was in the side to replace Leslie Johnstone, the latter having been transferred back to Clyde for £10,000. The other three goals came from Ormond, Turnbull and Combe, with many fans expressing the view that right-back Jock Govan had pushed Reilly hard for man of the match with his swashbuckling runs.

Those two wins preceded a visit to Ibrox to face the league leaders. It would be nip and tuck all season between the two. On this occasion, the home side won out and took both points with a 2–1 victory after Hibs had scored first through Bobby Combe.

Lowly Morton were the next side Hibs faced and the green and whites had to play most of the game with just ten men after defender Peter Aird had to go off injured. The visiting side took the lead, but five minutes from time Ormond got a huge cheer from the Easter Road crowd when he netted a deserved equaliser.

On 1 November 1947 Hibs travelled to Fir Park to face Motherwell and began a spell of three games where Gordon Smith grabbed all the headlines. The winger got both goals to beat Motherwell 2–0, the first of those being described as a wonder strike after he had beaten five defenders in a great dribbling run in the build-up. Next, Third Lanark conceded eight without reply at Easter Road and Smith got five of them, only to say after the game that he was disappointed with his own performance and felt he had not played well! Finally, Dundee went down 2–1 at Easter Road and Smith scored the winner while Turnbull got the other. Those results put Hibs at the top of the table, but a 3–1 defeat at Falkirk with Linwood the scorer allowed Rangers back into the mix in a league title campaign that already had the look of a two-horse race.

A hat-trick from Willie Ormond – two goals coming from the penalty spot – and a double from Smith helped Hibs towards a 5–0 home win over St Mirren and started a sequence of results that would see the club go on a long undefeated run.

Pushing hard on the tails of Rangers and Hibs at the top of the table were Partick Thistle and it was to Firhill that Hibs next travelled at the start of December. Combe gave Hibs the lead in the first-half, but a late penalty conversion by Wright meant Hibs had to be content with a point.

A week later, Celtic visited Easter Road and snatched a point in a 1–1 draw despite Hibs being by far the better outfit on the day. Cuthbertson scored in the first-half and it looked as though the home side would get more, but Miller in the Celtic goal was inspired in holding them at bay. Sadly, Paton equalised in the second-half and another vital point had been dropped.

The Saturday before Christmas saw Hibs secure a 4–0 win over Aberdeen at home and although that result looked good on paper it is only fair to point out that the Dons finished the match with just nine men, having lost two through injury. That win over Aberdeen, with the goals coming from Smith, Linwood and a double by Ormond, put Hibs back at the top on goal average, but Rangers had three games in hand and so remained firm favourites to lift the title.

On the last Saturday of the year, Hibs went to Broomfield and won 3–0 against bottom-of-the-table Airdrie. On a day when the wind was of gale-force proportions with the rain lashing down it was a good outcome for the green and whites, who scored through Smith, Linwood and Combe.

The New Year didn't bring much improvement in the weather conditions, but the Edinburgh derby survived on a day when a number of games were postponed. Going into the game, Hearts were confident, having won the three previous encounters of the season, but their confidence was misplaced as Hibs set about taking total control of the game. That it was 0–0 at half-time is a miracle, but goals did come in the second-half, which was just ten minutes old when Bobby Parker handled in the box for Ormond to convert the penalty and Linwood soon added a second. A mini fightback saw Hearts score through Dixon, but Turnbull sealed the win with a third for Hibs. The vast majority of the 45,000 crowd went home happy while the Hearts fans were left to ponder whether the £10,000 spent for Flavell from Airdrie had been money well spent.

Two days later, Hibs were at Shawfield fighting out a 2–2 draw with Clyde. The visitors had the better of the early exchanges, Linwood firing Hibs ahead only to see McPhail cancel that out at the other end. Next, Long put the hosts ahead, but Hibs fans in the 20,000 crowd were delighted when Cuthbertson scored an equaliser.

Seven days after that, Hibs entertained Queen's Park at Easter Road and secured the points with a convincing 4–0 win. In its match report, *The Scotsman* commented on the 'wanderings' of Gordon Smith, querying as to his effectiveness when doing so. Smith's two goals should have given the reporter a clue that this Hibs side didn't hold with convention as their forwards often switched around to confuse the opposition. The other two goals were scored by Combe and Turnbull, neither of whom was accused of 'wandering'!

Palmerston Park hosted the next match as Hibs took on Queen of the South. A 3–0 win was achieved thanks to a Cuthbertson hat-trick, with all of the goals being set up by the wizardry of Gordon Smith. That result would have taken Hibs to the top of the league had it not been for the fact that Rangers scraped a 2–0 win against Motherwell with two very late goals. Over the years, strikes late in the game would serve Rangers well as this was a club with a never-say-die attitude.

The Scottish Cup draw had paired Hibs with Albion Rovers at Coat-bridge and that game was less than a minute old when the home side had a golden chance to take the lead, but Kerr saved and no further chances would be forthcoming. The visitors secured progress with a double from Cuthbertson, whose scoring form was good at this time. Joy at the result was short-lived when it was made known that Willie McCartney had taken ill at that game and had been taken home only to collapse and die later that evening. This was truly devastating news, and the whole of Edinburgh's footballing public went into mourning. In his 16 years as manager of Hearts, where he succeeded his father, John, he did not win any major trophies but would forever be remembered as the man who discovered Tommy Walker and many other Hearts stalwarts. Ten months after resigning at Tynecastle, he took over the reins at Easter Road and guided Hibs' fortunes in an upward direction, signing the players who will forever be remembered as the Famous Five.

A week later, Hibs hosted Rangers in a top-of-the-table clash. Going into the game, the visitors had a three-point advantage over their opponents. It was wet and windy in Leith that day, but that didn't deter 52,000 fans watching on as both teams served up some fantastic football without really looking as though they might score. With just seconds remaining, Alex Linwood chased a ball that looked as though it might be going out for a goal kick to Rangers, right down near the corner flag. Linwood reached the ball in time, fired over a brilliant cross and joined in the roar of celebration as Cuthbertson headed past Bobby Brown from six yards to win the points for Hibs. Willie McCartney would have been so proud of his charges and especially in the way that they had played to the final whistle.

It was 'game on' for the title now and Hibs knew that they could not afford to drop many points in the run-in. Of course they were still in the cup and easily disposed of Arbroath 4–0 at Easter Road in round two with goals from Smith, who got two, Linwood and Combe doing the business.

On Valentine's Day 1948 the green and whites travelled to Greenock, a notoriously difficult venue at which to gain points and won 2–1 with Smith striking the winner in the dying moments of the game.

Round three of the cup brought Aberdeen to Easter Road. These two sides had contested the final last season and Hibs were keen on revenge, something they achieved despite having only ten men for the whole of the second-half after Willie Ormond was unable to continue. The home side were a Cuthbertson goal up in the first minute and though Aberdeen equalised when both Ormond and Jimmy Kerr were off the park being treated, they were never in front at any stage. Further goals from Cuthbertson, Smith and Linwood carried Hibs through 4–2 and into the quarter-finals.

Following the untimely death of Willie McCartney, Hibs appointed

Hugh Shaw as his successor and he was in place to guide the club to a stirring 4–1 win at Cathkin over Third Lanark. With young George Farm in goals for the injured Kerr, his team-mate Cuthbertson grabbed a brace before Mitchell pulled one back, but further goals from Aitkenhead and Combe carried Hibs through and ensured the two points. To make Farm's day, he saved a penalty in an all-round good performance from the debutant. That same day a stunning scoreline was being fed through from Ibrox as Rangers went down 3–2 to relegation-threatened Queen of the South. The combination of those two results put Hibs back at the top of the table.

March 1948 began for Hibs with a home Scottish Cup tie against St Mirren where all the goals came in the first-half. After Combe scored, Linwood added two more before Mitchell pulled one back for the Buddies. But it would be Hibs at Hampden for the semi – and their opponents would be Rangers.

Ahead of that cup tie, Hibs faced two important league challenges if they were to continue holding aspirations of becoming champions. The first brought Falkirk to Easter Road. An early injury to Combe upset the balance of the home side, but they still secured the points with a 2–0 win, courtesy of goals from Linwood and Buchanan.

On 20 March 1948 Hibs went to Paisley to face St Mirren in yet another vital league clash and won both points with a stirring display that produced a 4–2 scoreline. Although the home side competed well and scored through Crowe and Lesz, the visitors were majestic and won with goals by Smith (2), Cuthbertson and Linwood. On the same day Rangers were involved in yet another shock scoreline as lowly Queen's Park won 2–1 at Ibrox. Who would have thought Queens would down Rangers twice! The combination of those results put Hibs three points clear at the top, although Rangers had two games in hand.

With the league race so finely balanced, it is hardly surprising that the Scottish Cup semi-final between Rangers and Hibs at Hampden a week later caused a frenzy of excitement. Astonishingly, the match attracted 143,570 fans, a record to this day for two clubs meeting in domestic competition, outside of a cup final. Sadly for Hibs, they would go out to a single goal scored by Willie Thornton after Jimmy Kerr's replacement, George Farm, made a catastrophic error in goals.

The cup dream was over yet again, but Hibs had their eye firmly fixed on the league title and their chances of lifting it were increased the following Saturday when they won 4–2 at Parkhead. Celtic made Hibs fight all the way and scored through Lavery and Evans, but Hibs won the day with goals from Linwood and Turnbull, who each scored a double. That same day, Rangers could manage only a point from a draw at Pittodrie. Hibs now had a three-point lead with three games to play while

Rangers had four to play. It was shaping for a thrilling close to the season.

Another week further on and Hibs won a crucial two points at home to a very strong Partick Thistle, thanks to a solitary strike from Eddie Turnbull. On the same day, Rangers were facing and drawing 1–1 after extra time with Morton in the Scottish Cup final, which would mean a replay. Elsewhere, Celtic won 3–2 at Dundee with a Jock Weir hat-trick and put to rest any thoughts of relegation.

Two days later, Hibs trounced Motherwell 5–0 at Easter Road to all but win the title. Goals from Combe, Turnbull, Smith and a double from Linwood had the huge Edinburgh crowd roaring. Although Hibs subsequently lost their final league match 3–1 at Dundee on the last day of the season, when Reilly scored the Hibs goal, they were still crowned champions as Rangers could no longer catch them. It was a great day for Hibernian even if tinged with sadness following the loss of Willie McCartney who was not around to see his 'babes' lift the league flag. As a footnote, it is worth pointing out that Hibs also won the reserve league and their newly created third team were also crowned champions of their league. All of this brought a degree of bright optimism to everyone associated with the club.

A short tour of Belgium was the reward for the players. While they were there, presumably unwinding after a hard campaign, they played a few games, among which were a 2–1 defeat by Standard Liege and a 2–2 draw with a Liege select.

Chapter Three

1948/49

BIRTH OF THE FIVE

When the new season started with a visit from East Fife, the league flag fluttered proudly over Easter Road and some 35,000 fans turned out to watch their favourites. An injury to Turnbull caused him to leave the field for 20 minutes for treatment and when he returned with his head heavily bandaged, Hibs were already a goal down. With eleven men on the park again, however, the hosts went into overdrive and goals from Smith, Linwood and Turnbull gave them a 3–1 half-time lead. A double from Aitkenhead, either side of a goal by Morris, secured Hibs the points in a 5–2 win. During the following week, Hibs travelled to Palmerston Park, Dumfries, and gained a point in a hard fought 1–1 draw with Queen of the South. Smith grabbed the vital goal.

Just 24 hours later, the Danish side Frem Copenhagen were at Easter Road for a friendly match and found Hibs too hot to handle with the home side cruising to a 4–0 win thanks to goals from Jimmy Cairns, Reilly, Smith, Bobby Johnstone and Jackie Bradley. Both Johnstone and Bradley had been impressing in the reserves and so manager Hugh Shaw took the chance to play them in the first team. Neither player let him down.

Saturday 21 August was Derby Day in Scotland and it was the turn of Hibs to host their fixture with Hearts. The champions had little difficulty in disposing of their visitors and only in a brief 15-minute patch in the second-half did Hearts look dangerous. They scored in that period, but they were already behind as Linwood had scored two first-half goals. Turnbull restored Hibs' two-goal advantage and but for the brilliance of Brown in the visitors' goal the defeat might have been much heavier.

On the Monday following, Hibs sent a side to Inverness to face Caledonian in a benefit match and won 6–2 with the goals coming from Combe, Aitkenhead and Smith, plus a hat-trick from Lawrie Reilly.

The last Saturday of August served up a cracker of a match when Hibs visited Shawfield to play Clyde. The hosts had looked the better side in the first-half and were unlucky to go in a goal down after Cuthbertson scored. Linwood then put Hibs two up, but Clyde got back level through goals by Wright and Davies only for the green and whites to step it up again with Reilly and Cuthbertson giving them a 4–2 advantage. Plucky Clyde struck again through Wright, but a dreadful blunder by the home keeper allowed Linwood to complete the scoring and secure a 5–3 win.

The following Wednesday, Hibs were involved in another eight-goal exchange but this time they had to settle for a point as newly promoted Albion Rovers, 4–1 down with ten minutes to go, punished slackness in the home rearguard with three goals. Inspired by Smith at his best, Reilly grabbed a hat-trick and Cuthbertson the other. Rovers countered through Craig, Love and Smith and a penalty by their central defender, one Jock Stein.

One more league match would take place before League Cup games began to enter the fixture list and that was at Pittodrie against Aberdeen. A double from Cuthbertson sealed the win, a penalty from Baird late in the game making the match look much closer than it actually was. One thing that Hugh Shaw took note of and spoke to his players about was the worrying trend of conceding penalties.

A more difficult League Cup section was hard to imagine as Hibs found themselves drawn with Rangers, Celtic and Clyde. The first match took place at Parkhead in front of 55,000 fans. Charlie Tully was outstanding for the hosts, who took the points with a single goal scored by former Hibs man Jock Weir in the third minute. Next up was a home tie with Rangers. Hibs had the better of the play but neither side could score, much to the disappointment of the 47,000 fans in attendance. Interestingly, *The Scotsman* reporter at the game later wrote that the game was 'marred by several incidents' – polite speak for tough tackling.

In the following midweek Hibs entertained Manchester United at Easter Road in a match where the proceeds went to the Willie McCartney Memorial Fund. The visitors won 1–0 with a goal from Buckle, although Hibs could and should have won the match – they were thwarted by a combination of poor finishing and great goalkeeping by the visiting keeper. A fabulous crowd of 35,000 enjoyed the spectacle and many were for the first time seeing a white ball used as the referee insisted on a change due to the failing light.

It was back to League Cup business on the Saturday and a visit from Clyde saw yet another penalty being awarded. Thankfully, it was to Hibs this time and Turnbull duly converted. A double from Cuthbertson and a fine strike by Linwood had Hibs 4–0 up at the interval and that's how the game finished.

A week later Celtic visited Easter Road and Hibs gained revenge for their earlier defeat by winning a thrilling match 4–2. It must be said that but for the form of Miller in the Celtic goal the margin of victory would have been far greater. Time after time he defied the Hibs attempts. Linwood put the hosts ahead and then as the home players swarmed around the referee claiming a penalty, Celtic broke forward and equalised through Gallagher. The non-award seemed to rattle Hibs because they conceded a second to the same player just after the interval. That acted as a wake-up call and the hosts poured forward in search of victory, securing it in style with goals by Smith, who got two – one from the penalty spot – and Reilly.

Ibrox was the next port of call and once again the robust tackling proved the talking point as Hibs went down 1–0 to a Thornton header that went in off an upright. It was tough luck on the visitors, with most reports suggesting a draw would have been a fairer result.

A gallant effort to push into the qualifying spot by beating Clyde 4–1 at Shawfield was thwarted when Rangers defeated Celtic to win the section. The Ibrox side went on to win the trophy by beating Raith Rovers 2–0 in the final. At Shawfield, Linwood grabbed a double and Smith and Cuthbertson one each but it proved not to be enough.

Hibs were back in Glasgow a week later to face Partick Thistle as the league campaign resumed and handed out a bit of a thumping to the Jags despite being under strength due to international call-ups. Wright and O'Donnell managed to count for the home side while every Hibs forward found the net – Turnbull, Cuthbertson, Aitkenhead, Linwood and Smith, who got a double. The result put Hibs on top of the league after Rangers fell 2–0 to bottom club Hearts at Tynecastle.

The stay at the top was short-lived. In their very next game, Hibs lost 2–1 at home to a struggling Celtic. Cuthbertson found the net for the home side but ironically, Leslie Johnstone, who had left Clyde again and signed on at Parkhead, scored a double to secure the points for his new club.

A week later Hibs faced the other half of the Old Firm when they travelled to Ibrox and played their hosts off the park with Gordon Smith in superlative form. The winger put Hibs ahead before Cuthbertson and Turnbull ensured a half-time lead of 3–0. The home side came out all guns blazing in the second-half and pulled one back through Thornton, but then came the goal of the game when Smith collected the ball some 30 yards out and crashed a shot high into the net to stun the home support into silence. A late goal by Gillick reduced the deficit, but the visitors were well worthy of their 4–2 victory.

It seemed that scoring goals away from home was coming easily. The home form, however, took another hit when Morton took both points in a seven-goal thriller. It was a game in which Hibs never held the lead and although Reilly hit the net in the last minute, something for which he would soon become renowned, it was too little too late for the green and whites, who now found themselves in second spot behind East Fife.

When the home crowd at Fir Park watched Hibs dominate the opening 35 minutes of the game they must surely have thought that Hibs were showing the kind of away form that had won them matches. They could not have been more wrong. Johnston put Motherwell ahead in 37 minutes and in the second-half the visitors were run ragged, losing four more goals and the game 5–1. Mathie, Goodall and two from Watson met only with a single response from Linwood in a game that Hibs would quickly want to forget.

As November drew to a close and the weather worsened, Hibs got back to winning ways, but had to thank Eddie Turnbull for scoring the only goal of the game against Third Lanark at Easter Road. That result and results elsewhere put Hibs back to the top of the table. In truth, though, the championship race was wide open as Dundee and Falkirk had entered the fight at the top. Meanwhile, Hearts hauled themselves off bottom spot after an excellent 2–0 win away to Morton.

The month of December opened for Hibs with a good 2–1 home win over Dundee. This would start a run of four games without defeat, but sadly the three other games played all resulted in draws. In the Dundee match the home side welcomed back Linwood and Smith from injury but lost Kean and Aird, which meant the squad was always running a little light. The first of those matches drawn was at Brockville where Falkirk lost a man to injury when they led by a goal from Inglis. Linwood equalised for the visitors following a Smith free kick, but the Bairns defended stoutly to see out the match and earn a worthy point. Hibs were still top but, ominously, Rangers had closed the gap to two points with two games in hand.

In mid-December Hibs welcomed a good-going St Mirren to Easter Road and proceeded to pound their goalmouth for 60 minutes without reward. The home crowd was stunned when a rare attack by the Buddies resulted in a goal after Kerr had fumbled a shot and Stewart scored from the resultant corner. A siege of the visitors' goal developed but it was not until the 86th minute that Hibs finally got the goal their play so richly deserved. Smith went on a mazy run down the right and then delivered the perfect cross for Reilly to head into the net.

On Christmas Day 1948, Hibs welcomed Queen of the South to Easter Road, where Davie Shaw lasted just 20 minutes before having to limp off injured. Shaw could not return and so Hibs played three-quarters of the match with just ten men. Quite late in the game, Reilly fired them ahead. The lead lasted just four minutes, Jenkins capitalising on an error by Kerr to shoot home an equaliser. This was the latest in a series of errors by the normally dependable Hibs goalie, but it must be said his general form was excellent and the mistakes very uncharacteristic.

A fast-improving Hearts side faced Hibs at Tynecastle on 1 January 1949 and within 20 minutes they were 2–0 up following goals from

Flavell and Bauld. A spirited Hibs fought back bravely and when Angus Plumb missed the ball in front of goal his team-mate Reilly was there to pounce and reduce the leeway with a low shot. With just four minutes left, a rejuvenated Hibs got level when Bobby Combe scored. With their tails up they went in search of a winner, but their misplaced enthusiasm cost them dear when a long clearance by the Hearts defence found Bauld out wide and his pass to Conn allowed the latter to race through and score a late winner. If ever there had been a time just to close a game out, this was it, but it was not in the nature of this Hibs team to do anything but try and score goals.

Forty-eight hours later, Hibs faced Clyde at Easter Road in front of 30,000 fans. In a bright first-half, the home side scored twice through Combe and Plumb. Linwood, who had left the Easter Road club and signed for Clyde, tested Kerr on two occasions but found the keeper in top form. The visitors lost Dunn to injury in the second-half, but they held out until the closing moments when Plumb got his second and Hibs' third in a merited 3–0 win.

The following Saturday, Hibs crossed the Forth to face East Fife at Methil on a day when the conditions underfoot were not ideal. The hard and bumpy surface often put a stop to creative play. Nevertheless, both sides served up a game worth watching. Fleming put the Fifers ahead. Plumb equalised and then got a second to give Hibs the lead. Adams scored next to level the tie, but inside the final ten minutes, Combe struck what proved to be the winning goal.

Lowly Aberdeen presented the next challenge at Easter Road. It was a close-fought affair in the first-half, but after the interval Hibs stepped up a gear and scored three times in a ten-minute spell to effectively kill off the challenge. The first count came from Plumb, who was certainly in form, and the third via Smith's deflected shot. It was the second that caused all the debate after the game. Ormond was felled and the referee pointed to the spot. He was immediately surrounded by Aberdeen players, who argued that the tackle had been made just outside the 18-yard line. Needless to say, the referee stuck to his guns and Jimmy Cairns duly converted the award. A goal by Hamilton reduced the deficit, but Ormond completed the scoring in the 4–1 win late in the game.

The Scottish Cup draw sent Hibs to Station Park, Forfar, where they won 4–0 in a game marred by tough tackling and poor playing conditions. Ormond and Turnbull gave Hibs a 2–0 half-time lead before Robbie hit the Hibs post with a penalty. Further Hibs goals from Plumb and Ormond should have sent Hibs and their fans home happy, but celebrations were muted following the sight of Gordon Smith being carried off on a stretcher three minutes from time following a particularly brutal challenge by Shaw, the Forfar centre-half.

Thankfully, Smith's injury was not as bad as first feared and he was in his familiar number seven jersey for the next match, which took Hibs to Coatbridge to meet Albion Rovers on league duty. With a strong wind at their backs the visitors were soon in attack and opened the scoring when Jock Stein was short with a pass back and Plumb added to his recent impressive tally by rolling the ball into the empty net. Smith then lit the game up with a stunning run and strike: the ball was in the net almost before the Rovers keeper moved. A penalty looked likely to increase the advantage, but the shot by Cairns struck the outside of the post. A third goal did arrive in the last minute when Smith doubled his tally. That win took Hibs back to the top of the table, the skill of Smith and the goals from Plumb having played a major part in putting them there.

Round two of the Scottish Cup brought Raith Rovers to Easter Road, where they went a goal down in nine minutes after Plumb finished off a three-man move with a crisp shot. The Fifers fought gamely and a goal from Brady near the end meant a replay the following midweek at Stark's Park. Ahead of that match there came an announcement from the Secretary of State for Scotland via the Scottish Home Department that following completion of this replay any draw in a first meeting would lead automatically to 30 minutes of extra time to minimise the need for midweek replays. Although perhaps considered an unlikely source for such an announcement, it was made with the full agreement of the SFA and the league management committee. The reason given was that it was designed to reduce absenteeism from the workplace. Clearly, avid supporters were attending such replays rather than going to work!

The Scottish Cup has a habit of throwing up thrilling games now and again and this clash fell into that category as Hibs scraped through by the odd goal in seven. A double from Collins and a strike by Penman had the home fans hoping for a giant-killing act, but while Raith were gathering their three-goal haul, Hibs were accumulating a four-goal response with Plumb, Ormond and Sammy Kean seeing their strikes joined by the unfortunate Colville, who put through his own net.

There would be three more league games before Hibs faced East Fife at Easter Road in the cup and the first of those took the Easter Road men to Parkhead to face Celtic. Hibs were intent on revenge following a home defeat to the Glasgow outfit earlier in the season and they succeeded in exacting that revenge by taking the points in a 2–1 win. With two former Hibees, Weir and Johnstone, in their forward line, the home side pressed hard in the early stages but were stung by an opener from Smith, whose shot somehow squirmed through Miller's hands and into the net. A penalty equaliser from McPhail lifted the spirits of the home support, but Miller blundered a second time to allow Plumb to score what proved to be the winning goal. The hosts fought hard to gain an equaliser, but Kerr was back to his best in the Hibs goal and denied them at every turn.

As defending champions and with hopes of retaining the title, Hibs next faced their strongest rivals when Rangers came to Easter Road. With more than 40,000 watching, the sides served up a thrilling first-half of end-to-end play, but neither side broke the deadlock. A fierce challenge by Woodburn left Combe a virtual passenger for most of the second-half and the visitors capitalised on what was basically a man advantage when Paton headed home from a Waddell cross. Hibs fought hard to get level and Smith thought he'd pulled it off late in the game only to watch in disbelief as Brown dived superbly to turn the ball behind for a corner. As the dust settled after the game, there was a realisation that this was the one game Hibs needed to win to retain their title and that their failure to do so had put Rangers firmly in the driving seat.

The last Saturday in February saw Hibs at Cappielow to face a struggling Morton side in quite atrocious weather conditions. The pitch was like a bog and there was a near gale-force wind blowing when the sides kicked off. Within 30 minutes Hibs were down to ten men after Davie Shaw, just back from injury, crumpled in a tackle and was carried off. Despite that loss, Hibs took the lead through Smith before Farquhar ensured level-pegging at half-time. In the second-half, with Turnbull immense and seeming to cover both his own position and that of the departed Shaw, Hibs hit a mini purple patch and scored twice through Reilly before Cairns missed from the spot. At the death, Orr scored for the home side but the points were going back to Edinburgh following a spirited display by the green and whites.

March 1949 began with the Scottish Cup visit of East Fife and once again playing conditions were poor as the pitch was very muddy follow-ing several days of heavy rain. The passing game at which Hibs often excelled was missing as both sets of players slugged it out against the elements while serving up a decent cup tie to entertain the spectators. Right on the interval, Davidson put the visitors ahead. In the second-half it was all Hibs with the East Fife goal area seeing lots of action. Time and again the Fifers defied Hibs with stout defending and the home side was unlucky not to get a penalty when Smith was hauled down, the referee insisting the challenge had been outside the box. With the clock ticking down, Cuthbertson missed a glorious chance to level the tie and then moments later Fleming fired in a long-range shot to win the match 2–0 for East Fife and send Hibs crashing out of the tournament yet again.

Dundee were among the main contenders for the title, and so it was no easy matter for Hibs when they visited Dens Park in mid-March, even though the home side were coming off the back of a heavy defeat away to St Mirren. From the first whistle, both sides went at each other and at times it was more like a cup game with play raging from end-to-end. Just four minutes had elapsed when Turnbull fired Hibs ahead. Patillo equalised five minutes later, only for Cuthbertson to restore the Hibs lead. The visitors were playing some lovely football and on another day would have had more than the two goals for their efforts so far, but Dundee were still a very lively and dangerous outfit. In a six-minute spell early in the second period the home side ran riot, scoring three goals through Stott, Bruce and Hill before Turnbull, the best Hibs man on the day, reduced the leeway near the end. Sadly, that was not enough and Hibs lost the points with, in all probability, any hopes of retaining their title.

Any lingering hopes of being champions again were finally extinguished after Hibs went down 2–0 to St Mirren at Paisley in early April. Gordon Smith was out injured. His place on the right wing was taken by Lawrie Reilly and Hibs gave a debut to Alex Bruce at centre forward. Also in the team that day was Bobby Johnstone, who gave his all but ended on the losing side. Poor Bruce, who was making his one and only appearance for Hibs, was totally dominated by Telfer the home centre half. At the other end, goals from the Polish winger Lesz and former Hibs man Milne ensured victory for the Buddies.

Seven days later, while Lawrie Reilly was playing for and scoring in a Scotland side that defeated England 3–1 at Wembley, Hibs welcomed Partick Thistle to Easter Road. Tommy Younger made his debut in the home goal as Kerr was out injured. The big keeper gave a first-class account of himself, although the sterling work of the defenders in front of him ensured he was well protected. Hibs took the lead when a clever lobbed cross from Johnstone allowed Turnbull to score with his head and then, after a number of further chances had been squandered, Smith scored a second for Hibs with a raking left-foot drive. Walker scored for Thistle late in the game, but the points belonged to the home side and left them in third place behind Rangers and Dundee, who both had games in hand.

There was a short break from league football during the following week when Hibs went to Tynecastle to face Hearts in the final of the East of Scotland Shield, held over from the previous season. The visitors defended well with young John Paterson in particular having a solid game against Bauld. Up front, they found the net three times through Smith, Turnbull and Cuthbertson to ensure at least one piece of silverware for the season.

Back in November at Fir Park, Motherwell had dished out a very painful 5–1 thrashing to Hibs and so a chance for revenge was on the cards when the Lanarkshire outfit visited Easter Road in the return fixture. A goal by Mathie was all the visitors had to show for their efforts, but Hibs had a good day and scored five times with Reilly and Cuthbertson each getting two and Smith the other. It was a crushing result for Motherwell who now found themselves down among the clubs fighting relegation.

There was still a chance that Hibs might finish runners-up but those hopes took a severe dent the following Saturday when a visit to Cathkin Park brought a 3–2 defeat by Third Lanark. Once again, playing conditions were not ideal, but that was no excuse for some sloppy play by the visitors, who really didn't deserve to take anything from the game. Staroscik put Thirds ahead inside ten minutes and doubled his tally minutes later when Paterson was adjudged to have handled in the box. A cracking left-foot drive by Smith made it 2–1 at the interval, but a goal by McCulloch early in the second-half took it to 3–1. Only a late strike by Cuthbertson made the scoreline more respectable.

The following Monday evening ensured that the date 21 April 1949 would attain huge significance in the history of Hibernian Football Club. Fulfilling an obligation to play a friendly match in the Borders against Nithsdale Wanderers, Hibs duly obliged by thrashing their hosts 8–1. It was not the scoreline that would hold any significance, but rather the names of the Hibs forwards that night. For the first time, Smith, Johnstone, Reilly, Turnbull and Ormond would play as a unit and little did those present realise that the names of those Famous Five would be talked of for decades to come. For the record, Thomson scored for Nithsdale while Ormond (2), Turnbull (2), Reilly (2), Mick Gallagher and Smith netted for Hibs.

Only one league match remained for Hibs and that was against Falkirk at Easter Road, with the home side securing the points after Cuthbertson and Turnbull gave them a 2–0 win, ensuring a third-place finish behind Rangers and Dundee.

That next weekend saw two Scottish clubs in friendly action against English opposition with both Hibs and Celtic in London. The Glasgow outfit went down 3–2 against Millwall at The Den and Hibs triumphed 5–2 against Spurs at White Hart Lane in a cracking match that saw Hibs trailing 2–1 with just ten minutes to go, Johnstone having opened the scoring in the first-half. In those final minutes the visitors struck four more through Ogilvie, who got two, an own goal and Smith. A few days later, and at the other end of the country, a young Hibs side lost 1–0 to a North of Scotland Select, while a few first-team players were drafted in to help the reserves defeat Hearts 3–1 in the Reserve League Cup final.

A short hop across the Irish Sea to Belfast saw Hibs face an Irish League XI in a match designed to raise funds for the building of a war memorial. The hosts had undertaken to meet all expenses incurred by Hibs, but upon arrival chairman Harry Swan announced that he would foot that bill so that the fund would benefit more from the match income. The Irish authorities were delighted with that gesture and presented each of the 26 that travelled with a box of Irish Linen handkerchiefs as well as organising a sightseeing trip to the Mountains of Mourne and a slap-up lunch. As to the game itself, the visitors won comfortably scoring two goals in each half without conceding. The Hibs marksmen were Johnstone, who got two, Turnbull and Smith.

The season ended with Hibs going on a European tour, during which a number of friendlies were played, including a fantastic 6–1 win against Bayern Munich where Smith (2), Reilly, Souness and Ormond were the scorers.

The willingness to take a team on tour to foreign places was not always popular with Scottish clubs, but Hibs saw it as a good thing and in the not too distant future their efforts would be remembered when there was talk of a tournament where European clubs would play against each other.

Chapter Four

1949/50

PIPPED AT THE POST

In a change to the previous arrangements for the playing of League Cup ties, the authorities decided that the domestic season should commence with the cup ties and that league football would need to wait until the sections were complete. Hibs found themselves in a section with Falkirk, Third Lanark and Queen of the South, not the most demanding group on paper, but this was a Hibs side with youngsters coming through to fight for first-team places.

In the first game, Easter Road housed around 35,000 fans for the visit of Falkirk. It would be a drab 90 minutes, with only one goal scored. It was, though, something special as visiting keeper Carrie fisted away a Smith cross and the ball reached Ormond some 12 yards from goal. Quick as a flash, the little number eleven got his head to the ball and looped a header into the opposite top corner. The rest of the game threw up little of note, although John Ogilvie and Matt McNeil in the Hibs rearguard caught the eye with assured displays.

Game two had Hibs at Cathkin Park, where they faced a stubborn Third Lanark outfit. Gordon Smith was at his brilliant best and the home side just couldn't figure out how to cope with him. Even with McNeil off the park getting treatment for ten first-half minutes, Hibs still looked the better side and opened with a goal in just 30 seconds when Turnbull headed on a cross from Ormond and Smith darted in ahead of keeper Fraser to net. At the other end, Cuthbertson, surprisingly sold during the close season, tried hard to level the game but found Younger in good form. Two minutes from the break, Hibs doubled their lead when Smith reacted quickest to a shot from Ormond being parried by Fraser. Around 25,000 watched as Thirds huffed and puffed in the second-half and yet it was Hibs who might have scored again had Turnbull not missed a penalty in the closing minutes.

On the road again for their next match, Hibs were in Dumfries to face Queen of the South. Thanks to their flying wingers, Smith and Ormond, they won the game 2–1 to stay at the top of their section having achieved maximum points from their opening three games.

In the following midweek, Hibs took a side north to face Dundee at the official opening of Dundee Violet's Glenesk Ground in a match that attracted around 15,000 spectators. The hosts began well and were soon two goals ahead, Gerrie getting both, but Hibs fought back and a double from Combe and one from Smith meant a 3–2 win. The green and whites failed to carry their goalscoring form into their match at Brockville the following Saturday and as a result lost their unbeaten record. Dawson opened the scoring for Falkirk after 14 minutes as his defensive colleagues were winning the battle against the Hibs forwards. Inglis added a second for the Bairns near the hour mark and although Turnbull pulled one back the visitors couldn't find that elusive equaliser.

Knowing that the result in the home tie with Third Lanark might well determine which club won the section, more than 30,000 attended at Easter Road to watch a six-goal thriller in which Reilly claimed a hat-trick and Smith scored a fine header to guide Hibs to a 4–2 win. Thirds were unlucky to lose Staroscik to injury during the game and did well to score twice through Friel and Staroscik prior to the latter going off. The home side deserved their win however, and could already look forward to a quarter-final outing.

The result of the final game had no bearing on qualification but Hibs wanted to finish the section with a flourish and to reward another big home crowd when Queen of the South visited. The Doonhamers had clearly not read the script as they quickly raced into a two-goal lead thanks to Johnstone and Brown and they held on to that until the interval. Presumably some plain talking took place in the home dressing room because within ten minutes of the restart Hibs were 3–2 up with two goals from Combe and one from Ormond. Pretty soon Ormond hit the target again and Hibs went nap as Combe completed his hat-trick. Johnstone did get another for Queens, but by then the damage was done.

Newly promoted Raith Rovers provided the opposition for the opening league game of the season in Fife and they must have wondered what they'd let themselves in for after Hibs scored six times without reply. Shots rained in on the home goal and it was a miracle that only Smith found the target in the first-half. After the interval the visitors picked up where they had left off, with Smith grabbing his second before Reilly made it three. The home fans were stunned as Turnbull, Combe and Reilly doubled the total, with the final whistle coming as a blessed relief to the hosts and their fans.

A week later Hibs were at Firhill for the first leg of their League Cup quarter-final against Partick Thistle. Once again, they were involved in a six-goal thriller, but this time they were on the losing side. Without the injured Smith, the visitors fought off the early attacking of the home side and Reilly put the green and whites a goal up after 18 minutes. Fifteen minutes later, Davidson levelled with a well-struck free kick. As the half-time whistle approached, the hosts took the lead when a shot by Kinnell was deflected past the stranded Younger. In the second-half, Davidson converted another free kick and Walker added a fourth before Johnstone pulled one back with time running out.

Four days later the second leg took place at Easter Road. Around 35,000 roared Hibs on as within the first ten minutes they had levelled the tie. Smith was back from injury and he combined with Turnbull to set Reilly up for the opener before Ormond doubled the tally with a long-range effort. At the other end, Kerr had little to do although he had to look sharp at one point to deny Kinnell. With 20 minutes left, Combe put Hibs ahead in the tie and with Thistle still reeling, Reilly added a fourth just two minutes later to win the game 4–2 and the tie 6–4 on aggregate.

If confidence was high after that fine aggregate win, it soon crashed back to earth with a thump as Hibs were blown away by their oldest rivals in a derby at Tynecastle. Some 40,000 were there to watch as the Gorgie men dominated from the off, racing in to a two-goal lead after just ten minutes of play. Conn and Bauld exposed glaring holes in the visitors' defence and cashed in accordingly. Somehow Hibs managed to reach the interval without conceding again but any half-time hopes of a revival were quickly lost as Hearts blasted three more goals in a devastating ten-minute spell, also contriving to miss a penalty. Scorers of goals three, four and five were Conn, Flavell and Bauld, Flavell being the man guilty of the penalty miss. The hosts appeared to ease off at this point and allowed Hibs to score a couple of consolation goals through Combe and Smith. But there was no disguising the fact that the men from Leith had been comprehensively outplayed.

With Smith and Reilly away on international duty and both Ogilvie and Govan out injured, Hibs next faced Aberdeen with four reserves in the starting eleven. The best of those on the day was Tommy McDonald, who wore number seven. While his play did not match what might have been offered by Smith he did not let himself or the club down with his solid display. In goal, Younger had three excellent first-half saves and it was not until ten minutes into the second that Hibs broke the deadlock when Ormond sent a rocket shot past Curran in the visiting goal. Ten minutes further on, Turnbull, playing in the unfamiliar role of centre forward, got the second and last goal of the game with a neatly placed low shot from around 12 yards.

The League Cup semi-final pitched Hibs up against Dunfermline at neutral Tynecastle. The Hibs fans in the 31,600 crowd must have anticipated a trip to Hampden when Lawrie Reilly fired the green and whites in front, but the Pars equalised in controversial fashion when Turnbull was clearly tripped in the Dunfermline box. All around that area stopped in anticipation of a whistle by the referee, but he ignored the incident and Dunfermline raced to the other end to draw the game level. Whether that incident upset the Hibs men we shall probably never know, but suffice to say they did not play well for the remainder of the game and that allowed the Pars to score a second and decisive goal. Salt was rubbed in the wound by the fact that both Dunfermline goals were scored by ex-Hibs player Gerry Mayes.

Remarkably, the cup setback seemed to galvanise Hibs as they proceeded to go on an unbeaten run of 11 games that took them right through to the end of 1949. Many have argued that the cup defeat was what prompted manager Shaw to rejig his half-back line and the statistics seem to show there is a great deal of merit in that argument because, as a unit, Bobby Combe, John Paterson and Archie Buchanan became quite formidable over the years.

The first in the run was against Queen of the South at Easter Road and thankfully Smith was back from injury to bring creativity to the right side of the attack. In the match programme for that game the winger had offered a tip to budding young players along the lines of being willing to use either foot at any time. Proof of that pudding came with the first goal of the game when Gordon controlled the ball with his right foot before switching it to his left and crashing home a low drive. Turnbull added a second to complete the scoring. Hibs might have had five but for three very dodgy offside decisions going against them. One point worth noting was the display of young John Paterson at centre half as he gave the free-scoring Scotland forward, Billy Houliston, no shooting opportunities at all.

A second consecutive home match meant that Hibs next faced Partick Thistle and the visitors defended exceptionally well until the 55th minute when Smith caught them unawares by taking a quick throw-in to Johnstone, who shuttled the ball into the path of Combe, the number four scoring with a drive into the top corner of the net. Some 20 minutes later Govan dispossessed the Thistle left winger in his own penalty area and set off on one of his trademark mazy runs that took him right to the other end of the park. He picked out Turnbull in the box and as quick as a flash the ball was in the net for number two. A couple of late good saves by Younger ensured Hibs took both points for the second week in succession.

A week later at Parkhead, with Combe, Smith, Reilly and Turnbull at their best, Hibs were two goals up and cruising when out of the blue Celtic pulled one back with a deflected shot that sent Younger the wrong way. Still the visitors looked safe for the points, but with the last action of the game Evans headed home an equaliser that delighted the home support but caused disbelief among the Hibs players and fans.

Having dropped that point at Parkhead, Hibs were determined to get back to winning ways as quickly as possible and could not have chosen more difficult opponents against which to try. Unbeaten Rangers came to Edinburgh as league leaders and with a quite awesome defensive record that had the sporting press describing the Rangers back line as the blue wall of steel. A fantastic crowd of 52,000 included an estimated 20,000 Rangers fans and no one was able to take their eyes off the play for long as the game flowed from end-to-end. One goal settled the matter and it came 14 minutes into the second-half from the boot of Turnbull. Defensively, the ever-improving Paterson was the rock upon which Rangers perished and it's worth listing the starting eleven here as this would largely be the side responsible for future successes: Tommy Younger, Jock Govan, Jimmy Cairns, Bobby Combe, John Paterson, Archie Buchanan, Gordon Smith, Bobby Johnstone, Lawrie Reilly, Eddie Turnbull and Willie Ormond.

With St Mirren leading the way in the league, Hibs were closing in and a combination of the next results of each club had the Edinburgh side at the top of the league. While St Mirren, who lost top scorer Crowe with a broken leg, were going down 1–0 to Rangers, Hibs were at Fir Park collecting all three points in a fine 3–1 win. Buchanan got the ball rolling with a smart left-foot drive and then just a few minutes later Johnstone was coolness personified as he stroked the ball home from a tight angle. Smith added another with Humphries getting the consolation for Motherwell towards the end of the match.

A week later, on a cold but crisp afternoon at Easter Road, Hibs took on an East Fife side weakened by international call-ups and injury and cruised to an impressive 4–1 win. With Govan injured, Shaw slotted in at right back and had a good game, combining well with Combe and Smith down the right. Two goals inside the first 20 minutes brought roars of pleasure from the home fans in the 35,000 crowd, but those soon turned to groans as both strikes were cancelled due to offside. A rare headed goal by the in-form Johnstone put Hibs one up just after the half hour and the lead was doubled on the stroke of half-time by Ormond. Soon after the restart the crowd was cheering with delight at it watched Gordon Smith take a high ball on his head and proceed to run into the East Fife box juggling said ball on his head, only to see his final header just fail to beat the visiting keeper. It was astonishing stuff and so typical of a hugely talented footballer. When both first-half scorers repeated that feat in the second, the points were won, but in fairness to the visitors they never gave up and were rewarded with a late goal by Black. That win kept Hibs at the top, one point ahead of Dundee but with a game in hand. Two points behind were Rangers, who had played a game less than Hibs, and Celtic were fourth. Hearts, who had started the campaign very poorly, had managed to find the form that destroyed Hibs and were now mid-table as a result.

As November drew to a close, Hibs visited Third Lanark and found that even though they were not at their best on the day they still had too much firepower for the home side. Johnstone got the first Hibs goal after a neat back-heel from Reilly set him up and Reilly himself got the second and last of the game after being put through on goal by a wonderful pass from Combe. For Thirds, only Ally MacLeod sparkled in his left-wing berth and it took a fine save from Younger to deny the future Scotland manager a goal.

The first of five games in December 1949 took Hibs to Dens Park to face a very strong Dundee. The first-half was even, but devoid of any real scoring opportunities as the two sides cancelled each other out. The deadlock was only broken with 15 minutes left to play as Rattray fired the home side ahead. The loss of the goal seemed to inspire Hibs to greater efforts and they were soon level when Smith beat Lynch in the home goal. With the referee closely examining his watch with a view to ending the game, Ormond sent over a teasing cross and Reilly dashed in to send a firm header into the net to win the game 2–1 for Hibs. On the same day the normally close-to-invincible Rangers defence lost a staggering four goals to Clyde – but still managed to win the game by scoring five of their own!

Falkirk were the next club to try and halt the green and white machine of Hibernian but well as they played they still left Easter Road empty handed. A magnificent display of goalscoring by Smith saw him hit the target four times. Johnstone added another as Hibs went nap. The Bairns got a consolation goal through Whitelaw, but the cheering was muted compared to that which greeted each of the Hibernian strikes. Contemporary reports suggest that even the loudest of cheers for Smith's goals was beaten by the roar which greeted the half-time news from Fir Park where Motherwell were beating Rangers 3–0.

One of the clubs still in the mix for the league title were St Mirren and when Hibs visited Love Street in mid-December the weather was freezing but the football on offer soon warmed up those hardly souls watching from the terraces. Both sides played really well and it was no surprise when St Mirren broke the deadlock. The surprise was in the manner in which the goal was scored. A 60-yard clearance from Martin in the home defence totally confused the Hibs keeper, who allowed the ball to sail over his head and into the net. Undaunted, the visitors kept their cool and equalised through Reilly after good lead-up work from Smith and Turnbull. Johnstone gave Hibs the lead with a smart shot and then ex-Hibee Arthur Milne thought he had equalised only to have the goal chalked off before Turnbull settled the whole affair with a third for Hibs.

Christmas is a time for giving and when Hibs faced Raith on the eve of that big day they seemed to be in giving mood. Thankfully, the Rovers goalkeeper McGregor was similarly minded. Hugh Shaw's men were way below their best but still managed to score a couple of early goals through Johnstone and Reilly, only to gift their visitors two in return with Garth and Maule the marksmen. Those two goals were scored either side of a third for Hibs by Reilly and the game was finally settled when a long-range effort by Smith somehow wriggled under the diving body of the Rovers custodian.

New Year's Eve saw Hibs fighting out a dour battle with Clyde at Shawfield where there was plenty of effort from both sides but very little by way of flowing football. The game was settled by a single goal, scored for the league leaders by Buchanan.

It was as leaders that Hibs welcomed local rivals Hearts to Easter Road on 2 January 1950. The lengthy unbeaten run by the home side and an equally impressive one by the visitors, together with the fact that it was a holiday, boosted the crowd to a record 65,850, a figure not surpassed before or since for a game outside of Glasgow. Reports suggest that many more were in attendance having entered the ground by 'less conventional' methods than paying at the gate. There was certainly a problem when more than 30 fans had to receive medical attention as hundreds escaped the crush by jumping over the wall on to the track around the pitch.

As to the play, Hibs were much improved from their last meeting with Hearts and they had the better of the first-half, scoring a wonderful goal on the half hour. Ormond dashed down the left, sold not one but two outrageous dummies to Hearts defenders and then sent over a head-high cross which Smith diverted wide of Brown and into the net. The second-half was a different matter with Hearts in the ascendancy and it was no surprise when Conn equalised early on. With fewer than 15 minutes left to play, Wardhaugh scored what proved to be the winner. That result ended a 14-game unbeaten run for Hibs and extended the unbeaten run of Hearts to 12 but it was a painful one for the followers of the Easter Road club.

Twenty-four hours later, a long journey north was undertaken and a great display ensured that Hibs got back to winning ways. Aberdeen had the better of the first-half, but the visitors defended well and that was the foundation for three second-half goals, Ormond getting the first and Smith the other two. Hibs even had the luxury of missing a penalty when Turnbull crashed his shot so hard off the post the ball bounced back almost to the centre circle.

It was back to Saturday games next and although it was very cold and the pitches were a bit hard they were playable as Hibs hosted a visit from Stirling Albion. Once again the defence had to be on top form. Albion attacked frequently, but found Younger in particular to be at the top of his game. On the quarter-hour, Turnbull beat the offside trap and Albion's Polish keeper Gerhard to open the scoring. Within a minute, Guy had equalised. Late in the half, Reilly restored the Hibs lead and they added two more in the second-half through Combe, whose long-range effort somehow slipped through the keeper's hands, and Ormond. For the second game in succession, Turnbull failed from the spot, only this time the ball sailed over the bar.

In mid-January Hibs travelled to Dumfries and thanks to a very sluggish start were two goals down in no time. Both Brown and McEvoy beat Younger, who was to blame for neither as his defensive colleagues were slow to cover. This would be a game of two halves, however, and Turnbull, by far the best player on show, struck twice to earn the visitors a point.

The Scottish Cup draw gave Hibs a home tie against Partick Thistle, but that was still a week away and the green and whites had first to travel to Firhill to face the Jags in a league match. Atrocious underfoot conditions failed to stop this game turning into a real belter with both sides pressing forward at every opportunity. Indeed, it fell into that category of games often described as being like a cup tie, but of course that was still a week away. Turnbull continued his good scoring form by giving Hibs the lead just after the half hour. Before the break, McCallum shot home a fine equaliser. The second-half was only minutes old when Stott's quickly-taken free kick was thumped into the net by Gibb, but the best goal of the game was yet to come. A corner kick from Ormond was delivered at pace to the back post where Smith controlled the ball brilliantly with his first touch before sending a wonderful shot into the net off the bar from an incredible angle. Both sides went looking for a winner, but neither succeeded and a share of the points was about right on the day.

The kind of play fought out in the league match was replicated when the sides met in the cup. Hibs, shooting up the slope and into the wind in the first-half, hit the woodwork twice and Henderson saved brilliantly from a fierce drive by Smith. The Jags were little seen as an attacking force, but just a few minutes into the second-half a corner from Walker found McCallum totally unmarked and the Thistle man headed home strongly. Down the slope, Hibs bombarded the Thistle goal, but Henderson stood firm and yet another year passed since the last time the home club had lifted the trophy. The Scottish Cup really was a hoodoo as far as the green and whites were concerned and though their exit from the competition over the years had often just been to better sides on the day, this latest one was sore to bear as there is no doubt Hugh Shaw's men were by far the superior outfit.

Out of the cup, Hibs needed to concentrate on their league challenge and their next result gave them a perfect platform from which to relaunch. In a quite thrilling 90 minutes the home side took the points with a 4–1 win but there is some story behind that scoreline and both Turnbull and left back Willie Clark would have good reason to recall it in future years. In a stormy start to the game, the Celtic centre half McGrory seemed to foul Reilly every time the Hibs man had the ball. When he did so around the 20 minute mark it was in the box and the referee awarded a penalty which Turnbull duly converted. Eleven minutes later Clark tripped ex-Hibs man Weir and another penalty award followed. Collins, the Celtic outside right, had to take the kick twice after the referee saw an infringement at the point of the first attempt. The ball was fired home on both occasions, although only the second counted, and so it was now 1–1. At this point Hibs lost Younger to injury and Clark had to take over in goals. The Hibs man must have been glad to volunteer his services as Collins had been giving him a hard afternoon. Remarkably, this would be Clark's only appearance of the season! With half-time fast approaching, McGrory fouled Johnstone and referee Mowat awarded another penalty which Turnbull fired home. Five minutes after the restart, Turnbull completed his hat-trick after good work by Smith and then amazingly scored a fourth with yet another penalty 20 minutes from the end. A truly stunning game, no doubt thoroughly enjoyed by the majority of the 40,000 on the terracings.

The next Saturday was a Scottish Cup day and given Hibs' lack of involvement the club travelled to Birmingham to face Aston Villa in a friendly. Things started well enough with Reilly putting the visitors ahead inside the first five minutes but thereafter it was all Villa as they scored five in a row to decimate the Edinburgh side. Goffin and Ford made it 2–1 at half-time before Dixon, Ford again and Smith made it 5–1. Ormond converted a penalty near the end to make the final score 5–2.

Another seven-goal game took place a week later at Easter Road. This time, it was Hibs who dominated. Opponents Motherwell had an early Kelly miss and a goal by Watson, but that was pretty much all they could claim to as the home side found the net six times. On another day they might have had ten such was their dominance. Smith and Ormond on the wings were at their best while Johnstone patrolled the midfield, firing passes left, right and centre. Smith opened the scoring for Hibs and Turnbull added a second with a trademark thunderbolt of a shot that flew past Hamilton in the 'Well goal at a frightening speed. Then came Watson's goal to reduce the leeway, but Ormond soon restored the two-goal advantage and before the half-time whistle had sounded Smith scored another two giving him a hat-trick and Hibs a 5–1 lead. The second-half saw the Motherwell goal lead a charmed life until seven minutes from time when Reilly got the goal his performance richly deserved.

A visit to Bayview followed and with the winter sun low in the sky, both sides served up an entertaining 90 minutes and a goal apiece. Somewhat against the run of play Johnstone put the visitors one up but Fleming equalised for East Fife when he headed home a corner early in the second-half. On the day, Govan, Paterson and Johnstone were best for Hibs with Smith and Ormond strangely subdued and Reilly well marked by the home defence. Without knowing it at the time, these dropped points in drawn games would cost Hibs dear, although the Fifers would finish the season strongly in fourth place.

If the dropped point at Methil was disappointing, the two points dropped in the next match against Third Lanark at home were a total disaster in terms of championship aspirations. With Turnbull out injured and replaced by Dennis McGurk in his only appearance for the club, the home side lacked drive when going forward and lost the game 1–0 to send many of the 20,000 spectators home disconsolate.

A second successive home game offered the chance to quickly make amends to the fans and that chance was duly taken, as much due to a horror performance by Dundee's young goalkeeper Brown as to good play by Hibs. The first goal was controversial when Brown and Reilly clashed, the keeper holding the Hibs centre back, but as the ball rolled free and crossed the line the referee awarded a goal rather than a penalty. Eight minutes later, a high and hopeful ball from Smith somehow dropped over the keeper and into the empty net before Reilly added a third when Brown failed to hold a pretty tame shot. The visitors pulled one back through Gerrie, but hopes of a revival were crushed when Johnstone scored a fourth for Hibs and though Gerrie scored again it was in the final minute and counted for little. As Turnbull was again absent through injury, Combe took the number ten shirt, allowing Hugh Howie, back after a very lengthy illness, to don the number four.

Heavy rain in the days preceding the next match ensured that the pitch at Brockville was both muddy and slippy when Falkirk welcomed Hibs in mid-March. Despite the conditions, both sides served up decent football and it was a blow to the Bairns when keeper Nicol hurt himself in a challenge with Reilly and had to leave the field for treatment. During his absence, Combe netted from close range on the hour mark. Within five minutes Falkirk drew level when Hibs old boy Angus Plumb beat Younger with a fierce drive before the home side were restored to full strength with the return of Nicol. The game ebbed and flowed as the final whistle approached and it was Reilly who ensured the points for Hibs, keeping their championship hopes alive.

With spring in the air, Hibs next faced St Mirren at Easter Road. The

Buddies played quite well but still contrived to lose the game 5–0. They were good to watch when going forward but were shot-shy when they reached the Hibs box and the home side made them pay dearly for that. Ormond opened the scoring after ten minutes before Smith had the fans roaring in delight as he gathered the ball on the half-way line, dribbled past three defenders and then fired a rocket shot at the Saints goal, only to see the ball hit the bar and bounce clear. The winger didn't have to wait long to end his disappointment as moments later he was on hand to head home an Ormond cross. The players reversed roles when Ormond headed home a cross from Smith to make it 3–0 at half-time. The Buddies were better for the bulk of the second-half but still lost another two goals, the first from the ever hard-working Reilly and the second from Smith right on the final whistle.

Just three games remained and Hibs had to win them all to have any chance of the title. The first took them to Annfield to face doomed Stirling Albion. As is often the case, relegated teams can relax and play better once their fate is sealed, and the home side gave Hibs a torrid 90 minutes. Thankfully, Smith was at his majestic best and he helped himself to a first-half hat-trick with all three goals from his left boot – pretty impressive for a right winger! Miller had countered for the home side prior to the second-half getting under way, but Reilly made it 4–1 early in the second-half before Anderson once again reduced the margin. A late Ormond penalty secured the points although Anderson got a third for Albion with virtually the last kick of the game.

The penultimate league game of the season was at Easter Road against Clyde. A light drizzle welcomed the sides as they took to the field and that made the surface a little slick with the ball skidding across it on numerous occasions. It was the kind of surface that defenders don't particularly enjoy and that might help explain why no fewer than nine goals were scored in the match. On the plus side, every Hibs forward found the net, but the Bully Wee seemed to find some alarming gaps in the Hibs rearguard. Johnstone fired Hibs ahead, but worryingly the home side appeared hesitant in the early part of the game and it looked ominous when Cairns conceded a penalty. Clyde's South African forward Acker-man blazed the ball high over the bar from the spot. Relief was short-lived because soon after the same player made amends with a strong shot that beat Younger from 25 yards. With nerves beginning to jangle on the terraces, Smith took control of the game by scoring himself and then setting Turnbull up for a third before the interval. Early in the second-half Reilly brilliantly sped away from his marker to fire home a fourth before Barclay made it 4–2, shooting through a ruck of players to beat the unsighted Younger. A smart double by Ormond ensured a 6–3 win for the home side, Barclay having netted for Clyde late in the game.

One game of huge importance remained and the tension was palpable both on and off the park as Hibs faced Rangers in Glasgow knowing that the destiny of the league title was at stake. An incredible 101,000 packed into Ibrox, but no one would leave with any real sense of satisfaction as a tense affair ended up at 0–0. That game completed Hibs' fixtures and they were top, one point ahead of Rangers. The Glasgow club, however, still had one game to play.

On the following Monday night, Hibs were in London facing Spurs at White Hart Lane in front of 34,000 spectators. One wonders whether their minds were truly on the job rather than on the fact that around 400 miles away Rangers were playing Third Lanark: if they lost, the league flag would be coming to Edinburgh. In London the game was won by a single goal from the boot of Willie Ormond while at Cathkin Park Rangers were involved in huge controversy when Willie Thornton barged Thirds keeper Lou Goram over the line and the referee awarded the goal. In those days barging the keeper was part and parcel of the game – acceptable provided that the keeper had the ball under his control. In this case, Goram, whose son, Andy, would later play for both Hibs and Rangers, did not actually have the ball under his control at the point of contact. An upset home side went further behind when Rutherford fired home a deflected effort, but they fought back and Mason reduced the leeway before the break. Thirds then won a penalty which Henderson sent wide of the target. Ex-Hibs man Johnny Cuthbertson levelled the game on the night, but try as they did the hosts could not find a winner and as a result Rangers won the title on goal average.

Chapter Five

1950/51

RUNAWAY WINNERS

After a long hot summer, Hibs got down to business in mid-August when the League Cup section matches began. This year, all six games would be played before the league got under way and the green and whites found themselves sharing a section with Dundee, St Mirren and Falkirk. The Dens Park outfit visited Easter Road for the opening game. With over 40,000 inside the ground it took the home side until the 52nd minute to break down a resolute visiting defence. When it came it was a goal to remember as Johnstone dribbled past three defenders, slipped the ball to Ormond and then ran into the box to head the cross from the winger strongly past Rennie in the Dundee goal. The cheering had hardly subsided when it rose in volume again after Smith cut in from the right and sent a piledriver of a shot into the net off his left boot. The resultant 2–0 win got Hibs off to a winning start.

The same eleven turned out for the next game, a midweek tussle with St Mirren at Love Street. This time, Hibs struck twice in the first-half with Reilly getting both goals. Any thoughts of resting on that were soon dispelled as the visitors ran riot in the second period when Reilly completed his hat-trick, Johnstone scored twice and Smith ensured a very impressive 6–0 win.

Saturday 19 August 1950 was a day to remember for those fans attending the Falkirk v Hibs game at Brockville. Initially the Hibs fans in the crowd must have been mightily depressed as former player Angus Plumb put the hosts ahead before a Hibs player had even touched the ball. By the 18th minute the Bairns were 3–0 up as first Wright and then Plumb capitalised on some poor defending, but before the interval the green and whites rallied and pulled two goals back thanks to Smith and Turnbull, the latter smashing in a trademark shot from well outside the box. Within eight minutes of the restart Smith had the visitors level, but then Falkirk got a penalty which Wright converted to make it 4–3. Still the Hibs would not give up and Ormond brought them level again. With the final whistle only moments away, Smith completed his hat-trick to win the game 5–4 for the Easter Road men.

Six points from three games and 13 goals scored had the players in confident mood and that confidence had them 2–0 up at Dens Park, Reilly getting both when the referee abandoned the game with just over 20 minutes to play. A torrential and concerted downpour caused flooding in some parts of the playing surface, making it unsafe and all concerned agreed the decision was correct. A nominal date for replaying the Dundee match was agreed but in the end the authorities decided it was not needed as it would not affect the final placings in the section, regardless of the score.

Two more section matches remained, both at Easter Road. The first was against a St Mirren side that had shipped six goals in the first clash. With the home side playing such expansive football it is unsurprising that more than 30,000 fans were in the ground to see the Buddies demolished for a second time as the green and whites ran out 5–0 winners thanks to goals from Reilly (2), Turnbull (2) and Smith.

A similar number of fans attended for the sixth and final section clash with Falkirk. Despite Smith being injured early on and limping out on his wing until he finally left the field with 20 minutes left, the green and whites still managed to score four times without reply, the marksmen being Ormond, who got two, Johnstone and Turnbull.

By sheer chance it would be the Bairns that Hibs faced in their first league match of the season. On this occasion, Smith would not be fit to play and as Jimmy Souness, his normal replacement, was also unfit, the number seven jersey went to Jim Gunning, who would be making his one and only first-team start. An eighth-minute opener from Reilly was added to near the interval from a Turnbull penalty, but it was in the second-half that a poor Falkirk side were overrun. Four more goals were scored without reply, with excellent set-up play by Johnstone and Turnbull helping Reilly score three more before the little centre forward returned the compliment by setting up Turnbull to score the final goal in a comprehensive 6–0 victory.

During the following week Hibs travelled to Somerset Park to play in a benefit match for long-serving Ayr United player Norrie McNeil and found themselves 4–1 down after just 22 minutes. Thereafter a remarkable comeback was staged, and by full-time the score was 5–5. Thyne and Goldie had the hosts in front, but Reilly pulled one back before Goldie again and Beattie made it 4–1. By half-time it was 4–4 after Turnbull, Ormond and Johnstone had all found the mark. Honours were even in the second-half with Beattie for the hosts and Reilly for Hibs completing the scoring in what must surely have been a memorable event for Ayr's McNeil.

The six-goal win over Falkirk put Hibs in good mood for their next challenge which came in the shape of a League Cup quarter-final first-leg match against Aberdeen at Pittodrie. Smith was still unfit, but Souness had recovered and took his place on the right wing. Although the first-half was fairly even, the visitors went in a goal up after Johnstone scored following a good move. The second-half was a different story altogether as the hosts hit top form and scored four times through Hather, Emery (from a hotly disputed penalty), Yorston and Hamilton. Hibs were stunned to lose the game 4–1 and would have it all to do in the second leg.

The story goes that Smith, who had travelled to Pittodrie but not played, persuaded Hugh Shaw as the players travelled back to Edinburgh, that he should play in the second leg as he felt sure he could exploit weaknesses he had spotted in the Aberdeen rearguard. With his leg heavily strapped Smith started the game and soon began to find those weaknesses. With more than 60,000 in the ground the winger hustled and harried centre half Anderson, causing him to make a hash of a pass-back and put the ball into the Aberdeen net after just three minutes of play. Thereafter, play raged from end-to-end. The Hibs defence stood firm, however, while the home forwards hit woodwork on no fewer than three occasions, making them most unfortunate to take only a 1–0 lead into the half-time break. Within 15 minutes of the restart the wily and hugely talented Johnstone made it 2–0 and the roar of the crowd seemed to grow even louder. Five minutes later, Smith set up Ormond for number three and by now the noise was deafening as the sides were level on aggregate, away goals not being decisive in games back then. Extra time was required and in the first minute Reilly pounced to get a fourth for Hibs and put them in front, to the unbridled joy of the home support. Darkness was falling rapidly as the game drew to a close. Disastrously for Hibs, Yorston struck for the visitors with virtually the last kick of the game. The 4–1 scoreline obviously mirrored the outcome of the Pittodrie clash and so a replay would be required.

Ahead of that cup tie, two league games were scheduled, the first bringing Hearts to Easter Road for the Edinburgh derby. More than 50,000 came through the turnstiles, and it would be those wearing maroon and white colours who would leave the game with a smile. Try as they might the home side could not find a way past Brown in the Hearts goal, while at the other end a headed goal by Sloan secured the points for the visitors. It was undoubtedly the case that the Hibs men were weary after their cup exploits, but the disappointment on their faces as they left the pitch showed how much they had wanted to win this game.

The league fixture card ensured that Hibs and Aberdeen would become well acquainted given that they'd already met twice in the League Cup and would do so again in the forthcoming replay, but on this occasion it was points at stake for the match at Pittodrie. Eddie Turnbull gave the visitors the best possible start by scoring inside the opening minute. The Dons gradually fought their way back into the game and winger Pearson drew them level before the break. A string of fine saves by Martin in the home goal stopped Hibs from regaining the lead and then disaster struck as Yorston broke free on the left before passing the ball to Baird who set Hamilton up for what proved to be the winning strike.

On the following Monday evening the sides faced up to each other once again for the cup replay, staged at neutral Ibrox. A first-half goal by Turnbull put Hibs in command but the Dons fought back and had several near things before Baird equalised to take the game into extra time. Both teams, though tiring on the muddy pitch, went out to win the tie, with Smith lofting a golden chance over the bar from inside the six-yard box and then Younger saving brilliantly from a Yorston drive. Neither side could find a goal and so would be required to play again to find a winner. Amazingly, the authorities set the tie for the following evening at Hampden with a 4.40pm kick off.

Despite the early kick-off time, some 30,000 were in the stadium at the start, a good number of those having travelled through on the football special which left Edinburgh at 2.30pm. It can only be assumed that absenteeism from work was rife that day! At Ibrox, the sides had been very even in terms of their play, but on this occasion the green and whites would rule the roost and run out impressive 5–1 winners. Turnbull and Smith combined well to allow Johnstone a headed goal after thirteen minutes and six minutes later Turnbull thundered home a second to put Aberdeen on the ropes. Only three more minutes passed before Johnstone was on the mark again but to their credit Aberdeen soon pulled one back through Baird. After the break, Smith and Reilly scored again for Hibs and took them into a semi-final clash with Queen of the South.

That semi was played on the next Saturday at neutral Tynecastle, a ground that had not always served Hibs well in such situations, but the green and whites soon mastered the blustery conditions and swarmed around the Queens goal. It came as something of a shock therefore when the Dumfries outfit took the lead through their veteran outside left Johnstone. The Easter Road men were soon level after Turnbull shot into the top corner of the net, giving Henderson no chance. The half-time break allowed each manager to offer fresh advice and it was Hugh Shaw's that had the greater effect as Turnbull hit the net again, this time from the penalty spot. Late in the game Turnbull secured his hat-trick, ensuring a 3–1 win and the right to face Motherwell in the final.

The fixture card threw Hibs and Motherwell together for a league game at Fir Park and needless to say it was billed as a cup final rehearsal by the press. In a quite devastating display of football the visitors ran out 6–2 winners despite Smith being injured and limping for most of the match. The Hibs captain showed all present just why he was so special: despite limited movement he still managed to spray around a number of telling passes that had the 'Well defence in all sorts of bother. Ormond and Johnstone got two goals each, the others coming from Reilly and a Turnbull penalty, while Forrest and ex-Hibs man Aitkenhead struck for the home side. The final was just two weeks away, the following Saturday being one when international matches were being played. The gap would give Smith more time to recover, while Reilly would be turning out for Scotland.

Hampden Park housed 64,000 fans for the League Cup final and in the crowd rather than on the park was the injured Eddie Turnbull whose number ten jersey went to Ormond, with Jackie Bradley wearing the winger's customary number eleven. A great player but not in the engine-room role, Ormond tried his utmost but found it difficult and Bradley showed some nice touches without ever setting the game alight. Mother-well, still smarting from that earlier 6–2 defeat at home, were consider-ably tighter defensively and though Hibs enjoyed the better possession they could not find the crucial opening goal. Instead it looked as though maybe a replay would be needed until the Lanarkshire outfit silenced the majority of the crowd with a 75th-minute strike by Kelly and then doubled their advantage just three minutes later through Forrest. By that time Hibs were a beaten side and when Younger miskicked in trying to clear, allowing Watters to add a third, the cup was lost. It was a bit of a tragedy for Younger, who had otherwise had a fine game.

A week later Hibs were back in Glasgow, this time to face Rangers in the league in front of 80,000 spectators and once again Younger was at the heart of a key moment in the game, although he was entirely blameless. A long punt upfield by a Rangers defender fell to Paterson, who could have sent it straight back but didn't. Younger obviously expected him to and so was as surprised as everyone else in the stadium when Paterson attempted a pass-back that flew past the keeper and into the net. Needless to say that caused the home side to push on looking for a second, but Younger was immense in saving from both Waddell and Paton and when the half-time whistle went there was still only the one goal in it. Early in the second-half the Ibrox defence was bamboozled as the Hibs forwards interchanged during a passing move and that allowed Reilly to head an equaliser from an Ormond cross. The visitors then took control of the game, creating a number of chances but finding the Rangers keeper in top form, and ultimately the sides had to settle for a draw.

Fixtures had kept Hibs away from home for a month, but on 7 November 1950, Easter Road was back in use with the visit of Morton, which attracted a crowd of 35,000. As the home side took the field a rousing cheer went up as though the fans were acknowledging the disappointment the players must have felt in not winning the League Cup. The visitors gave a good account of themselves in the first-half with centre forward Mochan and keeper Cowan catching the eye while Combe and Johnstone did sterling work for Hibs. Into the second-half and the game poised at 0–0, Hibs flowed down that famous old slope of theirs and took the points with two headed goals, the first from Reilly and the second from Ormond, who was brave in meeting Turnbull's fierce cross on the full when many a player might have ducked out of the way.

Seven days later Hibs were at Bayview to face a stuffy East Fife side that was going well in the league. The visitors started slowly and paid the penalty when Morris put the Fifers ahead after 12 minutes and almost immediately forced Younger into a fantastic save to deny a second. Hibs then began to play and Reilly levelled it with a tap-in after he reacted quickest to a ball dropped by the home keeper. That seemed to galvanise the green and whites and they went on to take the points thanks to a second-half header by Buchanan.

With a midweek international match looming, the four Hibs forwards chosen to represent Scotland all turned out at Easter Road in a side that had the better of visitors Airdrie from the off and cantered to a convincing 5–0 win. Stuffy defending prevented the home side from scoring until the 34th minute, by which time two strong penalty claims had been turned down by referee Main. This time, however, he pointed to the spot and Turnbull sent keeper Fraser the wrong way with his kick. It was 2–0 before the break after the impressive Johnstone headed home a Smith cross, and almost immediately from the restart Reilly made it three. Thereafter Hibs went into cruise mode but still managed to add two late goals, both from Turnbull, the second from the spot to give him his hat-trick. That result confirmed Hibs as genuine contenders in the league race with Rangers, Dundee and Hearts also in the hunt.

A hectic December, during which Hibs would play five games, began with the visit of Dundee, a side whose tremendous recent form helped swell the attendance to 40,000. On the day Hibs won out and scored two goals without reply. Indeed the goals themselves typified how the game went for Hibs with the first a scrappy affair and the second a goal of real quality. It was no coincidence that both were scored by Reilly, easily the man of the match. The visitors missed a penalty after Combe was adjudged to have handled but otherwise they didn't feature much, with international striker Billy Little getting few sightings of the ball thanks to the good marking of John Ogilvie, who had taken over at left back in place of long-term injury victim Jimmy Cairns.

A poor start to the season was a thing of the past for Third Lanark when they hosted Hibs on 9 December, the home side having hit a rich vein of form. Once again the visitors started the game slowly and might have gone behind in the first minute but for Younger brilliantly turning a Mason shot round his post. Hibs began to get forward and in 22 minutes Smith saw a weak-looking shot somehow deceive the home keeper and creep into the net to make it 1–0. On the hour mark, McColl equalised and then Turnbull missed a penalty, which must have disappointed him. Worse was to come as he was sent off with about five minutes remaining. Despite being a man down, Hibs went looking for a winner and got it in the final minute from that man Reilly.

The dismissal of Turnbull at Cathkin a week earlier meant he had to sit out the match with St Mirren at Easter Road. His place was taken by 17-year-old, Musselburgh-born Robert Wood, who celebrated his call-up by having a fine game and scoring the opening goal after 17 minutes. Within moments he almost repeated that feat but was denied when a defender kicked the ball off the goal line. Wood it was again who featured next as it was his cross that Smith headed home to put Hibs 2–0 ahead at the break. Five minutes after the restart the former Rangers man Duncanson headed a goal for the Buddies, but an Ormond penalty sealed the win and the points to keep Hibs in a good challenging position. After the game it became known that the Scottish Cup first-round draw gave Hibs an away tie with, coincidentally, St Mirren.

Two days before Christmas, Hibs were at Brockville to play a game that might easily have been postponed but for the sterling efforts of the Falkirk groundstaff, who managed to ensure no puddles of surface water following a torrential downpour earlier that day. By the time the final whistle sounded those groundstaff might have wondered whether they should have bothered as Hibs eased to a comprehensive 5–1 win. Man of the match Buchanan opened the scoring before Turnbull, back from suspension, added a second. Johnstone made it 3–0 at the break and though Brown scored a good goal for the hosts, Ormond and Turnbull were on target for the green and whites. A week later Hibs narrowly defeated a plucky Clyde outfit 1–0 to ensure they would go into 1951 leading the title race. It was not a great game, but to play below par and yet still take the points was a good indicator that Hibs were genuine title challengers.

On the first day of the year there were four clubs in a cluster that had aspirations of league title success and intriguingly the Old Firm were not among them. Joining Hibs were Dundee, Aberdeen and Hearts, the last named being the customary opponents for Hibs on New Year's Day. The match at Tynecastle attracted a capacity crowd and turned out to be one of the most exciting derby matches in years. The visitors had to take the field without the injured Govan and Turnbull, but in Howie and Wood they had fine deputies. After a flurry of half chances in the opening exchanges, Hearts grabbed the lead in the 11th minute when Cox, who went on to be man of the match, played a slide-rule pass through the centre of the Hibs defence for Conn to collect and shoot past Younger. With around ten minutes of the half to go, Hearts' keeper Brown was injured and had to leave the field for treatment, inspiring Hibs to pour forward in search of an equaliser. It was the ten men, however, who scored again through Sloan. Brown reappeared for the second-half and had a string of wonderful saves, being beaten only once in the last ten minutes by a strong shot from Smith.

Twenty-four hours later, a crowd of 45,000 turned out on a cold afternoon at Easter Road to watch the home side take on another of the clubs chasing the title. Aberdeen had been regular opponents already this season with a league match being added to by the four clashes required to separate the clubs in the League Cup. Lots of goals had been scored in those games and this latest encounter would add eight more to the total. Barely sixty seconds had elapsed when Hibs fell asleep at a Dons throw-in, allowing Hamilton to put the visitors a goal up. A few minutes later, Ormond and Smith combined well to set up Johnstone for the equaliser. Undaunted, Aberdeen got straight back at Hibs with a cracking second goal when Pearson gathered the ball in the centre circle, skipped past Paterson and, with the Hibs man pursuing him all the way, strode right into the penalty box before firing a low shot under the diving body of Younger. Next, Gordon Smith, who was on fire throughout, drove a shot which Curran could only parry and that allowed Reilly to fire in a second equaliser just before half-time. With the second period just a minute old, Reilly pounced on a loose ball to make it 3–2 and Hibs began to run riot. Four minutes later, Smith scored with a header from a Buchanan free kick before Smith was again involved, his shot saved but not held by Curran, allowing Wood to make it 5–2. Then came the goal of the game as Howie gathered the ball in his own 18-yard box and rolled it forward to Smith, who played a one-two with Reilly and then set off down the right wing before hitting a cross to the back post. Wood headed it down into the path of Johnstone, who cracked home the sixth and last of the game. That magnificent win put Hibs into third place behind Dundee and Aberdeen with Hearts one behind in fourth.

On the following Saturday, Hibs travelled across the Forth to take on Raith Rovers at Stark's Park. It was a horribly cold and wet afternoon and, of course, there was no road bridge in those days. So the fact that thousands of Hibs fans helped swell the attendance to over 20,000, the biggest of the season to date for Rovers, was pretty impressive. Once again Govan and Turnbull were out injured and had now been joined by Ormond meaning that Fife-born Willie Allen was drafted in for his debut. In fact, this would be his only first-team game, but he acquitted himself well. After four minutes of play, the home side were awarded a disputed penalty when Paterson was adjudged to have handled the ball in the box. In fact, the ball had hit Paterson in the chest and a large muddy mark on his strip seemed to offer evidence of that fact. The referee, who had been at least 50 yards away, was having none of it and Colville duly fired the Rovers in front. This seemed to get the dander of the visiting players up and they set about righting the wrong by equalising in the 30th minute when Johnstone, who had a brilliant game, shot home strongly from 12 yards. That equaliser brought great cheers from the Hibs fans and their day was made complete when Willie Allen twice delivered pinpoint crosses for Smith to score a brace and win the points for Hibs in a 3–1 scoreline. Results elsewhere meant that the win took Hibs into second place behind Dundee.

The weather in mid-January meant a depleted card of fixtures. One game that did survive was the meeting at Easter Road between Hibs and Motherwell. Many Hibs fans and most probably many if not all Hibs players felt that when these sides had clashed in the League Cup final back in October, only the fact that the green and whites had played most of the game with ten men stopped them from winning that trophy. Around 40,000 spectators turned out for this latest encounter and watched Smith and Reilly shine in what was a real team effort. The hosts went ahead in spectacular style as a parried shot saw Smith, with his back to goal, perform an overhead kick to send the ball into the roof of the Motherwell net. Early in the second-half, Ormond fired in a stinging shot that flew past the 'Well keeper and earned the Hibs winger a pat on the back from his marker! Next, Smith went on one of his marauding runs down the right, beating several defenders before switching the ball to his left foot and crashing a shot into the net to make it 3–0. It has to be said that but for the heroics of Hamilton in the visiting goal there might have been more than the three goals for the huge Hibs support to celebrate, but only one more goal was scored in the game and that was late on when Forrest made the final score 3–1. The win made Hibs joint top, leading on goal average from Aberdeen, with the Pittodrie club having played three games more. Dundee were third and Hearts fourth, although the Gorgie side had played five more games than Hibs.

A second consecutive home game brought a stuffy Partick Thistle to Easter Road the following weekend and once again a big crowd turned out, hoping to see Hibs continue their winning ways, but in a keenly fought match played in good spirit the visitors merited the point they gained from a 1–1 draw. Johnstone scored the Hibs goal and, perhaps fittingly, Sharp scored for the Jags. With Aberdeen winning away at Clyde, the Dons now occupied top place on their own.

The Scottish Cup draw had been made and Hibs faced a trip to Love Street in the first round. A good-sized crowd, including the Secretary of

State for Scotland and several visiting dignitaries, watched as Combe took an early knock that saw him play out the remainder of the game on the right wing, even though his mobility was severely restricted. The Hibs right back, Jock Govan, was famed for his overlapping runs down the right wing. On this occasion he was pretty well restricted to his defensive duties as Lesz, the home side's Polish winger, was having an excellent game and indeed it was he who set Crowe up to score for the Buddies. Thankfully, Buchanan responded for Hibs so that the game finished at a goal apiece, one of seven first-round ties that would require a replay.

As the draw for the second round had already been made, Hibs and St Mirren knew when they met the following Wednesday that the prize for the winners would be a visit to Ibrox in round two. If the first tie had been very even the replay turned into a bit of a no contest as Hibs scored five without reply. Just six minutes had elapsed when Ormond headed home a Turnbull cross and he repeated the trick on the quarter-hour when Smith was the provider. Given the relatively diminutive stature of players such as Johnstone, Reilly and Ormond, it was amazing how many headed goals they managed when up against much taller defenders. Perhaps that was as much down to the accuracy of the crosses and the clever positional play of the three as anything else. By half-time Hibs had doubled their tally after Smith and Turnbull had set up Johnstone and then Reilly scored from an Ormond pass. With the job done, the second-half was not nearly as exciting, but Johnstone did find the net again to set up the clash with Rangers, who had won the Scottish Cup for the previous three years.

Ahead of that cup tie, Hibs had to visit Glasgow in early February to face Celtic and they did so on a day when heavy snow had fallen. The game went ahead after the lines were cleared. Some 60,000 hardy souls turned up, some of the younger ones amusing themselves by throwing snowballs at the policemen walking around the track. Wearing rubber-soled boots both sides tried hard to play a passing game but it was difficult on such a slippy surface and only one goal was scored. Thankfully, it was by Turnbull early in the second-half and worthy of winning the two points. Up at Pittodrie, the match had also survived the weather but although Aberdeen scored twice they conceded four to Rangers, the combination of the two results putting Hibs back to the top of the league.

Undoubtedly the game of the day was at Ibrox where holders Rangers hosted league leaders Hibs in the second round of the Scottish Cup in front of a full house, many Hibs fans having made the journey through on 'football special' trains. An early goal by Simpson put the hosts ahead and for a period Hibs looked very nervy. Gradually, they began to get their passing game going and deservedly equalised right on the stroke of half-time when Smith met an Ormond cross on the volley and the ball fairly flew into the net. Lessons from the first-half had clearly not been learned:

within two minutes of the restart the Northern Ireland internationalist Simpson scored his and Rangers' second. Fatally for the home side, they decided to revert to their more accustomed style of play, which was to put up a thick blue wall of players between their opponents and the goal. Against many clubs that would probably have worked, but Hibs were famed for their inventive play and Johnstone and Combe soon took the game by the scruff of the neck, firing pinpoint passes to team-mates and generally upsetting the Rangers rearguard. Soon, Turnbull rattled in an equaliser with one of his 'specials' and Rangers found themselves in a quandary, unable to revert to an attacking style and struggling to cope defensively. With nine minutes to go, Hibs sealed the win with a very special goal. A free kick some 20 yards from goal had the hosts putting up a seven-man wall to try and block Turnbull's expected thunderbolt. The Hibs man fooled them all by laying the ball sideways to Ormond who quickly passed it on to Johnstone. The Hibs number eight fired home a historic winner.

With confidence sky high after that cup win, Hibs next travelled through to Cappielow to face a gritty Morton outfit fighting hard to stay clear of the relegation battle. Unsurprisingly in mid-February, the weather was a factor. On this particular winter weekend it was at its worst with blizzards in some parts that were so bad they caused 300 passengers to be trapped overnight in a train in Perthshire. In the west, it was gale-force winds rather than snow, so both teams had to face that as well as each other. Just past the quarter-hour, Reilly opened the scoring with a clever lob over the stranded Morton keeper and ten minutes later Turnbull sent a strong shot into the bottom of the net to double Hibs' lead. On the stroke of half-time, McGarrity took advantage of a slip by Govan to reduce the leeway. Reilly restored the two-goal advantage early in the second-half. Jimmy Cowan in the Morton goal had damaged his shoulder earlier in the game, but he still denied Reilly a hat-trick when the Hibs player sent a powerful header towards goal. A Turnbull rocket did beat him, however, and that made it 4–1 to Hibs before Aitken struck a late second for the hosts. That win put Hibs at the top of the table, one point ahead of Dundee and with three games in hand.

After three successive away games, Hibs finally got to play in front of a home crowd on 24 February when a struggling East Fife provided the opposition. Anyone not aware of the respective league positions would have thought, on the evidence of the first 45 minutes, that the Fifers were chasing the title, but Hibs raised their game in the second period and took the points with goals from Turnbull and Reilly, the latter scoring in the last minute.

On the first two Saturdays of March, Hibs would face Airdrie at Broomfield in first a league and then a cup fixture. The hosts had started the season really badly and looked early candidates for the drop but the new year brought a change in fortunes and they had yet to suffer a defeat in 1951. A sixth minute header from McCulloch resulted in a goal for Airdrie when the Hibs defence switched off defending a corner and thereafter there was some hefty tackling. Right on the interval, Turnbull crossed a ball into the centre and Johnstone rushed in to head an equaliser. It was end-to-end in the second-half with both sides coming close, but eventually McCulloch found the target again with what proved to be the winning goal. Luckily for the green and whites both Dundee and Aberdeen also dropped points that day, but fourth-placed Hearts took advantage of Jimmy Cowan's absence due to injury to slam eight goals past Morton at Tynecastle. Even with that impressive win, Hearts remained eight points behind Hibs and had played a game more.

After their league win of seven days earlier, Airdrie were super-confident going into the third round cup tie and soon set about trying to upset the rhythm of the visitors. Strong challenges kept the referee busy, but in the first-half neither keeper could claim the same and so the sides turned round at 0–0, although Reilly had been unlucky to see a goal ruled out for offside. Within two minutes of the restart, Reilly put Hibs a goal ahead, at which point the Airdrie players seemed to lose their cool and begin to concede foul after foul. Centre half Kelly seemed more intent on getting the man than the ball and as a result Hibs doubled their lead when Reilly slipped in to steer a loose ball into the Airdrie net. A crunching challenge on Johnstone earned Kelly a booking and in truth the big defender was lucky not to be sent off, but his misery was complete when he attempted to head the ball back to his keeper, was woefully short with the effort and Reilly duly nabbed his hat-trick, taking Hibs into round four in the process.

Third Lanark were next on the agenda for Hibs and a good-sized crowd turned out at Easter Road to see if the green and whites could maintain their league challenge. This was a game that had one or two controversial incidents and by the time the final whistle blew, those incidents would lead to as much discussion as the result itself. Firstly, as Aitken of Third Lanark was taking a throw-in, Buchanan jumped up in front of him to block the ball with his hands. It was a bizarre incident and only Buchanan would know why he did it, but he was very lucky as the only action taken by the referee was to have the throw taken again. Not long afterwards, Hibs took the lead with a simple goal from Johnstone and then the strike that doubled the advantage of the home side provided another controversial moment. Reilly was fouled near the edge of the box and as Buchanan set about placing the ball for the free kick the visiting defenders began to form their wall. Before they could do so, Turnbull rushed forward and hammered the ball into the net. The visitors were raging but the referee allowed the goal to stand. With five minutes of the game left and the points looking safe, ex-Hibs man Cuthbertson pulled one back and caused a few nervous moments until Ormond raced clear and shot low into the net with his trusty left foot. Elsewhere, Aberdeen drew, Dundee lost at home to East Fife and in the surprise result of the day Hearts lost 5–4 at Brockville to struggling Falkirk. As a result, Hibs' position at the top was strengthened.

The fourth of six games in March took Hibs to Love Street where the hosts enjoyed the upper hand for long periods but could not find a way past Younger and his defensive colleagues. As it was, Johnstone won the points for Hibs with the only goal of the game in 52 minutes when he headed home an inch-perfect cross from Smith.

The Scottish Cup fourth round (quarter-final) tie at Easter Road against League Cup holders Motherwell was a 48,000 sell-out as the vast majority inside the ground looked for Hibs to get some revenge as beaten League Cup finalists. It was a match full of incident and the excitement began as early as the first minute when Kelly put the visitors ahead. On the quarter-hour mark a cruel blow to the home side saw Ogilvie suffer a double leg break as he bravely got in a challenge to avoid the loss of a second goal. It was completely accidental but devastating for the player and a real problem for the home side, who had to move Combe to left back, meaning that his creativity in midfield would be lost to the side. Despite all of that, Reilly levelled before the interval. As the referee checked his watch for a final time, Kelly scored again to make it 2–1 for Motherwell. Early in the second-half, McLeod made it 3–1 only for Reilly to reduce the deficit within a minute. Huge effort was made by the ten men to try and secure even a replay, but it was not to be and as the Hibs fans left the stadium they must surely have felt that but for the tragic injury to Ogilvie, it would be their team moving through rather than Motherwell – the Lanarkshire side now having the chance to secure a cup double.

The long-term loss of Ogilvie was added to by the short-term injuries to both Ormond and Smith when Hibs had to make the difficult trip to Dens Park at the beginning of April. The Dark Blues were still very much in the league race and must have been buoyant when first Hill in the fifth minute and then Steel in the 67th had them 2–0 ahead, but the team spirit of the green and whites ensured they would fight until the end and Combe's strike a minute later came as no surprise to the travelling fans who now roared on their favourites and were rewarded by a second Combe goal in the 81st minute when he headed home a Turnbull corner. With the game in its final throes, Combe, the little man with the big heart, was so unlucky to see a fierce shot crash back off the crossbar to safety. A point from a 2–2 draw was a good result for Hibs, all things considered, and brought about a set of circumstances where they could, results allowing, win the title in their next outing.

Minus the services of Smith, Reilly and Ormond, Hibs took the field on the night of Wednesday 11 April 1951 at Shawfield against Clyde. Souness, Mulkerrin and Hugh Higgins were the Hibs deputies and despite the fact that it was midweek a huge travelling support witnessed the visitors dominate throughout, scoring four times in the second-half without reply through Souness, who got two, Mulkerrin and Buchanan to lift the league championship with four matches still to play.

Following an international break, Hibs were next in action at Firhill where they met a determined Partick Thistle side intent on showing the newly crowned champions that they were a pretty good outfit too. It was a decent game with a fair amount of goalmouth action, but neither side could score and the spoils were shared. For those Hibs fans that travelled through that day there was a sense that the Scottish Cup final, being played at Hampden that afternoon between Celtic and Motherwell, should have been a battle of the greens but for the unfortunate defeat inflicted by Motherwell in the quarter-final. Had Hibs made it they may well have ended a 50-year wait as they had the measure of Celtic. Ironically, the cup was presented with green and white ribbons attached but sadly it followed a 1–0 Celtic victory.

In the first home game after the championship win, Hibs ran out to a full house to face Raith Rovers and had Alex Bruce in goal, replacing the injured Younger in what would be his one and only first-team game for the club. By chance, Rovers also had their substitute goalkeeper on duty that day, and while Bruce was a virtual spectator, Johnstone had to pick the ball out of his net three times, courtesy of goals by Turnbull, Combe and Reilly.

Back in season 1941/42, Hibs had thrashed a full-strength Rangers 8–1 at Easter Road in a Southern League match and sent shock waves reverberating around the country as a result. When the sides met at Easter Road in the penultimate game of this current season it could so easily have happened again, so dominant were the men in green and white. A combination of good goalkeeping/poor finishing/bad luck meant that Hibs only managed four this time, two in each half, the goals in the first period coming from Johnstone and Reilly headers – quite something when considering the height of the Hibs forwards in comparison to Young in the Rangers defence. Combe and Reilly each set up a goal for Smith before Woodburn ensured a final score of 4–1 with a goal in the last minute.

The final game of the season pitched the title winners up against the Scottish Cup winners when Celtic visited Easter Road on the last day of April. Although there was nothing at stake, both sides served up an entertaining 90 minutes with the hosts coming out on top in a 3–1 win. Smith and Reilly combined well to set Buchanan up for the opener before a little piece of magic from Reilly made it two. Turnbull had headed the ball forward and towards the edge of the Celtic box whereupon Reilly, with his back to goal, allowed the ball to go over his shoulder before spinning and volleying a left-foot shot into the net. Ex-Hibee Jock Weir pulled one back, but Hibs ensured victory and two points when Reilly scored what was becoming his customary last-minute goal. It's fair to say here that although Lawrie scored a number of late goals in his career he was always at pains to say, and rightly so, that he scored lots of other goals too.

The following morning the Scottish League champions flew out to France for a short post-season tour/break and 24 hours after arriving they faced Racing Club de Paris at the Parc des Princes in front of around 20,000 spectators. After an even first-half, Smith opened the scoring early in the second but then the Hibs man was adjudged to have handled the ball in his own box. It was a harsh decision because a shot had been driven straight at him and he had no time to get out of the way. Gudmundsson converted the kick and the game slowed down in pace thereafter. In the last minute, a short free kick from Reilly saw Turnbull fire the ball home only for the referee to order it to be taken again and when it was he blew his whistle for full-time immediately the ball was kicked.

Next it was off to the south of France to face Olympique Nice, where the visitors controlled the game for the most part and won it with a solitary goal scored by Reilly.

Back home in Scotland, the players enjoyed a couple of weeks off before making the short trip to Tynecastle to face Hearts in the final of the East of Scotland Shield. The visitors were without four of their strongest team but started the game well and as half-time approached took the lead when Turnbull drove home a low shot from just inside the area. The home side fought back well in the second-half and deserved their equalising goal ten minutes from the end, despite its fortuitous nature. In trying to head the ball back to Younger, Cairns was short with his effort and that allowed Bauld to nip in and score. Such a late goal might have deflated Hibs' confidence but instead it fired them up again and they went looking for a winner, which duly arrived when Buchanan's long ball down the middle witnessed the Hearts defender Dougan ducking under it, presumably having received a shout from Brown. The ball bounced high and to the keeper's left and rolled into the unguarded net to win Hibs the match.

Four days later, Hibs welcomed Rapide Vienna to Easter Road for a glamour friendly that attracted more than 30,000 spectators. Austrian football was very strong in those days and the Vienna team boasted a few international caps in its starting line-up. Hibs were missing Reilly, Ogilvie and Ormond and it showed as the visitors coasted to a 5–3 win. Goals from Koerner and Dignat gave Rapide a 2–0 half-time lead and that prompted Hugh Shaw to make a few positional changes for the second-half. Those changes worked to a degree because Hibs scored three goals through Turnbull, who got two, including a penalty, and Smith. Unfortunately, Vienna also scored three through Probat, who got two, and Reigler. Although the match was lost it was an entertaining game for the big crowd and invaluable experience for the Scottish side, in terms of facing European competition.

Chapter Six

1951/52

CHAMPIONS AGAIN

Following the summer break, the new season began for Hibs with an invitation to take part in the St Mungo's Cup, a tournament organised as part of the Festival of Britain event. Third Lanark provided the first opposition and because their bus broke down on the way to Easter Road the match kicked off 15 minutes late. Despite not having enough of a chance to warm up the visitors held out until the hour mark when a cross-cum-shot by Turnbull flew past their keeper Petrie and into the net. Then a Smith shot was only parried out and Johnstone reacted quickly to double Hibs' lead. Thirds then pulled one back when former Hearts man Currie passed to former Hibs man Bradley, who shot low into the net from close range. The final goal of the game was engineered by Turnbull. He played a short corner to Reilly, received the return ball and fired a strong low shot that looked as if it might go past the far post until Johnstone dived full length to head it past Petrie and make it 3–1.

The tournament was principally based in Glasgow and so when Hibs met Motherwell in the next round the tie was played at neutral Parkhead. Without the injured Combe, Hibs struggled in the first-half and constantly fell foul of Motherwell's well-executed offside trap. At the other end, Humphries shot home from 30 yards to give his side the interval lead, but early in the second-half Reilly was fouled in the box and Turnbull converted the penalty to level things up. On the hour mark a Johnstone cross was headed home well by Jimmy Souness and then a minute later Johnstone himself settled the tie with a brilliant solo goal after he dribbled past three Motherwell defenders and beat the keeper with a fierce drive from around 12 yards.

Four days later, Hibs were back at Parkhead for a semi-final clash with Aberdeen that drew a crowd of around 27,000. It was pretty even for most of the first-half. Hibs made the breakthrough when Reilly and Johnstone fed Smith, who looked up, saw keeper Martin off his line and calmly lobbed the ball into the empty net. Early in the second-half Delaney found Hamilton unmarked in the box and the latter shot an equaliser before, on the hour mark, Kerr brilliantly saved Hamilton's penalty to keep Hibs level. The match ended in a draw and as there was no suitable venue for a replay in Glasgow the sides agreed to host it, with a toss of the coin determining that the venue would be Pittodrie. There, goalkeeper Martin would have a wonderful game, saving shots from Turnbull, Johnstone and Willie Allan that lesser goalkeepers might have conceded. Eventually he was beaten when Thomson handled the ball in the box and Turnbull converted the penalty, but within minutes the match was all-square when Hamilton screwed a low shot under the diving Kerr. It could have gone either way, but it was the Dons who triumphed when Yorston beat Cairns before shooting high into the Hibs net. The result meant that Aberdeen would meet Celtic in the final after the Parkhead side had defeated Raith Rovers in their semi. For the record, Celtic went on to win the final.

Prior to the season commencing with League Cup ties, an Edinburgh Select side met Liverpool at Easter Road for the Allison Cup, and the game attracted a bumper crowd of 40,000. A goal by Lawrie Reilly had the select ahead after seven minutes and then Liverpool keeper Ashcroft had a string of fine saves – and a bit of luck when the woodwork saved him three times – before Billy Liddell equalised. In the second-half, Liddell struck again to win the game for Liverpool. The big talking point for the fans was the performance of Jock Govan. Gordon Smith suffered an early injury and as the sides had agreed on replacements the Hibs right back took Gordon's number seven jersey and played on the right wing, where he thoroughly enjoyed the experience and certainly didn't look out of place. To add to his enjoyment he was then switched to centre forward when Reilly took a knock and moved to the wing! The select team was Brown, Parker and McSpadyen (Hearts), Buchanan (Hibs), Dougan and Laing (Hearts), Smith, Johnstone and Reilly (Hibs), Wardhaugh (Hearts) and Combe (Hibs).

The League Cup draw placed Hibs in a section with Partick Thistle, Motherwell and Stirling Albion, the opening match taking the green and whites to Firhill. A bright start to the game saw Hibs take the lead through Turnbull on the quarter-hour, but in three disastrous minutes just before the interval the Jags hit a hat-trick of goals through Stott, who got two, and Walker. A shellshocked Hibs began the second-half with a comeback in mind and after 68 minutes a Turnbull penalty offered them hope, but as they pressed for the equaliser Crawford raced clear to win the game 4–2 for the hosts. An incredible 71 goals were scored that day and as well as the six at Firhill, Aberdeen trounced Queen of the South 9–0 and Motherwell beat Stirling Albion 6–4.

The next day, Hibs took to a field with a difference as they faced Grange in a charity cricket match and surprisingly won by one wicket, Jimmy Souness scoring a wonderful 98 not out.

Easter Road was packed the following Wednesday evening as the Hibs fans turned out in force to watch the league champions take on League Cup holders Motherwell. The 'Well fans in the 40,000 crowd must have gone home to Lanarkshire very happy after watching their side trounce Hibs 4–0. Press reports indicate that Hibs didn't play all that badly but that Motherwell produced the best football seen by a visiting side in many a long year. Leading 1–0 at half-time with a Forrest goal, the visitors hit three in the second through Forrest again, Humphries and Kelly.

Those two defeats had Hibs rock bottom in their group, but they got back to winning ways on the Saturday when Stirling Albion visited Easter Road. In the opening quarter of the game it was the Hibs of old and two goals were soon scored. After that, they got a little sloppy and although they scored two more they also conceded two. The Hibs scorers were Johnstone, Ormond, Souness and Turnbull, with Anderson and a Dick penalty counting for Albion. On the same day in Paisley, the Buddies drew 5–5 with Hearts in a game worthy of mention because Willie Bauld scored all five for the Gorgie outfit.

The fixtures now reversed and that meant Partick Thistle visited Easter Road towards the end of August 1951. The Jags had beaten Hibs in the first encounter, but now found themselves facing the side that won the league with cracking displays. It was all Hibs for most of the game and the 5–1 scoreline does not flatter the victors at all. Scorers for Hibs were Turnbull, who got two, including a penalty, Johnstone, who also got two, and Reilly. The last named had a fine game as he led his marker a merry dance by constantly interchanging position with his fellow forwards. Thistle's consolation was scored by Crawford. Motherwell, meanwhile, had suffered a shock defeat away to Stirling Albion, so Hibs were right back in the hunt to qualify.

A large following ensured Hibs were well supported at Fir Park the following Wednesday, but too many players were below par and the hosts won 1–0, effectively ending Hibs' League Cup campaign. On a day when only Kerr, Paterson, Johnstone and Souness played to form it was ironic that the winning goal was scored by ex-Hibs man Johnny Aitkenhead.

The result of the final game was purely academic, but it's worth noting that Hibs played poorly on a bumpy Annfield pitch and yet still managed a 1–1 draw against Stirling Albion. Jimmy Kerr had a great game in goal and Lawrie Reilly never stopped trying, his reward being the Hibs goal. Laird scored for the home side. At Tynecastle, Hearts beat St Mirren 3–1, but the conceded goal, sloppy though it was, cost them a place in the quarter-finals on goal average. For comparison's sake, Hearts scored 15 and lost ten while Hibs scored 12 but lost 13, the figures pretty much speaking for themselves.

The League Cup now out of the way, the champions turned their attention to retaining the league title and began the campaign by crossing the Forth to face Raith Rovers at Stark's Park. There was a welcome return to action for Gordon Smith and although lacking a bit of sharpness he was to have a significant impact on the result. Pat Ward, in for the injured Bobby Combe, laid on the opening goal for Johnstone who rifled a low shot into the net from 12 yards. By half-time it was 2–0 after Smith converted a Johnstone cross and that's how it finished, giving Hibs a winning start.

During the League Cup campaign Hibs had been guilty on a number of occasions of turning in a Jekyll and Hyde performance, and when Aberdeen arrived at Easter Road on league business the green and whites were at it again. In a blistering first-half the home side scored four goals, Johnstone and Reilly getting two each while Harris counted for the Dons. However, Hibs' performance in the second-half was poor, even though the visitors were without Young for a period when he went off injured. Perhaps Hibs thought the points were safe, but they suffered a rude awakening when Yorston made it 4–2 before Young returned to the pitch and scored almost right away to make it 4–3. Hibs were at sixes and sevens by now and it was no real surprise when Boag equalised near the end.

Next up was a visit to Tynecastle for the derby and with a full house at this all-ticket match it was Reilly who opened the scoring after ten minutes following good play by Smith, Combe and Johnstone but the lead was short-lived as Conn soon scored the equaliser. There were no more goals but it was an entertaining match that saw the fans inter-mingling without the slightest hint of trouble.

With Jimmy Kerr injured, Hibs gave a debut to young Willie Bruce for the visit of Third Lanark at the end of September. It has to be said that Bruce looked nervous throughout and conceded twice, but Gordon Smith was at his sparkling best and hugely involved in helping his side score five times. In the first-half it was Petrie in the other goal who saw all the action with Hibs hitting woodwork on no fewer than four occasions before Ormond finally got one on target to make it 1–0 at the break. Three minutes into the second-half, Henderson beat Bruce to make it 1–1, but a further three minutes on Reilly restored the lead. Five minutes later, Bruce dropped a cross and Goodall made it 2–2, at which point Smith came into his own in setting up another for Reilly and two for Johnstone.

The following Saturday Hibs had to do without the services of Reilly and Johnstone, who were in Belfast playing for Scotland against Ireland. As Johnstone was bagging two of the goals in a 3–0 win, his club side were facing Stirling Albion at Annfield and cruising to a worthy 4–1 win in a game where they scored all five goals. Unlucky Jock Govan put through his own net, but Combe and Ormond each scored a double and the result put Hibs to the top of the table as the only undefeated side in the league.

Undoubtedly the best goalkeeper in Scotland at that time was Jimmy Cowan of Morton and it was against Cowan and his team-mates that Hibs next played. Around 30,000 turned out at Easter Road and watched Cowan defy Hibs time and again. He was beaten twice in the game, but only one counted thanks to a quite bizarre decision by the referee. Right on half-time Hibs won a free kick which Turnbull flighted into the box for Smith to head home. Everyone heard the whistle and assumed the break had been reached, but the referee announced to the stunned Hibs players that he'd blown the whistle after Turnbull's free kick but before Smith's header. Luckily the second attempt counted as a glancing header from Ormond sailed past Cowan's outstretched hand and went in off a post. The narrow win put Hibs in second place because the new leaders, East Fife, had played twice that week and won on both occasions.

A second successive home game drew a second successive 30,000 as Hibs next faced Partick Thistle. Hibs sparkled and led 2–0 at the interval thanks to goals by Johnstone and Reilly. There would be no collapse in the style shown weeks earlier against Aberdeen, and Hibs struck three more times through Smith, Reilly and Johnstone to win the match 5–0 and go back to the top of the table. Two points worth noting from this match were the outstanding performance of Bobby Combe, who was involved in setting up four of the five goals, and the strange case of the Hibs fan who sat behind the press box and barracked Turnbull throughout. *The Scotsman* reporter expressed the view that Turnbull had enjoyed a good 90 minutes, which made the criticism hard to understand. It is true to say that the fan might not have been quite so vociferous had Turnbull taken him to task – he was most certainly a man you would not want to upset!

On the day that Dundee scored a last-minute goal at Hampden to beat Rangers in the final of the League Cup, Hibs were also in Glasgow to face Celtic at Parkhead. Going into the game, the hosts were struggling near the foot of the table, but they managed to secure a draw with McPhail's goal balancing out one from Ormond. That result meant East Fife leapfrogged Hibs to the top, but the men from Easter Road had thirteen points from eight starts, were still unbeaten and had scored twenty-three goals for the loss of just eight.

It was the other half of the Old Firm next when Rangers came to Easter Road, bringing with them a sizeable support that helped swell the attendance to 50,000. Leading by a goal from Findlay, the visitors sat back and relied upon their famous Iron Curtain defence to win them the game. For a long time it looked as if the tactic might works as Hibs' small forwards struggled against the giants in the Rangers back line. Then Jock

Govan took matters in hand for Hibs. The long-legged right back went on a marauding run down the right and almost reached the byline before firing a low cross into the box for Smith to force home the equaliser and secure a point for his side.

During the following week, Hibs travelled to Ochilview to face Stenhousemuir in a friendly and secured a fine 5–3 win with a side made up of first-team regulars and a few reserves. Miller, Kerr and Allan scored for the home side with Jimmy Mulkerrin (2), Johnstone, Souness and Turnbull all finding the net for the visitors.

Although Hibs had not yet faced all of the other sides in the league, their next fixture took them to Cappielow to face the Morton side they had narrowly beaten just five weeks earlier. The pitch was very muddy, as seemed normal for that venue, and the visitors got off to the worst possible start when their former player Linwood scored in the first minute. Ten minutes later Reilly was pulled down in the box, but Jimmy Cowan made a wonderful save at Turnbull's effort to keep his side in front. Midway through the half an Ormond cross allowed Reilly to equalise before McGarrity made it 2–1 for the hosts. The second-half witnessed a string of wonderful saves by Cowan, but no more goals as Hibs slipped to their first league defeat of the season.

A home tie against league leaders East Fife drew a crowd in excess of 40,000. Those supporting Hibs were met by the news that Combe was injured and his place had been given to young Michael Gallagher. The new man had a solid game. With Hibs shooting down the slope in the first-half, Reilly earned a penalty for Turnbull to convert and Ormond scored a second after Duncan had equalised. The same player made it 2–2 shortly after the break, but Hibs upped their game and Buchanan and Johnstone got the goals to secure a 4–2 win. The Fifers, however, stayed at the top with 18 points from 12 starts. Hibs were second, having earned 16 points from 11 starts.

With November nearing its end, Hibs next travelled to Broomfield to face Airdrie in what would be a black day for Willie Ormond. The hosts were known for their robust style and during the game Ormond sustained a suspected broken leg, Paterson a suspected fractured rib and Younger a heavy knock to his ankle. Despite all of that, the visitors still took the points thanks to goals by Ormond and Johnstone.

The first of five games scheduled for December took Hibs to Dens Park to face a struggling Dundee and the points were won in some style as Johnstone and Turnbull each grabbed a double, with only Ewan on target for the hosts.

With a light frost on the pitch and a strong wind blowing across the park, Hibs welcomed Queen of the South to Easter Road in front of a sizeable home crowd. The visitors were stuffy in defence in the first-half, restricting Hibs to just the one goal from Reilly, but in the second their game plan disappeared as the hosts added four more through Reilly, Smith and Johnstone, who got two.

Goals seemed to be coming easily for this Hibs side and that trend continued at Love Street when four were scored against St Mirren without reply. Johnstone grabbed another double, Smith and Combe getting the others. The two points ensured that Hibs retained second spot with their game in hand over East Fife. Hearts were third, some five points behind while Rangers sat fourth a further three points adrift, but with three games in hand over Hibs.

The Saturday before Christmas brought Raith Rovers to Easter Road and unluckily for them they encountered a Hibs side at its best with the forwards interchanging positions throughout and thoroughly confusing the Rovers defenders in the process. Had all of the chances been taken, double figures would have been achieved, but the woodwork and some good goalkeeping restricted the scoreline to 5–0. Once again Johnstone got a double as did Combe, with Reilly getting the other.

A six-game unbeaten run came to an end in the last fixture of the year when Hibs faced Motherwell at Fir Park and lost 3–1. The hosts had been struggling in the league and had signed Sloan and Cox from Hearts in a bid to improve their results. The double signing worked to good effect with Sloan getting the third goal after former Hibs favourite Johnny Aitkenhead had hit a double. Ironically, it would be a Motherwell player by the name of Kilmarnock who scored the Hibs goal, but there was some good news as East Fife also lost that day. At Tynecastle, Hearts reduced the gap by beating Airdrie 6–1, all of the goals being scored in the first-half.

The New Year derby on 1 January 1952 saw Easter Road packed almost to capacity and the vast majority must surely have left around 4.45pm wondering how on earth Hibs had lost. The home side dominated huge periods of the play but couldn't finish off numerous promising moves with vital goals. Instead, Hearts took the lead through Wardhaugh in the 18th minute and then Bauld got a second some 11 minutes later. Reilly pulled one back within 60 seconds, but seven minutes from the break Bauld restored Hearts' two-goal lead. Good combination play by Smith and Turnbull set Reilly up to reduce the deficit before Smith was carried off on a stretcher following a quite savage foul by Conn. The winger returned after treatment but looked shaken and was quiet thereafter. A late penalty award gave Hibs the chance to save a point, but Turnbull put his shot high over the bar and the game was lost.

The very next day, on a snow-covered pitch with the lines cleared, Hibs faced Third Lanark at Cathkin and hit top form to easily earn the two points on offer. Reilly beat two defenders to slot home the first just past the quarter-hour mark and before half-time he'd scored again, as had Johnstone, to make it 3–0. It must be said that the right-wing partnership of Govan and Smith was causing the home side great difficulty and both were involved in setting Reilly up for his hat-trick goal before Combe completed the scoring with a smart shot on the turn. Had it not been for some heroics by Robertson in the home goal the winning margin of 5–0 would surely have been much greater.

On the following Saturday the wintry weather gripping Scotland caused a number of postponements, but the Hibs v Stirling Albion match survived and was played on a snowy surface that cut up easily. How the Albion men must have wished the game was postponed as they were taught a footballing lesson by a sparkling Hibs eleven. The home side scored three goals in the opening quarter of an hour and all came from Gordon Smith crosses, converted by Reilly twice and Combe. Both of those scorers went on to secure hat-tricks while Turnbull got two, one from the penalty spot. Smith may not have scored, but he was brilliant throughout with his clever play and delivery of crosses. The 8–0 win meant Hibs had scored 65 goals in 20 starts.

A week later Hibs made the long journey north to Aberdeen on a day when a freezing wind was blowing in off the North Sea, creating very difficult playing conditions. It wasn't until the 63rd minute that the deadlock was broken. Turnbull and Reilly combined to set up Johnstone, who fired a low shot under the diving body of Watson in the Aberdeen goal. The visitors were in control now but didn't score again until two minutes from time when Smith sent a fierce drive into the bottom corner. With literally the last kick of the ball Yorston put a more respectable look on the final score, but Hibs were worthy winners on the day.

It was Firhill for thrills the following Saturday afternoon when a capacity crowd watched Gordon Smith at his bewildering best and at the root of everything good from Hibernian. On the half hour he released Combe down the right and the Hibs man cut in on his left foot and sent a blistering drive past Ledgerwood into the far corner of the net. A freezing fog was hovering over the stadium, but the game was never under threat. The home side earned a 50th-minute equaliser when Walker scored a carbon copy of the Combe goal. The visitors pushed and pushed for a winner, getting it in the 89th minute when Combe's corner was headed home by Buchanan. On the same day, Hearts drew 2–2 with Rangers at Tynecastle – good news for the green and whites, who moved another point clear of them both.

The Scottish Cup first-round draw sent Hibs to Stark's Park to face Raith Rovers. The record crowd of 30,206 would all go home disappointed as it was a poor game on a treacherous surface and neither side found the net. Meanwhile, Hearts were losing 3–0 at Pittodrie in the league, thereby passing up the chance to leapfrog Hibs, but the news was not so good from Love Street where Rangers won 5–0.

On the following Wednesday evening the replay was expected by most to go Hibs' way, but no one had told the Raith players, who set about dominating periods of the game and defying the Hibs forwards at every turn. Even with 30 minutes of extra time played, neither side could score and so a second replay would be required.

Ahead of that replay, Hibs hosted a good-going Celtic side at Easter Road, where the crowd exceeded 40,000. The home side looked the better outfit throughout with Paterson and Smith in particular catching the eye. Paterson nullified the threat of McPhail very effectively while Smith taunted and tormented the Celtic rearguard. It was the Hibs winger that almost opened the scoring when he dashed down the right and let fly a crashing shot that came back off the crossbar with Bonnar beaten all ends up. On the quarter-hour, Smith took a short free kick to Turnbull and the latter hammered a low shot into the Celtic net. As half-time approached Younger couldn't get his punched clearance to safety and Walsh pounced to equalise. Down the slope in the second-half, Hibs were all over their visitors with the forward line leading their defenders a merry dance. Ten minutes in, Smith crossed for Reilly to head home and five minutes from time Johnstone raced through the middle to beat Bonnar and secure a 3–1 home win and two very good points.

Next up was the second cup replay against Raith Rovers, which the SFA had decided should be played at neutral Tynecastle. It would be easy for Hibs to blame a poor playing surface or indeed point to the fact that the venue had never been kind to them in cup ties, but the plain truth is that Raith Rovers got their game plan spot-on and deservedly won 4–1 on the night. A goal up in two minutes through Penman, the Fifers always looked comfortable and all the more so on the quarter-hour when Younger was lobbed and McIntyre rushed in to finish. Hibs started the second-half by scoring before a Rovers player had touched the ball, Reilly finishing the move, but two goals in two minutes from Penman and Kelly ended Hibs' hopes of advancement for yet another year.

The league now became the sole target and the outcome of the next match would give an indication as to how things might turn out at the season's end. Hibs were at Ibrox with a big following helping to swell the crowd to 70,000. There was to be fast, clever football from both sides and though Young and Reilly were booked and there were two penalties, it was never a dirty game. In the fifth minute Young was adjudged to have handled in his box and though he protested his innocence a penalty was awarded: Turnbull fired it home, sending Brown the wrong way. The home side equalised in strange fashion when McCulloch crossed from the byline and under pressure from Woodburn, Younger contrived to punch the ball into his own net. Big Tommy made up for his error later with two or three stunning saves. In the second-half Rangers applied pressure, but Hibs soaked it up before breaking out and storming downfield for Reilly to make it 2–1 with a clever lob over Brown's head. Before the end, Howie was found guilty of handling in the box and Young converted the penalty to make the final score 2–2. A point each was a fair reflection on the game, although that outcome favoured Hibs more than it did their hosts.

In mid-February St Mirren visited Easter Road and from the off they were under the cosh with keeper Crabtree making two quite stunning saves early on to deny Reilly and Turnbull. It took the home side until the 35th minute to make the breakthrough, when Reilly was on the end of a fine cross from Ormond, and two minutes later he scored again, with Smith the provider on this occasion. Seven minutes into the second-half Ormond scored from a Turnbull pass and before the final whistle had blown Smith and Ormond also found the net to ensure a 5–0 win. Hibs now had 39 points from 25 starts with Rangers in second on 32 from 23 and Hearts third, also on 32 but from 25 games. Hibs were also top scorers with 79 goals.

The journey to Methil to face East Fife at Bayview was made without goalkeeper Tommy Younger as he was in Germany playing for a British Army XI. His place in the Hibs side was taken by Kerr. Unluckily for the stand-in he lost three goals, but none could be considered errors on his part as it was his defensive colleagues who made the mistakes. It all started brightly for the visitors, who took the lead in the tenth minute through Smith, but from then on the home side ruled and took the points with goals from Christie, Bonthrone and a Duncan penalty.

On 1 March, Hibs played the first of six games scheduled for that month when they took on Airdrie at Easter Road. Reilly gave them an early lead but Younger, back from Germany, made three outstanding saves to deny the Diamonds an equaliser. Reilly was then tripped in the box and Ormond's penalty was pushed out by the keeper, but Willie reacted quickly to score on the rebound. Early in the second-half Smith set Reilly up for number three and then Johnstone completed the scoring before the end. A 4–0 win sounds convincing but those early saves by Younger were crucial. Just below *The Scotsman* match report from that Hibs game was a little article advising that Celtic had continued to fly the Eire flag over Parkhead despite being instructed by the SFA not to do so. The logic behind the instruction to remove it was that it might help reduce the sectarian-based fighting between Celtic and Rangers fans.

In the following midweek, Hibs travelled south to face Doncaster Rovers under their new floodlights – seven lights along each side and one in each corner. The set-up met with approval and Hibs enjoyed it as they won 3–0, thanks to a Johnstone double and one from Ormond.

On the Saturday, with cup ties the order of the day and Hibs without one to play, the Easter Road men travelled to face Manchester City at Maine Road and won 4–1 in front of more than 35,000 fans. The City team had been made aware that Gordon Smith was unable to play and so they paid little attention to Jimmy Souness who replaced him on the right wing. It was a fatal error on their part as Jimmy scored all four Hibs goals, the City strike coming from Don Revie.

The third-last league game of the season took Hibs to Palmerston Park where Queen of the South were in fine form and won the game 5–2 very much against the expectations of most. Brown got one for the home side and Paterson the other four. Reilly and Johnstone were on the mark for Hibs, who now had 41 points from 28 games with Rangers on 38 from 26 and Hearts and Celtic close behind.

The next outing for Hibs was a friendly against St Mirren at Easter Road where Buchanan, Reilly, Turnbull and Ormond all found the net in a 4-1 victory, Crowe scoring for the Buddies.

Another trip to Manchester followed. This time it was to face United at Old Trafford and once again Hibs returned home unbeaten, although on this occasion the outcome was a 1–1 draw with Turnbull the marksman.

With two games left to play, Hibs clinched the championship when they beat Dundee 3–1 at Easter Road on 9 April 1952. Somewhat disappointingly, only 25,000 turned up for the match, but those who did were entertained to an enthralling 90 minutes. Early in the proceedings, Christie lobbed a ball towards the Hibs goal. At the fatal moment, Younger slipped and the ball sailed past him into the empty net. The home crowd, however, got right behind their favourites and soon a corner from Smith was headed home by Ormond, for the equaliser. A little later Smith found Combe, who in turn found Ormond and it was 2–1. Later, Combe made it 3–1 and Younger redeemed himself by making two great saves late in the game. The biggest cheer of the day was reserved for right back Jock Govan, who ran the length of the park, beating several Dundee men on the way including the goalie, only to loft his final shot over the bar. It was a glaring miss, but the fans loved Govan and so forgave him in the euphoria surrounding the winning of the title.

Another friendly took Hibs to Love Street to face St Mirren and once again the green and whites came out on top, winning 3–0 with goals from Ormond and Reilly, who got a double.

The last league game of the season brought Scottish Cup winners Motherwell to Easter Road in a game that attracted upwards of 35,000 spectators. In the fifth minute Paton downed Reilly in the box, but Johnston saved Turnbull's penalty. The opener was delayed only another three minutes as Reilly scored a lovely solo goal after beating two defenders. In the 14th minute Reilly turned provider when he released Smith who in turn found Ormond, and the outside left made it 2–0. Barely another five minutes had passed before Hibs struck again, Combe the scorer on this occasion as he finished off a four-man move. The hosts relaxed now and though they lost a goal to Kelly on the hour mark the result was never in doubt.

Two days later Hibs were at White Hart Lane facing and beating Tottenham Hotspur, who opened the scoring through Ramsay but then conceded twice to Smith. On the same evening Hearts led 2–0 at Stamford Bridge, but Chelsea fought back to win 3–2.

On the Thursday evening, Bolton Wanderers arrived at Easter Road for a floodlit friendly that attracted a healthy crowd of more than 33,000. It was end-to-end in the first-half with only goals missing from the spectacle, but just two minutes into the second-half Govan crossed and Reilly trapped, controlled and swivelled on the ball to make it 1–0. Next, the legendary Nat Lofthouse scored a goal that had the whole crowd applauding. He collected a ball on the half-way line and set off for the Hibs goalmouth, leaving Paterson and Govan in his wake before slamming the ball past McQueen, the Kilbirnie Ladeside keeper deputising for Younger. Hibs took the game to Bolton, but it was Lofthouse who scored the next goal against the run of play before Smith beat off two challenges, fed Reilly and watched as the centre scored a fine equalising goal.

That game against Bolton set Hibs up nicely for a trip to Tynecastle to meet Hearts in the final of the East of Scotland Shield. After 16 minutes Smith left the field with a painful face knock and though he never returned the ten men still won the game handsomely with goals from Reilly and Combe, who got two.

A short end-of-season tour of Germany saw Hibs beat a Limburg Select 4–2 with goals from Combe, Reilly, Smith and Turnbull. That night the players had a few beers to unwind and encountered a couple of Cologne players in the hotel bar. The Germans expressed surprise that the Hibs men were drinking on the night before a game, but of course the Scots responded with a 'We'll beat you anyway'. The next evening the score was Cologne 4 Hibs 1, Combe the scorer, so those words uttered in confidence the previous evening had come back to haunt the Easter Road men.

Three days later, in front of a massive 40,000-plus crowd, Hibs faced Borussia Dortmund and won 2–1. The crowd was greatly swelled by the presence of British Forces personnel and Hibs were well cheered in their victory. The local newspaper, *Wesser Kurier*, proclaimed in its match report that 'Hibernian's football was the most beautiful and accurate play seen in Dortmund since the war'. Fluegel got the Dortmund goal, while

Reilly grabbed a double for the visitors. Next it was on to a tie against Werder Bremen which Hibs justly won 3–2. Reilly got another double and Souness the other, but poor Willie Ormond was sent off by the local referee, who was lambasted in the press the following day! The tour ended with a 1–1 draw against St Pauli, Buchanan getting the Hibs goal.

Chapter Seven

1952/53

GOAL AVERAGE AGONY

Having enjoyed a couple of months off, the Hibs players reported for the new season and set about getting themselves fit for the long league and cup campaigns ahead. It is said that very little work was done with the ball and that when Eddie Turnbull asked Hugh Shaw why that was, he responded by saying if the players didn't see the ball much during the week they'd be hungrier for it on a Saturday. It's not clear what Turnbull's reaction was to that, but it doesn't take much of an imagination to guess!

The first game for Hibs was in the League Cup against Partick Thistle at Firhill. The Jags, St Mirren and Celtic made up the section and it was a tough opening game which Hibs won handsomely 5–1. In the opening moments, Sharp stung the fingers of Tommy Younger with a fierce drive, but the ball rebounded into play and was collected by Lawrie Reilly, who quickly shuttled it on to Bobby Combe before racing off downfield. Combe lobbed a perfectly weighted ball over the heads of the Thistle defenders and there was Reilly racing through to score. Prior to half-time, Combe added a second and soon after the break Reilly made it three before Stott pulled one back, but it meant little as Reilly went on to complete his hat-trick and Turnbull added another to make the final score 5–1. It was truly a good day for Edinburgh: over at Tynecastle, Hearts hammered a full-strength Rangers 5–0.

On 13 August 1952, in front of more than 40,000 fans, the League Championship flag was unfurled at Easter Road ahead of Hibs facing St Mirren in their first competitive home fixture of the season. The joyous celebrations became somewhat muted after four minutes when McGill put the Buddies a goal in front, but it was cheers all the way when Reilly equalised on 24 following a defence-splitting pass from Smith. Surely Hibs would go on to score more now. Indeed, on the half hour, Smith evaded two challenges before lashing a shot toward goal which the keeper parried only for Smith to follow up and net the rebound. Early in the second-half Combe made it 3–1 and then Ormond got a fourth before

Duncanson made it 4–2. With time running out Turnbull made it 5–2 and Hibs topped the section with ten goals for and three against.

On to Parkhead for the next challenge, and it was a close game played out in front of a big and noisy crowd. Chances were few at either end and eventually the game was won for Celtic by an 80th-minute strike from McPhail.

The fixtures now reversed and that meant a home tie against Partick Thistle. In a rough and tumble game, Hibs started slowly and didn't seem to be on top of their game but still took a one-goal lead in at the interval after Turnbull had been fouled in the area and got up to take and convert the penalty in the 40th minute. On the hour mark, Sharp equalised after some poor defending from the home side, but with 15 minutes left Hibs restored their lead with the best move of the match. Smith found Ormond on the left and the winger picked out Combe, whose goalbound shot was handled by Collins. Turnbull netted the resultant penalty. Right at the end, Combe made it 3–1 and Hibs stayed top of the section.

On arrival at Love Street the following midweek, Hibs found that there was a gale-force wind blowing from one end of the pitch to the other. The home side won the toss and elected to play with the wind at their backs. It proved to be a good choice as they led 3–0 at the break. A first-minute penalty from Telfer was brilliantly saved by McCracken, deputising for the injured Younger, but just 60 seconds later he was beaten by Stewart and then twice more by McGill before the sides changed ends. Unfortunately, Hibs didn't harness the wind as well as their hosts had and could only manage one goal, Bobby Johnstone the scorer, before the end.

The final game in the group brought Celtic to Easter Road for a winner-takes-all showdown against a Hibs side determined to earn the points needed to qualify for the quarter-finals. It soon became clear that both sides were prepared to get physical if needed, but referee McKerchar was outstanding and kept a firm grip on the game, much to the surprise of the crowd of over 50,000. Hibs were on fire and a rapier-like attack ended with Turnbull firing a rocket shot into the net for a 1–0 lead. Celtic tried to fight back, but Hibs stood firm and when a corner from Smith was headed against the bar by Buchanan, Reilly was first to react to the rebound to give his side a 2–0 interval lead. The second-half started as the first ended with Hibs in the ascendancy and after Ormond had missed two decent chances, Reilly beat his man to the ball and added a third goal. The visitors poured men forward now, but the Hibs defence, with Howie deputising for the injured Paterson at centre half, was magnificent. The 3–0 win meant both clubs finished on the same points, but Hibs had a superior goal average and so qualified as a result.

On 6 September 1952 Gordon Smith reached the personal milestone of having played 500 games for the club (all games including those played during the Second World War included) when he and his team-mates faced Queen of the South at Easter Road in the first league match of the season. Sadly for Gordon, it would turn out to be a day he'd rather forget as Hibs lost 3–1 to a good Queens side. Smith did score the Hibs goal, but Johnston and Paterson twice counted for the visitors. Throughout the game there had been a number of somewhat dubious decisions going against Hibs and the home fans showed their frustration on the final whistle when they booed the referee off the park. Their view was that he had failed miserably to live up to his name – Mr Faultless from Glasgow.

The following Saturday Hibs were at Cappielow to face Morton in the first leg of the quarter-final of the League Cup and they ran riot. Apparently the admission money for these quarter-final matches was increased by sixpence, but those Hibs fans in Greenock for the tie would surely not have begrudged paying up when they got the chance to see Johnstone and Ormond score two each and Turnbull and Smith get singles to make the final score 6–0 to the visitors. All the more remarkable was the fact that prior to this match Morton had not been beaten at home this season.

As a long and faithful servant of Hibernian FC, having joined the club at just 16 years of age and now having more than 500 appearances under his belt, Gordon Smith was awarded a testimonial match and the opposition would be no less a team than the English First Division champions, Manchester United. A football feast was possible, given the number of highly skilled players on either side, and it is safe to say that the fans got that feast and more, with the football correspondent from *The Scotsman* later writing: 'The match provided the finest football entertainment that I have ever seen as in football artistry it surpassed anything ever seen in Edinburgh.'

As to the game, it was unsurprisingly end-to-end stuff and the result could have gone either way despite the 'evidence' of the final scoreline. The first goal arrived on the quarter-hour, a typical Turnbull rocket from distance. Seven minutes later the brilliant Arthur Rowley fired past McCracken from 20 yards to level. The same player scored again on the half-hour, but Turnbull also got his second when his penalty was saved but not held and Eddie netted the rebound. Pearson restored the United lead, which they carried into the second-half but after a Reilly shot had hit the post, Ormond pounced to equalise and then Turnbull converted another penalty to make it 4–3. A chance for the visitors to equalise was lost when Carey missed a penalty and Smith punished them by scoring at the other end to increase the Hibs lead. The crowd loved this flowing football and the cheering was virtually constant throughout the game. Two more goals by Reilly made the final score 7–3 to Hibs and provided the Prince of Wingers with a night to remember.

Two nights later, Hibs were at home again when Morton visited with the impossible task of overhauling a six-goal deficit in the League Cup tie. Needless to say, they didn't manage it, but they did score three goals through Quinn, who got two, and Linwood. Unfortunately for the visitors, Hibs scored six again, four of those coming in a devastating opening 25 minutes. Ormond, two from Johnstone and one from Reilly were added to after the break when both Reilly and Ormond secured their doubles. The aggregate score of 12–3 was really tough on Morton keeper Jimmy Cowan, a star performer who was badly let down by his team-mates over the two games.

Having scored 20 goals in their previous three matches, Hibs were hoping to carry that sort of form into their next match which brought Hearts to Easter Road for the first derby of the season. In the past, the free-scoring Hibs had seemed to falter at times against their oldest rivals. On this occasion, the visitors had to thank keeper Watters and the woodwork for preventing an absolute mauling by the green and whites. Hibs were immense and dictated long periods of the game, starting with the opening goal from Reilly in the eleventh minute when he latched on to a good through ball from Smith. Two minutes from the break Jock Govan swung over a brilliant cross from the right and there was Reilly to steer the ball past Watters to make it 2–0. Twice Ormond hit the woodwork and three times Watters defied first Smith and then Johnstone before Reilly secured his hat-trick following great build-up play from Ormond and Turnbull. The end of the match was fast approaching when Younger, who had the ball firmly clasped to his chest, was, in the style of play in those days, charged by Durkin who tried to push him into the net. Younger was a big lad and stood firm while pushing Durkin away. Astonishingly, referee Jack Mowatt pointed to the spot for a Hearts penalty. It was a ludicrous decision and even some of the Hearts players looked embarrassed by it, but ultimately the kick was taken and converted by Bobby Parker to make the final score 3–1.

Years later when I was in conversation with Lawrie Reilly, he told me how outraged he had been when one of the local newspapers led its match report with the headline PARKER PENALTY FAILS TO SAVE HEARTS – Lawrie was quite rightly miffed and felt that the headline should have been about his hat-trick or even the fact that Hearts were both outplayed and outclassed.

Another week on and Hibs were banging in the goals again in a display that prompted one West of Scotland newsman to write that such was the display of this Hibernian team that nine of the eleven should be selected to play for Scotland against Wales in an upcoming international. The article went on to explain that the writer would have said all eleven but that Gallagher (Irish) and Paterson (English) were not eligible. The game that brought forward these words was at Fir Park, and Hibs won it 7–3. Two from Reilly and another two from Johnstone ensured a 4–1 half-time lead with ex-Hibs man Aitkenhead scoring for Motherwell. Early in the second-half Humphries and Kelly got the hosts back to 4–3, but a Turnbull penalty and two more from Reilly made it 7–3 at the end. It has to be said that Lawrie Reilly was at his very best in these recent matches – and he wasn't the only one.

After the international break, Hibs next faced Dundee at neutral Tynecastle in the semi-final of the League Cup. This was not a happy hunting ground for Hibs in terms of semi-final matches and once again they would fall at the last but one hurdle in front of 46,000 spectators. It had started well enough, with the in-form Reilly firing Hibs ahead, but Steel got the Dark Blues level and former Hearts man Flavell struck what proved to be the winning goal on his old home patch.

That disappointment was not allowed to linger and a few days later Hibs got it out of their system in the best possible way by going to Ibrox and silencing the majority of the 60,000 crowd by winning 2–1. The visitors were the better side throughout and although Grierson struck first to put Rangers ahead it was Hibs who dominated the play, Reilly getting them level by the break. Early in the second-half Turnbull hammered home a fierce drive and the points were destined for Edinburgh.

Around this time it was reported that Turnbull had tabled a transfer request some weeks earlier. At least two English clubs were interested, with Newcastle very keen indeed. The board and manager did not want the player to leave and so decided to let Turnbull decide for himself. Happily, Eddie stayed – and did so to the end of his playing career.

A week after that great win at Ibrox, Hibs faced Falkirk at Easter Road without the services of Reilly and Smith, who were both playing for Scotland. The replacements were Jimmy Mulkerrin and Jimmy Souness and it seemed as though the visitors felt that an apparently weakened Hibernian could be there for the taking. The Bairns started the match well and were ahead after ten minutes when Howie felled former Hibs man Angus Plumb in the box and Duncan converted the spot kick. Seventeen minutes later Duncan repeated that feat after Paterson was adjudged to have handled in the box. Hibs were now 2–0 down, with their home crowd pretty quiet. If anything, however, the loss of the second goal kick-started Hibs into action and by the break they were level thanks to goals from Ormond and Turnbull. The tide had now turned and the home side were in control, reinforcing that point by scoring another two goals without reply through Souness and Turnbull.

During the following week Hibs travelled south to face Arsenal at Highbury, where everything that could go wrong for them did. Conversely, everything Arsenal tried seemed to come off and as a result they beat their Scottish opponents 7–1. With the Duke of Edinburgh in the 55,000 crowd and learning later that the gate receipts had reached £11,545, with the money going to his playing fields appeal, Roper scored five of the home goals, Lishman getting the other two and Reilly scoring for Hibs. Years later, Lawrie Reilly told me that when the Hibs men got back to the dressing room at the final whistle there was deathly silence and much holding of heads in hands. The bold Lawrie then declared to his defensive team-mates: 'Well, I did my job, what happened to you guys?' It was typical Reilly, but don't forget he was always the first to talk of what he called the Stupendous Six, referring to those behind the Famous Five without whom Hibs would not have achieved league title success.

On the next Saturday the opponents were Clyde at Shawfield Stadium in Glasgow. Johnstone and Ormond scored either side of a goal by Robertson to make it 2–1 at the break before Johnstone got another on the hour mark and Buchanan hit a late consolation for the hosts. Elsewhere in Glasgow that day, Dundee were beating Kilmarnock in the final of the League Cup to be the first side to win it in successive years. Dundee had of course beaten Hibs in the semi, and so at least the Hibs fans could say their side had been knocked out by the trophy winners.

Going along quite nicely in the league, the green and whites came down to earth with a bit of a bump when they lost to a struggling Third Lanark at Cathkin Park by a scoreline of 2–0 with Dobbie getting both goals. Just how Hibs contrived to lose a game they dominated throughout defies description, but the effect of that loss was to hand East Fife and Celtic joint top spot in the league.

At home the following weekend Hibs looked somewhat nervy against mid-table Airdrie and that was reflected in a first-half that had no goals and precious few chances. The second period was a different story as a Turnbull double and a fine solo goal from Ormond were met with only one goal by Airdrie from Seawright.

In mid-November Dundee were the visitors to Easter Road for what many predicted would be a difficult game given the recent success by the Dark Blues in winning the League Cup. The Dens Park outfit were big and strong, especially in defence, but they made the mistake of trying to dominate Hibs using aerial football, while the home side played their passing game to good effect. In 36 minutes Combe sliced the home defence open with a glorious pass that released Johnstone, who scored from around 12 yards. More chances were created but it wasn't until the 78th minute that the second goal came along when Reilly sent a rasping shot past Henderson and into the net. The final whistle was getting close when Turnbull scored from the spot to make it 3–0.

On 22 November the green and whites travelled over the Forth to face league leaders East Fife knowing that they'd have to be at their best against a very good Bayview outfit. As expected the Fifers attacked from the off, but by half-time their dominance had yielded just the one goal by Gardner. In the second-half, presumably after a robust pep talk from Hugh Shaw, the Hibees came out with all guns blazing and scored five times. The ever alert Reilly got a hat-trick with Smith and Turnbull also finding the net, but the home side made a game of it and scored two of their own through Gardner again and a penalty from Emery. Despite losing, East Fife stayed top by one point from Hibs, who had two games in hand.

November ended as it had started for Hibs, with an unexpected defeat. On a frosty Easter Road pitch the hosts did everything but score while their visitors St Mirren bagged two through Gemmell and Stewart. Throughout the 90 minutes Hibs had peppered the Saints goal but either missed, hit woodwork or found keeper Park equal to the task. In fairness St Mirren had a good side and that win actually took them to the top of the table.

A second successive home game saw Celtic as visitors to Easter Road at the start of December. The Parkhead side had struggled the previous season and had actually looked like relegation candidates at one point, but the current campaign was a different story and it was no surprise that they played well enough to secure a 1–1 draw. In a very entertaining game, McIlroy opened the scoring for Celtic but that goal was cancelled out by a strike from Lawrie Reilly. It must be said that this was proving to be the tightest league race in a long while with Hibs, Hearts, Celtic, Rangers, St Mirren and East Fife all very much in the hunt.

Another side trying hard to join the leading group were Partick Thistle and they helped their cause enormously by beating Hibs at Firhill in a nine-goal thriller. On a bumpy and partly rutted surface both sides provided an absorbing and exciting encounter. Walker put the hosts ahead only for Reilly to equalise and then, right on the interval, Ormond put Hibs 2–1 up. It was looking good for Hibs but in a devastating three-minute spell early in the second-half the Jags shot into a 4–2 lead with goals from Walker, who got two to complete his hat-trick, and Davidson. Many teams would have folded at that point but not Hibs and they hauled themselves level with goals from Reilly and Smith. With the clock ticking down, both sides went all out for the winner and it was the classy Walker who settled matters with his fourth of the game to win the match 5–4 for Thistle.

Back in September on the first day of the league season, Queen of the South had arrived at Easter Road and shocked just about everyone by winning the game 3–1, so when the sides met again on the Saturday before Christmas at Palmerston it was anticipated that the hosts would again cause problems. The first-half certainly bore out that argument as the sides went in level at 1–1, Smith scoring for Hibs and Johnstone for Queens. The second-half was a different story altogether as Smith scored twice to get his hat-trick and Reilly nabbed two, as did Turnbull, taking the Hibs tally to seven. Paterson got a goal for the hosts, but in truth they were swept away by the slick passing and interchanging of the Hibs forwards and a 2–7 result was fair on the balance of play.

The last Saturday in 1952 brought Aberdeen to Easter Road and once again Hibs were in devastating form with the Dons owing a huge debt of gratitude to keeper Martin, who pulled off save after save to stop the home side from running riot. As it was, he did concede three but it could have been an awful lot more. The first-half had witnessed many close things until in the final minute Ormond and Johnstone combined well to set up Smith for the opening goal. That was a landmark moment for Gordon: his 300th for Hibs, including war time games and friendlies – a remarkable feat by a truly remarkable player. While Hibs dominated, Aberdeen had their moments but found Younger well shielded by Paterson, Howie and Willie Clark. The visitors were finally killed off by two late goals from Reilly and Ormond, the two points earned taking them back to the top of the league.

New Year's Day derbies at Tynecastle had not provided happy memories for some years as Hearts had tended to accrue good results, but the 1953 version would prove somewhat different. A near capacity crowd watched Hibs control large passages of play and the only disappointment for the fans wearing green and white was that a 2–1 win could have been much more emphatic. A combination of poor finishing, good goalkeeping by Watters and a tendency by the Hibs forwards to be over-elaborate in their build-up meant only Reilly and Turnbull found the mark while Urquhart scored for Hearts. One of the main talking points arising out of this game was the majestic performance from Bobby Combe, who had been head and shoulders above anyone else on the park that day. It is unfortunate that while the Famous Five are remembered as legends, players like Bobby Combe do not always get the recognition they deserve. Once again Lawrie Reilly sums things up succinctly in saying that Bobby was the sixth member of the Famous Five. The derby win consolidated Hibs' position at the head of the pack while consigning their oldest rivals to second-bottom spot.

At the end of September 1952 Hibs had gone to Fir Park and thrashed Motherwell 7–3 with a blistering display of passing football. Against that backdrop the Lanarkshire side visited Easter Road two days after Hibs had won the Edinburgh derby. This time, the elaborate play that restricted the number of goals scored at Tynecastle paid off handsomely as once again Motherwell conceded seven while scoring only two of their own. Make no mistake, this was a masterclass in the art of creating and taking chances, and the chief lecturer was Bobby Combe, who sprayed passes all over the park to the feet of his willingly running team-mates. Just past the quarter-hour, Combe picked out Reilly and it was 1–0. Ten minutes later Reilly was tripped in the box and Turnbull blasted home the spot kick. Soon after, with Hibs upfield seeking a third, the visitors broke away and Sloan reduced the deficit. It was short-lived joy for the 'Well fans as before half-time Reilly had completed his hat-trick and Ormond had chipped in with another to make it 5–1. Early in the second-half Sloan scored again, but it was too little too late as Turnbull and Smith added a sixth and seventh for the rampant Hibees.

If Hibs had been brilliant against Motherwell, and they were, the performance in the next outing must have left Hugh Shaw scratching his head in wonder. The venue was Stark's Park and the opponents were bottom-of-the-table Raith Rovers. With the hosts leading 2–1 following goals by Copeland and McIntyre against one from Ormond, Hibs missed a penalty when Turnbull screwed his shot wide. That seemed to energise the hosts. Copeland deservedly completed his hat-trick and only Combe scored for Hibs, meaning the visitors had lost 4–2.

A week later at Easter Road, in front of a near capacity crowd, Hibs met Rangers in what many were billing as the championship decider – perhaps a little unfair on East Fife, St Mirren and Celtic, who were all still very much in the hunt. As it was, Hibs dominated for around two-thirds of the game but had to settle for a 1–1 draw with only the large travelling support feeling their side was not in any way lucky to get a point. A Turnbull penalty was cancelled out by Grierson. Hibs should have won in some comfort, but for once their finishing deserted them.

The Scottish Cup first-round draw paired Hibs with Stenhousemuir at Easter Road for what turned out to be a complete mismatch. At times the game resembled an exhibition game as Hibs toyed with their opponents and even though Eddie Turnbull was missing due to injury the green and whites were far too strong for their lower league visitors. Combe started the scoring in the seventh minute and although the maroon-shirted Stenhousemuir held out until the half hour it was all downhill for them after Smith made it 2–0. By the interval it was 4–0, Ormond scoring twice against his former team. Early in the second-half Aikman struck for the Warriors and a fine goal it was too. Chipping the ball over Paterson's head, he raced on to collect it before rounding Younger and firing home a goal that even the home fans cheered, such was its quality. Further Hibs goals arrived from Combe, Ormond for his hat-trick and Johnstone, at which point loud cries of 'Gie the ba' tae Reilly' began to echo around the ground. When Johnstone broke clear and could easily have scored he spotted Reilly arriving and duly passed the honour to the Hibs number nine, earning a loud cheer in the process. Final score 8–1 and passage into round two was assured.

Ahead of that cup tie Hibs faced a tricky league match against Falkirk at Brockville on the last day of January. The weather was foul, with snow, sleet and rain all falling at different intervals during the game. The home side settled the quicker and were a goal up in three minutes through Brown. Thereafter it was all Hibs and a Reilly double plus a Turnbull penalty secured the points to take them back to the top of the league.

Another home tie in the Scottish Cup brought amateurs Queen's Park to Edinburgh and at first it seemed as though the Hibs players were taking it for granted that they'd progress easily into round three as Hastie opened the scoring for the Spiders following some quite woeful defending that would become a feature of the game. Johnstone and Smith combined well to set up the equaliser for Reilly and the same player scored again early in the second-half. Although O'Connell levelled it once more, the visitors tired and in the final 20 minutes Combe and Reilly's hat-trick goal made the final score 4–2.

Valentine's Day brought Clyde to Easter Road on league business and although no massacre ensued the hosts were easy winners in the end. Tommy Ring had shot Clyde ahead but they were little seen after that as Reilly equalised and got a second just after half-time. A double from Smith and a Clark penalty rounded it off at 5–1 and kept Hibs top with East Fife second and Rangers, having dropped a point at Dens Park, third.

On the following Monday Hibs travelled to Boothferry Park to face Hull City in a floodlit friendly and won 3–2. The Tigers scored through Cripsey and Lineker while Hibs got two from Johnstone and one from Reilly, his 50th of the season in all competitions and friendlies.

Having disposed of East Fife in the previous round, Airdrie fancied their chances when they met Hibs at Broomfield in the Scottish Cup, but they were totally outplayed by their classy visitors, who refused to bend under the pressure of the home side's somewhat physical style. Gordon Smith was on the top of his game and scored a wonderful hat-trick. Reilly was also on the scoresheet in a 4–0 win that would take them into a quarter-final tie against Aberdeen.

A week later Hibs were back at Broomfield, this time in search of league points. The hosts must have hoped for a better outcome but although they scored three times they still ended up losing as Hibs ran riot and scored seven. Airdrie drew first blood when Quinn scored after just 12 minutes, but by half-time it was 4–1 after Combe scored a double, with singles from Smith and Johnstone. The break didn't really interrupt the flow of the game and Johnstone soon made it five before Pryde got one back, only for Combe to take his personal tally to four and Hibs' to seven. At the death, Lennox got a third for the Diamonds, but in truth the hosts were never going to win this match once the Hibs goal machine got going. The two points put Hibs on to 32 points from 22 starts with East Fife, having lost at home to Partick Thistle, on 30 from 23 and Rangers on 29 from 20.

After losing at home to Partick, it seemed to many that East Fife's challenge was over, but in early March Hibs went to Dens Park and surprisingly lost 2–0 to put the Fifers, who beat Airdrie 3–0 that same day, right back in the frame. At Dens, Reilly had the ball in the net after 20 minutes. Although the referee initially awarded the goal he was persuaded by the home defenders to consult his linesman and having done so he changed his mind, saying that the ball had not crossed the line. The man in the middle then further infuriated the Hibs players and fans by failing to award a penalty when it seemed clear to everyone else in the ground that Reilly had been fouled. Those incidents seemed to upset the visitors and Dundee took full advantage by scoring twice through Flavell and Steel to secure the points. Elsewhere, Clyde did Hibs a favour by winning at Ibrox in a bad-tempered game that saw Buchanan of the Bully Wee carried off with a broken leg and three players sent off – Woodburn and Simpson of Rangers and Murphy of Clyde.

The Scottish Cup fourth round pitched Hibs up against Aberdeen at Easter Road and with 47,500 in the ground the sides served up an enthralling tie that fell into the old category of a game of two halves. The Dons ran the show in the first period and were a goal up after Rodger sent a strong header past Younger in the tenth minute. Howie was then injured and Hibs had to reshuffle with the injured man playing on the wing but restricted in terms of mobility. The game got a bit fiery in the second-half and Hay of Aberdeen nearly came to blows with Reilly but neither player suffered any punishment. Hibs pushed forward more and more in search of an equaliser and it finally came late in the game when Buchanan fired home a Smith cross. The huge crowd produced gate receipts of £4,083 but it was reported that the figure did not include the stand or taxes, which might give an indication of why, in years to come, attendance figures were often thought to exclude those in the stand. It's not clear why these figures were omitted, but remember that in those days only one stand existed, the other three parts of the ground being given over to terracing.

The replay took place at Pittodrie the following Wednesday and Aberdeen chose to drop Hay after his altercation with Reilly. They replaced him with the veteran Hamilton and it proved to be a good move as the replacement scored both goals in a 2–0 win. The first was a header in the twelfth minute and the second a low drive just four minutes into the second-half. The Dons were the better side on the day, though Hibs could point to the fact that Smith being out injured did them no favours. That was no excuse really as they created few goalscoring opportunities throughout. On the same day Rangers played Raith Rovers at Stark's Park in one of their league games in hand, and the Fifers did Hibs a massive favour by winning 3–1.

With Gordon Smith still on the injury list, Hibs next travelled to Love Street to face a good-going St Mirren side who took the lead with a 23rd-minute penalty by Lapsley. As the interval approached, Ormond took a knock and was limping for the rest of the match. Even with that setback the visitors equalised early in the second-half through Johnstone and then took the lead through Reilly. The clock was ticking down and it looked as though a win was on the cards until three minutes from the end when Saints were awarded a second penalty and Lapsley scored again to secure his side a point. That same afternoon, East Fife beat Celtic 4–1 and Rangers secured a like result against Motherwell, which meant the Fifers went top, Hibs were second and Rangers third.

On the following Wednesday, the Scottish League met the English League at Ibrox and originally all five Hibs forwards had been selected to play, but injuries to Smith, Turnbull and Ormond prevented that from occurring. Johnstone and Reilly did play, however, and the Scots won 1–0 thanks to a move started by Johnstone and finished by Reilly in the 38th minute. The English League side boasted a number of top-rated players, including Billy Wright, Tom Finney and Nat Lofthouse, but even then the Scots proved too strong and were worthy winners.

A third consecutive away game took Hibs to Parkhead to face Celtic and the good news was that Smith was back in the side, although in truth he did not look 100 per cent fit. Even then he was fully involved: it was his corner that Johnstone headed Hibs ahead from midway through the first-half and it was his clever interplay with Reilly that allowed the last named to make it 2–0 at the break. A bizarre second-half moment had everyone scratching their heads as Fernie shot home to pull a goal back for the hosts, only to realise that the referee had awarded a penalty instead. There would be a goal, however, as Collins converted the kick – although Younger very nearly saved it and the ball just trickled over the line. As Celtic pushed for an equaliser, Hibs held firm with Paterson and Howie outstanding at the back, and this allowed the visitors to grab a third with five minutes left when Johnstone sent a cheeky back-heel into the net from around eight yards. Rangers drew at Aberdeen that day and East Fife beat Third Lanark, so there was no change in the positions at the top.

April 1953 began with a visit from Partick Thistle and once again Smith was in the starting line-up but still not looking fully fit. Given his performance at Parkhead the previous week it was obvious as to why a chance was taken in playing him because he was such an influential player for Hibs. Thistle played the game as if it was a cup tie and so an end-to-end tussle ensued with Reilly and Johnstone going close for Hibs while Henderson and Sharp tested Younger at the other end. The first-half brought no goals, but that would change in the second when young Mick Gallagher dived full length to send a bullet header into the net from a Johnstone cross. Stott equalised ten minutes later and a precious home point was dropped, but in fairness Thistle deserved the draw as they had played very well. East Fife beat St Mirren 7–0 and stayed top while Rangers were busy knocking Hearts out of the Scottish Cup in a Hampden semi-final. Those latter two met again on the Monday in the league and Rangers won 3–0 to keep the pressure on the top two.

On that same Monday, Hibs sent a young side to Selkirk to play in a friendly and won by the very convincing score of 7–0 with Mackie getting five, Bill Anderson and Bobby Nicol scoring the others.

Aberdeen, fresh from a cup semi-final replay win over Third Lanark, were somewhat less successful in terms of league performances and were too close to the relegation fight for comfort, so when they entertained Hibs at Pittodrie, both sides had plenty of incentive to win the match. The game started badly for Hibs. Just three minutes had elapsed when a long high ball had Jock Govan challenging in the air with Buckley and the ball fell near the edge of the Hibs box. Younger rushed out to collect, but before he could get there Hather nipped in to screw the ball past the keeper and into the net. The lead was short-lived, however, as seven minutes later Smith fed Turnbull who rolled the ball into the path of Reilly and the centre netted with a fierce right-foot shot. Thereafter both sides tried and failed to secure a winner, Hibs having Tommy Younger to thank on a few occasions when the big keeper made some vital saves. Rangers won that day and East Fife didn't play, but on the following Monday at Ibrox the home side demolished a poor Airdrie side 8–2 and moved into top spot as a result.

On the day that Rangers went top, Hibs were in Europe facing Austria Vienna in a friendly. Komisnek put the Austrians in front, but Johnstone soon equalised and it was even at half-time. An early second-half strike by Turnbull put Hibs ahead, but before the end Melchior netted twice to win the game in front of more than 30,000 fans.

On 18 April Hibs were not in action, but Scotland played England at Wembley that day and took a very creditable 2–2 draw in front of a capacity crowd. Both Johnstone and Reilly played and the latter scored both of the Scotland goals, the second coming in the final minute of the match, earning Lawrie the nickname of 'Last-minute Reilly'. That came about after some enterprising sports reporter did a bit of research and discovered that Reilly had scored a fair few last-minute goals in his time.

Hibs had just three league games remaining. To stand any chance at all of retaining the title, they had to win them all and hope that the others slipped up elsewhere. It certainly helped that all three games would be at Easter Road and the first brought East Fife to Edinburgh for a match that, if won by either side, would effectively end the title hopes of the other. The Fifers arrived on the back of a 1–1 draw with Celtic that had put them a point ahead of Hibs, but after meeting the Easter Road side they would have just one more game to play. Although a huge home crowd played its part in roaring Hibs on, the occasion was clearly having an effect on both sides and the game was littered with fouls, which meant neither outfit could settle into their normal style of play. The Hibs defenders had decided to clear their lines with long punts down the park, playing right into the hands of the tall Fife defence, and there reached a stage when Reilly could clearly be heard shouting to his team-mates to keep the ball low. It seemed to work as a flowing 13th-minute move saw Howie feed Turnbull, who in turn laid the ball in front of Johnstone and the little inside right scampered through to shoot past Curran and make it 1–0. Eleven minutes later East Fife were level when Matthews ran down the right and delivered a deep cross into the Hibs box for Bonthrone to head past Younger. The Methil side had brought a good support and their fans showed their delight with loud cheers. By the time the half-time whistle sounded Hibs had scored three more goals – but, to the disgust of players and fans alike, all three had been ruled out for offside. Certainly one had been but the other two seemed harsh decisions on the home side. Eleven minutes into the second-half, Smith sent over a cross at about knee height and Ormond threw himself full length to head home at the back post. This time there was no hint of offside so Hibs were 2–1 up and that's how it finished, although there was a scare in the last minute when Fleming hit Younger's crossbar with a header. Rangers beat Motherwell 3–0 that day and so were top with 40 points from 28 starts with Hibs next on 39 from the same number of starts and East Fife third with 39 from 29. It was possible that goal average might come into play and at that stage Rangers had scored 76 and conceded 37 while Hibs had scored 82 and conceded 49.

Five days later, while Rangers and Aberdeen were playing out a 1–1 draw in the Scottish Cup final at Hampden, Hibs were giving their goal average a distinct boost by thrashing Third Lanark 7–1 at Easter Road. Had it not been for Robertson in the visiting goal, the home side could have easily reached double figures. Indeed, Robertson made a string of quite wonderful saves, including one from a Turnbull penalty, but even then he found Hibs at their sparkling best with Bobby Johnstone the pick of a very good bunch. He had a hat-trick after just 25 minutes and Smith added a fourth on the stroke of half-time. There would be no rest for the beleaguered visitors as Ormond, Turnbull and Smith took the total to seven. Two minutes from the end they got their consolation when Henderson let fly from 30 yards to beat Younger all ends up.

Four days later Hibs played their final league game of the season with the opposition being provided by Raith Rovers. The Kirkcaldy side would be no pushovers and had recently beaten Rangers 3–1. A scrappy first-half burst into life six minutes from the break when Turnbull took a short free kick to Johnstone, who raced into the box, beat two defenders and shot low into the net to make it 1–0. Two minutes after the restart, Smith sent in a corner that Johnstone headed home, but seven minutes later Young beat off both Howie and Paterson before driving the ball at goal. Younger seemed to have it in his grasp, but somehow the ball squirmed free and rolled into the net. With six minutes left Johnstone fed Reilly, who made it 3–1, and then right on the whistle the scorer turned provider when his short free kick to Turnbull was lashed home by the big number ten.

Hibs had completed all their fixtures and from the 30 games they had amassed 43 points, scoring 93 goals and conceding 51, giving them a goal average of 1.83. Incidentally, for younger readers, I should point out that before the days of goal difference, goal average was used to separate teams and that was calculated by dividing the number of goals scored by the number of goals conceded. Rangers did not play a league match that day, but were at Hampden narrowly beating Aberdeen 1–0 to lift the Scottish Cup. They had two more league games left to try and do the double and prior to those games they had played 28, and had 40 points. They had 76 goals for and 37 against, producing a goal average of 2.05 which was superior to that of Hibs.

Things didn't get any better for the Easter Road men when Rangers beat Dundee 3–1 in their next outing and salt was rubbed in the wound when it was later reported that both the second and third goals scored by the men from Ibrox had more than a hint of offside about them. The win put Rangers on 42 points, one behind Hibs with one to play.

On Thursday 7 May, Hibs were at home facing Hearts in the final of the East of Scotland Shield. Hugh Shaw surprised many present by switching Paterson to left back and Howie to centre half. The change certainly worked to good effect and Hibs proved to be the classier outfit on the day. The visitors were at full strength, but with Ormond out injured the home side gave the number eleven jersey to young Alex Duchart. After just five minutes of play a Govan cross was headed home by Reilly and the same player doubled the lead 60 seconds later after a Duchart run and cross had caused Watters to fumble the ball and Lawrie nipped in to score. Ten minutes from the break, Smith made it 3–0 when Johnstone carved open the home defence with a wonderful pass. Before the half had ended, Wardhaugh had beaten Younger from close range to hand the visitors a lifeline. Early in the second-half Hibs had a real let-off when a Parker shot hit the post, rolled along the line and hit the other post before Govan raced in to clear, but the warning had not been heeded and when Blackwood's powerful shot could not be held by Younger, Ward-haugh was there to make it 3–2. With twenty minutes left and Hibs very much in the ascendancy, McKenzie handled in the area and Turnbull duly thundered home the spot kick to make the final score 4–2.

On the same day, Rangers were at Palmerston Park facing Queen of the South in their final league match. The home side dominated the first-half and were a goal to the good at half-time. Crucially however, they missed a penalty and 20 minutes from the end Willie Waddell broke down the right, cut inside on to his left foot, beat three defenders and scored the goal that would take the league flag to Ibrox. Hibs and Rangers finished on 43 points, but the Ibrox side had the superior goal average. Ironically, if the present-day method of goal difference had been used the title would have come to Easter Road as Hibs finished +42 and Rangers +41.

The league season may well have been over, but Hibs still had a number of games to play before the players could get a well-earned rest. With 1953 being the year of the Coronation of Queen Elizabeth II, the football authorities decided to arrange a cross-border competition, fittingly known as the Coronation Cup, with four sides each from Scotland and England competing and all the matches being played in Glasgow. The sides taking part were Celtic, Rangers, Aberdeen and Hibs from Scotland and Arsenal, Spurs, Manchester United and Newcastle from England, each of the four quarter-final ties matching a Scots club with an English one. While Celtic were beating Arsenal and Manchester United beating Rangers, Newcastle were disposing of Aberdeen and Hibs drew a crowd of 45,000 to Ibrox for their clash with Spurs. As early as the ninth minute Hibs were ahead when Ormond took a short corner to Reilly, whose delivery into the box picked out Smith to make it 1–0. On the brink of half-time Bailey crossed for Walters to beat Younger with a header and that proved to be the last goal of the game, after 30 minutes of extra time were played. It's worth pointing out that a new lighter ball was being used in these games and that both sides seemed to struggle to adapt.

Twenty-four hours later, at the same venue but in front of a much-reduced attendance, the sides met again and in a pretty even first-half both goalkeepers were well protected by their defence until the 28th minute when McClellan fired home from close range to put Spurs 1–0 up. The second-half witnessed Hibs taking command of the game and so it was no surprise when on the hour mark Govan's free kick was smacked into the net by the predatory Reilly. Then a superb drive from Smith was brilliantly tipped over the bar by Reynolds and you got the feeling a winner must surely come for the Edinburgh men. It did, but not until the 90th minute, when Johnstone's inch-perfect cross was met by the head of Reilly and the ball flew past Reynolds to put Hibs into a semi-final match against Newcastle.

Four days later, at a packed Ibrox Park, Hibs dominated the match for almost the entire 90 minutes against Newcastle and deservedly qualified to play in the final. The Geordies started brightly enough and Younger had two fantastic early saves to deny them, but after that it was virtually all Hibs and once Turnbull scored in the 16th minute the writing was on the wall for the Magpies. Turnbull turned provider to set up Reilly, who made it 2–0 before the break, and then early in the second period a three-man move put Johnstone free and he notched a third before Turnbull completed the scoring late on. Prior to the match, Newcastle had been thought of as certainties to at least reach the final, if not win it, but their hopes were dashed by a very good Hibernian side that cantered to a 4–0 win. In the other semi-final at Hampden, Celtic also pulled off a shock win in beating Manchester United 2–1 with goals by Peacock and Mochan, Rowley scoring for the reds.

The all-Scottish final took place at Hampden on 20 May in front of a staggering 107,060 supporters, thousands of whom had travelled through from Edinburgh to cheer Hibs on. The story of the match really revolves around the Celtic goalkeeper Johnny Bonnar and their recent signing from Middlesbrough, Neil Mochan, as one defied Hibs at every turn while the other scored a wonderful goal and led the Hibs defence a merry dance throughout. This was no one-sided affair, however, and among the hearts broken by Bonnar were Buchanan, Johnstone and Reilly, all of whom thought they had scored only to watch in dismay as the Celtic keeper somehow kept the ball out of the net. Younger was also performing heroics in denying Evans, Fernie and Mochan, but the last named finally beat him with a fierce drive from all of 35 yards in the 29th minute. Hibs poured forward at every opportunity and Smith's lob beat Bonnar, but landed on the roof of the net. Reilly then saw his shot deflect off Stein and head for the bottom corner, but somehow Bonnar diverted the ball round the post for a corner. With just two minutes left the match was settled when a shot by Jimmy Walsh was blocked by Howie and the Celtic man fired the rebound home to make the final score 2–0. Against the odds, Celtic had won the cup deservedly, while Hibs had thoroughly entertained all who had watched them, not just in the final but in the two games against Spurs and the one against Newcastle too.

The last event of an already long season saw Hibs flying out to Brazil to participate in what the Brazilian FA called the World Club Championship. The tournament went by the grand name of the Octagonal Rivadavia Correa Meyer. As the name suggests it involved eight teams, but the only non-Brazilian sides were Hibs, Olympia of Paraguay and Sporting Lisbon from Portugal, so the World Club Championship was probably stretching things a little. It took Hibs a gruelling 29 hours to get there. Once they arrived, they were delighted to find out they were staying in a hotel on Copacabana Beach in Rio, so the journey didn't seem so bad after that. The first match saw them take on Vasco da Gama in the Maracana Stadium and the Scots earned a very creditable 3–3 draw with Turnbull getting the first and Reilly the other two. There were claims and justifiable ones too that the third goal for Vasco was offside, but the local referee unsurprisingly disagreed. Both Turnbull and Johnstone hit the bar in the second-half, but the most bizarre situation at the game was the sight of the fans fighting on the terracing. Fiercely loyal the Hibs fans unquestionably were, but following them to Rio was perhaps a step too far, and so it can only be assumed that local rivalries were at play. Two more matches brought defeat and exit from the competition as Botafogo won 3–1, with Reilly the Hibs marksman, and then in sweltering heat that floored Hibs Fluminense beat them 3–0.

One footnote from that trip makes fascinating reading. Apparently a football encyclopedia published in the 1960s in Brazil had a whole section dedicated to the skills and play of the Famous Five, with great emphasis on the fact that the five often interchanged during games in order to confuse defenders. It can surely be no coincidence that in later years the likes of Pele, Gerson, Tostao, Rivelino and Jairzinho did that to wonderful effect when winning World Cups!

Finally the season was over. Hibs travelled back on their 29-hour journey knowing that they'd have several weeks off before the new campaign began.

Chapter Eight

1953/54

CRUCIAL INJURIES AND ILLNESSES TAKE THEIR TOLL

After a relaxing summer break, the players returned for pre-season training, all that is except Lawrie Reilly, who found himself in dispute with the club. Essentially Reilly was disgruntled, and rightly so, that Hibs were refusing to award him a testimonial match along the lines of that granted previously to Gordon Smith. It was a situation that would rumble on for some weeks, during which time Lawrie went back to his trade as a painter. The centre forward was a very determined character and was resolute in his view that he would not return until the club changed its mind.

The season for Edinburgh football fans began with a challenge match between an Edinburgh Select and Wolves which drew a crowd of 50,000 to Easter Road. Lawrie Reilly had been selected to play at centre forward, but withdrew because of his dispute, and so the jersey went to Willie Bauld of Hearts – who found himself wearing a Hibs strip for the occasion! A fast and entertaining game brought a first goal to the visitors when Wilshaw scored in the 19th minute, but within 60 seconds Davie Laing set Bauld free and the Hearts man fired home the equaliser. Twelve minutes into the second-half, a fantastic five-man move by the visitors ended with Swinburne heading Wolves 2–1 in front. Such was the quality of the goal that the huge crowd cheered and clapped to show their appreciation for good football. They were cheering again soon after when Ormond set Smith up for the equaliser and the final goal of the game went to Bauld, who was set up to score by Turnbull. The Select side was Younger (Hibs), Parker, McKenzie, Laing, Dougan (Hearts), Combe, Smith, Johnstone (Hibs), Bauld (Hearts), Turnbull and Ormond (Hibs).

The League Cup threw Hibs together with Queen of the South, St Mirren and Falkirk in Section A and it was to Palmerston that Hibs travelled for their opening game in the competition. Without Reilly, Hibs included young Jimmy Mulkerrin in their line-up and he had a good game, scoring one of the goals in a convincing 4–0 win. The other goals came from Smith who got two and Ormond.

A home tie against Falkirk came next and it is safe to say that Hibs were not firing on all cylinders. The Bairns lost Delaney to injury early in the first-half, but even with ten men they still managed to go in at the interval enjoying the 0–0 scoreline. Early in the second-half Falkirk suffered again following an injury to Kelly, who limped out the rest of the game on the wing, but it was only then that Hibs started to threaten McFeat in the visiting goal. The keeper was having an outstanding game and could count himself unlucky when an overhead kick by Johnstone took a deflection off a defender and wrong-footed the keeper as Hibs took the lead. Ten minutes later a Turnbull piledriver hit the bar and bounced down over the line. As Turnbull went off to celebrate, young Tommy D'Arcy rushed to head the ball into the net just in case the referee was unsure as to whether it had crossed the line. Straight from kick-off, with the home fans still cheering, the Bairns went up the park and pulled a goal back through Angus Plumb. Not long after that, Smith was tackled in the box and got up to go and take a corner only to be stunned when the referee pointed to the penalty spot. It seemed a very harsh decision and perhaps justice was done when McFeat saved Turnbull's kick. With around ten minutes to go Smith popped up on the left and hit a wonderful right-foot drive past McFeat from a tight angle. The ball hit the far post then bounced towards the prone McFeat, hit his back and rolled into the net. Falkirk were beaten now, and just to rub salt into the wound Smith scored another in the last minute to make the final score 4–1.

A beautiful, sunny mid-August afternoon greeted Hibs and their travelling fans as they arrived at Love Street for the game with St Mirren. It's perhaps just as well that the sun was bright as it gave the spectators a chance to top up their tans as they watched a dismal first 45 minutes devoid of goals and with little to cheer. Things got better after the break and Younger distinguished himself with a wonderful save from Stewart before the hosts finally broke the deadlock when Stewart did find a way past the Hibs keeper. Hibs were soon level when Smith found Turnbull with a slide-rule pass and the number ten fired home a low drive. McGill then put the Buddies ahead, but a glorious 30-yard left-foot drive from Ormond whistled past the keeper and into the net to earn Hibs a point in a 2–2 draw.

The fixtures now reversed and so Hibs faced Queen of the South again, this time at home. D'Arcy retained his place in the attack and he was a willing enough runner, but he lacked the experience of Lawrie Reilly and Hibs struggled to get any shots on goal. Around the 25-minute mark a fan sitting just behind the press box shouted 'send fir Reilly' and almost immediately D'Arcy raced clear down the right before sending over a low cross that Ormond slammed home from 12 yards. It was huff and puff a lot after that but the hosts managed to go further in front with about 20 minutes left. And what a goal it was by Ormond. The wee winger was coming into the box and was hugging the byline. His low drive went past keeper Henderson and swerved into the net at the far post to make it 2–0. Eight minutes later Oakes crossed for Black to head past Younger. This led to a nervy finish, but thankfully Hibs held out.

Heading to Brockville for the next match, Hibs knew that if they won it they would qualify for the quarter-finals even with one game still to play. The home side started well, but all attacks were successfully repelled before Hibs opened the scoring in the 21st minute. Ormond was in a central position and found Smith on the right and the winger then sent a cross into the box that D'Arcy knocked home, much to the delight of the travelling fans as well as the player himself – he returned to the centre sporting a huge smile. D'Arcy was involved again early in the second-half as his telling pass allowed Johnstone to make it 2–0. With 20 minutes left, Gallagher pulled one back for the home side. It was too little too late, and Hibs had qualified along with unbeaten Rangers, the other sections needing to wait until the final round of games before qualifiers were established.

Around 20,000 fans turned out to watch Hibs take on St Mirren and although there was nothing at stake it was a keenly contested match with four players booked for rash challenges. Only three minutes had elapsed before Hibs took the lead when Ormond's cross was knocked past Park by Turnbull. Eight minutes later, Younger did well to parry a fierce Lapsley free kick, but was helpless to stop Gemmell racing in to net the rebound. On the quarter-hour there was a bit of genius from the mercurial Bobby Johnstone, who looked up and saw Park fractionally off his line and promptly lobbed the keeper from 20 yards to make it 2–1. From then on, Hibs came close through Smith, Johnstone and D'Arcy but the next goal would be St Mirren's when Rice made it 2–2 just before the hour. Although keeper Park was making some useful saves, he was finally beaten again ten minutes from time when Smith carved open the Buddies defence with a run and pass to set Johnstone up for the third and winning goal. The sections now complete, the draw was made for the quarter-finals and Hibs were paired with Third Lanark for a tie that would be played over two legs.

After that bright start the club now turned its attention to the league campaign and got off to the worst possible start when they made the trip to Kirkcaldy and were hammered by Raith Rovers. Gone was the flowing football and in its place there was a nervousness that was hard to fathom. Goals from Young, who got two, Copland and Kelly put Hibs to the sword and the misery was made complete late in the game when Eddie Turnbull was sent off.

The reverse at Stark's Park was hardly the ideal preparation for a midweek trip to Cathkin to face Third Lanark in the first leg of the League Cup quarter-finals, but on this occasion it was the confident Hibs side that turned up and from early in the game it was clear which side would win. Bobby Combe was at centre forward, but it was the other Bobby who shone throughout the 90 minutes. Johnstone was a revelation and he opened the scoring after 20 minutes when he lobbed the keeper after taking a nice pass from Turnbull. The home side got to the break without conceding again, but after the interval Ormond soon made it two and then Johnstone scored the goal of the game. Looking up, he saw his forward colleagues were offside and so he ran through on his own, holding off three challenges before driving a low shot into the net. Turnbull then missed a penalty, but before the end Johnstone got his hat-trick and ensured the 4–0 win would make the return leg on the next Saturday easier than it might otherwise have been. So it proved to be as the green and whites notched up another 4–0 win. Had it not been for Robertson in the Thirds goal, there's no telling how many Hibs might have scored, but he was immense and totally blameless for the goals conceded to Johnstone and a fine hat-trick from Tommy D'Arcy.

Safely into the semi-final, Hibs next faced Hearts at Tynecastle in a league match and sadly it was the nervous Hibs who turned up for this one. It started well enough and the Hibs fans in the 40,000 crowd were enthused as first Smith and then Turnbull rattled the woodwork, but Watters stood firm in goal and Hearts opened the scoring after 25 minutes when Laing's free kick was headed in by Conn. The visitors had a few half chances but couldn't find that elusive equaliser and were punished close to the hour mark when a hand-ball in the box allowed Parker to make it 2–0 from the spot. Four minutes later, Bauld scored a magnificent goal when he went on a run down the left, beat Govan and Howie then cut inside to fire a cracking shot past Younger from a tight angle. The green and whites were a beaten lot now, but Hearts weren't finished as Wardhaugh added a fourth near the end. Although it was only two games into the campaign, Hibs were rock bottom with no points, no goals and eight conceded. Reilly was sorely missed and perhaps D'Arcy should have led the line at Tynecastle, but the number nine jersey was given instead to Combe and he was out of sorts for the whole game.

The holiday Monday provided two lots of bad news for Hibs. Firstly it was announced that Eddie Turnbull would serve a three-week suspension following his recent ordering off and then Spurs, who drew a crowd in excess of 25,000 to Easter Road, won the friendly 1–0. The goal was scored by Wetton, ensuring his side would enjoy their first victory over Hibs since 1949, the sides having met on a fairly regular basis. It wasn't that Hibs played all that badly, but the legendary Spurs keeper Ted

Ditchburn was in unbeatable form and denied the hosts on numerous occasions.

Having performed so well against Spurs it was hoped by the Hibs fans that the team could carry that form into the next match, which brought Hamilton to Easter Road. Tommy D'Arcy was restored at centre forward and might have had a goal or two with better luck. Thankfully, his team-mates were in the mood and after 19 minutes went a goal up after Ormond's cross had been cleverly left by D'Arcy to allow Johnstone to blast the ball into the net at the back post. The green and whites didn't score again until the 57th minute when Johnstone turned provider in helping Ormond set up Combe to make it 2–0. Relaxing a bit now, Hibs scored again just four minutes later when Combe beat keeper Scott with a rasping drive and then 12 minutes from time Johnstone was fouled in the box and Ormond took on the task vacated by the suspended Turnbull and duly converted the kick. Shearer scored a consolation for Hamilton, but the other thing worth noting was that Hibs gave starting places in defence to both Willie MacFarlane, who would one day manage the club, and Pat Ward.

The following midweek Hibs travelled south to face Manchester United in a floodlit friendly and perhaps the most important thing about that game was that it marked the return in a Hibs jersey of Lawrie Reilly. The dispute with the club had been at an impasse, with the board sticking to their guns regarding a testimonial and Reilly refusing to return until one was granted. The matter was taken in hand by Sir George Graham, chairman of the Scotland selectors, who had 'urged' Hibs to end the matter by granting a testimonial, which Sir George himself would oversee and provide suitable opposition. The matter settled, Reilly soon got back into his old ways and, with Hibs trailing to goals from Taylor and Aston, he nabbed two second-half goals to secure a draw. It must not be forgotten that Lawrie had signed for Hibs at 16 years of age and had been a loyal servant to both club and country, much the same as Gordon Smith who had been the beneficiary of a testimonial. The only puzzle in all of that is why Hibs were so reluctant in the first place.

The surprise package so far in the league were Queen of the South, who sat in first place undefeated when Hibs visited them at the start of October 1953. In a cracking match it was Hibs who struck first when Reilly set up Smith in the 25th minute. Seven minutes later Rothera equalised after Younger had misjudged a cross. Reilly then made it 2–1, but before the interval Rothera struck again following a second uncharacteristic gaffe by Younger. After the break both sides strove to win the match but it looked as though they'd have to settle for a point each until Rothera popped in his third goal just minutes from the end.

A week later, Hibs were at neutral Tynecastle to face East Fife in the semi-final of the League Cup. With more than 40,000 in the ground, the Fifers struck first when Bonthrone looped a clever header over the keeper and under the bar in the 34th minute. Referee Jack Mowat then incensed the Hibs support by awarding a goal-kick after Smith was clearly fouled in the box. To his credit, Smith just looked at the ref, shrugged his shoulders and got on with it. Very few chances were created by either side, but the game suddenly burst into life ten minutes from the end when East Fife keeper Curran collected a cross and as he landed on his goal line Reilly barged him and the ball into the net. The referee allowed it, as that was legal in those times. Three minutes later Reilly struck again and it looked as though Hibs might exorcise their Tynecastle ghost until Hugh Howie had a mad five minutes. First, he jumped in his own box and inexplicably grasped the ball firmly in both hands. This time Mr Mowat did point to the spot, allowing Emery to get his side level. Moments later, with no apparent threat to Younger's goal, Howie clearly tripped Bonthrone in the box and conceded another penalty. Emery struck the shot well, but Younger blocked it only to see Emery follow up and blast the ball home to take East Fife into the final where they would meet and beat Partick Thistle.

Games against Falkirk at Brockville were never easy, and so it proved when Hibs found themselves a goal down after Sinclair scored in the second minute. The green and whites fought back and by half-time Johnstone had set up two goals for Reilly. The return of the centre forward made Hibs dangerous opponents and Reilly emphasised that point by scoring a third before Turnbull made it four from the spot. Campbell pulled one back late in the game, but the points were bound for Easter Road.

On 24 October the Famous Five all played for the first time in the season when they and their team-mates took on Clyde at Easter Road. Willie Ormond had been a pre-match doubt and though he started the game he did not look completely fit. A goal came for Hibs when Reilly was through on the keeper and hauled down before amusing the crowd by carefully planting the ball on the spot almost before the referee had finished blowing his whistle. Turnbull thundered the ball home. Hibs were ahead and never looked like losing, especially after Buchanan fired a shot through a maze of legs and into the net to double the lead. Smith added two more after the break. The first was set up for him by Johnstone and Reilly. The second was pure Smith magic as he raced from the half-way line, beat Baird and Haddock and then drilled a low shot past Wilson from the tightest of angles. It cannot be emphasised enough that when Smith was in that kind of form he was nigh on unstoppable. Though the mists of time make us all believe he always played like that, he didn't. But he did more often than not, and that made him worth paying the entrance fee to watch.

During the following week the green and whites travelled south to face Derby County at the Baseball Ground in a friendly. An entertaining game saw the spoils shared in a 3–3 draw with Turnbull nabbing a hat-trick.

The ups and downs of supporting Hibs continued in the next match when Partick Thistle arrived at Easter Road and left with the points following a 2–1 win. The first Jags goal was scored by McKenzie from all of 30 yards, but in defence of Tommy Younger the keeper had a lot of players between the ball and his goal and seemed unsighted. With Ormond unfit Alex Duchart deputised and both he and Johnstone hit woodwork while Thistle keeper Ledgerwood pulled off a host of good saves throughout the game and was beaten only when a Johnstone shot hit a defender on the way in. A soft penalty gave Hibs the chance to go ahead. Turnbull failed from the spot when Ledgerwood brilliantly dived full length to push the ball round the post. A Walker goal in the second-half won the visitors the game, leaving their hosts fifth from bottom in a league topped by Queen of the South.

Around this time Hibs lost the services of Hugh Howie following his enforced retirement due to ill health. Howie had been a hugely influential player in the side and was so unlucky to have to stop playing when at his peak. A career in journalism followed, but sadly he would later be killed in a fatal road accident.

Parkhead was the next port of call and match reports of the game suggest Hibs were lucky to get a point in a 2–2 draw, but fans who travelled felt Celtic were the lucky ones. Collins shot Celtic ahead and then Charlie Tully was injured and limped out the rest of the game on the wing. Hibs used their man advantage and Reilly scored twice with the points looking won until Stein's late header levelled things up.

On the following Monday evening, Hibs were at Elland Road to mark the 'opening' of Leeds United's floodlights. More than 31,500, the biggest crowd of the season, watched on as the hosts won 4–1 in a game closer than the final scoreline might suggest. Leeds were 3–1 up at half-time and Hibs just couldn't find a way through. The home side scored through Charles and Carter, who both got two, while Duchart counted for Hibs. On the same night, Hearts were also in Yorkshire to face Doncaster Rovers and they won 3–1, which probably made up at least in part for their last visit south of the border when they'd been thrashed 7–0 at Upton Park by West Ham.

Back to league duty the following weekend, Hibs faced St Mirren at Love Street in what turned out to be a great game despite the best efforts of the referee to steal the limelight. Blyth, Lapsley and Stewart all found the net for the hosts, with Reilly and a double from Johnstone securing a point. With two minutes left, Reilly was clearly tripped but the referee waved play on until he was surrounded by protesting Hibs players. His decision was that he'd consult his linesman and after a brief chat he awarded Hibs a free kick on the edge of the box when it was blatantly obvious that the trip had been in the area. Perhaps the fact that the consulted linesman looked mortified as he shook his head in bewilderment told its own story.

With Tommy Younger away doing his National Service, Hibs drafted in young Donald Hamilton to play in goals and his first outing came at Easter Road against East Fife. The game opened with a whirlwind first goal for the hosts when Smith went on a dazzling run before setting Reilly up to score, but the visitors hit back when a Stewart cross was gathered in the jump by Hamilton. As he came down he collided with Bonthrone and Ward and ended up in the net with the ball still firmly clutched in his grasp. A cute lobbed pass by Smith set Reilly up for what proved to be the winning goal, and that lifted Hibs to tenth place in a table still topped by Queen of the South, with Hearts, Dundee and Aberdeen in hot pursuit. Interestingly, Rangers, the club who had with Hibs been the strongest in Scotland for a good number of years, languished in eighth place and many of the supporters who packed Ibrox most weeks were beginning to make noises about a change in management.

November 1953 ended for Hibs with a visit to Dens Park to face a Dundee side without Billy Steel. It was said he was being rested, but it seemed an open secret that he was in dispute with the club. In the event, the Dark Blues didn't need the mercurial talents of Steel as a goal by Cowie was enough to beat Hibs on a very cold afternoon.

The disappointing start to the season continued when Hibs travelled to play struggling Airdrie at Broomfield without the services of the injured Gordon Smith. Baird put the hosts ahead on the half hour but four minutes from the break Ormond set up Tommy McDonald for the equaliser. The second-half was pretty even until Brown put the Diamonds 2–1 ahead, but their joy was short-lived as Turnbull scored from the spot 60 seconds later to earn his side a draw. As was often the way when Airdrie were the opponents, a few Hibs players limped off the pitch at the final whistle.

In mid-December, Stirling Albion were the visitors to Easter Road and faced a Hibs side that did not have the services of Govan, Smith or Reilly. The Albion sported red and white strips in the style of Arsenal, though it must be stressed that the similarity ended there. Strangely, they wore no numbers on their backs, which prompted one bright spark to suggest that they'd probably bought the kit on the way to Edinburgh. All of that aside, the visitors were mid-table and doing ok, so it was perhaps not such a great surprise when they took the lead in the 12th minute, a corner from Allan being headed in by ex-Hearts and Aberdeen centre forward Kelly. A roar erupted when D'Arcy appeared to level, but referee Murphy had blown for an earlier infringement when playing advantage would have been the correct call. A second for Kelly after the break was responded to by Johnstone. Despite their best efforts, Hibs could not salvage a point and that meant from 13 starts they had amassed only 11 points while league leaders Queen of the South had 22 points although they'd played two games more.

The Saturday before Christmas brought Raith Rovers to Easter Road in a game that would forever be remembered by Gordon Smith – but not for the right reasons. Thirteen minutes in, Reilly raced clear, rounded keeper Drummond and rolled the ball into the net to make it 1–0. Nine minutes later a wonderful pass from Johnstone set Turnbull up to score a second and then he scored again to make it 3–0 and put Hibs on easy street. On the half hour, a Smith rocket made it 4–0 and then, after Turnbull had smashed a penalty over the bar, Smith got number five with a header. It was all good news so far. But then tragedy struck. Smith collided with keeper Drummond and suffered a broken leg. Minutes from time, Buchanan limped off with what was later diagnosed as cartilage trouble. Although Hibs had won 5–0, the victory came at a price.

On Boxing Day 1953, Hibs went to Ibrox to face a Rangers side under enormous pressure from its support to start winning games. Decimated by injury, the visitors tried to make a game of it on a pitch that was cutting up badly, but it was the hosts that triumphed, scoring three goals without reply. In fairness, when Gardiner scored in the first-half it was against the run of play but a second from the same player and another from Prentice sealed the win. Result of the day might have gone to ever-improving Celtic following their 7–1 win against Clyde at Shawfield, but the award actually went to Aberdeen who thrashed Stirling Albion 8–0 at Pittodrie. All of that simply served to highlight just how much off the pace Hibs were as Celtic and Aberdeen fought it out with Hearts to see which club if any could catch and overtake Queen of the South. There is absolutely no doubt the long-term injuries to Smith and Buchanan would test Hibs to the limit. If nothing else, it presented an opportunity for others to step in and show what they were capable of.

The 1954 New Year Derby pitched a struggling Hibs up against high-flying Hearts at Easter Road and more than 50,000 fans braved the elements to see these old enemies face up to each other. Hibs handed the number seven jersey to Tommy McDonald, who was a completely different style of player to Smith, but that didn't stop him taking a Reilly pass in his stride to open the scoring just before half-time. Indeed, the home side had enjoyed the better of the first-half but missed chances and found Watters in good form or the lead might have been greater. In the second-half a long punted clearance by Cumming completely deceived young Donald Hamilton and ex-Hibs man Jimmy Souness raced in to score. Both sides then went looking for a winner and sadly for Hibs it came from the boot of the immensely talented Willie Bauld.

Losing the derby was painful but Hibs found a cure for their ills in their next outing when they went to Douglas Park to face basement boys Hamilton. The opening minutes gave no clue as to what would follow because Accies came close to snatching the lead on two occasions, but once Hibs went ahead with a tenth-minute strike from McDonald the floodgates opened and by half-time McDonald scored again, Willie Ormond found the net and Reilly bagged a double. Early in the second-half Crawford reduced the leeway but Johnstone soon restored it and Martin's late strike was most definitely in the consolation category. On the same day, Hearts beat Airdrie 4–3 and Queen of the South lost at home to Partick, which put the Tynecastle club at the top of the table.

A week later, Queen of the South were at Easter Road where, on a fine, sunny but cold afternoon, 25,000 fans turned out and watched Hibs play most of the football and yet have to rely on an error by the visitors to secure the points. Only ten minutes remained when Sharpe was short with a pass back, which allowed Ormond to nip in ahead of the quaintly named centre half Hollywood and get the game's only goal. That was game 18 in the league and Hibs had won only seven, lost eight and drawn three.

A tough assignment in their next game took Hibs to face an Aberdeen side who had a very impressive home record. With Govan out injured, George Boyle played at right back and was involved in the seventh-minute move that set Combe up to give the Hibs a lead. Half an hour later Yorston slipped his marker to equalise, but an injury to Hather in the second-half weakened the home side and both Reilly and Johnstone found the net from Combe passes to win the game 3–1.

Only one game remained before Hibs started their Scottish Cup run, and that brought Falkirk to Leith on a cold and wet Saturday towards the end of January. After a pretty dull first-half, the game burst into life in the second with the home side making all the running but suffering a double sucker punch when first Morrison took advantage of some hesitation from Hamilton and then Plumb, after a terrible mix-up in the Hibs defence, made it 2–0 to the visitors. Within a minute of losing that second goal, Reilly pulled one back from a McDonald corner and ten minutes later the same player scored again to make it 2–2. The home fans roared their heroes forward but lessons had not been learnt and a third, decisive goal from McCrae on the breakaway won the points for the visitors. News from elsewhere showed that Hearts had won 4–2 at Dundee to go four points clear, although Queen of the South and a fast-improving Celtic were still very much in the hunt. The frustrating thing for Hibs and their fans was that the gap was still not so wide that it could not be closed, but the fluctuation in form convinced most that Hibs would not be at the top of the heap this time around.

A tricky Scottish Cup draw meant Hibs had to face second division St Johnstone at Muirton Park and although Reilly's pass to McDonald allowed the young winger to open the scoring after just six minutes the hosts were always dangerous in attack and got their reward on the hour mark when Landells was upended in the box and Ewen converted the penalty to get Saints level. A shock result was a possibility. In the end, a huge slice of luck carried Hibs through after Saints defender Woodcock, chasing a through ball with Reilly, attempted to chip a pass back to his goalkeeper but only succeeded in lofting it over his head and into the net. Over the years, Hibs had suffered some horrendous bad luck in this tournament and so when something positive happened it was firmly grasped in both hands.

By chance the next league match Hibs faced was against Clyde, the side they would also meet in the next round of the cup. This first meeting was at Shawfield, while the cup tie would take place at Easter Road in a week's time, but the venue meant nothing to a Hibs side firing on all cylinders and so it was to be in this first encounter, with the visitors 2–0 ahead after just eight minutes, the goals coming from McDonald and Johnstone. Tommy Ring pulled one back for Clyde, but by half-time Johnstone had completed his hat-trick and Ormond had also scored to make it 5–1 at that stage, though it might have been six had Wilson not saved a Turnbull penalty. Early in the second-half Clyde were awarded a penalty of their own which Baird converted, but a third penalty of the match was scored by Ormond to make the final score 6–2. That same day, Hearts beat Celtic 3–2 at Tynecastle and the popular money was going on the Gorgie club to lift the title.

On the following Monday evening Hibs were at Roker Park for a floodlit friendly against Sunderland on a freezing cold night and on a rock-hard pitch that had a covering of snow. In front of a crowd of more than 14,000, the hosts went two up with goals from Chisholm and Wright, but Hibs kept plugging away and in the last ten minutes scored through McDonald and then Ormond to earn a deserved draw.

Having hit Clyde for six on their own patch a week earlier, Hibs set about demolishing them again when they came to Easter Road for the Scottish Cup tie, only this time the hosts went one better in winning 7–0. It was a classy display of attacking football, but credit must also go to young Donald Hamilton and his defensive colleagues for keeping a clean sheet. Star of the show was Bobby Johnstone, who was involved in everything constructive and was part of moves setting up goals for McDonald, Turnbull and Reilly in the first-half. In the second-half

McDonald got his second, Johnstone rattled in two of his own and Ormond completed the rout in the last minute.

One of the clubs still in contention at the top were Partick Thistle, but their hopes of league title glory took a significant knock when Hibs visited Firhill on 20 February. The visitors were the better side for the bulk of the game and took the lead on the half hour when a McDonald free kick was headed home by Ormond and then ten minutes later Turnbull scored from a Reilly pass to deservedly win the points for Hibs.

The last Saturday in February brought another dose of Scottish Cup misery to Hibernian and their fans when Aberdeen came to Easter Road and were two goals up inside the first six minutes. Hather, the English left winger for the Dons, led Jock Govan a merry dance and twice left him in his wake when going on to beat Hamilton in the Hibs goal. The painful thing was that both goals were almost identical and that was surprising because Govan had enjoyed good form against Hather in past encounters. An early second-half strike from Buckley sealed Hibs' fate and their fans in the biggest crowd of the day at 47,692 must have been thinking of their journey home before Johnstone struck a late consolation. Shock of the round came at Shielfield, where Berwick Rangers beat Dundee 3–0, while it took a last-gasp goal at Annfield to take Celtic through 4–3 against Stirling Albion.

Further bad news descended upon Easter Road during the following week when it became known that Lawrie Reilly, who had been feeling unwell for a few weeks, had been diagnosed with pleurisy and would be out for some weeks. Pleurisy is essentially a lung disorder that severely affects a sufferer's breathing as well as causing very low energy levels.

With Reilly out, Hibs introduced Dougie Moran at centre forward for the next match against St Mirren at Easter Road. Also in the side that day was Buchanan, now recovered from his cartilage operation, which had kept him out for 12 weeks. Willie MacFarlane played at right back, though press reports suggest that his robust style of play was not to everyone's liking! This reshuffled Hibs side took time to get going but still took the lead seven minutes from the break with a Turnbull shot that was hit so hard it was in the net before keeper Crabtree moved. Midway through the second-half St Mirren enjoyed a spell of dominance and took advantage of that when Stewart equalised. Nine minutes later a Willie Ormond cross was knocked home by Moran and that proved to be the winning goal. Hibs were now mid-table, some nine points behind leaders Hearts but with three games in hand. Unfortunately, they had only seven games left and so it would take a minor miracle for Hibs to overtake their oldest rivals.

Any chance of catching Hearts would mean winning those remaining games and Hibs got off to a good start when they went to Bayview and inflicted a first home league defeat of the season on East Fife. Leading by a first-half Turnbull strike, the visitors added two more in the second through Ormond and Johnstone before Gardiner scored a late consolation for the home team.

In recent years Hibs had enjoyed a good run of home success against Dundee and that continued in their next meeting, with the home side winning 2–0. The game itself was far from a classic but the Scotland selectors were there and must have been impressed by Combe and Johnstone, together with Cowie of Dundee. Both goals came in the second-half, the first a flashing header by Johnstone and the second a typical piledriver from Turnbull. The win moved Hibs up to fourth and with Hearts losing 1–0 at Pittodrie, Celtic closed the gap by defeating Partick Thistle 3–1 at Firhill.

The following Tuesday evening Hibs were at Bramall Lane to face Sheffield United in a floodlit friendly. Both sides served up a pacy and entertaining 90 minutes. The hosts went ahead just before the interval through Cross, but two early second-half goals from Combe and McDonald put Hibs ahead. Hawksworth then grabbed a double for the hosts, Turnbull earning the visitors a draw with a late equaliser.

On the day that four horses were killed in the Grand National at Aintree, sparking an official inquiry into the safety of the event, Hibs were entertaining second-bottom Airdrie and it was a great pity that the game attracted the lowest attendance of the season as there were goals galore. The stay-away fans missed a hat-trick from Turnbull, two each from McDonald and Mulkerrin and a solo effort from Ormond, while McMillan scored for the Diamonds to make the final score 8–1. Although Bobby Johnstone didn't score he was at the centre of all things good from the home side and would be happy that the victory took Hibs up into third place.

Yet another floodlit friendly took Hibs to White Hart Lane at the start of April 1954, but the journey to London turned out to be an unsuccessful one. With 20 minutes played Buchanan and Turnbull combined to set Govan up for the opening goal as a strong header flew past Ditchburn. The keeper then denied Combe, Johnstone and Ormond with top-drawer saves and that helped build the confidence of the home side, who equalised through Burgess early in the second-half. Sixty seconds later Robb put Spurs 2–1 ahead, but Hibs kept plugging away and Bill Anderson equalised ten minutes from time. In the final minute Duquemin grabbed the winner for the hosts. Not involved in that game was Tommy McDonald, who had been sold to Wolves for a fee reported as £10,000.

Hibs had four more league games to play and the first of those took place at Annfield, where hosts Stirling Albion achieved the double against their visitors. Turnbull went close early on and then Ferguson cleared off his own line when Mulkerrin looked to have scored. Pat Ward and George Boyle then repeated Ferguson's feat at the other end, but Albion finally broke through in the 55th minute when poor handling from Hamilton allowed Rattray to fire home. Ten minutes later the home defence got into a tangle and Ormond swooped to level the tie. With three minutes left on the clock, Chalmers scored a breakaway goal to win the points for his side.

Three days later a disappointing crowd of only 20,000 turned out at Tynecastle to watch Hearts face Hibs in the final of the East of Scotland Shield. In modern times such an attendance would be a miracle, but back then it was second v fourth in the league and so should have generated more interest. Perhaps many decided to stay at home to listen to the Scottish Cup semi-final on the wireless – and if they had they must surely have been as astonished as the rest of Scotland when Aberdeen thrashed Rangers 6–0. The Shield match was a good if not great game, with both sides blooding youngsters – Dave Mackay for Hearts and Jimmy Thomson for Hibs. The game was settled in the end by a 34th-minute strike by Jimmy Wardhaugh, the only goal of the game.

The final three league matches, against Celtic, Aberdeen and Rangers, would all be tough albeit all three would be at Easter Road. Champions-elect Celtic were first to arrive and brought with them a huge travelling support that swelled the attendance to over 45,000. In just two minutes Mochan played a short corner to Fallon and then took the return pass before firing a magnificent swerving shot into the Hibs net, which resulted in a massive roar of approval from their fans. For the rest of the first-half, it was the home supporters doing all the cheering as their heroes pounded the Celtic goal, but try as they might they could not get level. In the first-half Hibs had been caught cold by an early goal and the same thing happened in the second when Mochan scored his second to double the Celtic lead with a shot that Younger got to but could not hold. Again the Hibs charged forward and again they failed to breach the Celtic defence and so a third late goal by Higgins meant the points going to Celtic.

The following Monday Hibs faced Aberdeen, who included several reserves in their line-up in preparation for the cup final. Hibs handed the number four shirt to John Campbell, who would be making one of only two starts in league matches. Also in the home line-up were goalkeeper Willie Miller and forward Tommy Preston. The former made a very small number of appearances in his Hibs career, but the latter would be a long-serving and valued member of the squad. Once again there was an early goal, this time in favour of the home side when Thomson's header sneaked over the line despite the best attempts of Aberdeen goalkeeper Martin in trying to stop it. On the half hour Johnstone drove a low ball across the six-yard box and Ormond knocked in number two. Thereafter the game got bogged down in midfield until ten minutes from the end when Combe, Preston and Turnbull combined well to set up the final goal for man of the match Willie Ormond.

The final curtain fell on a very long season when Rangers arrived in Edinburgh for what would be their last game under manager Bill Struth who, at 78, was to retire from the post. With ten minutes on the clock a Prentice cross resulted in Ward and Campbell leaving the ball to each other, which allowed Gardiner to nip in, waltz round Miller and roll the ball into the empty net to make it 1–0. Thereafter Hibs chased the game and finally got their just reward 20 minutes from the end with the best move of the match. Preston picked the ball up in the centre of the park and fed it to Thomson who spotted Johnstone scurrying down the left. The pass was made and Bobby took the ball round the full back before rolling it into the path of Turnbull, who crashed a fantastic drive into the top corner from 20 yards. With the goal celebrations still going on around the ground, Hibs were caught napping at the back and Paton scored with a header to restore the Rangers lead. Within two minutes, and this time without the elaborate and skilful build-up, Turnbull sent another thunderbolt into the same top corner to earn Hibs a point.

Elsewhere, Celtic won the cup and the league title without losing a home game in the entire season.

There was no doubt that the illness which had incapacitated Lawrie Reilly was having an adverse effect on results and performances and all at Easter Road hoped fervently for a quick and full recovery.

A short European tour at the end of the season took Hibs to Germany and Czechoslovakia, where they first played against Nuremberg. *The Scotsman* news report for that match begins with a headline 'Beaten by clever football and continental refereeing' and that was the case as the Edinburgh side went down 6–1 in a match where even the 17,000 local fans were booing the ludicrous refereeing of the game. The Hibs goal was scored by Burns but even then the referee looked as though he might disallow it until he was surrounded by protesting players – from the home side! From Germany it was on to Czechoslovakia to meet Ostrava, although in truth it was the Czech National XI as they prepared for the World Cup. An amazing crowd of 43,000 watched on as Bobby Combe opened the scoring after 12 minutes only for Hemele to equalise and then give the hosts the lead. Minutes later Paszicky headed a third and then added a fourth before full-time, when Hibs were tiring badly in the oppressive heat. Next it was on to Prague, where a Willie Ormond goal earned a draw against Sparta. Finally the tourists faced Bochum in Germany and lost 3–1, Johnstone the Hibs scorer.

Chapter Nine

1954/55

JOHNSTONE DEPARTS

Mid-August saw competitive football get under way once again with the six League Cup matches and Hibs started badly in going down 3–1 at Bayview to East Fife. In fairness this was a very good East Fife side and it was no surprise when they raced to a 3–0 half-time lead through goals from Bonthrone and Gardiner, who got a double. Hibs rallied a bit in the second-half and Tommy Preston pulled a goal back, but unfortunately it was too little too late for the visitors.

Next up was a home tie against Scottish Cup holders Aberdeen where there were signs of a good understanding developing between Gordon Smith and Tommy Preston. Indeed, it was a shot by Smith which deflected to Preston that allowed the youngster to fire home through a ruck of players and put his side ahead. At that point Bobby Johnstone was off the park receiving treatment after he'd suffered a couple of hefty challenges by the Aberdeen rearguard, and so it was to Hibs' credit that they scored when a man short. With five minutes to go until the break, O'Neill erred in trying to clear his lines and Preston pounced to make it 2–0. With Reilly incapacitated, Preston was doing his best to cover and though their styles were completely different and young Tommy lacked the experience he was still making a good fist of things.

A second successive home game brought Queen of the South to Edinburgh and on a day when heavy rain throughout the 90 minutes threatened to spoil the spectacle, both sets of players served up an exciting game and Hibs were soon 2–0 ahead thanks to a double scored by Preston and set up by Smith. Just before the break Queens pulled one back through Black and that seemed to unsettle the home side, who looked for a time as though they might concede again. Thankfully, Turnbull sealed the win in the 90th minute. On the same day Aberdeen beat East Fife and so those two and Hibs were all on four points after three games.

In the following midweek Hibs took on a side from Scottish Command and the servicemen found it tough going, even though the home side played a number of reserves in their starting eleven. One of those reserves, Pat Walker scored four times and Ormond once to secure a 5–0 win. Bizarrely, Walker would never make a first-team appearance for Hibs.

As holders, East Fife came to Easter Road knowing that if they wanted to retain the trophy they'd have to win. A very close and exciting game witnessed chances galore being created at either end, but the Fifers had an ace up their sleeve in little Charlie Fleming, who was superb throughout. Fleming actually missed the chance of the match when he rounded Younger and then proceeded to fire the ball wide of the goal with the net gaping, but otherwise his display was flawless. Hibs took the lead in the 15th minute when Preston scored his sixth in four games, but seconds later Gardiner equalised from a Fleming pass and that served to cut short the celebrations of the home fans in the 28,000 crowd. On the half hour Christie put the Fifers ahead and although Smith and Ormond both hit woodwork later, the green and whites could not get level. Only a glimmer of hope regarding qualification remained for Hibs after it was learned that Queen of the South had surprisingly beaten Aberdeen.

The penultimate game of the section took Hibs to Pittodrie. They swarmed all over Aberdeen for almost the whole 90 minutes but passed up chance after chance in front of goal. Even when they were on target, Martin was in inspired form in the home goal. Hibs started the game in whirlwind fashion, but typically were caught on the break after 12 minutes when a pass from Hather allowed Hamilton to fire home from close range. Ten minutes from the end Hibs finally scored when Johnstone was downed in the box and Ormond rattled home the penalty. Hibs could and should have won but it would make no difference to their chances of qualifying as East Fife's 3–0 win over Queen of the South won the section for the Methil men, Fleming scoring a hat-trick.

The final match brought eight goals at Dumfries, three of those coming from the penalty spot. In an exciting tussle, Paterson of Queens scored a hat-trick, two of those coming from the spot, while Johnstone and Preston each got a double and Ormond converted a penalty to make the final score 5–3 in favour of the visitors.

One encouraging aspect of an otherwise unsuccessful League Cup campaign was the goal scoring form of Tommy Preston and the youngster would be looking to carry that form into the league programme.

It would be hard to imagine a tougher start to the league race than that faced by Hibs as they travelled to Ibrox on the opening day and played in front of a 50,000 crowd, the majority of whom wore red, white and blue. Given the time of year it might be thought that the fans would be in shirt sleeves, but in fact it rained throughout the whole match, which in the terms of that well known football cliché was one 'of two halves'. The home side shaded the first and went in a goal ahead thanks to Grierson's

21st-minute effort but the second belonged to Hibs and they got their deserved equaliser and a point after Smith and Turnbull combined to set up Preston.

The tough start continued as Hibs welcomed Hearts to Easter Road for the Edinburgh derby. A thrilling 45 minutes saw Hibs go close on numerous occasions and yet still go in 1–0 down at the break after Conn's 19th-minute strike. Duff in the Hearts goal seemed by far the busier keeper, but his efforts and a touch of both bad luck and poor finishing kept his goal intact. Early in the second-half the visitors twice struck woodwork as Wardhaugh, by far the outstanding player on display, prompted his team-mates with telling passes, but it was Johnstone who caught the eye for Hibs when he raced clear to fire an equaliser. Next a penalty was converted by Ormond but just 60 seconds later Wardhaugh took a pass from Bauld in his stride and cracked home the equaliser. As time ran down and a draw looked to be on the cards, Wardhaugh wrong-footed the Hibs defenders in back-heeling the ball into the path of Conn, who scored the winning goal.

On the following Monday evening Hibs welcomed Spartak Sokolovo of Prague to Easter Road for a return friendly that attracted a crowd of around 20,000. The visitors were champions of their own league and played some wonderful free-flowing football, but seemed very reluctant to have anything to do with tackling! With Smith playing like his old self, having now fully recovered from the leg break that had kept him out at the end of the previous season, Hibs started brightly but fell a goal behind when keeper Donald Hamilton could only partially clear a shot, and when the second effort was arrowing towards the net, Buchanan elected to punch it clear and the resulting penalty was converted by Crha. After Preston had come close on a couple of occasions the Spartak goal was finally breached in the 27th minute when Ormond headed home a Smith corner. Brilliant play from Ormond and Smith then set Johnstone up to make it 2–1 at the break. In the first minute of the second-half Preston made it three and minutes later scored a fourth for the home side. Prague were then awarded a second penalty as that man Buchanan conceded again and Crha found the target from 12 yards, but Hibs were not finished yet and ten minutes from time Smith made it 5–2 before Ormond added a sixth on the final whistle.

While it was nice to win such games, an improvement in league form was a priority. It would not come in the next match as Hibs had to play for 50 minutes with just ten men after the unfortunate Archie Buchanan was carried off with a broken leg. The venue was Pittodrie and Aberdeen made full use of their man advantage with only the form of Younger saving the visitors from a heavy defeat. Trailing to a sixth-minute goal by Yorston, Hibs got level close to the half hour after Preston was felled in the box and Johnstone converted the penalty. Second-half goals from O'Neill and Yorston meant Hibs made the long journey home without any points.

On 29 September 1954, when Hibs were down in Leeds for a floodlit friendly, a significant event was taking place at Tynecastle, where Hearts met Hibs in a 'C' Division clash in which Lawrie Reilly played for the visitors. Hibs lost 2–0, but the significant thing was that Reilly was back playing after an eight month absence. Meanwhile, Leeds were going down 3–1 at Elland Road, where Smith scored two and Ormond the other.

Still without a win in the league, Hibs next faced Falkirk in front of 25,000 fans at Easter Road with that crowd being treated to a fantastic display of fast movement and passing. Sadly, it was the visitors who provided that entertainment. The young Falkirk side were reminiscent of Hibs in days gone by as they deservedly won the game 1–0. Ironically, it was an Ormond penalty that settled matters, scored by Willie's brother Robert. The three draws and one defeat to date left Hibs joint-bottom of the league.

With Lawrie Reilly in the travelling party, Hibs next faced Queen of the South at Palmerston Park, Dumfries. The centre didn't play, but he must have enjoyed watching his team-mates finally get that elusive win with a touch of Gordon Smith genius setting the foundation as he weaved through the home defence to put the green and whites a goal ahead in eight minutes. Willie Ormond then scored a second and the visitors simply sat on that lead to earn a much needed two points.

With Hibs still seeking a first home win in the league campaign things looked bleak in their next match when visitors Raith Rovers took a 12th-minute lead. MacFarlane had misjudged the flight of the ball and Duncan raced clear to shoot past Younger. Debutant Jock Buchanan equalised with a close-range shot and then Ormond missed a penalty as the home side bombarded Raith's goal. Shooting down their famous slope Hibs piled on the pressure but the ball just wouldn't go into the net until finally Pat Ward popped up 90 seconds from the end to knock the ball home after Rovers had failed to clear a corner kick. The back-to-back wins moved Hibs up to eleventh, some five points behind leaders Aberdeen.

On 18 October 1954 history was made at Easter Road as Hibs played their first ever match under the newly installed floodlights. Around 25,000 turned out to watch Hearts provide the opposition, but it's possible a number of that 25,000 attended more due to the novelty of the occasion as both sides had indicated they might not field their strongest eleven. The first-half witnessed a few quite curious incidents as shots at goal were fluffed and easy saves mishandled. The problem was that the photographers behind each goal had to use flash bulbs to take their pictures and that was causing problems for the players! Early in the second-half Tulloch put the visitors ahead and then 20 minutes from time Whittle settled it for Hearts with the second and last goal of the game. The game was a friendly, but it still rankled with the Hibs fans that their side had lost to Hearts.

Two evenings later Hibs were in Reading to play a floodlit friendly which marked the return to the first team of Lawrie Reilly. Some 14,594 fans paid to watch an entertaining game in which Livingstone gave the home side the lead only for Johnstone to first equalise and then put the visitors ahead. With three minutes left, Hinshelwood made it 2–2 and although Reilly did not score he showed much of his old skill was intact.

On 23 October, while Hibs were at Shawfield facing Clyde in the league, Hearts were across the city at Hampden beating Motherwell 4–2 in the final of the League Cup. Unlike modern-day attitudes, many Hibs fans will have been delighted to see Hearts bring a trophy east, but that delight would be tempered on the day by the fact that Hibs were thrashed 6–3 at Shawfield. Although the Famous Five were together for the first time in ten months it was another five that caught the eye – that was the number of goals Clyde scored in the opening 25 minutes. Reilly did reduce the leeway just before the break and a late double from Johnstone was only met by one more goal from the Bully Wee to make the final score 6–3.

On the following Monday evening Hibs entertained Newcastle in a floodlit friendly that turned out to be a real cracker. Chances galore ensured that both Willie Miller in the home goal and Ronnie Simpson at the other end were kept busy. Miller had joined Hibs from Clyde as cover for Younger and Hamilton, and although his Easter Road career was short he certainly caught the eye in this game with a string of fine saves. Simpson, of course, had first played senior football when only 15 and on this evening he was also in tip-top form. It took until the 70th minute for the first goal to be scored and it went to Hibs as Reilly's cute pass allowed Smith to dash in and score. With only three minutes left, Miller blotted his copybook when he inexplicably allowed a harmless effort from Crowe to bounce between his legs on its way into the net. On the night, Reilly looked a lot like his old self and there were good performances too from Johnstone and 17-year-old central defender Jackie Plenderleith, who had recently joined the club from Armadale.

Kilmarnock were next to visit Easter Road and with three minutes of that match remaining it looked as though Hibs were down and out as they trailed 2–1, but when Johnstone was tripped in the box, Turnbull slammed home the penalty and then a mere two minutes later Johnstone himself skipped past two lunging challenges and slotted home a most welcome winner.

Even at this early point in the season it was obvious that Stirling Albion would struggle to stay up as they had adopted a policy of developing youth players rather than signing ones from elsewhere. In itself there was little wrong with that philosophy, but it did mean that experienced teams would cause them problems and that's exactly what Hibs did when they travelled to Annfield in early November. To their credit the home side started well and were a goal up in two minutes through Whitehead, but Hugh Shaw's men soon got things back in their favour and so by the time Albion added a second goal through Docherty late in the game their opponents had scored four through Bobby Johnstone, who got two, Tommy Preston and Willie Ormond.

A week later Motherwell arrived at Easter Road hoping to improve on what had been a dismal start to the season for them but it was not to be as Hibs were in sparkling form and mastered the slippery conditions much better than the men from Lanarkshire. Bobby Johnstone gave a majestic performance that surely caught the eye of several scouts in the stand while Lawrie Reilly was back to something like his best and grabbed two goals to prove it. In addition, Reilly foxed two defenders with a drop of the shoulder and paved the way for Tommy Preston to get a third while Johnstone bagged the fourth and a late Motherwell strike did nothing to take the shine off of a super performance by the home side.

After three straight league wins, Hibs were involved in a glamour friendly against Manchester United at Easter Road in mid-November. The Old Trafford outfit had crashed 7–3 on their last visit to mark the occasion of Gordon Smith's testimonial, but on this occasion they would fare much better. In fact Hibs took the lead in the 19th minute when Reilly headed home a Smith cross and then Dougie Moran, who was in for the injured Johnstone, twice went close to increasing the lead before the break. Ten minutes into the second-half the Hibs defence fell asleep and allowed Blanchflower to equalise. A further 11 minutes on they hadn't learned their lesson and Scanlon put the visitors 2–1 up. Hibs then pummelled the United goal and Moran thought he'd scored but the referee adjudged the ball not to have crossed the line. The man in black was busy again minutes later when Reilly was clearly tripped inside the box, only for Mr Whittle of Glasgow to give a free kick outside the area. A late breakaway goal brought a second for Blanchflower and ensured a 3–1 win for the Red Devils.

Having lost the services of key players Merchant and Roy for several weeks, Dundee were delighted to welcome them back for an Easter Road clash with Hibs, but what they hadn't reckoned on was that Jackie Plenderleith for all his youthful inexperience would totally eclipse Merchant from the game. Hibs took the lead when Reilly fed Smith down the right and then made his way into the box to meet the winger's pinpoint cross and steer a strong header past the hapless visiting keeper. Reilly got the second, and what a peach it was as he raced into the Dundee box, evaded two defenders and fired a hard low shot into the net. Smith added a third before the home defence forgot the golden rule of playing to the whistle and as they anticipated offside, Roy was able to run clear and beat the advancing Younger to make the final score 3–1.

On the following Monday evening Hibs entertained a side with a difference when they met a Scotland XI at Easter Road. It was the practice in those days for the selectors to put together a squad and then test it in challenge matches against club opposition. On this occasion it would mean Bobby Johnstone wearing the dark blue instead of his customary green and white. The tie certainly fired the imagination of the Edinburgh public as more than 35,000 turned out on a cold crisp night and they were rewarded with a decent game. By half-time Hibs were down to ten men and trailing 2–0 as Smith was unable to continue after an injury, while goals from Johnstone and Bauld must surely have impressed the selectors. Indeed, Johnstone was man of the match and laid on a third which Jimmy Wardhaugh scored to make the final score 3–0.

League-wise, it had been a good month for Hibs with three wins out of three and that form continued in their next outing when, despite not having Smith available and then losing Turnbull to injury after 55 minutes, they still managed to thrash East Fife 5–1 at Bayview. Smith's place was taken by John Fraser, who had an excellent 90 minutes and was involved in at least three of the goals. In an exciting first-half Johnstone and Ormond had Hibs ahead, although Gardner ensured it was only 2–1 at the turnaround. Second-half goals saw Johnstone secure his hat-trick and Ormond his brace and although Reilly didn't score it was largely due to his unselfish work that his team-mates did.

'Lucky Hibs' was *The Scotsman* headline in its match report for the home game against St Mirren on 4 December. 'Reilly's poor form' offered the sub-heading before then describing how the Buddies had taken a first-half lead through Callan only to lose the game to goals by Reilly and Combe. Indeed, in describing Reilly's goal the thought that he 'showed why he has been chosen to play for Scotland' somewhat contradicted his alleged poor form! In fact the report indicates that defensively Hibs played well.

The win over St Mirren extended the unbeaten run to six games, but the next side Hibs had to face at Easter Road were high-flying Celtic who very much had their eye on the title and arrived determined not to lose ground on Aberdeen and Rangers above them. A close first-half saw Walsh getting the only goal for the visitors, but it was an altogether different story in the second-half as Walsh scored again, Fernie got two and Higgins the final goal in a 5–0 win for the Glasgow outfit.

Following that thrashing Hibs welcomed Rapid Vienna to Easter Road on the Monday night for a floodlit friendly and it has to be said that the Austrian team were quite brilliant at times with the football free flowing, although they often let themselves down in the final third. Hibs, who gave starting places to Jimmy Thomson and John Grant, took the lead after 32 minutes when a mazy run from Smith ended with the winger firing home a low drive, but two minutes from the break a shot from Probst seemed to deceive Willie Miller, who let the ball trundle through his legs and into the net for an equaliser. The second-half went much the same way as the first with both sides playing neat passing football. The tie was decided on the hour when Hallas sent a blistering drive past Miller from around 25 yards.

On the back of those two defeats in a row, Hibs next travelled to Firhill to face a good-going Partick Thistle on what turned out to be a quagmire of a pitch. Despite the conditions Hibs adapted well and with Smith in sparkling form they never looked like losing. The Prince of Wingers set Reilly up for the first goal, which was well taken by the Scotland man, and then Smith himself scored a second with a fabulous free kick. Goal number three saw Smith's shot parried by the keeper and that allowed Reilly to claim the ball and roll it to the unmarked Ormond, who slotted it into an unguarded net. All three of those goals came in the first-half and although the home side saw more of the ball after the break their efforts brought no reward.

A full card of fixtures took place on Christmas Day 1954 and Hibs had the task of facing Rangers at Easter Road in front of a huge crowd. Christmas may be the time of giving, but this Hibs side were not in that frame of mind as they set about attacking the Rangers rearguard at every opportunity. In a counter-attack Rangers were incensed when the referee refused to award them a penalty and the anger grew considerably more when Pat Ward sent a long ball forward to Ormond, who blasted home a second goal for Hibs, Combe having earlier opened the scoring. Late in the second-half Grierson did pull a goal back, but it was not enough for the visitors and the Hibs fans streamed out of the stadium on full-time in a very festive mood.

It's fair to say that 1954 was not the best of years for Hibs and sadly 1955 didn't start much better as Hibs went to Tynecastle for the derby on New Year's Day. A relatively even first-half which Hearts shaded on possession and led through a smart strike by Conn following a Souness cross, gave no clue as to what was about to unfold. Seconds after the restart Hibs came close to equalising, but Combe's shot was cleared and Hearts raced downfield to double their lead through Bauld. A Johnstone penalty offered brief hope, but further strikes by Bauld, Souness and Wardhaugh gave the home side a stunning 5–1 win.

Having suffered that major setback in the derby, Hibs next faced league leaders Aberdeen at Easter Road. The key to the success of this Dons team was to defend in numbers and look to score on the break, which is exactly what they did as Buckley scored the only goal of the game. Watching Aberdeen that day it was easy to see why they were doing so well as their defence had conceded just 12 goals in 17 games, but in truth if Hibs had converted even a small percentage of the chances they created they would have severely damaged that defensive record and collected the two points their attacking play deserved.

The trip to Falkirk is a relatively short one and for those Hibs fans who made it, it was also a frustrating one as the visitors dominated a goalless first-half and scored early in the second through Johnstone only to see Willie Ormond's brother, Robert, level soon after and then get a second just minutes later. Ten minutes from the end, with Hibs pushing for an equaliser, Davidson made the points safe for the Bairns and ensured that Hibs were still without even a point in January.

Towards the end of the following week Scotland was subjected to severe snowstorms that wiped out most of the games scheduled for the Saturday, but for some reason the Hibs game at home to Queen of the South was given the go-ahead, even though the pitch was covered in hard-packed snow and the terraces were treacherous. Around 6,000 fans braved the elements as Mr Whittle of Glasgow got the game under way. Despite the underfoot conditions both sides played well, and it took the green and whites until the 36th minute to open the scoring through Bobby Johnstone, who added a second two minutes later. A further snowfall around half-time meant work for the groundstaff in clearing the lines, but if anything conditions were getting worse. Still the game continued and after 69 minutes Johnstone completed his hat-trick. Just minutes later, with the snow covering the lines again the referee had little choice but to abandon the match – which, if nothing else, was tough luck on Bobby Johnstone, whose hat-trick would not stand as part of his goal tally for the club.

Little did the Hibs fans know but that 'non' hat-trick by Johnstone would be his last goals for the club for some time as Manchester City came in with a bid of around £22,000, quite a considerable sum in those days and Hibs reluctantly accepted. 'Nicker' had been a fabulous servant to the club and fully deserved this chance to play on a bigger stage.

Further bad weather meant that Hibs were not in action again until the end of January when they faced Clyde at home. Despite the awful weather a good number of fans turned out, hoping that the home side could get back to winning ways. The spirits of the Hibs fans were lifted by two quite wonderful goals by Reilly and Ormond, but a ten-minute lapse midway through the second-half saw Clyde first level and then take what proved to be a winning lead with two goals from Buchanan and one from Ring. That defeat was heralded by an amount of booing from the terraces, Hibs fans having watched on in disbelief as a side containing four of the Famous Five in its number was once again left pointless. There was a growing feeling that changes were needed, but in those days fans had no vehicle through which to make their concerns known other than by either staying away or booing when things went wrong.

Winless Hibs began February in the hardest possible way with a trip to Tynecastle in the Scottish cup. They'd shipped five goals the last time they were there just a few weeks earlier and disappointingly they did so again as they crashed out of the Cup. *The Scotsman* newspaper summed things up nicely with its headline for the match report: 'Hibernians Beat Themselves – defence crumbles.' It could have been so very different as the green and whites were rampant in the opening 15 minutes during which time Ormond, Reilly twice, Turnbull and Combe all came close, but a 17th-minute strike by Wardhaugh seemed to knock all the spirit out of the visitors and it was all downhill from then on. A further goal from Wardhaugh, two from Bauld and one from Conn gave the hosts a 5–0 win and helped increase the dissenting voices among the Hibs support in terms of their dwindling faith in manager Hugh Shaw and their displeasure with the efforts of the players.

The criticism of the fans could be argued to have had a positive effect as on their next outing, when they made the difficult trip to Rugby Park to face Kilmarnock, the green and whites completely outplayed their hosts from start to finish. A second-minute goal by Reilly set Hibs up nicely and the Hibs centre went on to get two more as his side recorded their first victory of 1955.

The win at Rugby Park brought some confidence back into the team and so they were looking for good things when they visited a struggling Motherwell in early March. The green and whites started well and made several chances without converting any when a sharp counter-attack saw Bain put the home side ahead. The home fans were still celebrating when Smith released Reilly and the Hibs number nine guided home an equaliser past keeper McIntyre. This Hibs side were a delight to watch when they played their close passing game, but it's goals that win games and the next Hibs goal didn't come until almost an hour had been played, Reilly's cheeky chip allowing Smith to head home from close range. Moments later Combe made it 3–1 when he finished off a superb three-man move and then five minutes from time an own goal compounded the misery for the home fans, many of whom had left before Smith got another to make the final score 5–1.

They say that football is a funny old game and by way of example on the day Hibs visited Dens Park to face Dundee a story was unfolding over the border,where Third Division York City defied all odds in beating First Division Notts County to reach the semi-finals of the FA Cup. Back to Dens Park, where Hibs had a poor first-half and trailed 2–0 following goals by Merchant and Christie, but the visitors showed great resolve and came roaring back in the second-half, scoring twice in three minutes through Reilly and Smith. Reilly's goal, a 20-yard screamer, brought the house down and Hibs came so close to winning the game, but Smith's late piledriver was brilliantly tipped over the bar by Dundee keeper Brown.

On the following Monday evening Hibs took on Spurs at Easter Road in a floodlit friendly and rested Smith, Combe and Preston while giving starting places to John Fraser, Jimmy Thomson and young Eddie Gray, who had joined the club from Kirkintilloch Rob Roy. In an entertaining game, McClellan gave the visitors a first-half lead but that was cancelled out on the hour mark when Ormond flashed a low drive across the box and Fraser steered it back from whence it came, which foxed keeper Reynolds and allowed Reilly to slot it home. It was a good performance from Reilly, who found himself up against Spurs' record signing Blanchflower and he did not allow the marked difference in stature to affect him one bit. As to Eddie Gray, he played well enough but his chances at Easter Road would be limited and he soon left to try his luck elsewhere. Incidently, this was not the same Eddie Gray who would star for Leeds United and Scotland at a future date.

Earlier in the season Hibs had gone to Bayview and thrashed East Fife 5–1 without Smith and having only ten men for the final 25 minutes of the game. Since then the Fifers had struggled badly and were in the relegation fight when they arrived at Easter Road in mid-March. Needless to say the home fans expected another five goals at least, but the visitors fought tooth and nail for every ball and Hibs just couldn't break them down. The consequence was a 0–0 draw which was a rare beast indeed for this Hibs side. The fans, not best pleased, barracked the team and kept up a pattern of slow handclapping throughout the game. It seems as though their anger was aimed mainly at Younger and Turnbull, though why that should be is a mystery as neither was the worst player on the park that day. Only the Fifers and their fans had reason to celebrate, an unexpected point helping their cause.

Having performed so dismally against East Fife it would be interesting to see how well Hibs would get on in their next outing, which brought Arsenal to Easter Road for a floodlit friendly. The game attracted 25,000 through the gates, though it seems likely that given the calibre of opposition, fans of other clubs had come along to see them play. Somewhat surprisingly to most, the home side set about their opponents in a brisk fashion and before long were camped in the Arsenal half. An early header by Smith looked netbound until Sutherland in the Arsenal goal tipped it behind for a corner and it was Smith again with the next chance, but he uncharacteristically sent a shot high over the bar when well placed to score. Three minutes from the break Reilly flashed home a header from 12 yards after a Turnbull cross was delivered with power and accuracy and then, after only seven minutes of the second-half, Turnbull himself blasted Hibs two goals ahead. Inside the last ten minutes of the game, when Plenderleith was off getting treatment for a knock, Lishman and Bloomfield scored the goals that would earn the Gunners a draw.

Forty-eight hours later some 24,000 of those fans in attendance at the Arsenal game chose to stay at home as the Hibs v Stirling Albion attendance barely scraped into four figures. There is no obvious reason why this happened as even a Hibs side losing regularly would attract a bigger turnout than that. It's true to say that Albion were a side already doomed to relegation, but you might think that would pull the fans in as surely Hibs could score a few against the Annfield side. In any event, those who stayed away missed seeing John Fraser, in for the injured Reilly, score in the 18th and 25th minutes before Smith pulled one back for the visitors. Further goals from Ormond and Turnbull secured the points for Hibs.

On the following Saturday afternoon the terraces were once again teeming with fans but sadly they were there to watch Aberdeen and Clyde draw 2–2 in a Scottish Cup semi-final. Meanwhile Hibs were in Paisley facing St Mirren and losing 4–2. The home side always seemed to have the edge and scored through Wilson, Anderson and Telfer, who got two, while a jaded Hibs eleven countered through Smith and Ormond.

Going into April the title race was still being fought out between Aberdeen, Rangers, Celtic and Hearts, but the hopes of the Parkhead club at least were snuffed out after Hibs had the audacity to go to a packed Parkhead and win 2–1. The home side scored through the immensely talented Charlie Tully, but his goal counted for nothing following strikes by Smith and Fraser. Elsewhere it looked as though Rangers might be faltering but there were still three games to play and it looked as if it might go right down to the wire.

On 9 April the destination of the league flag was decided when Aberdeen went to Shawfield and defeated Clyde 1–0 while Rangers were hammering the final nail in the coffin of Hearts' hopes by beating them 2–1. It was the first time in Aberdeen's history that they had been crowned champions and in truth no one could begrudge them the honour as they had been the best and most consistent side all season, winning 24 of their 30 games. Away from all of that Hibs were facing mid-table Partick Thistle at Easter Road in what proved to be a typical end-of-season affair. Reilly, Smith and a Turnbull penalty won the day, although Thistle did get one back through Crowe. Worth mentioning is the fact that Jimmy Thomson had a first-class game at right half.

Only two games remained and while neither held much value for Hibs, both matches did for their opponents. First up was a visit from Queen of the South, the Dumfries outfit still not sure of retaining their place in the top division. As Hibs ran out that day there was a murmur of surprise around the ground as goalkeeper Tommy Younger, recently installed as first choice for Scotland, was sporting a rather natty corduroy cap, which was odd because the day was overcast! Around 15,000 fans had a smile at the eccentricity and then set about enjoying a pretty decent game in which Reilly secured a half-time lead for Hibs. To their credit the Doonhamers came out in the second-half and attacked Hibs at every opportunity with McBain striking a worthy equaliser and earning his side a crucial point.

The final game of the league season had Hibs at Stark's Park where Raith Rovers knew they had to win to be sure of staying up. A goal after just three minutes by Kelly set the home fans in the substantial crowd cheering and the noise level grew still further when Young added a second before the break. A different Hibs turned up for the second-half and Turnbull got a goal back to set the nerves jangling for Rovers' players and fans alike. The visitors dominated the play but Rovers gave a fantastic backs-to-the-wall performance and ran out 2–1 winners to leave Motherwell and Stirling Albion in the relegation positions.

As it turned out, neither Motherwell nor Stirling Albion were relegated as the football authorities decided to increase the number of clubs in the top league from 16 to 18. The additions for the coming season were Dunfermline and Airdrie.

The curtain finally came down on the 1954/55 season with a match against Hearts at Easter Road in the final of the East of Scotland Shield. Somewhat surprisingly, both sides fielded strong teams and after a fairly dull start the game burst into life and proved to be highly entertaining from thereon in. A hat-trick from Urquhart was answered by two from Turnbull and one from Ormond but three minutes from time Jimmy Wardhaugh struck the winner for Hearts.

Chapter Ten

1955/56

EUROPEAN CUP PIONEERS

For many years Hibernian Football Club had been pioneers of the sport and had played in foreign tours as far afield as the South American continent. The Scottish press made little of that fact, while down south the English press was quick to nominate Wolverhampton Wanderers as Champions of the World after a successful run of good results playing friendlies in Europe. The French were particularly aggrieved by this turn of events and Gabriel Hanot, sports journalist and editor of the famous French football magazine *L'Équipe*, took it upon himself to organise a European Cup where the best sides from a number of European countries would play each other home and away for a handsome trophy. The inaugural tournament was by invitation and although Hibs were not the Scottish champions they were selected to take part because the French sporting press at least recognised the fact that the Easter Road club had played many times in Europe in friendly matches.

As well as Hibs, the tournament was entered by Sporting Lisbon (Portugal), Partisan Belgrade (Serbia), Voros Lobogo (Hungary), Anderlecht (Belgium), Servette (Switzerland), Real Madrid (Spain), Rot Weiss Essen (Germany), Djurgaardens (Sweden), Guardia Warsaw (Poland), Aarhus (Denmark), Stade Reims (France), Rapid Vienna (Austria), PSV Eindhoven (Holland), AC Milan (Italy) and Saarbrucken (Germany). There would be no English club, as they were quite happy to keep plugging the Wolverhampton cause. In the draw for the first round Hibs were paired with Rot Weiss Essen, the matches due to commence in mid-September. Ahead of that Hibs had to battle out with Aberdeen, Clyde and Dunfermline to see which club would progress into the last eight of the League Cup.

A difficult opening game brought league champions Aberdeen to Easter Road on 13 August under the guidance of new manager Davy Shaw, who was well known to the Hibs fans as captain of the side that brought the 1947/48 league title to Edinburgh. The Dons had based their side in the title-winning season on a strong defence and a pacy attack to hit on the break and those tactics paid off for them again on this occasion as Hibs were the better side over the 90 minutes and yet still lost to a single goal from star forward Buckley. Special mention must also be made of keeper Martin, who pulled off save after save to hold Hibs at bay.

A midweek trip to Shawfield followed with Scottish Cup holders Clyde the opponents. Once again Hibs dominated for long spells and yet failed to win. Early on in the game an outrageous lob by Smith looked bound for the net until keeper Hawkins pulled off a wonderful save to deny the Hibs number seven. At the other end a slip by full back John Higgins allowed Currie to race in and put the hosts 1–0 up against the run of play. After Smith had again gone close in hitting a post, the winger set up Ormond to make it 1–1. A second Ormond goal looked to have won the points for the visitors, but right at the death Currie scored again to earn his side a point.

Three penalties in one game is relatively rare,but that's exactly what happened when Hibs next faced Dunfermline at Easter Road. Twice Pars defenders used their hands to stop certain goals and twice Eddie Turnbull smashed home the resultant penalties, those goals coming either side of one from Smith. Late in the game the visitors were awarded a penalty which Duthie converted to make the final score 3–1. Interestingly, there is no note of either of the Dunfermline players being booked for deliberate hand-ball: a similar offence today would bring an automatic red card for the offender. Dunfermline, of course, had just been promoted to the 'A' Division and first impressions indicated they would more than hold their own.

To have any chance of progressing to the quarter-final stages of the League Cup Hibs would need to beat Aberdeen at Pittodrie and that was a tall order. In an even first-half the visitors took a late chance and went in 1–0 up at the break thanks to Lawrie Reilly. In the second-half Hibs had chances to increase that lead but in fairness the hosts were also pushing hard and that made for a fantastic game of football. In time Buckley equalised for the Dons, but a draw was no use to Hibs and so they pushed on looking for a winner. That left inevitable gaps at the back and when O'Neill blasted a rocket shot past Younger it meant the hosts would qualify.

With nothing to play for but pride and the chance to improve match fitness, Hibs next faced Clyde at Easter Road and gave starting places to Joe McClelland at left back and Des Fox in the forward line. Young Fox enjoyed his first-team debut and made an excellent start to the game, the home fans offering warm applause for his clever play. After 13 minutes Reilly set up Turnbull with a chance and the ball was in the net before the keeper moved, but two minutes later in a rare attack McPhaill equalised for the Bully Wee so that the sides went in level at the break. Barely a minute of the second-half had elapsed before a Turnbull shot hit the post and Smith reacted quickly to put Hibs a goal ahead and although both sides had chances after that the game ended 2–1 in favour of the hosts.

The last game in the section took Hibs to East End Park where they were often second best and yet still managed to win. With Younger in great form, the home side were restricted to a Mailer goal at the break while Hibs had struck twice through Fox, getting his first goal for the club, and Reilly. A late goal from Ormond secured a 3–1 win for the visitors. On the same day at Brockville there were ugly scenes when Falkirk hosted Celtic. Two home players were hit by bottles and glasses thrown from the crowd after Celtic had been denied a penalty. These events would lead to a major inquiry by both the SFA and the Scottish League. I highlight this event to show that contrary to popular belief football hooliganism was not as many believe an invention of 1970s fans.

Already having played and lost twice to Aberdeen, Hibs opened their league campaign with a trip to Pittodrie where they were involved in an eight-goal thriller. The reigning champions were anxious not to give up that title easily and on the day were a better side than Hibs. Two goals down inside the first ten minutes meant on early warning for the visitors as Buckley and Leggat danced past defenders and beat Younger with ease. Reilly pulled one back, but the same duo that got goals one and two then got goals three and four prior to the first-half ending. In the second, Buckley completed his hat-trick and Yorston added a sixth while Hibs' only reply in a 6–2 thrashing came from Turnbull.

A heavy defeat was hardly the best preparation for Hibs' European adventure, but when they travelled in the following midweek to face German cracks Rot Weiss Essen they put all thoughts of that reversal behind them. In a match dominated throughout by the Scots, Turnbull scored twice, laid one on for Reilly and watched on happily as Ormond added a fourth before the end. The German side was rarely seen in attack and their international goalkeeper Herkenrath stood no chance with any of the goals he conceded.

Back in Scotland for their weekend fixture, Hibs were once again on duty at Shawfield where last time out they had run the show but had to settle for a point in a 2–2 draw. This time it would be the home side that had the better of the game, although it took goals by Reilly and Ormond to spark them into life. Midway through the second-half Robertson made it 2–1 and in the dying moments Lennie levelled from the penalty spot after international winger Tommy Ring had been tripped in the box. At the end of the day it was a point each and on balance that was a fair outcome.

'Hibs' convincing win over Manchester United' is not a headline that can be easily ignored! On 19 September the Manchester club came to

Easter Road for a floodlit friendly that was played in front of more than 35,000 fans. Hibs were minus Preston and Combe and so drafted in John Grant and Jimmy Mulkerrin while the visitors were more or less at full strength. In a first-half blitz the green and whites scored four times without reply while playing some fabulous passing football. Goal one arrived in nine minutes courtesy of Ormond, who finished off a three-man move from close range. Five minutes later there was a second goal, again following a brilliant build-up, with Reilly completing the move in firing home a 25-yard rocket. More pass and move action brought a third from Smith and the visitors must have been shell-shocked when Ormond's blocked free kick was pounced upon by Reilly, who made it 4–0. Whatever the visitors discussed at half-time, whatever game plan they proposed to use received a major setback just two minutes in as Reilly got his hat-trick with the last goal of the game. It had been great entertainment for the watching fans and surely a confidence booster for the Hibs players.

A week later at Tynecastle Hearts set out to prolong a run of avoiding home defeat in a derby since season 1952/53, but like Hibs they played with a hesitancy that was creeping into such fixtures, where players seemed more determined not to lose than to win. On balance Hibs had the edge and five minutes from time Jimmy Mulkerrin struck the goal that both won the points and ended that dismal Tynecastle run. Mulkerrin had fired a strong shot at goal which Watters did well to save, but he couldn't hold it and the Hibs man reacted quickly to drive the loose ball into the net, sending thousands of Hibs fans home with smiles on their faces.

A young, lively and very talented Kilmarnock came to Easter Road for the next match and within five minutes were a goal ahead after Catterson steered home a pass from Harvey. For the next ten minutes or so Younger's goal was under siege, but the home defence stood firm and at the other end a corner taken by Grant was strongly headed home by Mulkerrin to bring the sides level. The youngsters from Ayrshire tried everything they knew to break Hibs down again but they failed and must have had the stuffing knocked out of them when an 'old head' in Reilly nabbed the winning goal following a pinpoint cross by Smith.

Another floodlit friendly followed on the Monday evening when Hibs travelled down to Preston to face North End at Deepdale. Things were pretty close until Mattinson had the misfortune to score an own goal but that sparked Hibs. They controlled the rest of the match and scored again through Turnbull, who got two, one of those from the penalty spot, and Reilly.

With Smith, Reilly and Younger rested and Hibs already leading 4–0 from the first leg, Hugh Shaw drafted in Jock Buchanan, Jimmy

Mulkerrin and goalkeeper Adams for the return tie with Rot Weiss Essen. Around 30,000 fans attended, but it was not a great game as Hibs scored through Mulkerrin after five minutes and in reality the Germans were out. The home side took their foot off the gas, but the visitors kept plugging away and a quite wonderful goal by Abromeit, the German forward thumping home the kind of shot Eddie Turnbull would have been proud of, was met by appreciative applause from the home fans.

It was back to league business again on the Saturday with another home match as a good-going Falkirk side came to Edinburgh. The visitors started brightly enough without really threatening to score, while at the other end Bert Slater was at his very best in denying Combe an opener. As the first-half was drawing to a close Hibs struck twice in 90 seconds through Ormond and Combe, a setback the visitors failed to overcome despite playing quite well after the interval.

Yet another floodlit match the following Wednesday evening took Hibs to St James' Park to face Newcastle in front of around 18,000 fans. The visitors were in great form and after 12 minutes they went ahead through the ever reliable Lawrie Reilly. An interval lead was pegged back six minutes in when Whyte equalised following a free kick and it's safe to say the crowd was enjoying the match. When Combe beat Ronnie Simpson in the Newcastle goal with what proved to be the winner the home fans cheered what was a fantastic finish.

Since going down heavily at Pittodrie on the opening day Hibs had enjoyed a run of seven wins and two draws from league matches, European ties and friendlies, but they came back down to earth with a bump at East End Park towards the end of October. It was the day upon which Aberdeen, the only other side to have beaten Hibs, won the League Cup with victory over St Mirren in the final. While the Dons fans would have been celebrating that win, Hibs fans who made the trip to Fife were first elated when Reilly struck after ten minutes and then deflated when his namesake in the Dunfermline forward line equalised. Then Baikie got a second and decisive goal after the interval.

One of the teams going well in the league were new boys Airdrie, who were flying high when they visited Easter Road. An opener from Reilly in the 31st minute was cancelled out by McMillan six minutes later, the goal coming from the penalty spot after Younger had fouled McCulloch. As half-time approached Turnbull fired the hosts ahead and then the same player scored again just after the break. The Airdrie players were not about to give up and soon they pulled a goal back from a hotly disputed penalty which McMillan converted before McCulloch made it 3–3 and ensured a share of the points for the men from Lanarkshire.

A number of games had taken place under floodlights this season and Hibs were yet to be beaten, so the task for visitors Manchester City was obvious. Returning to Easter Road with City was Bobby Johnstone, who got a really warm welcome from the home supporters in the 29,000 crowd. 'Nicker' played well, as did centre forward Don Revie, but the Hibs defence, anchored around the impressive John Paterson, was in no mood to concede. After just eight minutes Reilly beat Bert Trautmann in the City goal with a close-range effort after Turnbull's original shot was deflected into his path. Twenty minutes from the break Jackie Plenderleith and Cunliffe collided, but the City winger recovered quickly to hit a low shot past the advancing Younger. That leveller was cancelled out seven minutes later after Turnbull set Ormond up and the home side went into the break with a goal advantage. The second-half was as exciting as the first but held no goals and so Hibs had managed to maintain their floodlit record.

The good form shown in the Manchester City game by Reilly and Smith was timely as Scotland were soon to face Wales and both Hibs men hoped to be selected. Their chances were further enhanced in Hibs' next game, against Raith Rovers at Stark's Park, where Reilly almost opened the scoring after a defence-splitting pass from Smith had created the chance. Minutes later Reilly was felled in the box and Turnbull converted the resultant penalty and then Reilly demonstrated his awareness by back-heeling a second goal into the Rovers net. The Edinburgh men were running riot now and before half-time Combe and Turnbull had added a third and fourth goal to the total. In the second-half the visitors eased off, knowing the job was done, but even then Younger was rarely troubled in goal.

Having disposed of one Fife opponent, Hibs next faced East Fife at Easter Road. The Bayview men were struggling somewhat and would find it difficult to halt the Hibernian goal scoring machine. To their credit they gave a very spirited performance and actually took the lead through Jimmy Bonthrone, but Hibs were soon level thanks to Ormond. Further goals from Reilly and Combe secured the points that took Hibs into third spot in the league behind Celtic and Queen of the South, although the men from Easter Road had played one game less.

With fog hanging over most of the east coast, Hibs welcomed Newcastle United to Easter Road for a floodlit friendly the following midweek. A sizeable crowd was in the ground as the fog thickened and had it not been for the fact that the visitors were stripped and ready and the fans had paid their money the game might not have been given the go-ahead. With conditions steadily worsening, Newcastle might have gone ahead when Jackie Milburn created a chance for himself but Younger was equal to the task. Play flowed to the other end where Turnbull was successful in beating Ronnie Simpson to put the hosts 1–0 up. Late in the second-half Turnbull scored again but by that time many of the fans were struggling to see what was actually going on and the referee, after consulting both managers, called a halt early.

On the next Saturday Hibs faced an important and tricky fixture at Palmerston Park against a high-flying Queen of the South. Over the 90 minutes it would be Younger and Reilly who played the key roles in winning the points for Hibs. Leading 2–0 at the break following excellent goals from Ormond and Combe, the visitors found that the Doonhamers were going to do everything in their power to claw back the deficit and as a result Younger's goal was under siege for long periods of play. In time Paterson pulled one goal back but otherwise Younger was immense, pulling off a string of superb saves to deny an equaliser. Late in the game Hibs broke clear and when the ball reached Reilly he struck a superb shot past the diving Henderson to secure a 3–1 win for his side.

Having already disposed of German champions Rot Weiss Essen in the European Cup, Hibs next faced the Swedish champions Djurgaardens, who had elected to play their home tie at Firhill in Glasgow due to the winter weather in their home town making their pitch unplayable. Hibs went into the tie minus the services of Lawrie Reilly, who had contracted a chest infection, and his place at centre forward was entrusted to young Jimmy Mulkerrin. In a pulsating start to the game Hibs were caught cold after just 90 seconds when Edlund broke free of his marker and fired in a powerful shot from 18 yards. Moments later Sandberg stung Younger's fingers with another try but the Hibs fans in the 22,000 crowd then witnessed a 'waking up' by their favourites. Twice in quick succession Ormond went close to scoring. The pressure was building and after 20 minutes Smith lobbed the ball over a Djurgaardens defender and Combe met it on the drop to volley home the equaliser. Early in the second-half a clearance by Plenderleith reached Mulkerrin, who raced past two defenders before shooting home from an angle. Then, after the same player was tripped in the box, Turnbull shot the resultant penalty wide of the goal. Around this time the Swedes began to get a lot more physical, but strong refereeing by Englishman Arthur Ellis kept them in check and five minutes from time Turnbull atoned for his penalty miss by cracking in a third goal for the Scots.

Prior to the second leg, Hibs had a league fixture to fulfil when Partick Thistle came to Easter Road. The Djurgaardens squad had stayed in Scotland and were in the stand watching on as Hibs went nap in what turned out to be a very one-sided match. The visitors were without two of their key players, but the home side suffered too as Reilly was still not fit to play. Just what the watching Swedes thought was anyone's guess as Gordon Smith turned in a masterclass display in laying on the first three goals with pinpoint crosses. Mulkerrin and Ormond twice turned those crosses into a 3–0 lead and though Wright pulled one back, Combe and

Turnbull took the goals tally to five and another two points were safely added to the total.

On the following Monday, in front of a huge crowd, the Swedish visitors impressed with some neat passing play, but they lacked a finisher and even when they did get shots on target Younger was at his best in the Hibs goal. At the centre of the home defence, John Paterson and Jackie Plenderleith were both in fine form and from that foundation the Hibees went on to win the match by scoring the only goal, 20 minutes from time, after Ormond was tripped in the box and Turnbull hammered the penalty past Arvidsson. That win took Hibs into the semi-finals and all the talk was that they stood a chance of facing the mighty Real Madrid or AC Milan, as both sides were still in the competition along with the representatives of France, Hungary and Austria, those teams not having yet played their quarter-finals.

Moving into December, Hibs next faced St Mirren at Love Street, where the pitch was hard and bumpy and did not lend itself to good football. Nevertheless, both sides put on a good show. Defences were very much on top and it was late in the game when the winning goal was scored by Mulkerrin, the points gained moving Hibs up to second behind Celtic but with a game in hand. Encouragingly for Edinburgh football fans, Hearts were third, two points behind Hibs and on the same number of games played.

A week later Dundee were the visitors to Easter Road and they played a significant part in a nine-goal thriller. The weather was awful and the entire game was played out in torrential rain with the fans on the open terracing getting soaked but hardly caring because the football was so exciting. Given the conditions it was perhaps surprising that the first-half belonged to the goalkeepers, Younger and Brown confidently handling just about everything that came their way. Only Brown was beaten once when he failed to stop a Turnbull piledriver from fully 25 yards. The second-half was quite different as goals began to fly in from all directions. Hibs struck first blood as Ormond raced down the right wing before cutting inside and cracking home a beauty with his left foot. Perhaps the players had heard the crowd roar at half-time when news came through that Kilmarnock were winning at Parkhead because further goals by Ormond, Combe and Smith and an own goal by Cowie took the total to six. To their credit Dundee still went forward when they could and were rewarded by goals from Merchant, Smith and Christie. When the full-time whistle blew, Hibs topped the league as Celtic ended up losing 3–0.

For some time there had been disquiet among both fans of the game and players over the rule that allowed a forward to score a goal by barging the goalkeeper into his net while he had the ball in his arms. It was hugely unpopular, with critics suggesting it was more akin to rugby than football. Even Lawrie Reilly, who had scored a few that way, was not its biggest fan and like most he felt a review of the rule was long overdue. The whole topic came to a head for Hibs when they visited Ibrox in mid-December. Playing well and leading by an Ormond goal, Hibs were outraged when Younger leapt to gather a cross and before he could collect it he was barged over his goal line by Simpson, the ball bouncing into the net. The referee allowed it and following significant protest by the visiting players, Reilly was booked. Early in the second-half Younger gathered a ball in safely and then braced himself for the inevitable challenge, which this time came from Kitchenbrand. As the Rangers man made contact with the Hibs goalie he basically bounced off and landed in a heap, whereupon referee Liston promptly awarded a penalty. It was a quite ludicrous decision and it knocked the stuffing out of Hibs, who went on to lose 4–1. The Rangers 'goals', incidentally, were scored by Hubbard, who got two, Kitchenbrand and Simpson. Results elsewhere ensured that it would get ever tighter at the top of the table.

As if they had not had enough bother with the referee at Ibrox, Hibs again seemed to suffer in their next match against Celtic at Easter Road on Christmas Eve. Mr Youngson of Aberdeen caused incredulity not just on the terraces but also in the press box when he blew the final whistle with still a full four minutes left to play. At that point Celtic led 3–2, but Hibs were swarming around their goal in search of an equaliser and might well have scored had the game run its regulation length of time. In fairness, Celtic proved very good on the day and even had to play with just ten men for a while as Fernie was off the park getting a lengthy dose of treatment. Their goals came from Mochan, who got two, and Sharkey, while Hibs countered through Ormond and Turnbull. That result and results elsewhere meant Hibs dropped to fourth behind the Old Firm and Hearts.

Incredibly, the Celtic match was the first of six home games that would take Hibs into the middle of January 1956 before an away trip was required. The second of the six games brought bottom club Stirling Albion to town on Hogmanay and Hibs set about giving their fans something to warm them up on a cold day by winning at a canter by six goals to one. Goals came at fairly regular intervals, the scorers being Smith, who got two, as did Combe, with singles from Reilly and Ormond.

Going into January 1956 both Edinburgh clubs were valid contenders for the title and so it was no surprise that a crowd of 60,800 made their way to Easter Road on 2 January. A tense first-half was evenly fought as both sets of players seemed more intent on not making mistakes rather than scoring goals, but the game burst into life ten minutes after the interval when Ormond got on the end of an inch-perfect cross from Smith to open the scoring. Four minutes later a swirling cross from Reilly on the left wing completely deceived Duff in the Hearts goal and crept in at his back post. The visitors were stung by this double strike and soon laid siege to the Hibs goal. Just after the hour Bauld pulled one back for the Gorgie outfit. Minutes later Wardhaugh's shot caused confusion between Younger and MacFarlane and Conn nipped in to grab the equaliser. There were no more goals as the sides drew for the first time at Easter Road since the end of the Second World War. As Rangers beat Celtic 1–0 that day it meant that the top five clubs were covered by just three points.

A mere 24 hours later Hibs were again in action when they faced second-bottom club Clyde. That lowly position was surprising as the side were virtually unaltered since lifting the Scottish Cup the previous season, and it's true to say that they very nearly were a match for Hibs in this tussle. Only a 66th-minute penalty scored by Turnbull separated the sides, but the two points won put Hibs back at the top, level with Celtic.

An icy Easter Road came into use again as Hibs faced the Scotland Under-23 side in a challenge match. In the dark blue that day were Jimmy Thomson and Jackie Plenderleith of Hibs along with Duff, Young and Hamilton of Hearts. In at centre for Hibs was Jimmy Mulkerrin, who set up the first goal, scored by Turnbull after just three minutes of play. Ormond was then injured and had to leave the field, but both camps had agreed on the use of replacements and that allowed young Johnny Frye to make his first-team debut. On the half hour Turnbull scored again, this time from a MacFarlane cross, and seven minutes later Frye made it 3–0. Midway through the second-half Scott of Rangers pulled one back, but before the end Turnbull got his third and Hibs' fourth to make the final score 4–1.

On 14 January Hibs hosted the reigning title holders Aberdeen. Although going into the game both sides enjoyed quite similar figures in the goals for and against columns, the Dons were in the middle of a purple patch, scoring 18 in their last four games, a complete contrast to their usual 1–0 or 2–1 wins. The Dons obviously knew that to retain their title they'd need to beat fellow contenders like Hibs, so as the game unfolded it was slightly surprising to see the home side dominate for long periods. Sadly, Hibs could not turn the pressure into goals and went down 3–1 after Boyd, who got two, and Wishart both beat Younger, whereas only Reilly scored for the hosts. A 2–0 win at Dundee on the same day took Hearts to the top of the pile.

Rugby Park was always a difficult venue and mid-table Kilmarnock ensured that Hibs had to fight all the way to secure a 1–0 win. It took a flash of Smith and Reilly genius to create and score the goal late in the game, the players playing a one-two before Reilly slid the ball into the net. The hosts might have earned a point when awarded a late penalty, but Watson blasted the ball high over Younger's bar.

Hibs were back in Edinburgh for their next outing against a Motherwell side who had earned a top half of the table position based largely on a very successful offside trap. They arrived at Easter Road having conceded only 30 goals in 18 games, but the wheels came well and truly off their bus on this occasion, in a game where Gordon Smith was back to his very best. The Prince of Wingers laid on no fewer than five goals as well as scoring one himself. The final score of 7–0 did not flatter Hibs in any way whatsoever as the total could indeed have been higher on the day. The goals came from Smith, Combe, Mulkerrin, Reilly and Turnbull, who got three, including a penalty. Mulkerrin, who played centre with Reilly on the left in place of the injured Ormond, was apparently the subject of some speculation as to his future as it had been rumoured that he'd asked for a move. After the match, Hibs chairman Harry Swan said: 'I've heard these rumours but that is all they are, rumours.'

February was scheduled to start for Hibs with a home tie against Raith Rovers in the Scottish Cup, but heavy fog and foul weather caused a postponement for that tie and several others. This led to the affected clubs seeking permission from the SFA to play the games in midweek under floodlights. After deliberation the SFA gave its permission and so on the Wednesday evening Raith Rovers faced a side that had been undefeated in floodlit games, in front of a partisan Easter Road crowd of 26,024. As it turned out the Fifers more than held their own and led through a McEwan goal until Turnbull forced home an equaliser four minutes from time. In fact there were six 'goals' during the game, but each side had two disallowed by the referee. Once the dust had settled it meant a replay at Stark's Park during the following midweek.

In the meantime Hibs' hopes of league title success took a severe bashing on the Saturday when they travelled to Brockville to face Falkirk. An incident-packed game saw the visitors strike the woodwork no fewer than four times and at the other end Tommy Younger saved a penalty, taken by Parker. Sadly, however, the Hibs keeper had earlier made a mistake that allowed McCrae to put the Bairns ahead and despite heroic efforts to get level again the green and whites actually conceded a second goal scored by Sinclair. The defeat left Hibs in third, three points behind leaders Rangers but with a game more played.

A tie against Second Division leaders Queen's Park awaited the winners of the replay at Stark's Park, where a crowd in excess of 13,000 turned out, many of them having made the trip across the Forth in football special trains courtesy of British Rail. Opening exchanges in the game were brisk and after 15 minutes McEwan put the hosts ahead. A second goal arrived fairly soon after from the head of Copland. The men from Edinburgh were struggling to get their game going and it was all over bar the shouting when Copland struck again early in the second-half. Hibs went on to finish the stronger side, but Raith had clearly decided to protect what they had and so Reilly's late goal was no more than a consolation. At the railway station after the game the travelling party were met by an amount of booing from disgruntled fans, unhappy at the poor showing and yet another exit from the Scottish Cup.

With no game the following Saturday due to that cup exit, Hibs travelled down to Lancashire, where they faced Bury at Gigg Lane in a floodlit friendly. The men from Edinburgh never really got going on a very difficult surface and went down by four goals to nil after Robinson, May (2) and Kelly had beaten Younger. The nearest Hibs got to a goal was from a penalty, but Turnbull missed the chance.

During the following week Hibs learned of their fate in the European Cup as the semi-final draw had paired them with French champions Stade Reims, the first leg to be played in France. As a matter of interest the other semi paired Real Madrid with AC Milan, so Hibs were moving in exalted company.

The post-match criticism of the players at Kirkcaldy railway station had clearly hit the mark because in their next league outing against Dunfermline at Easter Road, Hibs played out of their skins and delighted the home fans with their display. Once again it was Gordon Smith who led the charge, the winger, now in his fifteenth year at the club, being still able to play at a very high level. At times his play mesmerised the opposition defenders and he had a hand in a few goals that day as the Pars were thumped 7–1. Reilly got two, Turnbull went one better with a hat-trick while Smith himself and Ormond completed the rout, with Miller on target for the visitors. Making his senior debut at centre half that day was Bobby Nicol, who gave a solid display throughout.

Another vacant Saturday caused by cup ties meant that Hibs once again headed south, this time to Yorkshire, where they faced Huddersfield and lost 3–2, the Hibs goals being scored by Reilly and Ormond. Back at home the cup semi-finalists were established as Celtic beat Airdrie 2–1, Hearts crushed Rangers 4–0, Queen of the South lost 4–2 at home to Clyde and Hibs' conquerors Raith Rovers beat Partick Thistle 2–1.

Despite recent setbacks Hibs still held a flickering flame of hope that the title could be won, but that flame was more or less extinguished when a visit to Broomfield ended in a defeat by three goals to one. In a rough and tumble encounter, Baird fired the hosts ahead after 26 minutes, but nine minutes later Ormond got Hibs level. A couple of quite dramatic minutes early in the second-half basically saw the match won and lost. First, McCulloch tangled with MacFarlane in the Hibs penalty area and incredibly the referee awarded a penalty when it seemed obvious to everyone that the Airdrie man had committed the foul. Undeterred by the ruckus that decision caused, McMillan slotted home the spot kick. From the kick-off, Hibs swept down the park and Reilly was sent crashing to the ground in the Airdrie 18-yard box and could only join everyone else in the stadium in looking on in disbelief as the referee waved play on. Three minutes from the end Baird made it 3–1, making debutant Jimmy Harrower's experience an unpleasant one for the young lad to remember.

Although now all but out of the league race, Hibs had to try and keep their performance level high as they had a European Cup semi-final to play in just a few weeks' time. Perhaps with that thought in mind and taking into consideration the unavailability through injury of Turnbull, Reilly and Combe, manager Hugh Shaw fielded Jimmy Harrower, John Grant and Jock Buchanan in the next match at home to Raith Rovers. Also in the starting eleven that day was goalkeeper Jim Rollo because Younger was nursing a twisted knee. Goals by old heads Smith and Ormond were cancelled out by Young and Kelly as both sides settled for a point and the overall impression for the home fans was that although they tried very hard the incoming youngsters found the pace of the game too much for them at times.

In mid-March Hibs were at Bayview and once again found themselves involved in refereeing controversy, only this time it was the other team who felt hard done by. With 20 minutes on the clock a penalty was given for hand-ball by an East Fife defender, but the home players swarmed around the referee insisting the offence had taken place outside the 18-yard box. Eventually the whistler consulted his linesman, but then stuck to his decision, which allowed Turnbull to fire Hibs in front. On the stroke of half-time Leishman equalised, but within two minutes of the restart the visitors struck again when Jimmy Thomson scored what turned out to be the winning goal. Like Hibs, Celtic had dropped away in the race for the title and it now seemed certain the flag would fly at Ibrox, Tynecastle or Pittodrie.

When Queen of the South visited Easter Road on 21 March, Hugh Shaw fielded his new-look half-back line of Jock Buchanan, John Grant and Bobby Combe to great effect as the home side were dominant throughout and cruised to a 4–1 win. A lively opening saw the visitors strike first blood through Black, but from then until the end Hibs were the better team and scored goals through Smith, Reilly, who got two, and Ormond.

Only one game remained before the first leg of the European Cup semi-final and that took Hibs to Firhill to face Partick Thistle. In an even game the Jags gave as good as they got and Davidson gave them the lead, but Hibs fought back and thanks to a Jimmy Thomson goal they shared the points in a 1–1 draw.

From Firhill to the Parc des Princes is quite a leap, but that's what Hibs did when they travelled to France to face a very strong Stade Reims outfit the following midweek. With 36,000 fans in the stadium an intriguing match saw both sides create but miss early chances and indeed the scoresheet remained blank at half-time. With Smith and Ormond in good form there was always a chance Hibs might score, but Reilly was being kept quiet in the centre by the Reims international centre half Jonquet and so openings for him were rare. At the other end Younger had three amazing saves to deny Kopa, but with around 20 minutes left he was finally beaten when Leblond headed home from a corner and then, with almost the last kick of the game, Bilard made it 2–0, setting the Edinburgh side a hard task for the return leg.

It was back to the bread and butter of league football next and a visit from St Mirren, who were struggling near the foot of the table. The game was not great in truth as the Hibs players looked a bit heavy-legged after their midweek tie, but they still had enough going for them to record a 2–0 win with a double by Ormond.

The following Saturday, Younger, Smith and Reilly played for Scotland against England with the match finishing 1–1. On the Monday after that Hibs were at Fir Park, but only two of the three Scotland caps were on duty, Reilly sitting the match out and being replaced by Mulkerrin. In a hard-fought game the visitors earned a point, but it came at a price as at the end of the game Grant, Paterson and Mulkerrin all limped off having been injured. The home side had scored through Quinn but Hibs earned their deserved point with a strike from Turnbull.

It would prove to be a tale of glorious failure in the European Cup semi-final second leg against Stade Reims as Hibs were superb throughout, thrilling the record midweek crowd of 46,000 but failing to find the target. It had not seemed likely that the hosts would fail to score because they launched attack after attack, but the ball just would not go in the net. Needless to say, all that attacking left spaces at the back and when Kopa fed a ball through to Glovakie the Reims man fired it past Younger to make it 1–0 on the night and 3–0 on aggregate. Loud claims for offside against Glovakie seemed justified but were ignored and that goal proved to be the only one of the game. Despite losing, Hibs did not do their reputation or indeed the reputation of Scottish football any harm what-soever and drew many compliments regarding their playing style. In the other semi, Real Madrid defeated AC Milan and went on to beat Reims in the final, the first of an incredible seven consecutive European Cup wins for the Spanish outfit.

Just three days later, while Hearts were at Hampden beating Celtic in the Scottish Cup final, Hibs were hosting newly crowned champions Rangers and fighting out an entertaining 2–2 draw. Scorers for Hibs were Turnbull and Reilly, with the Rangers strikes coming from Murray and Baird.

The season was nearing its end now and fixtures were being squeezed in over a short space of time. As a result Hibs were once again in action on the Monday when they visited Dens Park, where around 10,000 fans witnessed a game not at all in keeping with standard end-of-season fare. Both sides played open and attractive football, the visitors taking a third-minute lead through Reilly. As half-time drew near, Merchant secured an equaliser with a cracking drive from distance. Early in the second-half Christie put the hosts ahead, but on the hour mark a Dundee defender put the ball into his own goal under pressure from Reilly. Near the end, Merchant headed what turned out to be the winning goal.

Unlike the game at Dens, the match at Parkhead just 48 hours later saw a lethargic looking home side fall to a very good Hibs outfit, for whom Reilly scored all the goals in a 3–0 win. The fact that only 7,000 fans turned out can be measured against the fact that Celtic had lost out in the league race to Rangers despite the fact that for a long while the flag looked destined for Parkhead.

The last league game of the season was a drab affair at Annfield where only a quite stunning goal from Turnbull lit the place up. That was one of three scored without reply, the others coming from Ormond and John Fraser.

Crack Brazilian outfit Vasco da Gama were in the UK on a short tour and had lost 6–3 to Everton before facing Hibs at Easter Road on the last day of April. The home side were missing Younger, Smith and Reilly, while the visitors were playing in the knowledge that the Brazilian international team selectors were in the stand watching as they worked towards picking a squad for that season's World Cup tournament, which would be preceded by a friendly international against England at Wembley. After ten minutes Combe released Turnbull and the ball was in the net almost before keeper Heilo moved. When Livinho equalised prior to the break an element of farce ensued as the scorer and two of his team-mates decided to celebrate by lying on the ground and wriggling about. The visiting bench promptly sent on three substitutes, clearly thinking their men injured, but no one went off and it took the attention of the Hibs players to make referee Bobby Davidson of Airdrie aware that Vasco had 14 players on the park! By half-time Jimmy Harrower had restored the Hibs lead and in the final minute of the game Turnbull scored again to make it 3–1.

On 5 May Hibs were at Tynecastle to face new Scottish Cup holders Hearts in the final of the East of Scotland Shield. Higgins made his first-team debut for the green and whites, who were without Smith and Reilly, but the game was won by Hearts. They took the lead through Ward and were then pegged back by Ormond, only for Wardhaugh to score a very late winner. On the same day at Wembley, Bobby Johnstone scored one of the goals for Manchester City, who beat Birmingham City 3–1 in the FA Cup final.

In mid-May, Hibs embarked on a short tour of France and Switzerland where they had mixed fortunes. The tour opened with a match against French side Rouen and a victory for the tourists by three goals to one, with Reilly, Combe and Ormond the marksmen.

Eight days later Hibs were in Marseille, where there was a strange prelude to the match: instead of flipping a coin, the referee simply asked Hibs which way they would like to shoot. With that out of the way, the visitors kicked off in front of a poor crowd of around 5,000 and six minutes into the game Ormond scored with a fantastic drive from an oblique angle. Minutes later Frye should have scored a second but he screwed his shot wide. Hibs were playing fast open football, keeping the ball on the ground. A few niggling fouls began to enter the play and the referee called both captains together for a word. With the tension bubbling away there were no more goals until 16 minutes from time when Andersson equalised and that set up a great finish as both sides looked to win the match. Johansson then put Marseille ahead, but Reilly soon equalised and then in the dying seconds Andersson scored what proved to be the winner for the hosts.

Next up was a game against Strasbourg, an encounter which was to prompt the local newspaper to later describe the referee as indifferent and the linesmen as somnolent. This view was taken after the reporter had watched the home side push and shove its way through the game without incurring the wrath of the whistler, while every time a Hibs player made any physical contact a foul was given. Despite all of that the visitors took a first-half lead through Ormond and then the same player scored another, only to have it chalked off for a quite ludicrous offside decision by one of the 'somnolent' linesmen. A blatant push on Reilly in the box was a stonewall penalty, but nothing was given and a few minutes later Haan scored what proved to be both the equaliser and the last goal of the game.

The final game of the tour was in Switzerland against Basle and once again there was some dubious refereeing that seemed to confuse even the 5,000 home fans. The awarding of a penalty to the home side late in the game allowed Hugi to score the winning goal when the sides were level at 1–1 after Frye had shot Hibs ahead only for Stauble to equalise.

Chapter Eleven

1956/57

EASTER ROAD 'LIGHTS UP'

A new season dawned and it would surely be a difficult task to measure up to the last campaign when Hibernian became the first British club to compete in the European Cup and did fantastically well to reach the semi-finals in beating Rot Weiss Essen of Germany and Djurgaardens of Sweden before losing out to Stade Reims of France.

A huge effort would be required if success was the target and so there were a number of new faces around at Easter Road as the players returned from a shortened close-season break. The new guys must have wondered what lay ahead as Hibs slumped to an opening day League Cup defeat at Tynecastle by a very painful six goals to one with Eddie Turnbull the Hibs marksman. Manager Hugh Shaw was distraught at his charges and though not wishing to take anything away from a first-class performance by the Gorgie side he confirmed he would be looking for more spirited and coordinated performances from the greens in games to come, vowing to give youth its chance if the old heads failed to produce.

The line-up which crumbled at Tynecastle was Wren, J. Higgins, Paterson, Laing, Grant, Thomson, Smith, Turnbull, Reilly, Combe and Ormond, and looking at those players it seems inconceivable that they would lose so badly. If youth were to be given its chance, which reserve players might make the step up? Well, on the same day that the first eleven were struggling so badly against Hearts the sides also met in a reserve game at Easter Road in a game which finished 2–2 and which featured a Hibs line-up of Rollo, Brown, McClelland, H. Higgins, Muir, A. Buchanan, Frye, Gibson, Harrower, Moran and Harkes, only a handful of whom would become regular first-team men.

With that bad opening day result still hurting, the Hibs fans turned up at Easter Road the following Wednesday evening to see if their heroes could redeem themselves against a young and talented Falkirk outfit. In the match programme the editor advised of a busy season ahead with at least 47 games to be played – 34 in the League, at least six in the League Cup and at least one in the Scottish Cup. There would also be at least six in the newly created Anglo-Scottish Cup that saw Hibs matched up with FA Cup holders Manchester City as well as Newcastle and Spurs. The programme also contained its usual quota of adverts, encouraging fans to make use of goods and services provided by the likes of Hendry's Aerated Waters, Thornton's Sports and McEwan's Ales.

As to the Falkirk game itself, Hibs managed to huff and puff their way through the 90 minutes without ever really troubling the visiting defence while conceding a soft goal at the other end to lose the game 1–0. It really was an unsatisfactory start to the season and it went from bad to worse as Hibs crashed 4–1 away to Partick Thistle in their next League Cup tie. Once again it was Eddie Turnbull who found the target, but it was only Hibs' second goal in three games, with no fewer than eleven being conceded. Certainly it is true that a number of youngsters got their chance, with George Muir, Davie Gibson, Hugh Higgins and Joe McClelland all in the starting line-up. Three of the four played in defence and so perhaps a 4–1 reversal was not that bad as at least it let these youngsters taste first-team football.

The reserves hadn't fared a whole lot better, but at least new boy Alec Harkes was getting among the goals. The Port Seton and former Elphinstone Primrose boy had been signed from Musselburgh Windsor and though only five foot tall and lightly built he was thought to have a lot of promise. Goals against Hearts and Partick would not have done the youngster's confidence any harm.

The League Cup sections were such that an early chance to avenge defeat was always on the cards, but when Hearts made the short trip across the city on Saturday 1 September 1956 they proved too difficult a nut to crack, and although Gordon Smith scored a quite magnificent goal for the greens the visitors struck two in reply to leave Hibs firmly rooted to the bottom of the section. Those Hearts goals, scored by Alex Young and Jimmy Wardhaugh, were hard for the home fans to swallow as it is never a nice feeling to lose in a derby match, but they were a forgiving bunch, realising that there was a certain amount of rebuilding of the side going on with long-term injuries to the likes of Tommy Preston, Jimmy Mulkerrin and John Paterson hardly helping manager Hugh Shaw's cause. Making it all the harder was the stunning news that Gordon Smith, who had looked to be in sparkling form against Hearts, had actually limped out of that game only to have it diagnosed that he had broken a bone in his leg.

The League Cup was just a dream for Hibs now – or should that be a nightmare? – as they crashed 4–0 at Brockville in game five of the six scheduled. Once again the injury hoodoo struck as Willie Ormond was carried off with a suspected broken ankle, though that later proved to be a case of just severe bruising. The fact was, however, that another senior player would be on the treatment table when the side were already struggling in that regard. The Bairns were a better outfit on the night and goals from McCole (2), McCrae and Morrison saw them comfortably home.

Scorer of doubles in both the Hearts and Falkirk reserve fixtures was Walter McWilliams, nicknamed Gunner, who had left his native Pumpherston to ply his trade in the Irish League with Ards and Distillery while undertaking his National Service there. Upon his return to Scotland he joined Livingston United, for whom he banged goals in on a very regular basis, bringing him to Hibs' attention. Sadly for Walter, he would fail to make a big impact at Easter Road and would move on to other clubs, one of which would be Peebles Rovers, for whom he would score in a Scottish Cup tie at Easter Road in the years to come. No doubt Gunner enjoyed scoring that day but unfortunately for him, Hibs replied no fewer than 15 times with a certain Joe Baker grabbing nine.

The final League Cup fixture of the season brought a very talented Partick Thistle to Easter Road and in a cracking game the spoils were shared as goals from Reilly and a surprisingly fit-again Ormond earned a 2–2 draw, Wright and Smith scoring for the Jags. At least there was a point won for the efforts of the players, their first and only point in the League Cup section, offering some hope that league points might become easier to win.

The opening league game of the season brought Falkirk back to Easter Road and the Bairns must have arrived in confident mood having twice beaten their hosts in the League Cup, scoring five in total without reply. In goal for Hibs would be the newly conscripted Jackie Wren, but although the lad had been called up for his National Service, manager Hugh Shaw hoped that with him being stationed close by he would still be able to select his first-choice stopper more often than not. With John Fraser replacing the injured Gordon Smith on the right wing, Hibs suddenly struck the kind of form which swept aside opposition and Falkirk were roundly defeated 6–1 with Reilly grabbing a hat-trick and Turnbull, Ormond and Fraser himself getting the others. At the other end, a Thomson penalty was the only shot to beat Jackie Wren all day.

On the subject of Jackie Wren, it's worth recalling that the young goalkeeper arrived at Easter Road knowing that the jersey was very much up for grabs following the departure of Tommy Younger. Having joined Bo'ness from Gairdoch United, Wren had set about displacing both first and second choice at that club by making the number one jersey his own in a very short space of time. His display in a game for Bo'ness against a young Hibs outfit caught the eye of Hugh Shaw and he was soon persuaded to sign up at Easter Road.

With that thumping win over Falkirk under their belts, Hibs next hosted Liverpool in a Monday night floodlit challenge game at Easter Road and welcomed back Tommy Younger, who now kept goal in a very good Merseyside outfit which also included Ronnie Moran, Alan A'Court, Billy Liddell and Tony Rowley. Of course Hibs were still weakened by the absence through injury of Mulkerrin, Paterson, Preston, Grant and Smith, but those who played gave a decent account of themselves albeit in a 2–1 defeat. On target for Hibs was right back and future manager Willie MacFarlane, who beat Younger from the penalty spot, while young Lawrie Leslie, deputising for Wren in goal, was beaten by Stan Anderson and Billy Liddell.

The programme for that floodlit game makes interesting reading as apart from its usual quota of Hibs news and pen pictures of the opposing team's players it contained a 'Did You Know' section devoted to Liverpool. Among the usual information on most-capped player, attendance record, etc, was this little gem – 'It was a Liverpool man, Mr Brodie, who in 1890 invented and patented goal nets as we know them today. They were introduced in a North v South game in 1891.'

The following Saturday Hibs conceded another two goals, only this time it was in a league match against Queen of the South at Palmerston Park, Dumfries. Hibs could not find a way through the Doonhamers' defence and the game ended 2–0 to the home side with reports suggesting that was a fair result on the day. Back at Easter Road, the reserves were able to field a side which welcomed Jimmy Mulkerrin back from injury and he made his mark by scoring the first in a 2–1 win with Frye grabbing the other.

Two days after losing to Queens, Hibs welcomed Tottenham Hotspur to Easter Road for another of those floodlit challenge games and the London outfit went nap in thumping the greens 5–1. Willie MacFarlane again struck from the spot, but Spurs had Smith (2), Blanchflower, Harmer and Dyson to counter that. In goal for Hibs was 17-year-old debutant John Proudfoot, a real baptism of fire for the youngster, who had only signed a few weeks earlier and had just one reserve game under his belt. To be fair, Danny Blanchflower was only one of a number of star players in the Spurs line-up which also included goalkeeper Ted Ditchburn, Terry Medwin and Tony Marchi, all household names south of the border, and so the result was pretty much as expected.

With defeats in their last two games as the backdrop, Hibs next welcomed Hearts to Easter Road, the visitors having already inflicted two League Cup defeats on the greens. The Tynecastle men had enjoyed a far better League Cup campaign than Hibs, but had lost out on a quarter-final spot, Partick Thistle claiming that place. League games had produced a win away to Dunfermline and a home draw with St Mirren, meaning three points from two starts, but that would soon increase to five points as they defeated Hibs 3–2 in front of a big and noisy crowd. With Jackie Wren unable to play, Jim Rollo took his place in goal and was beaten twice by Wardhaugh and once by Mackenzie while Hearts' own young keeper, Wilson Brown, conceded to Reilly and Turnbull. In the Hibs side that day was Jock Buchanan, home on leave from Oswestry, where he was billeted along with fellow Hibee Lawrie Leslie.

Though the result brought no cheer, the match programme included the good news that young Des Anderson had joined the club from Edinburgh Thistle, following in the footsteps of Lawrie Reilly, Archie Buchanan, George Muir and John Fraser, all of whom had joined from the same outfit. Also in the programme was a snippet advising that some 40 fans had travelled down from Golspie in Sutherland, the exiled Hibs fans making a very long and tiring journey by coach. And finally, from that same programme, there was news that Jimmy Mulkerrin had returned to action in a reserve game while Tommy Preston, John Grant and John Paterson were all making good progress on the injury front.

Progress for Grant must have been even better than expected as he turned out at right back, in place of the now injured MacFarlane, when Hibs faced Aberdeen at Pittodrie on Saturday 29 September 1956. With home-on-leave Lawrie Leslie in goal and still-on-leave Jock Buchanan at outside right, Hibs were hoping to increase their points tally of two from three games, but came a cropper, losing 3–1 in a scrappy game with penalties converted by either side. Glen got that spot kick for the Dons and added another with Buckley getting the third while Turnbull scored the penalty for Hibs. Including the League Cup games and the floodlit challenge matches, Hibs had now played ten games with just one win, against Falkirk 6–1. A most unsatisfactory state of affairs, but Hugh Shaw had warned the fans early in proceedings that youth would have its day and it was taking time for the 'kids' to settle in.

Despite the Pittodrie setback it was generally agreed that young Lawrie Leslie had performed very well in goal having joined the club this season from Newtongrange. At just 21, Lawrie combined his football with learning his trade as a plumber and had been in Hibs' sights for some time before finally putting pen to paper after an impressive debut in a reserve game. Of course Lawrie was slap bang in the middle of doing his National Service and so his first-team appearances would be restricted to his availability to play and of course the form of first-choice keeper Jacky Wren.

The following midweek Hibs travelled to St James' Park to face Newcastle in the Anglo-Scottish Cup and for the third time lost out to English opposition with the Magpies recording a 2–1 win thanks to goals by Milburn and Hannah while Turnbull found the net for the greens. This tournament provided no relief to the miserable form already being displayed in the league and earlier in the League Cup.

Back from injury, both Gordon Smith and John Paterson were in the starting line-up to face Queen's Park on the first Saturday in October, but it would take a penalty goal from MacFarlane to secure a point in a hard-fought 1–1 draw, Cromar striking for the Glasgow side. It had been a long while since the Spiders had visited Easter Road and in recognition of their appearance in Edinburgh that day manager Hugh Shaw recalled a previous meeting between the sides when the Hampden-based outfit had, in 1924, provided the opposition on the day the new main stand was formally opened at Easter Road. The Hibs team that day had been Harper, McGinnigle, Dornan, Kerr, Miller, Shaw, Ritchie, Dunn, McColl, Halligan and Walker, with the greens winning 2–0.

Seven days after drawing 1–1 with Queen's Park, Hibs travelled to Kirkcaldy to face Raith Rovers and recorded an identical result, Ormond hitting the net for the visitors and Kelly beating Jacky Wren from the spot for the hosts. A point gained away from home gave some reason for optimism of better things to come, but the Hibernian cause was not helped when both Smith and Combe had to limp out of the action.

On the following Tuesday Hibs took a young team to Armadale to play their annual friendly under floodlights. The home side were nurturing four Hibernian youngsters, offering the lads the opportunity to play regularly at competitive level, and all four performed well despite the greens winning 4–1. The four Hibs men in the Armadale ranks that night were Tommy Miller, Johnny McLeod, Bobby Train and Joe Baker. Miller it was who bagged the Armadale goal while McWilliams and Des Anderson, making his first-team debut, each nabbed a brace for Hibs.

Anderson was another of the Easter Road new boys and was surely a natural to join Hibs, given that he was brought up in Lochend and attended Norton Park Primary School, which of course shared a boundary wall with the Hibs ground. An Edinburgh Thistle player, Des had been capped at both schoolboy and youth level for Scotland.

A talented and good-going Motherwell side provided the next league challenge for Hibs and for the third time in a row the game would finish 1–1. The home support was treated to a cracking game and gave a rousing cheer to Tommy Preston, back from injury, before watching a game which seemed more like a cup tie such was the flow of play, but both keepers were in good form, keeping the score down on the day. MacFarlane notched the Hibs goal from the spot while Tranent-born John Hunter netted for the visitors, beating Jacky Wren with a fine drive from just inside the box.

With league form slightly improved the grumblings of the home support, happy to see Hibs playing glamour games against top-class opposition but worried that such games meant players were tired when league points were at stake, subsided somewhat. The programme for the Motherwell game carried Hugh Shaw's thoughts on the matter and he wrote of having attended two floodlit games in the previous week, the first at Easter Road, when Hibs had allowed Hearts to play there against Tottenham, and the second when he had gone to Old Trafford where Manchester United entertained Borussia Dortmund. The first game had attracted 16,000 fans and the second 75,000, and so it was no surprise that Shaw favoured such encounters as they most definitely increased revenue to the clubs involved.

In that same programme was news of a glamour friendly: Manchester United would visit Easter Road towards the end of November or beginning of December after United, leading 3–2 from the first leg of their European Cup tie with Dortmund, had played the return in Germany.

A second home game in succession brought Kilmarnock to Easter Road on Saturday 27 October and the visitors arrived with a number of their star men on the injured list. Like Hibs they had started the season slowly and it was almost inevitable that this would be a dull affair, the final scoreline of 0–0 coming as little surprise. Of course this was a fourth successive draw for Hibs and as a result they were in the lower half of the table, but all at Easter Road hoped for better things if only a fit first eleven could be fielded. Losing players of the calibre of Smith, Combe, Turnbull and Paterson was bound to have a negative effect on results, although those players drafted in could be seen to be giving their all for the green jerseys.

Another bugbear for football clubs was the fact that players were being drafted for their National Service and while the loss of such players undoubtedly affected all teams, Hibs seemed to suffer more than others. Joe McClelland would be next to 'go' and the young left back had been turning in some impressive reserve team performances in recent weeks too. With players away for varying periods of time, each club tended to sign more youngsters than it might otherwise have done and one of those youngsters, invited along to Hibs, was Donald McCalman. His signing was a touch bizarre to say the least as he had been playing for Port Glasgow Rangers against Livingston when Hibs boss Hugh Shaw was watching the game. Donald was injured and the instant diagnosis seemed to be that it was cartilage trouble, Shaw being knowledgeable on such matters given his long years in the game. After the match Shaw drove the youngster home to Port Glasgow and promptly asked him to sign for Hibs!

In the midweek following the Kilmarnock game Hibs travelled south to meet Spurs at White Hart Lane in the Anglo-Scottish Cup and secured a very creditable 3–3 draw. With Jacky Wren and Lawrie Leslie unable to make the journey, young John Proudfoot played in goals and performed heroically as the home side tried hard to win the game. Although he was beaten by Brooks, Medwin and Hopkins he denied the last named on two occasions with quite wonderful saves, so impressive they even drew warm applause from the home support. On target for Hibs were Reilly, Grant and Higgins, but the night belonged to Proudfoot. He had only played a handful of first-team games but had already faced the might of Liverpool, Newcastle and Spurs!

Back home in Scotland Hibs faced a tough away trip to Ibrox where, despite striking three great goals, the defence had a bit of an off day and conceded five. Wren was back between the posts but could do little to stop goals by Murray (2), Scott, Simpson and Hubbard from the penalty spot. In reply, Ormond grabbed a double and Preston the other, with many match reports suggesting that Hibs were unlucky on the day. Still, at least the side were beginning to find the net more often with three in each of the games against Spurs and Rangers.

In the following midweek Lawrie Reilly played his 51st match for Scotland in full and league internationals and he was joined in the squad by Gordon Smith, named as a reserve.

With the newspapers carrying a story that Archie Buchanan had been placed on the open to transfer list after 13 seasons at the club, fans arrived at Easter Road on Saturday 10 November to read in the programme that the reports were inaccurate. In fact, Archie had recently repeated a request to move and the board had agreed to listen to offers and not to stand in his way if an offer came along, but that he had not been put up for sale. In effect the newspapers got it wrong – it was not the first time and it certainly wouldn't be the last.

The opposition that day were Dundee, who arrived under the leadership of Willie Thornton and included a number of first-class players in their squad. Doug Cowie, Albert Henderson, Bill Brown and Jim Watt would all make a name for themselves in the game and it was Watt who scored for the Dark Blues. Ironically, Archie Buchanan netted for Hibs in a game which ended in a 1–1 draw.

Also included in the match programme that day was news of a possible visit to Easter Road by the crack Austrian outfit Rapid Vienna, later in the season, while it was noted that Davie Laing, signed in the close season from Clyde, was now back in contention for first-team duties following a long injury layoff. A feature on Hugh Higgins made interesting reading as it described him as a 'new boy', which technically he was, having signed at the very end of the previous season. Higgins had arrived from Tranent Juniors and made his debut in an East of Scotland Shield game against Hearts. This season he had worn the number four shirt in most games played to date. From Falkirk originally, Higgins had played a trial game for Celtic, and Sunderland were keen to offer him the same chance before Hibs stepped in and secured his signature.

A week after drawing at home to Dundee, Hibs travelled to Firhill to meet a resurgent Partick Thistle outfit and crashed 3–0 thanks to a penalty by Kerr and goals from Smith and McIntosh. It was a poor performance by a jaded Hibs side and given that the season was not yet half-way over it was a worry for the manager and supporters.

Seven days later those worries disappeared as a rampant Hibs went on the road again and destroyed East Fife 6–1 at Methil. It was one of those days when everything went right for the greens as Ormond (2), Thomson (2), Reilly and Turnbull all found the net while only Stewart could find a way past Wren in the Hibs goal. This was the second time Hibs had won 6–1 this season and for those fans who made the relatively short trip over to Fife it was well worth the effort.

A look at how things were going for the reserve team brought a 'mixed bag' picture as their form rose and dipped depending upon who had been needed to fill injury gaps in the first eleven. A snapshot of their form shows that in three matches in November 1956 they won two and lost one. Dundee handed out a 3–1 defeat at Dens with Frye on target for Hibs while Partick Thistle and East Fife each suffered defeat at Easter Road, by 3–1 and 3–0 respectively, the Hibs scorers being Mulkerrin, Moran and Aitken (4), including a hat-trick against the Fifers.

Monday 26 November brought Newcastle to Easter Road with Hibs looking to avenge the 2–1 defeat suffered at St James' Park some weeks earlier. The Magpies really were a class outfit and included in their number Tyneside hero Jacky Milburn and Ronnie Simpson in goal. Once again young John Proudfoot would keep goal for Hibs and though the greens lost 3–1 the keeper had another fine game. Fraser struck for Hibs but Milburn (2) and White won the game for the Magpies. This was the last of these floodlit games and the table had Spurs on top followed by Newcastle, Hearts, Partick Thistle and in bottom spot Hibs.

In his programme notes manager Hugh Shaw explained that due to their European and domestic commitments, Manchester United would not now visit Easter Road until January or February but that in mid-December Hibs would entertain Red Banner of Hungary, a side that included no fewer than ten Hungarian international players, among them the legendary Nandor Hidegkuti. It was perhaps a measure of Hibs' standing in Europe that such clubs were willing to come to Easter Road and meet the side who had been European Cup semi-finalists last season.

Having played one team whose strip was black and white Hibs next entertained another when Ayr United arrived at Easter Road on the first day of December. The home support was anxious to see the turn in league fortunes brought about by that crushing win over East Fife carried forward into this match. They were not disappointed as the greens scored three and could have had more on the day. Fraser (2) and Smith, back from injury, were on target while Jacky Wren and his fellow defenders kept a welcome clean sheet.

Keeping an eye on the progress of those youngsters farmed out to Armadale Thistle was something that Hugh Shaw took seriously and he cannot have failed but to be impressed with two of that number: Bobby Train and Joe Baker. Train lived in Rossie Place, just off Easter Road, and had been reared on watching Hibs, so it was a proud day for him when the club signed him on provisional forms. His progress with Armadale was good and his performances at wing half were appreciated by the fans of that club. Joe Baker was born in Liverpool but grew up in Wishaw and Motherwell and was signed on provisional forms for Hibs after starring in a match for Lanarkshire Schools against Edinburgh Schools at Tyne-castle. Capped at schoolboy level, he was banging the goals in for Armadale on a regular basis while he waited to be called up to Easter Road.

The 3–0 win over Ayr saw Hibs travel to Airdrie the following Saturday in buoyant mood. Though they once again managed to find the net three times, Leslie in the Hibs goal conceded five as the defence had another one of their 'off' days. Reilly (2) and a Turnbull penalty brought no reward and goals from McMillan (2), Baird (2) and McCul-loch ensured the points would stay at Broomfield. The Hibs cause was not helped when Gordon Smith, the subject of some quite 'close' attention from the Airdrie defence, had to leave the field injured and the greens were left to see out the game with just ten men. It was the kind of attention Smith often attracted as defenders tried any way they could to stop him carving open their defence.

Unlike the first eleven, the reserves were bowling along quite nicely and sitting high in their league with Anderson, McWilliams and Mulkerrin regular marksmen. It seems likely the goals were coming at least in part due to the fact that Bobby Combe was often in the side to create numerous chances.

They say a week is a long time in football and that may well be so, but the week which followed the defeat at Airdrie was not long enough to see Gordon Smith return to fitness. He was not alone in that regard and other absences required that young Pat Hughes be promoted from the reserve side to wear the number six shirt against visitors St Mirren. The Hibs fans had a reputation for getting right behind youngsters thrown into the top team and Pat was no exception as he won the cheers of the support for his part in an exciting 1–1 draw. Turnbull found the net for Hibs while Wilson Humphries replied for the Buddies. In years to come Humphries would be back at Easter Road in a coaching role.

Hughes enjoyed a good debut at left half, the 18-year-old playing with a maturity beyond his years. A product of Holy Cross Academy, Pat spent some time with Whitburn Juniors while on the Hibs groundstaff and that certainly toughened him up for the rigours of league football. Still only a part-time Hibee, Pat was training as a coalmine manager, so it was a busy time for the youngster.

Immediately after the St Mirren game word swept around the terraces that Younger was back at Easter Road and there was some truth in the story, albeit he was only training with the team as his wife was back in Edinburgh and due to have their child.

The match programme for the St Mirren game contained an interesting pen picture of John McLeod, one of the young players farmed out to Armadale. McLeod was another picked up from Edinburgh Thistle having scored no fewer than 40 goals for them in the 1955/56 season. He took this form with him to West Lothian where in the first three months of the season he had scored 12 times. This was a lad who would go on to make many first-team appearances at Easter Road before eventually being transferred to Arsenal.

Had things gone according to plan, Hibs would have been at home again the following Tuesday but sadly their intended opponents Red Banner of Hungary were recalled to their homeland by the Hungarian FA, the reasons for which were not stated. A sizeable crowd had been expected and the proceeds were to have gone to the Hungarian Relief Fund.

In a way it was a blessing that the benefit match did not take place as it allowed the players a full week of preparation for their next test, an away game at Dunfermline's East End Park. Pat Hughes retained his place and Smith was still an injury absentee, but that did not stop the greens putting on a good show in winning 3–1. Dickson scored for the Pars, but a Turnbull double, one from the spot, and a single from Smith's stand-in, John Fraser, ensured the points would come back across the Forth to Edinburgh. Back at Easter Road that day the reserves won 4–1, with Jimmy Mulkerrin bagging all four, surely staking a claim for a first-team start in the process.

The busy festive period fixtures now lay in wait and the first of those brought Celtic to Easter Road on the Saturday between Christmas and New Year. Once again Hughes and Fraser retained their places and they combined for a Hibs goal, set up by Hughes and finished in style by Fraser. Hibs managed two more that day through Thomson and Reilly, but the Hoops also scored three, Ryan, Smith and Mochan their marksmen in a thoroughly entertaining game.

It had been a topsy-turvy season so far with too many 1–1 draws, especially at home, to allow Hibs a high position in the league. The stats showed that if Hibs had scored just six more goals in those drawn games they would have been lying in third or fourth place. These kind of statistical breakdowns are of course not worth the paper they are printed on, as every club could argue that if they'd scored more goals they'd have won more games – it's hardly rocket science! The figures were trotted out in the match programme for the Celtic game, but in fairness there were a couple of other articles in that issue which are of genuine interest.

Under a heading of 'Generous Celts!' there appeared an article explaining that as was the custom every time Celtic visited Easter Road there would be a collection among the fans of both clubs with the proceeds going to the Hospital Broadcast Fund. These donations ensured that patients in many Edinburgh hospitals would hear the 90 minutes broadcast to their bedsides, and although the article did not say so it would be good to think that Hibs fans reciprocated in a similar collection when they visited Celtic Park. The other item which caught the eye was news of the fact that the Hibs youngsters farmed out to Armadale had contributed no fewer than 53 of 'Dale's 82 goals to date with, you guessed it, Joe Baker leading the way on 25.

With high-flying Celtic held to a draw at Easter Road the Hibs had little time to reflect on their performance before making the short journey across the city to face Hearts at Tynecastle on 1 January 1957. The home side and their support were in confident mood as they had already won the three encounters so far this season, but that confidence was to be shattered as the green and whites dominated the match and were very worthy 2–0 winners with Turnbull and Fraser bagging the all important goals. It was a happy throng of Hibs supporters who made their way along Gorgie Road that night, but the celebrations would have to be light as the Hibees had another fixture to fulfil just 24 hours later.

Having lost to Queen of the South at Palmerston earlier in the season Hibs hoped for revenge, but the curse of the 1–1 draw struck again with Reilly scoring for Hibs and McMillan for the visitors. In truth, Hibs made enough chances to win half a dozen games but could only take the one thanks to a combination of good goalkeeping by Roy Henderson and poor finishing. Still, four points out of a possible six was a reasonable return for the festive period fixtures, especially as two of those points had been gained at Tynecastle.

With the news that Hibs had drawn Aberdeen at home in the cup, the Hibs players had a few more league games to play before that showdown. A visit to Brockville was always full of incident and this occasion proved no different with stretcher bearers being called onto the park on no fewer than three occasions, though thankfully no serious injuries occurred. In a close but very exciting game the sides were separated by one piece of opportunism by John Fraser, who snatched the only goal of the game and two more valuable points for Hibs. Making his first-team debut in this game was 21-year-old Andy Aitken, a local lad who was, ironically, first spotted strutting his stuff in Ireland with Cliftonville when he had been serving in the Army there. It was a decent debut and it seemed likely that further first-team chances would arrive for the former Edinburgh Emmet lad.

Also in the team for the Falkirk game were Hibs' regular central defensive pairing of Bobby Nicol and Jackie Plenderleith, both of whom were to find out that night they had been selected to represent Scotland at Under-23 level against England. A richly deserved honour for the youngsters and all at Easter Road were delighted for the pair.

In a dress rehearsal for the forthcoming cup tie, Hibs entertained Aberdeen on league business at Easter Road on Saturday 12 January. The Dons were a decent outfit, with Paddy Buckley and Graham Leggat in their ranks, while of course their manager Davie Shaw was a former Hibee. On the day everything went right for the green and whites as they swept Aberdeen aside in an impressive display of attacking football resulting in a fine 4–1 win. Reilly bagged two, Fraser added to his impressive recent tally and Ormond also hit the target. A disconsolate Dons outfit had to settle for a consolation strike by Leggat before facing the long coach journey home.

Hibs were in a rich vein of form now and happily travelled to Glasgow the following week to face the amateurs of Queen's Park at Hampden, perhaps dreaming that they might return there again this season with a chance of Scottish Cup glory. Whether those dreams filled the minds of the players on the day or whether the old Hampden hoodoo kicked in we shall never know, but the visitors contrived to put in a quite miserable performance in losing 2–1. Although plenty of possession was enjoyed there seemed to be no cutting edge and Reilly's consolation strike, his 13th goal of the season, was cancelled out with interest as McEwan fired home two for the Spiders.

That same weekend Hibs held their annual club dance, giving the players a chance to mingle socially with the board. Mingle they certainly did with it being reported that Joe Baker thrilled those assembled by dancing with chairman Harry Swan's wife to some 'up to date Rock 'n' Roll music' while later Willie Ormond took the microphone to offer his rendition of chart-topper Jimmy Young's finest songs!

The party over, Hibs returned to training and preparation for a home league tie with Raith Rovers, a side sitting just eight points behind league leaders Hearts. Make no mistake, Rovers were genuine championship contenders and they emphasised that point by thrashing Hibs 4–1, thanks to a double by Jackie Williamson and singles from Ernie Copland and Johnny Urquhart. Hibs scored through the ever dependable Lawrie Reilly but in truth they were never at the races and the visitors thoroughly deserved their victory and the two points.

Around this time several Hibs men were away on National Service duty, among them Des Fox, who was stationed in Dover and being allowed to turn out for Dover FC; Jock Buchanan, stationed in Oswestry and turning out for Oswestry Town, and John Baxter, stationed at Aldershot but due home any day now. Baxter would go on to star many times for Hibs, captain the side and be a leader on and off the park. Signed from Benburb, he was a wing half of some quality and his impending return to Easter Road was eagerly awaited.

Also around this time the reserves were still going strong and a massive 10–2 away win at Stark's Park certainly had an effect on the goalscoring charts. Jimmy Mulkerrin scored four, taking his total for the season to 14 and playmaker extraordinaire Bobby Combe was also among the marksmen that day.

Saturday 2 February saw Aberdeen back at Easter Road, this time on Scottish Cup duty and it was a confident Hibs who took the field that day, memories of their recent 4–1 win against the Dons still fresh in the mind. After 90 minutes of pulsating end-to-end football it would be Aberdeen who progressed as they ran out 4–3 winners with Wishart (2), Leggat and Yorston bagging the goals. In fact the Dons had raced into a 4–0 lead and Hibs had to fight back to even stand a chance of a replay. Although Smith, Reilly and Nicol found the net, time ran out on the green and whites as they strove for that all important equaliser.

It was a stunned Hibs support which trudged home that night and almost certainly it was a stunned first team which left the dressing room after the game. Grant, Wren, Nicol, Hughes and Fraser had hoped that their first-ever Hampden appearance, a week earlier against Queen's Park, would be followed by another but it would not be this season.

Leaving the club for certain that week was Archie Buchanan, granted a free transfer at his own request. Archie was the third-longest serving player on the staff, behind Smith and Combe and left with everyone's best wishes. Another who might have been leaving was Mulkerrin whose 14 goals for the reserves had caught the attention of clubs on both sides of the border. Curiously, the match programme suggested this interest might well mean Jimmy moving on, implying one would think that his goals were not going to win him a first-team place anytime soon.

Playing occasionally in the same reserve side as Mulkerrin was 17-year-old groundstaff boy Malcolm Bogie, who had been a target for Rangers when Hibs stepped in to sign him from Balgreen Rovers. An outside or inside right, Bogie was impressively compared by some as having the look of Tom Finney about him, high praise indeed given Finney's legendary status. Capped at Scottish schoolboy level, Malcolm was learning his trade both as a footballer and apprentice engineer.

Out of the cup and not challenging in the league, a situation becoming too familiar for the liking of all connected with the club, Hibs' next port of call was Fir Park, Motherwell, where it would seem the cup defeat hangover was still in evidence as the green and whites crashed 3–0 in a game in which they struggled throughout. It was poor fare from a jaded Hibs and the fans who had made the journey through were less than happy with the effort of the players.

Those who did not travel and chose instead to watch the reserves in action were rewarded with a fine 4–1 win against the second string from Motherwell in a match notable for the fact that inside left Jim Harrower scored all the Hibs goals, emulating the feat of Jimmy Mulkerrin a few weeks earlier against Raith Rovers.

A week later Hibs invited Leicester City to Easter Road as both sides were out of their respective cup competitions and had a blank Saturday. The Foxes arrived with a fair sprinkling of Scots in their side, including Pat Ward, Tommy McDonald, Dave McLaren and John Anderson. For a friendly it was a decent game with both sides eager to win, but it would be the visitors who triumphed, winning 3–2 thanks to a double from Ian McNeill and a solo effort from McDonald. Hibs replied through Fraser and Turnbull and the sizeable crowd seemed to go home content with the fare on offer. There would be further opportunities for the fans to see visitors from the south as both Cardiff City and Leeds United were said to be expected.

Having been rewarded for his four goals against Motherwell reserves by being called up to the first team for the visit of Leicester City, Jim Harrower retained the number ten jersey for the visit to Kilmarnock. Though he scored a fine goal, he had to watch as Killie got two at the other end – after Jackie Plenderleith had missed a penalty which would have put the greens 2–0 up – through Moir and Caven. Maybe Jim would have been better sticking with the reserves as they thumped wee Killie 6–1 at Easter Road. That man Mulkerrin was on target again, this time with a hat-trick, while Combe, Frye and Aitken each weighed in with a single.

Over quite recent seasons Rangers and Hibs had fought out a number of games which had been billed as league deciders and though that was not the case when the Ibrox men visited Easter Road on 2 March it was true to say that the result could have a bearing on where the league title ended up. Rangers were pushing strongly and two points from this tricky tie would do their chances no harm whatsoever. Hibs started with Smith and Reilly in the attack, even though both had been declared doubtful due to injury and illness. Harrower won the number eleven jersey after Ormond failed a fitness test. It was a cracking game, flowing from end-to-end with no quarter asked or given and when referee Mr Crossley of Motherwell blew the final whistle it was the visitors who breathed a sigh of relief having secured a hard-fought 3–2 win. Turnbull from the penalty spot and Harrower found the target for Hibs, but a Murray double and a single from Morrison took the points to Ibrox.

Fans at the Rangers game were advised in the match programme that a number of clubs were negotiating to play friendlies with Hibs at Easter Road, among them German side Cologne, Manchester United and Cardiff City. Time has now shown that these negotiations were only ever that, as none of the three sides mentioned ran on to the Easter Road turf that season.

With no 'foreign' visitors in sight, Hibs went about the business of training for their next league game, away at Dens Park against Dundee. It turned out to be a profitable day for the green and whites, who easily secured the two points with an emphatic 3–0 win thanks to goals from Reilly, Turnbull and Preston, the last named having returned to first-team action in the Rangers game.

The weather was being kind this winter and Hibs had no problems in staging their next match, which brought Partick Thistle to Easter Road. David Meiklejohn was hoping that the Jags could recapture the form that had seen them reach the League Cup final, which they lost only after a replay with Celtic. In his programme notes Hugh Shaw warned that this was the time of the season which brought shock results with those near the foot of the table fighting for their survival, but he needn't have worried on this occasion as his charges dominated from start to finish, even though the final scoreline of 2–0 made the game look a close-fought affair. Turnbull and Reilly hit the target but many more shots from them and others were either saved or flew wide.

In the same programme it was revealed that Hibs and East Fife were about to make history. Hibernian have been involved over the years in several 'firsts', and on this occasion it was the first ever floodlit league match at Easter Road on Saturday 23 March 1957. The game would kick off at 6.45pm in order to avoid clashing with the Scottish Cup semi-final tie being played at Tynecastle that afternoon between Falkirk and Raith Rovers. East Fife had already made their own little piece of history the previous season by playing the first floodlit Scottish Cup match against Stenhousemuir, a game that kicked off 15 minutes earlier than the Hibs v Raith Rovers match on the same night.

Monday 18 March saw Hibs under those self same lights as a star-studded Leeds United arrived to play a friendly. Under the guidance of Raich Carter, Leeds had become a formidable force in the English league with John Charles the jewel in their crown. Scotsmen Jimmy Dunn, Archie Gibson and George Meek were joined by Englishmen Jack Charlton, Chris Crowe, Harold Brook and Jack Overfield among others. Both sides served up a real match to remember for the 17,000 crowd, in drawing 4–4. Fraser, Harrower, Preston and Smith all found the net for

Hibs while Charles (2), Crowe and Bob Forrest netted for the men from Elland Road.

The programme notes for the Leeds game mentioned that utility man Jimmy Mulkerrin had been transferred to Accrington Stanley the previous Friday evening, just in time to play in their promotion clash on the Saturday against league leaders Derby County. No note was given of the score or whether Mulkerrin was on target, but the evidence clearly showed that Stanley had signed a player with an eye for goal.

The history-making clash with East Fife had now come around and after the excitement of the friendly against top-class English opposition in Leeds United it was back to the bread and butter of league points. The Fifers were languishing near the foot of the table and did their best to offer up resistance, but the green machine was in full flow as it steamrollered the Bayview men into the ground in a 4–0 win. Harrower netted two, Reilly one, his sixteenth of the season, and Jim Thomson rounded off the rout. Hibs had played their first floodlit match in October 1954, going down 2–0 to Hearts, and it would be 11 months later before the greens recorded their first floodlit win – but what a win it was as Manchester United were trounced 5–0.

The match programme for the East Fife game also carried the sad news that John Clapperton, assistant groundsman and long-time Hibs fan, had died at the age of 81. John had served the club well and was never shy to remind everyone that not only had he watched Hibs win the Scottish Cup in 1902 but he had become firm friends with the 11 men who brought that glory.

Seven days after disposing of East Fife, Hibs travelled to Somerset Park and in a thrilling game collected two points in a 3–2 victory. Aitken, Reilly and Harrower were on target for Hibs while Price and McMillan struck for the home side. All five goals were well crafted and taken, with perhaps the Reilly effort the pick of the bunch as he twisted and turned in the box before rifling home a low shot into the corner of the net. This would be Lawrie's last game for a week or two as he was called up for international duty and a wee visit to Wembley to face the Auld Enemy.

While Lawrie was no doubt preparing at home, Hibs took a strong side over to Northern Ireland to face Distillery in a floodlit friendly. As it happened, Distillery included several guest players and it was in effect an Irish League XI. They were played off the park by Hibs, but somehow contrived to win the game 2–1. In appalling conditions it was Hibs who played the good football but lacked the finish, and the local press reported afterwards that the hosts had completed a smash-and-grab raid on their visitors. That same press was full of praise for Hibernian, suggesting that the men from Leith had provided some of the best entertainment seen in

Belfast in a long while. Turnbull struck the Hibs goal while Forde and Dickson found the mark for the Irish.

Once back in Edinburgh, Hibs had to prepare for the visit of Airdrie to Easter Road in a match which would, once again, be played on a Saturday evening under floodlights. While the East Fife game had clashed with the League Cup semi-final at Tynecastle, this tie clashed with the England v Scotland tie at Wembley and it was felt that those Hibs fans who had not donned their tartan bunnets and made the trek south would at the very least want to listen to the live broadcast of the Wembley game on the 'wireless'.

And so it was that Hibs met Airdrie that Saturday night without Lawrie Reilly leading their attack. Reilly was instead leading the Scotland attack in London and unfortunately picked up a knee injury which kept him out of subsequent World Cup qualifying games. Mid-table Airdrie were generally a hard nut to crack, but the men from Lanarkshire met Hibs on a day when everything went right. If the chances made in Belfast had not been taken the same could certainly not be said about this game as the green and whites hit six without reply. Smith celebrated his call-up to the World Cup squad with a fine double, Nicol, Turnbull, McWilliams and Aitken completing the rout.

Meanwhile, as the season neared its end, the Hibs reserve side were riding high in the league, fourth behind Hearts, Aberdeen and Rangers, although just three points separated those sides. A 3–2 win away to East Fife and a 6–1 home thumping of Ayr United ensured that the wee Hibs were fighting to the end for that top spot. Walter McWilliams was finding the net regularly; hence his promotion to the first eleven against Airdrie, and it would be he who finished top scorer for the second string.

Six goals in the Airdrie game were matched in the next league tie, only this time just two were scored by Hibs as their hosts, St Mirren, grabbed four. End-of-season games can often be dull affairs, but these two sides served up a very entertaining 90 minutes, with Hibs scoring through a Turnbull penalty and a drive from Harrower.

The same could not be said, however, of the penultimate league game of the season against Dunfermline when Hibs played out a very tense 0–0 draw which saw the Pars fail to stave off relegation. Had they won they'd have stayed up. Queen of the South survived at the Fifers' expense.

Hearts came calling next for the final of the East of Scotland Shield and Hibs took the honours with a 2–1 win thanks to a Turnbull rocket and an own goal by Hearts stalwart Bobby Parker.

A long, demanding league season finally drew to a close with Hibs visiting Parkhead on 27 April 1957. Neither team really had anything to play for but both contrived to serve up an exciting game with the home side edging to a narrow 2–1 win, the Hibs goal coming from Fraser.

Above. Bobby Combe, Archie Buchanan, Tommy Younger and Hugh Howie, four stars of their era, leave Waverley Station in 1947. *Scran*

Left. Menu from League Champions Celebration Dinner, 1948. *Courtesy of Brian Johnson*

CELEBRATION DINNER
of the
HIBERNIAN
FOOTBALL CLUB
League Champions 1947-48
North British Station Hotel
Monday 18th October
1948

Chairman HARRY S. SWAN, ESQ., J.P.

HIBERNIANS CHAMPIONSHIP TEAM, 1951-52

BACK ROW:-   TRAINER McCOLL,   COMBE,   HOWIE,   PATERSON,   YOUNGER,
MR. HUGH SHAW,   GOVAN,   GALLAGHER,   BUCHANAN,   ASSISTANT TRAINER KEAN
FRONT ROW:-   DIRECTOR WILSON TERRIS,   JOHNSTONE,   SMITH (CAPT.)
CHAIRMAN HARRY SWAN,   REILLY,   TURNBULL,   ORMOND,   DIRECTOR TOM HARTLAND

Scottish First Division Champions 1951/52. *Courtesy of Brian Johnson*

The Famous Five. *Scran*

Training session at Hawkhill. *Courtesy of Brian Johnson*

The Dundee defence is in a tangle at Easter Road. *Courtesy of Brian Johnson*

Above. Davy Gibson and Johnny McLeod. *Scran*

Right. Away programme from European Cup semi-final against Stade Reims, 1956. *Courtesy of Brian Johnson*

Left. Home programme from European Cup semi-final against Stade Reims, 1956. *Courtesy of Brian Johnson*

Below. Hibs v Dundee, 1959. *Scran*

Above. Retiring Chairman Harry Swan shakes hands with his successor, William Harrower. The club enjoyed huge success during both their tenures. *Scran*

Right. Match programme from Barcelona v Hibs in the European Cup, 27 December 1960, when the Scots fought out a wonderful 4–4 draw at the Camp Nou. *Courtesy of Brian Johnson*

c. f. barcelona

Bobby Combe

Left. Bobby Combe – the 'sixth' member of the Famous Five.

Below. Action from Albion Rovers v Hibs in 1952 – note the size of the crowd! *Courtesy of Brian Johnson*

Hibs at the world famous Maracana Stadium, Brazil in 1953.

Hugh Shaw, who was manager of three league title winning sides. *Scran*

Above. Hearts v Hibs 1955. *Scran*

Left. Match programme for first ever European Cup tie involving a British side, October 1955. *Courtesy of Brian Johnson*

HIBERNIAN F.C. PROGRAMME

VOL. 7   No. 12   WEDNESDAY, 12th OCTOBER 1955   Kick off 7.15 p.m.

EUROPEAN CUP   FIRST ROUND
SECOND LEG

Photos by "Scottish Daily Mail"

HIBERNIAN   VERSUS   4 D

ROT-WEISS, ESSEN

Above. Hibs v Rot Weiss
Essen, October 1955.
Courtesy of Brian Johnson

Right. The Prince of Wingers
– Gordon Smith in full flow.
Courtesy of Brian Johnson

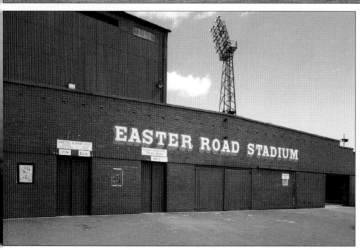

Top. Hibs v Third Lanark, 1960. *Scran*

Above. Baird heads the ball clear during the Falkirk versus Hibs match at Brockville Park. *Scran*

Left. The old main entrance to Easter Road. *Scran*

Hibs v Hearts at Easter Road, 1961 – Hamilton chases a high ball into the Hearts goal but it sails past. *Scran*

Barcelona, the European Cup holders, are defeated 7–6 on aggregate in 1961. *Scran*

Two days later Hibs played their last match when they travelled to Filbert Street to face Leicester City. Following a prolonged spell of dry weather the pitch was hard and flat, which suited Hibs. By half-time they were 3–0 up following goals from Frye, Harrower and Turnbull. Early in the second-half Frye got his own second and Hibs' fourth before Hogg grabbed a late consolation for the Foxes. After the game it emerged that Harrower had broken his wrist, and although in obvious pain he had insisted in staying on the park.

Chapter Twelve

1957/58

BAKER BREAKS THROUGH

As usual the new season got under way with a public trial match between Hibs and their reserve side, the 'big team' winning 5–3 in front of 5,000 fans. Among the goals for the reserves was Joe Baker, newly called up from his stint at Armadale, as was Johnny McLeod. A much larger crowd of 38,965 attended the next game, a friendly between an Edinburgh Select and Preston North End, with the Edinburgh men, including those guesting from Hearts, wearing Hibs strips. Some of the money raised from both the trial match and the friendly went to a number of local charities with only necessary expenses being deducted before the donations were made.

The League Cup matched Hibs with East Fife, Airdrie and Celtic and the opening tie brought the Fifers to Easter Road. Missing from the Hibs line-up was Lawrie Reilly, recovering from a close-season cartilage operation, but even without their main striker Hibs were able to cruise to a comfortable 4–0 win. Preston, Smith, Turnbull and Ormond all found a way past the Fife defence and it was as comprehensive a win as the scoreline suggests, although it is unclear whether young fans invaded the pitch at the end in search of autographs, despite a warning for them not to do so being carried in the match programme.

After the high of a good win came the low of a good thumping when Hibs travelled to Broomfield on the Wednesday night and were hammered 4–1. In fact, they did not play all that badly. Chances were made at either end, but all of Airdrie's seemed to go in while Hibs had clearly left their shooting boots at Easter Road and only Ormond found the net. The most memorable thing about this game, however, was that it marked the first-team debut of Joe Baker, who at just 17 found himself in direct competition with a massive centre half in Doug Baillie. Joe got bumped around a fair bit, but in what would soon be recognised as his never-say-die style he just kept picking himself up, dusting himself off and getting stuck in again.

With the Baker boy living just up the road in Motherwell there were a fair number of his friends and family in the crowd, though that number did not include elder brother Gerry, who was on the staff at Motherwell and who in time would follow in Joe's footsteps at Easter Road. Neither of the brothers were born in Scotland as Joe entered the world in Liverpool and Gerry in New York. The rules did not allow Joe to play at full international level for Scotland, but they did Gerry. At that time a player could play for Scotland if born of Scottish parents regardless of where in the world they were born – except England.

While the first team started with a win and a loss the reserves were banging in the goals in beating East Fife 8–1 at Bayview and Airdrie 4–0 at Easter Road. Alex Marshall bagged four at Methil and another two against Airdrie despite playing with a nagging injury and so at least the 'wee' team had started in winning ways.

Next up for Hibs there was a visit by a strong Celtic to Easter Road. Led by manager Jimmy McGrory, the Celts were sure to present a tough challenge to Hugh Shaw's men. That proved the case, but in a thrilling end-to-end cup tie it was Hibs who triumphed by a score of 3–1, thanks to goals from Ormond, Fraser and an own goal from the unfortunate Frank Meechan, who was forced into slicing the ball past his own keeper by the close attentions of John Fraser. Celtic were impressive that day and none more so than their goalscorer Bobby Collins, who was a step above the rest of his team-mates in quality.

Half-way through the League Cup section matches Hibs found them-selves with a win, a draw and a loss under their belts. Bayview was the next port of call and this time the Fife outfit gave a better account of themselves in forcing a 2–2 draw, with the home side beating Lawrie Leslie in the Hibs goal thanks to efforts from Bonthrone and Leishman while Ormond and Turnbull were on target for the visitors. Manager Hugh Shaw was very aware of the fact that the two wins had come on the big pitch at Easter Road while a defeat and a draw had been suffered on the tighter pitches at Broomfield and Bayview. His view was that it might take some time for his younger players to adjust to the differences in the size of the surface as a number of his more experienced men were fighting their way back to fitness.

With Airdrie the next visitors to Easter Road, Shaw would have an early chance to see if his men could avenge that 4–0 defeat on the bigger playing surface and he would not be disappointed as the Diamonds were crushed 5–1 in a cracking cup tie which had the home support cheering throughout. Two goals by Turnbull were added to by Smith, Fraser and Ormond, Price getting Airdrie's consolation from the penalty spot. This result effectively set Hibs up for a showdown at Parkhead with the winners from their game against Celtic going into the quarter-final draw to face newly promoted Third Lanark. In a tight game, it was the home side who triumphed in scoring twice without reply. Wilson and McPhail got the Celtic goals and Hibs had a few near things, but couldn't find the net and so dropped out of the competition. Manager Shaw blamed the poor away form for elimination and it was difficult to argue with him.

With the League Cup out of the way, the league campaign began with a tricky away tie at Pittodrie and the words of Hugh Shaw, regarding his players needing to show more fight and spirit away from home, must have sunk in as the Hibs won a tight game 1–0 with a solitary strike from Turnbull. The game marked a first-team debut for young John Baxter, who was handed the number six jersey, and he coped with the challenge like a veteran, showing glimpses of the form which would see him star in many Hibs games to come. Observers declared it to be a good game played in good spirits and the injuries suffered by Dons' Leggat and Young, together with Hughes and Ormond of Hibs, were not in any way due to it being a dirty game.

Incidentally, though the first team had fallen at the final hurdle in the League Cup qualifying stakes the reserves went one better and topped their group, losing only one of their six ties in going down 2–0 at Parkhead. In qualifying, they scored 16 goals and conceded only three, which earned them a place in the later stages. Their league campaign started with a narrow 1–0 win over Aberdeen at Easter Road. The winning goal in that game was a peach as Aitken's cross was dummied by Joe Baker, wrong-footing the keeper and letting Johnny Frye nip in to slam the ball home.

A week later the first team were at home to Motherwell and secured a narrow 2–1 win with goals from Harrower and Ormond. It was a hard-fought win and McPhee's goal for the visitors meant an anxious last ten minutes for the home support. Thankfully the Steelmen could not find a way past Lawrie Leslie and his fellow defenders, leaving Hibs with maximum points from their opening two games, a feat matched by the reserves, who won 4–3 at Fir Park, where Lawrie Reilly played to regain fitness after his cartilage operation and Joe Baker nabbed two of the goals.

Next up was the first Edinburgh derby, played at Tynecastle in front of a huge crowd. Hearts were in fantastic form, which would not desert them all season, and ran out worthy winners by 3–1 as Wardhaugh, Crawford and Murray found the target for the Maroons and Turnbull for Hibs. It was a cracking game with Hearts forcing the pace in the first-half and Hibs mounting an attempted comeback in the second. At the end of the day Hibs had Lawrie Leslie to thank for keeping it down to three, while the Hearts defence stood firm against wave after wave of attack in the second period. This would be a season when the Gorgie outfit were nigh-on invincible, losing only one league game and winning the title in scoring an amazing 132 goals.

Over at Easter Road the following Monday evening, the reserves fared no better as Hearts won 2–0, but if nothing else it gave Lawrie Reilly another 90 minutes to improve his match fitness. The most astonishing fact about this game, however, was that it drew a crowd of no less than 10,000, a remarkable figure for a reserve encounter.

A second consecutive away game for the first team took the green and whites on the short journey to Brockville where they overcame a gritty and determined Falkirk 3–1. Top scorer Eddie Turnbull took his tally for the season to eight by converting a spot kick while Preston and Harrower also found the target.

Two days later Hibs accepted an invitation from Hearts to travel across the city for a floodlit challenge match. Given the form of the Gorgie outfit it was somewhat of a surprise when Hibs ran out 4–2 winners in a match more noted for it being the first ever played under lights at Tynecastle. Hibs had fielded a weakened side because of injury and illness, but still managed to score four goals with Preston nabbing a hat-trick and young Joe Baker getting the other. Hearts counted through Willie Bauld and Jimmy Wardhaugh, but the general consensus was that Hibs merited their victory with a fine display.

Airdrie offered up the next challenge when they visited Easter Road on league duty towards the end of September, but they did so minus their star centre forward and the previous season's top league scorer, Hugh Baird, who had been transferred to Leeds United. His replacement, John Caven, was trying manfully to bridge the gap, but neither he nor any of his team-mates could find a way past Lawrie Leslie as Hibs cruised home with a very entertaining 4–0 win. Baxter, Turnbull, Reilly and Preston all found the mark and but for the heroics of Willie Goldie in goal for the Diamonds the winning margin could well have been much greater.

Newly promoted Queen's Park were October's first opponents and though they had not started their campaign particularly well they proved very stuffy in defence and only two flashes of genius from Joe Baker opened them up. Joe was already showing signs of being the goalscoring predator he would develop into as he formed a formidable strike partnership with Lawrie Reilly. The 2–0 victory set Hibs up nicely for their next challenge, which saw English giants Tottenham Hotspur visit Easter Road on Monday 14 October 1957.

Spurs were a big club with a big reputation and included none other than Danny Blanchflower among their number, but it was Hibs who stole the headlines under the floodlights that night. Smith scored two for Spurs but a Baker hat-trick and goals from Ormond and Frye sent the Londoners home with their tails somewhat between their legs.

Spirits were high in the Hibs squad as they travelled north to face Dundee at Dens Park, but this time it was the green and whites who had to go home somewhat humbled as the Dark Blues brushed them aside by three goals to nil. Goals from Sneddon, Christie and Black won the points and Hibs were a pale shadow of the free-scoring side who had disposed well of Hearts, Airdrie, Queen's Park and Spurs in their previous four encounters.

Raith Rovers, who had finished a very creditable fourth last season, arrived at Easter Road on the back of a good run and manager Bert Herdman had at his disposal a very useful squad of players, including Jackie Williamson, Willie Polland and ex-Hearts man Johnny Urquhart. In a match more like a cup tie the play flowed from end-to-end and when referee Tom 'Tiny' Wharton brought an end to the proceedings it was honours even in a 2–2 draw. The ever dependable Turnbull struck from the spot and Harrower got the other Hibs goal.

The following Monday evening Hibs welcomed Wolves to Easter Road for a floodlit challenge match and it was a star-studded side they faced, including England captain Billy Wright. Managed by Stan Cullis, Wolves led the English First Division and did so with the majority of their team having come up through the ranks from their youth team. A no-frills approach was the Cullis way and his motto, posted on the home dressing room wall at Molineux, was: 'There is no substitute for hard work'. It was hard work that won them the game that evening as they triumphed 3–2. Frye and Preston scored for Hibs, but it was not enough to topple the visitors. After the match Billy Wright was effusive in his praise of Hibernian, exclaiming that they would be more then capable of holding their own in the top league in England. High praise indeed!

The Scottish League was, however, the target for Hibs and in their next outing, at Love Street in Paisley, they won two valuable points in a thrilling 3–2 win over St Mirren. Having faced up to Billy Wright earlier in the week, Joe Baker had learned from the experience and gave the Paisley defence a torrid time as he notched a brilliant hat-trick. Baker was settling quickly and well into life in the first team and hat-tricks or better would follow him throughout his career. Special mention must be made of Johnny Frye's contribution in the game as it was from three of his perfect passes that Baker found the target. Indeed, Frye justified Hugh Shaw's decision to promote him from the reserves after the youngster had had a goalscoring outing against Raith Rovers the week before.

A week later Partick Thistle visited Easter Road and did so with a sprinkling of Scottish internationals in their line-up, but it would be the green and whites who lit up the play that day by recording a quite wonderful 5–1 win, in front of their ecstatic supporters. Not since the heady days of the Famous Five had Hibs fans witnessed such a good all-round team performance, though it's fair to say that two of the Five were still starring on the wings. Smith had a great game, although he eventually had to leave the field with a nasty ankle knock that threatened to keep him out of action for a spell but not before he had assisted his team-mates into an unassailable lead. On the left wing Ormond sparkled and nabbed a couple of goals into the bargain with Baker, Harrower and Turnbull, from the penalty spot, getting the others.

That win set Hibs up nicely for a visit to Merseyside two days later where they met Liverpool at Anfield in front of around 20,000 fans. The visit was marked by gifts being given to all of the players' wives as a memento of the occasion and their husbands added to the enjoyment by turning in a great display in a 3–3 draw. Remarkably, Gordon Smith travelled, played and scored despite that ankle knock taken just two days before, while Ormond and Baker, back in the city of his birth, also found the target.

These last two games set Hibs up nicely for their next challenge which involved an away tie at Broomfield. Airdrie always offered up tough resistance, especially at home, but Hibs were still in fine form and played in a very confident manner to secure their 4–1 win in Lanarkshire. In-form Willie Ormond scored twice with Baker and Turnbull getting the others in a game in which the green and whites were always in control. Both Turnbull and Ormond belied their advancing years by turning in five-star performances and the *Scottish Sunday Express* declared that Hibs had given 'a display of cool, casual and supreme football'. The only downside was that Smith took another knock on that ankle and once again had to limp off before the end.

Another trip south followed for a game with Manchester City. The visitors dominated in the first-half and had a goal disallowed. Manager Shaw later stated that he felt the cancellation of the strike was unfair but reflected the way the decisions went against his side throughout the 90 minutes. Phoenix scored the only goal of the game for City in the second-half with Hibs claiming in vain for offside. The game itself gave old acquaintances the opportunity to catch up with each other and Matt Busby, the man who would achieve immortality with Manchester United in the years ahead, was happy to see some of the friends he had made at Easter Road while guesting for the club during the war years. After the game, Busby stated: 'The happiest days of my playing career were spent with Hibs' – which I guess shows just what an impression all at Hibernian had made on the man.

That reversal at Maine Road saw a good little run of form come to an end and it was disappointing that a side who had been scoring freely suddenly saw the goals drying up. That could be put down to a number of factors, but it's tempting to say that one which had more influence than the others was the absence through injury of Gordon Smith. The Prince of Wingers would make no miraculous recovery this time and though his deputy on the right wing, Lawrie Reilly, did a fine job against visitors

Celtic the following Saturday, he could not find the target and nor could his team-mates as a solo strike from Sammy Wilson saw the points heading west. Celtic had a strong side and had won the League Cup the previous season, but Hibs could not break down their stout defence, though Turnbull did escape long enough to fire the ball home, only to have the goal disallowed.

Two days later Manchester City arrived to play the return tie of their floodlit challenge match. This was a strong City side, including Bert Trautmann, Ken Barnes, Dave Ewing and of course Bobby Johnstone. The last time they had been in Edinburgh, just a few weeks before, they had dumped Hearts 5–3 at Tynecastle and so the green and whites knew they would have a game on their hands. Thankfully, the goalscoring boots were found again and City perished 5–2 in front of a huge crowd. Ormond grabbed yet another brace with Turnbull, Baker and Harrower getting the others. Jimmy Harrower certainly had an eye for goal and his scoring exploits had not gone unnoticed south of the border, with Leeds United known to be very keen to sign him.

Just two days later Hibs travelled down to Teeside to meet Middlesbrough and once again went nap as they struck five without reply. Ormond only managed a single this time around, but both Harrower and Preston scored two with the home defence left in tatters by Hibs' crisp passing game. Young Des Anderson started the game and played exceptionally well despite an early injury. His contribution drew special praise from Hugh Shaw, who was delighted with the lad. The home crowd, appreciative of the Hibs performance, gave the visitors a standing ovation when they left the field at the end of the game. The win took Hibs to the top of the floodlit league, and deservedly so as the green and whites had lost only one game to date, that being the narrow loss at Maine Road.

Spirits were high therefore when, back in Scotland, Hibs travelled down to Dumfries to take on Queen of the South at Palmerston Park, but the wheels came well and truly off the Hibernian bus as they were thumped 3–0, showing signs of having had to play four games in just eight days. The floodlit league was all very well, but the form in domestic competition appeared to be suffering. Manager Shaw, however, felt that there were enough old heads in the team to know that each game was as important as the other.

Newly promoted Third Lanark were next to visit Easter Road and despite a patchy start to their season they had proved to be stuffy opposition for the most part though that was not the case on this occasion as the home side inflicted a 4–0 defeat on the Hi Hi. Preston (2), Baker and Ormond ensured the points would stay in Leith and that Hibs would remain in the top half of a table led by a rampant Hearts side who were banging in goals galore.

The festive period and its glut of fixtures were coming up fast and it was important that Hibs kept winning if they were to offer any challenge to their Edinburgh neighbours. The first test in that regard took Hibs to Bayview, Methil, where they faced a struggling East Fife and though they dominated proceedings throughout the visitors could only manage a 3–2 victory, with Preston again getting a double and Grant converting a penalty. The Fifers scored through Jimmy Bonthrone and Danny Duchart. It must be said that Hibs had been playing without the injured Gordon Smith and Johnny Frye and so it was encouraging that they were getting predominantly positive results with the promise of a stronger line-up once those injured men returned.

Down in Ayrshire, Kilmarnock were intent on mounting their own challenge to Hearts at the top of the league and their home form in particular was very impressive. All the more surprising then that Hibs arrived at Rugby Park on 21 December 1957 and left with the points after a quite stunning 4–1 win. The visitors dished up the kind of play seen earlier in the season when Airdrie had been dumped by the same scoreline at Broomfield, and they earned the same kind of plaudits from the press men, who described Hibs' play as 'silky and seamless, passing crisp and goals well struck'. Those goals came courtesy of McLeod (2), Harrower and the ever dependable Tommy Preston.

Christmas had been three days earlier, but Hibs were still in a giving mood when Clyde visited Easter Road and won 3–1 in front of a bumper holiday crowd. Injuries played a big part in Hibs' defeat, Preston, Harrower, Baker and McLeod all taking heavy knocks and all limping off at the end, by which time the damage had all been done as Dan Currie (2) and Tommy Ring beat Lawrie Leslie in the Hibs goal while only Baker could find a way past the Clyde number one Tommy McCulloch. It was bad news also from Shawfield, where the reserves went down 6–2 but much more importantly lost the services of young inside right Alex Marshall, who suffered a compound fracture to his leg, an injury that would take many months for him to recover from.

Those injuries meant enforced changes in the Hibs line-up to face Hearts at Easter Road on 1 January 1958. Preston and McLeod missed out altogether, unfortunate given their recent goalscoring exploits, while Baker and Harrower were not 100 per cent fit but started the game anyway. Nevertheless, the probability was that Hearts would win in any case as they were leading the league by a distance and had already recorded nine goals in each of three previous matches this season. Thankfully, they managed only two against Hibs, through Alec Young and Dave Mackay, but they were enough to take the points and send their fans away with smiles on their faces.

Just 24 hours later Hibs travelled through to Fir Park where a good-going Motherwell dispensed a 3–1 defeat, Smith hitting the goal for the green and whites and Quinn, McPhee and Gardiner finding the net for the Steelmen. It had been a disastrous festive period for Hibs with three straight defeats meaning they dropped down the league like a stone and waved goodbye to any thoughts of seriously challenging their Edinburgh neighbours for the title. Contrast that with the results from the previous festive period, when Hibs played four games in eight days and secured six points in the process by drawing with Celtic and Queen of the South and defeating Hearts and Falkirk.

As is always the way at football clubs, players come and players go and with the calling up from Armadale of Joe Baker and Johnny McLeod, coupled with the good form shown by youngsters Des Fox and Bobby Nicol, together with the signings of Brian Oliver and Ken Allison, there would be a mini-exodus from Easter Road as both Alec Harkes and Walter McWilliams joined Cowdenbeath and Hugh Higgins departed for Third Lanark. McWilliams had been in the shadow of Lawrie Reilly and now found his first-team chances severely restricted due to the electric form of Joe Baker, so the move was probably his best chance of regular first-team football. Tranen-born Higgins had flitted in and out of the first team and would get more chances at Cathkin Park where he starred in his debut as Thirds defeated Motherwell 4–2. Another who moved on was free-scoring Jimmy Harrower who it was thought was bound for Leeds United but who was snapped up instead by Liverpool.

Forty-eight hours after going down 3–1 at Fir Park, Hibs entertained Aberdeen at Easter Road and ended a miserable week with a 1–0 defeat as Dickie Ewen beat Leslie late in the game. While injury had certainly taken its toll on Hibs, that alone could not explain the alarming slump in form and it was a worried Hibs support that trudged out of Easter Road that evening.

A week later and with a still weakened team, Hibs took on Rangers at Ibrox and once again defeat was the outcome as the Light Blues triumphed 3–1. It was a fairly even game according to press reports at the time, but Hibs could not find their shooting boots and of the limited chances made only one was taken, a peach from Smith. Back in Edinburgh, the Hibs support was becoming increasingly worried by this poor run of form as the reserves were not doing a whole lot better and so there were few in that side who might assist the first team if promoted. All of this, however, seemed to pale into insignificance when, on the Tuesday following the defeat at Ibrox, news reached Easter Road that a former club stalwart had been tragically killed in a road accident.

Hugh Howie had played an integral part in Hibs winning league championships earlier in the decade and was a fine footballer and Hibs man. Illness and injury finally took their toll and he retired from the game in 1954 to pursue a career in sports reporting before his now untimely death. All connected with Hibs, be they players, staff or supporters, were greatly saddened by this news and there was a real sense of collective loss when those same players, staff and supporters gathered at Easter Road for Hibs' next league encounter against Falkirk. The Bairns, like Hibs, had been enduring a poor run of results and had found goals hard to come by. They rectified those faults in part when they put three past Lawrie Leslie. At least Hibs were able to do the same at the other end where Bert Slater was beaten by Smith, Baker and McLeod.

Finally the losing run had come to an end and manager Shaw was hopeful that the draw with Falkirk would lead to a change for the better in games to come. The chance to find that elusive win came when Hibs travelled through to Glasgow to face the amateurs of Queen's Park at Hampden. The Spiders had been having a torrid time of it and had been shipping goals galore, but Hibs made heavy weather of the game and only scraped through 2–1 thanks to goals from Frye and Baker. Not the best of performances by any degree of the imagination but a vital two points and, more importantly, a win at last.

Though the win at Hampden was welcome the game itself would have provided just another statistic for the record-keepers had it not been for the fact that this date would go down in Hibernian history as the first time since 15 October 1949 that there was not a member of the Famous Five in the forward line. It had been nine years since they first appeared together and in that time they had earned between them some 120 Scottish representative honours – Smith on 29, Johnstone on 23, Reilly on 51, Turnbull on 6 and Ormond on 11. Between them in those years they would score an astonishing 700 goals, with Smith on 110, Johnstone on 120, Reilly on 199, Turnbull on 145 and Ormond on 126. Phenomenal by any standards, both prior to their coming together and since they last appeared.

February 1958 commenced with Hibs entertaining Second Division Stirling Albion in a friendly at Easter Road. The green and whites fielded a mixture of first- and second-team players and won more comfortably than the 3–1 scoreline suggests with Frye and Baker (2) on target. The weather had taken its toll around the country, but once again Easter Road had beaten the freeze and a decent-sized crowd turned up for this match. Meanwhile, the second eleven had recaptured some form and were winning more often than not with young Des Fox frequently among the scorers.

Seven days later it was a different story as Edinburgh was hit by a blizzard. Even the groundstaff at Easter Road had to admit defeat on this occasion, and the scheduled league meeting with Dundee would have to take place later in the season. If nothing else, it gave those with injuries a little longer to recover and with the Scottish Cup about to start Hibs would need all the players they could muster.

In fact, the draw for the cup had been made and it paired Hibs with Second Division Dundee United at Tannadice. The sides had met before in this tournament, but always at Easter Road where in 1931/32 the visitors had shocked everyone by winning 3–2. An earlier meeting, in season 1923/24, saw Hibs scrape through 1–0 and indeed the green and whites went all the way to the final that year only to lose out to Airdrie.

The weather had been bad all through northern Europe and was the cause of an air tragedy which rocked British football to the core when a flight carrying the entire Manchester United playing pool and officials crashed on the runway at Munich Airport, with a number of passengers losing their lives and many others badly injured. Seven United players died as the plane carrying them caught fire shortly after take-off and the horror was added to as a further 14 people, including eight sports journalists and a number of Manchester United officials, also perished. The flight had been returning from Belgrade, where United had met Red Star in a European tie, and had stopped at Riem airport in Munich to refuel. On its third attempted take-off in quite horrendous blizzard conditions the plane overshot the runway, hit a house with its port wing, veered right, hit another building and burst into flames. The fuselage did not catch fire and a number of the surviving passengers went back into the aircraft to try and help others. Among those most seriously injured was manager Matt Busby and it would be many months before he regained full health.

Back in Scotland, football life carried on although there was a minute's silence at all senior grounds at the next opportunity as a mark of respect for those who lost their lives. That event occurred for Hibs at Tannadice, where they took on United in the second round of the Scottish Cup. After 90 gruelling minutes on a very heavy pitch the honours were even, with both defences keeping a clean sheet, and so a replay would be required to decide which club progressed into round three and a tantalising trip to Tynecastle to face the runaway league leaders and very much in-form Hearts.

Easter Road was pretty close to full as the cup replay kicked off on the evening of Wednesday 19 February 1958 and the home supporters were not to be disappointed as their favourites secured a 2–0 win and passage into that third-round tie at Tynecastle. It was a close game and Lawrie Leslie had to look lively early on to deny the United front men, but slowly Hibs took command and goals from Frye and a peach from Baker from a Baxter pass won the day.

Four days later and with the cup tie at Tynecastle due the following weekend, Hibs had St Mirren at Easter Road on league business and those fans present were treated to a humdinger of a game in which the sides shared ten goals. Hibs scored five, through Turnbull (2 penalties), Thomson, Baker and Ormond, but sadly the defence had a bit of an off day and so those five goals earned just a single point.

The snow earlier in the month may have put paid to the league game against Dundee, but it had also resulted in a match against a British Army eleven biting the dust. Committed to the game, Hibs chose to play it on the Monday before that Scottish Cup tie at Tynecastle, a risky decision as injuries were always a possibility, especially on a frosty surface. The game did go ahead, however, and intriguingly Hibs' own Jackie Plenderleith lined up at centre half for the Army side, who gave the greens a real workout in winning 4–2. Hibs scored through a Turnbull penalty and a Preston strike, but the visitors were worth their win over the piece.

Tynecastle Park had been something of a fortress this season with Hearts sweeping aside all that came before them, but that would not be the case in this Scottish Cup tie. The men from Leith made the short journey across town and duly dumped their oldest rivals out of the competition with a stunning 4–3 win. Stunning is the right word to use for more than one reason as firstly the Hearts defence was carved open almost at will and secondly, in a quite thrilling display of clinical finishing, Joe Baker scored all four Hibs goals. Make no mistake, this was the Baker boy at his best, scoring against Hearts, a task he never tired of whenever playing for Hibs.

The game opened at a frantic pace with Hearts pushing for an early strike which they succeeded in getting after 20 minutes when Johnny Hamilton fired home, but the lead was short-lived because 17-year-old Joe Baker equalised just two minutes later. The Hearts fans in the 41,666 crowd were rocked to the core as Hibs took command of the game and just six minutes later Baker doubled his and Hibs' tally. With half-time approaching, Baker almost got his hat-trick but was foiled by a quite brilliant from Gordon Marshall in the home goal, which meant the teams changed around with the visitors leading. Four minutes into the second-half, Wardhaugh powered home an equaliser and Tynecastle erupted as the Hearts fans, used to seeing their side win, anticipated that a winning goal would soon come along. After 66 minutes a goal did arrive, but to the undoubted disappointment of Hearts fans and players alike the scorer was Joe Baker and once more Hibs were dominating the game. Just nine minutes remained and Hearts were pushing forward at every opportunity only to lose a fourth goal to that man Baker again. Although Jimmy Murray pulled one back for Hearts in the dying moments, it would be Hibs who marched on into the next round and Baker who would grab all the headlines in the papers the next day.

In the midweek following the cup win at Tynecastle, Hibs travelled through to Glasgow to face Partick Thistle at Firhill and came a cropper on a tricky pitch, with the Jags doling out a 2–0 defeat. This proved a huge disappointment following the five-star display of just days before, but it seems that Thistle had done their homework on the Baker boy and he was well marked throughout the game, enduring a number of tough tackles – and, as always, getting up and going back for more.

With Third Lanark at Easter Road in the fourth round of the Scottish Cup looming on the horizon, Hugh Shaw decided to arrange a friendly against Airdrie to get his players back into shape for that important tie. The Second Division outfit proved a tough nut to crack, although in the end two goals from Ormond won the day at Easter Road. It was a good workout for the green and whites as the styles of Airdrie and Third Lanark were quite similar and a number of good lessons were learned.

While the first team had been doing quite well, especially in the Scottish Cup, the reserves had been getting a number of good results also and had qualified for the semi-final of the reserve cup, where they would face Aberdeen both home and away. In preparation, they too met an Airdrie side, this time at Broomfield and won handsomely 8–3, with Andy Aitken notching four of their goals in a side containing no fewer than three trialists. In those days a trialist was usually named as 'Newman' or 'A. N. Other' and fans didn't always get to know their real names unless the players had done enough to win a contract. One of the trialists against Airdrie was a lad named Alan Robertson and he must have impressed because he did indeed win a contract. What happened to the other guys we will probably never know!

With the Hibs support gearing itself up for the visit of Third Lanark on cup duty the game would be prefaced by some truly saddening news emanating from Easter Road. Star centre forward, former Famous Five member and most-capped Hibernian player Lawrie Reilly announced that he would retire at the end of the season due to injury. It is a difficult task to try and summarise what Reilly meant to Hibs in just a few sentences as he was a huge hero with the support, having spent his entire career at Easter Road. Lawrie made his debut in October 1945 at the age of 16 and went on to enjoy 13 seasons with the club he loved, scoring goals galore and making many others for team-mates. There was a sense of enormous sadness in hearing that at just 29 years of age he would be hanging up his boots and no more would the cry 'Gie the baw tae Reilly' be roared out from the terracing.

With that feeling of sadness hanging over the stadium, Hibs fans made their way to Easter Road on 15 March 1958 to see if their heroes could dispose of Third Lanark and thereby make progress in the Scottish Cup. The men from Cathkin would put up a stiff resistance in their quest to be the latest club to deny Hibs the chance of capturing that elusive cup, but a Baker double and a scorcher from Fraser took the Hibees through despite efforts from Matt Gray and Bobby Craig keeping the scoreline tight at 3–2. Results elsewhere meant that Hibs would be paired with Rangers in the semi-final, but ahead of that tie they faced more important league games, the first of which was at Parkhead.

In a quite dismal afternoon, the men from Leith conceded four goals to Celtic without reply to crash and burn in front of a huge crowd, the vast majority of whom were cheering the hosts. Hibs were most certainly missing the craft and guile of Smith, still recovering from injury, and the goalscoring experience of Reilly, but on the day they were simply outplayed by a good Celtic side that scored through a Sammy Wilson hat-trick and Billy McPhail.

Still smarting from that stinging defeat at Parkhead, Hibs next welcomed Queen of the South to Easter Road, the Doonhamers sharing ninth place in the table with their hosts. Johnny McLeod occupied the number seven jersey and scored the Hibs goal, but the visitors netted twice to leave the home fans in disgruntled mood as they worried over how this struggling Hibs side might fare against Rangers in the forthcoming cup tie. It was disappointing stuff from a side who were more than capable of playing at a much higher standard. Hibs would have only one more chance to sort out their problems before the visit to Hampden and that game took them to Cathkin Park to face the side defeated in the cup quarter-final, Third Lanark. In a close and keenly contested game the sides served up an entertaining 1–1 draw, Preston grabbing the Hibs goal that won them a league point.

At last the time had arrived for that eagerly anticipated clash with Rangers. Hibs took a huge support through with them, though many felt the journey was more in hope than anticipation. On the day, both sides served up a magnificent game of football, worthy of the hallowed ground at which it was played and the scene of many great games before. It was end-to-end all the way as the players gave their all and when referee Bobby Davidson blew the final whistle it was honours even at 2–2, the Hibs goalscoring heroes being Aitken and Preston.

Ever eager to have the tie decided, the SFA had ruled that the replay must take place the following midweek, but that did not deter another big support trekking through to Glasgow and making up a fair proportion of the 74,000 crowd. Hibs had been going through a few extra training sessions in the days before the tie and the extra effort paid off as they triumphed 2–1 and progressed to the final, where they would face Clyde. The replay goals were scored by Turnbull from the spot and Fraser, but every single player that night was a hero and the support travelled back to Edinburgh singing their praises. It had been 56 years since Hibs lifted that trophy and the win against Rangers gave them their first chance to do so since they had lost 2–1 in the 1947 final against Aberdeen.

There were important league games to play ahead of the final and it would give Hibs the chance to try and build up a head of steam if they could win a few and go into that game on a high. The first chance to shine came when Kilmarnock visited Easter Road in mid-April and they set about spoiling the party by defeating their hosts 2–1. A big crowd had turned out to cheer the men who had beaten Rangers, but they would go home disappointed with only a Baker goal to celebrate.

Many fans were worried that the poor league form might carry into the cup final and their concerns were not eased in any way at all when Hibs went south to face Tottenham in the floodlit league and were soundly thrashed 4–0. This game was played on the Monday after the loss to Kilmarnock. Two days after that, Hibs were in action again when they faced Dundee at Easter Road in the game postponed earlier in the season. On this occasion at least the green and whites managed to avoid defeat, but the win they so desperately wanted eluded them too as the sides drew 1–1, with Ormond netting from 30 yards for Hibs and Bonthrone for the Dark Blues. Worryingly, John Paterson was carried off injured. Thankfully, the injury proved not to be too serious and it was just before he rejoined the play that the visitors equalised to deny Hibs their first home league win since 7 December of the previous year.

The reserves were going along quite nicely, sitting third in the league and scoring a fair number of goals, with Des Anderson, Jimmy Gibson and Malcolm Bogie catching the eye, but would any of them manage to fight their way into the first team in time for the cup final? Certainly they had every incentive to do so, although manager Shaw would surely go with his most experienced men in such an important game.

The demand for cup tickets was overwhelming the office staff at Easter Road as thousands of Hibs fans made their postal applications in the hope that they would be successful in getting briefs – and perhaps the first to see a cup-winning team in many a long year. Tickets were also on sale at Thornton's Sports shop in Princes Street and large queues formed at their doors hours before the scheduled opening time. The club had received an equivalent number of tickets to that received for the semi-final against Rangers, but a spokesman admitted: 'It is almost impossible to devise a means of distribution which will please everyone but it is hoped that many loyal supporters were lucky enough to get a ticket. Certainly every available ticket was put at the disposal of the fans and though they were priced at £1.00, 10 shillings (50p) and 6 shillings (30p) they have been selling like hot cakes.'

There remained only two more league games before the cup final. The first of those was against an already relegated East Fife and the men from

Bayview did what many sides in their position do and played a relaxed game, which they won 1–0. The pressure was off the men from Methil while those in green and white looked as though they feared injury ahead of that Hampden tie.

The final home game of the league season fell to be played on Monday 21 April 1958 and it would bring Rangers to Easter Road on what was a hugely emotional night for everyone connected to Hibernian Football Club. Lawrie Reilly would pull on the green and white jersey for the last time, and it was perhaps fitting that Rangers should provide the opposition given the number of times Lawrie had faced and tormented their defence in years gone by as the Glasgow club battled with Hibs for the top prizes on offer in Scotland. Lawrie said then, and has repeated many times since, that 'the team to beat then (in his playing days) was Rangers. Celtic was nowhere near as powerful a side then and the Hearts were a decent team but Rangers were the ones to beat.' How wonderful it was, then, that in his very last game for Hibs the green and whites did just that in winning 3–1, the retiring Reilly finding the net along with Aitken and Baxter.

At last it was 26 April 1958, Hampden Park, Glasgow – the Scottish Cup final between Clyde and Hibernian. It seemed as though the whole of Leith had emptied as the fans travelled through in their droves, hopeful of a long-awaited triumph. Once again though, the Scottish Cup proved to be elusive as Clyde won the tie 1–0. Andy Aitken was badly injured after just 15 minutes and though he bravely stayed on the park he was but a passenger and the bad luck continued when John Baxter deflected a Coyle shot past Lawrie Leslie for the only goal of the game. Yet again, cup glory had eluded the Hibees and the disconsolate fans who travelled back from Glasgow that evening may well have felt a hundred times worse if they could have seen into the future, where that cup failure would go on and on and on.

There were two more league matches to play, although no one at the club was in the mood for them after that crushing Hampden disappointment, and so it was no surprise when Hibs failed to score at Stark's Park in going down 2–0 to Raith Rovers, while only Baker's goal raised a smile at Shawfield when Hibs lost again to Clyde.

The season ended with just 31 points from 34 games, a ninth-place finish, the retirement of star goalscorer Lawrie Reilly and a Scottish Cup final defeat, but still there was reason for a degree of optimism in the shape of Joe Baker, Johnny McLeod and John Baxter, three youngsters around whom Hugh Shaw could begin a rebuilding exercise.

Chapter Thirteen

1958/59

A TALE OF TWO STRIKERS

The summer of 1958 had held the promise of a pre-season tour of Italy but sadly, due to unforeseen circumstances, the tour had to be cancelled, which was a real disappointment to Hugh Shaw's men. All was not lost in terms of a trip abroad, however, as a late invite to the Festival Cup Tournament in Rotterdam saw the players take on Schalke of Germany and Valenciennes of France. In the Schalke game Hibs looked to take early command and scored a fine opener when Ormond cracked home a 25-yard piledriver, but in sweltering heat the Germans struck back to equalise on the stroke of half-time. Under the floodlights in the second-half, Hibs attacked from the off and Baker was unlucky when a crisp drive came back off a post. As the heat took its toll, the Hibs men flagged badly and the Germans scored five more goals to humble the Scots 6–1.

That defeat meant that Feyenoord would meet Schalke in the final while Hibs would face Valenciennes, 4–2 losers to the hosts in their first game, to decide which side finished third. A late McLeod goal won the game for Hibs and Feyenoord beat Schalke in the final.

Back home, Scotland suffered its wettest July on record for 18 years with widespread flooding in the Edinburgh area. Outside training was wholly impractical so instead Hibs joined Hearts and others in enjoying the shelter provided by an indoor five-a-side tournament held at Powderhall Stadium, where Hearts, with Hamilton, Blackwood, Milne, Cumming and Wardhaugh in their side, defeated Hibs 3–0 in the final, the Hibs five being Fox, Thomson, Turnbull, Ormond and Preston. There was no recognised goalkeeper in either side and Eddie Turnbull was between the sticks for Hibs.

In preparation for the months ahead, Hibs followed their usual routine of playing the first eleven against the second at Easter Road. These matches were open to the public and a fair crowd watched the reserves triumph 3–1, much to the surprise of most present. The reserves enjoyed top-quality performances from Tommy Kilbride, Davie Gibson, Malcolm Bogie, Donald McCalman and recent signing from West Calder, Ken

Allison, but the highlight of the game was Bobby Nicol's 25-yard strike which flew past Lawrie Leslie almost before he could move.

Those fans who attended the trial match were very concerned with the news that although Gordon Smith seemed to be recovering from an ankle injury he had not yet signed a new contract. The thought of Hibs without Smith was too much to bear as he was a huge favourite with the support. Manager Hugh Shaw did little to allay the fears when he described Smith's injury as 'very severe' and there would not be a Hibs fan alive who did not wish Gordon a full and total recovery. Further bad news arrived when it was revealed that John Fraser, carrying out his National Service, had been posted to the Middle East while big centre half John Paterson suffered a recurrence of his ankle problems and broke down in training before a ball had even been kicked in earnest.

Eddie Turnbull, freshly back from the World Cup in Sweden, would captain Hibs for the season and it was no more than 'Ned' deserved as he was a great example to both young and experienced players on the books at Easter Road.

The opening games would, as ever, involve League Cup matches in a group which this season saw Hibs paired with Falkirk, Aberdeen and Kilmarnock in what was sure to be a tough qualifying group. First up were Falkirk, who came to Leith with a strong side including Mussel-burgh-born goalkeeper Bert Slater, former Hibee Alex Wright and proven goalscorer John McCole. In a closely fought game in front of a bumper crowd Hibs scraped home 3–2 with goals from Baker, Aitken and an own goal from the unfortunate McCarry, while the Bairns countered through Sinclair and McCole. As ever the match programme that day held a few quite interesting advertisements including one for the Edinburgh Tattoo, which you could watch by purchasing tickets ranging in price from one shilling (5p) to 15 shillings (75p).

Around this time it was revealed that Newcastle United had been showing more than a passing interest in the Hibs youngster John Baxter, but the club declared it had no interest in selling the half back to Newcastle or anyone else for that matter.

The following midweek brought some great news for Hibs fans when it was announced that Gordon Smith had signed up for another season, his 17th with the club, and that thanks to his grit and determination he should be fit enough to play in the not too distant future. In addition to the treatment given by the medical staff at both Easter Road and the Royal Infirmary, Gordon had been bathing his ankle regularly in the cold sea water at Gullane and had cycled for miles each week to build up the strength in his legs. This typified the character of Smith, who refused to give in to an injury which might well have cost him his playing career, and when the news broke of his signing you can be sure there would not be one Hibs fan that didn't heave a sigh of relief.

The reserves had started their League Cup campaign with a disappointing 5–2 away defeat to Falkirk and things did not improve a great deal in their next outing when they went down 4–2 at home to Aberdeen. Des Fox and Ken Allison found the net for Hibs but defensive lapses cost them dear at the other end, where John Proudfoot stood no chance with any of the four strikes by the Dons. Spectators that evening got the first look at the newly painted lines on the Easter Road pitch as Hibs went for a four-inch thick marking instead of the 2.5 inches adopted by most other clubs. The maximum allowed was five inches and Hibs explained their reasons for changing the lines as being an aid to spectators behind one goal who would now be able to clearly see the goal line at the other end.

Twenty-four hours after the reserves lost at home the first team travelled to Pittodrie and fared much better in winning a cracking game 2–1. Wishart found the target for the home side, but goals from Aitken and Baker ensured the points would be taken back to Edinburgh and that Hibs would sit at the top of their qualifying section with two wins out of two. It had been a good game between two sides determined to play passing football and the sporting press was fulsome in its praise the following morning.

There was a new face at Easter Road this season and he was introduced to the support ahead of the game against Kilmarnock on Saturday 16 August 1958. Willie Redpath had won a Scottish Cup winners' medal with Motherwell in 1952 and now joined Hibs as assistant trainer and coach. Redpath won Scottish caps too and was a much respected figure in the Scottish game as well as being a first-class golfer. Quite what he thought as he watched Kilmarnock thump Hibs 3–0 is anybody's guess, but this was a game in which the scoreline flattered the victors as both Baker and Grant had goals disallowed and were outstanding throughout. Killie played a containing game and hit on the break to great effect as Joe McBride, Bertie Black and Tommy Henaughan all stuck the ball past a bemused Lawrie Leslie.

The League Cup sections had reached their midway point, but future games would be interspersed with league matches as the long campaign for the title commenced. By one of those quirks of fate which often occur in Scottish football Hibs found themselves facing Kilmarnock for the second time in four days, only this time the game would be played at Rugby Park. Killie boss Willie Waddell had assembled a good side and the Ayrshire outfit were looking to get off to a winning start in their attempt to better their fifth-place finish of the season before, but Hibs played well that day and held them to a deserved draw with each side scoring once, Baxter the marksman for Hibs.

Just a few days later it was League Cup time again and Hibs made the short trip to Brockville to face Falkirk, taking with them a quite sizeable number of supporters. The travelling fans were not to be let down as Hugh Shaw's men turned on the style in winning 4–0. The men in green and white were in fine form as they shut up shop defensively while probing away constantly at the home defence and it was no real surprise that their play brought four goals from Aitken, McLeod, Ormond and Preston. Poor Bert Slater in the Falkirk goal must have been quaking in his boots as it seemed every time Hibs came at him they might score and indeed had it not been for Slater's heroics the result would have been even more emphatic.

Aberdeen offered the next challenge and it was a League Cup game which Hibs must win in order to keep their hopes of qualifying from the group alive. Thankfully, the home support had plenty of reason to cheer as wingers McLeod and Ormond provided the ammunition for Baker to grab a hat-trick while Joe himself laid on a fourth Hibs goal when he fed the ball to Preston inside the box. This win put Hibs firmly in second place behind leaders Kilmarnock with the final sectional game to come at Rugby Park. Hibs went to Ayrshire knowing a draw was enough to see them through but Killie had other ideas and although McLeod scored a cracking goal from all of 25 yards the defence conceded two and the League Cup campaign once again ended at the group stages for Hibs.

Reigning league champions Hearts visited Easter Road in early September and they arrived having achieved something their hosts had not in that they had qualified from their League Cup section, where they had won five of their six games, losing only to Rangers at Ibrox. Among those games had been a nine-goal thriller at Cathkin Park where Third Lanark had finally gone down 5–4, Willie Bauld grabbing a hat-trick for the Gorgie side. They also arrived freshly back from Belgium where they had met Standard Liege in the first-round first leg of the European Cup. Sadly, they had only a goal from ex-Hibee Ian Crawford to celebrate as their usually solid defence caved in and conceded five. Although they would go on to win the return, the 2–1 victory was not enough to allow them to progress in that tournament, but there would be some consolation that season as they went on to defeat Partick Thistle 5–1 in the final of the League Cup.

Although still clearly hurting from that defeat in Belgium, this was a derby match and both sides were desperate to win it. Unfortunately for Hibs, their visitors seemed more determined and ran out handsome winners with a 4–0 scoreline that left the home support to trudge home feeling thoroughly miserable. That misery was somehow compounded by the fact that Crawford netted twice, Mackay and Murray getting the others.

The pain of losing a derby was still very much in the mind as Hibs next travelled to Fir Park to face a Motherwell side who had started the season in mixed form, but that pain was soon eradicated as the Hibees struck top form in demolishing their hosts 5–2. Aitken and Baker each grabbed a brace and chief provider Willie Ormond also hit the target. This was more like the Hibs side the fans longed to see and it was an ongoing concern for manager Shaw that his team often performed in a Jekyll and Hyde style. Make no mistake, however, this was a fine result against a very strong side and the sporting press was not slow to acknowledge that fact, the *Sunday Mail* reporter writing: 'Hibs combined quick, first-time accurate passing, intelligent spreading of the play and a ready eye for the slightest gap in the 'Well defence.' Locally the *Evening News* reported that 'Hibs finished this game at Fir Park as a confident, strong, fast moving combination reminiscent of the team in its heyday'. High praise indeed but on the evidence of that display it was certainly merited.

There was an exciting piece of news for Hibs fans in the week leading up to the next home game which would see Queen of the South visit Easter Road. Crack German outfit Bayern Munich were due at Easter Road and the tie was sure to attract a bumper crowd as the visitors were early favourites to win the German League championship and still had two in their side, Karl Mai and Hans Bauer, who had been World Cup winners for their country in 1954.

Further good news was received as John Grant was called up to play for the Scottish League against the League of Ireland on the Wednesday before the Queen of the South game and it came as little surprise to the Easter Road faithful who had watched Grant turn out high performances on a weekly basis. Of course, Grant had made his debut earlier in the month for the League side in Belfast and had impressed greatly. His reward was another call-up with the hope that another good performance might mean his position would be retained for the League game against England in October. Hibs goalkeeper Lawrie Leslie also got the call, though his place was as reserve to first-choice stopper Bill Brown.

After such a hectic news week the Hibs fans were happy to see Saturday arrive and with it a home league match against the men from Dumfries. In a somewhat one-sided affair the hosts won at a canter with McLeod in sparkling form as he scored two goals and laid others on for Baker and Aitken to secure a 4–0 win. Nine goals in the last two games were just what the Hibs fans needed after watching Hearts win so easily at Easter Road and it put everyone in the right frame of mind for that friendly with Munich.

Hibs had toured Germany just after the Second World War hostilities had ceased and all connected with the club at that time had been hugely impressed both with the friendly reception received wherever they played and with the high standard of football in a country still struggling to find some sort of normality after a long and bloody six years. This particular tie had come about when Hibs played Schalke in the Rotterdam-based Festival Cup and agreed a future friendly at Easter Road, only for the German side to have to scratch from that arrangement due to their own playing commitments. Hearing this news, the directors of Bayern Munich offered to come in their stead and that offer was warmly received by the Hibs board.

Along with their two World Cup winners the visitors boasted a host of great players, including inside right Erich Hahn, already capped at Under-23 level and on the verge of a call-up to the full side. It would be the Hibs inside right, however, who won the headlines as young Ken Allison was given a start in the side as a reward for his fine form in the reserves.

A sizeable crowd was in attendance and watched two sides playing football the way it should be played, with the ball being passed through the team and not just lofted up the park aimlessly. Hibs took the lead thanks to a characteristic Turnbull thunderbolt of a free kick and doubled their lead through Allison, who finished off a great three-man move which carved the German defence open. The third goal was a bit bizarre in that Frye shot for goal only for right half Mantey to try and stop the shot by punching it clear. Instead, his punch put the ball into the German net and referee Bobby Davidson took the view that the goal should stand rather than award a penalty. Although only a friendly, the game took on a European nights feel under the Easter Road floodlights with Bayern trying hard to crack the Hibs defence but without success as a highly entertaining game finished 3–0.

The form in recent league games and the friendly with Bayern were cause for encouragement as Hibs looked to build on the goals scored and position themselves for a tilt at the league title. One player who would not be there to help that cause was full back Willie MacFarlane, who had been in dispute with the club over the contract offered and then, having reached agreement, he was promptly bought by Raith Rovers. MacFarlane had been a good servant to Hibs and had defended stoutly throughout his time there as well as weighing in with a few goals and all at Easter Road wished him well at his new club. Whether those good wishes were still in evidence the following Saturday evening is a moot point as MacFarlane made his debut at Stark's Park against Hibs and helped his new team-mates dole out a 5–2 drubbing to the green and whites. Baker and Preston scored for Hibs, but in truth it was only consolation for a poor performance in which Hibs seemed always to be second to the ball.

On the international front John Grant had earned his three League 'caps' while that side was captained by Hibs veteran Eddie Turnbull and there would be further recognition for Hibs as Joe Baker was selected to play at centre forward for the English Under-23 side against Poland at Hillsborough. Baker was a big hit and the Scottish press was quick to praise him, the *Daily Express* journalist writing: 'The "babe" Baker was a success, his skill piercing through 90 minutes of rough handling.'

Back home in Scotland, Joe next lined up against Falkirk at Easter Road in a league match and he found the target twice despite some more of the 'rough handling' he'd endured in English colours. Sadly for Joe and for the Hibs fans present that day Falkirk scored three to take the points on offer.

Two days later Hibs faced a very strong British Army eleven under the floodlights at Easter Road. The visitors were able to call on the services of Bert Slater in goal, Hibs' own Jackie Plenderleith in defence and Alex Scott (Rangers), Peter Dobing (Blackburn) and George Mulhall (Aberdeen) in attack. The hosts put out a side peppered with young reserve players and paid the penalty in being trounced 6–1 with Ken Allison getting the Hibs goal. Much worse than the actual result, however, was that Hibs lost two players to injury, John Baxter and John Young both suffering ruptured knee ligaments.

Another home game brought Clyde to Easter Road, the Bully Wee having started the league campaign well, only to tail off in October. Restored to the Hibs first team that day was centre half Jackie Plenderleith. He had the misfortune to score an own goal, but his blushes were saved by the fact that he otherwise put in a superb display and helped Hibs win 2–1, goals from Preston and Allison securing the points.

Hibs' next game took them on the long journey north to Aberdeen where they would face a Dons side very much in form. It was the furthest away trip for any league game and perhaps the players were weary on arrival for they folded under incessant pressure and crashed to a humbling 4–0 defeat. The away league form was beginning to become a cause for concern: for every good win, such as the demolition of Motherwell, there was a worrying loss of form, as displayed at Pittodrie.

Another very long journey was undertaken just two days later as Hibs travelled to Boothferry Park to face Hull City in a floodlit challenge game. That apparent travel weariness struck again, and for the second time in three days Hibs were the victims of a 4–0 drubbing. The visitors never really got going and had to play the last 20 minutes without Joe Baker, who left the field after having appeared to pull a muscle.

Intensive treatment from the backroom staff at Easter Road ensured that Baker would be fit to face Airdrie in a league match which saw the Diamonds secure both points with a 3–2 win in front of an increasingly unhappy Hibs support that filed out at the end of the game wondering just where and why things were going wrong. Although Allison had found the net twice, Hibs never looked like winning and so those same thoughts must surely have been occupying the mind of Hugh Shaw as he took his players south again, although on this occasion the long miles travelled did not stop his players winning 1–0 against Sheffield United at Bramall Lane, Ormond getting the goal. In the crowd that evening was a scout from Newcastle United and the player under scrutiny was the Hibs half back John Baxter, but the Edinburgh club were quick to again state their young star was going nowhere and that news alone certainly cheered the supporters back home in Scotland.

It was around this time that Hibs announced a new signing with Jim Scott, brother of Rangers star winger Alex, joining the club from Bo'ness United. An apprentice painter, Jim was being closely tracked by Chelsea, Newcastle, Leeds, Manchester City, Aberdeen and Rangers, so it was little surprise that Hibs were delighted to secure his signature.

Some 6,000 fans turned out at Easter Road to watch the reserves playing Rangers on 1 November 1958, the main attraction being the return to action of Gordon Smith wearing that number seven jersey which he graced so wonderfully. The young Hibees played well in gaining a creditable 2–2 draw and it was noticeable that Smith laid on both Hibs goals for Jimmy Thomson and Donald McCalman. Rangers had fielded a side with all eleven players having featured in their first team, but all present agreed that the outstanding player on the park that day was Gordon Smith.

On that same day the first team were at Ibrox and once again were on the wrong end of a 4–0 scoreline as the spirit seemed to have drained out of the men from Leith. It was an exceptionally poor performance and saw Hibs slipping towards the wrong end of the league table, a fact which was of great concern to everyone associated with the club.

Off the park, the Supporters' Association was busy arranging a special evening of entertainment at which Lawrie Reilly would be guest of honour. Among the acts lined up for the Usher Hall were Jack Radcliffe, Johnny Victory, Pat Cassidy and Dennis Clancy. Also attending would be former team-mate and present Scotland manager Matt Busby as well as players from the four home countries – all gathered to honour the man who gave birth to the call 'Gie the baw tae Reilly'. The fans turned out in large numbers to enjoy the concert and to pay tribute to a legend, retiring from the game at just 29 years of age and a loyal Hibs man through and through, the Easter Road side being his only senior club. There had been times in his career when Lawrie could have left Hibs, with admirers on both sides of the border willing to offer the chance of a change, but Reilly only ever had eyes for Hibs and it was fitting that his tribute was such a success.

Another would be leaving Easter Road at this time too as Willie Redpath decided to part company with the club, citing a conflict of time available to undertake his football duties and run his public house in Motherwell. In Willie's defence, his concern was that the intensive coaching promised to the younger players was not being achieved in the time available to him and as he left, Eddie Turnbull and Willie Ormond took a greater part in that activity. In essence, this was the beginning of the coaching which both would carry out to great effect in the years ahead at Hibs and elsewhere.

The next challenge for Hibs came in the shape of a home league fixture against Third Lanark. The men from Cathkin brought a decent run of form into the game and in an eight-goal thriller they took a point away with them as the sides drew 4–4. A Baker hat-trick and a stunning volley from Allison were not enough to secure the points, and while it was extremely encouraging that the green and whites scored four goals it was more than a little worrying that they also managed to concede four, the point won doing little to ease the concern of being in the wrong half of the table.

The match programme for the Third Lanark game contained an interesting piece about a former Hibee, retiring from his current post. Matthew (Matta) Paterson was a stalwart of the side in the early 1900s and was a centre half of some considerable ability, leaving Hibs just as Hugh Shaw was breaking into the first team as a youngster in 1924. Matta took up employment as a chauffeur with Adam Cramond and Son in Edinburgh and gave them 35 years' service, performing his duties as he did his football, to the highest standard. In 35 years he never once had an accident and his duties involved driving for many dignitaries, including driving The Duchess of Kent on a number of occasions when she visited the capital.

The day after drawing 4–4 with Third Lanark, Hibs made the long journey south to face Tottenham Hotspur at White Hart Lane. This fixture had become something of an annual event as the sides had met at least once each year since 1949. Hibs held the edge going into this game, having won five, with Spurs on four and the other four drawn. In a highly entertaining 90 minutes the visitors had their chances and could bemoan some eccentric refereeing from whistler Mr Rose which denied them a goal when even the Spurs defenders were bamboozled by the whistle blowing to deny the strike. As it was, the home side ran out 5–2 winners, but Hibs were by no means disgraced and two late Spurs goals made the scoreline seem more emphatic. Baker and Fox scored for Hibs, the Baker boy being watched from the stands by the England manager and a host of First Division scouts.

Given that Baker had already managed to get the call for an Under-23 cap it seemed only a matter of time before a full honour would come along for the lad born in Liverpool but living in Lanarkshire and loving his time with Hibs.

The good form shown at White Hart Lane must have encouraged belief in the players that a much needed win could be achieved when they took the short journey across the Forth to play Dunfermline on 15 November 1958. Back in the team for the first time since early October, having had a few problems with both injury and form, Andy Aitken struck the winning goal and Des Fox got the other in a 2–1 victory. That win gave Hibs a timely boost and those fans that made the trip to watch the green and whites must have been heartened by the level of performance, which saw the Easter Road men win a lot more comfortably than the final scoreline would indicate.

In the midweek following that Dunfermline game the Hibs played a floodlit friendly against Orgryte of Sweden. The Gothenburg outfit were on a mini-tour of the UK and Hibs were delighted to face a side from the country whose national team had been runners-up in the World Cup earlier in 1958. Orgryte, who had put up a fine performance against Newcastle at St James' Park just two nights earlier, were a good outfit and gave Hibs a stiff challenge in a match which finished 1–1, a Turnbull penalty providing the Hibs goal.

Strong-running St Mirren presented Hibs with their next challenge as they travelled through to Love Street hoping to continue improving their league position. Half back John Baxter could have been excused had his mind not been fully on the task at hand for immediately after the game he would make the short journey into Glasgow where he would be married! As it was, Baxter played very well as did the rest of his colleagues, but missed chances and good goalkeeping kept Hibs down to just the one goal scored by Aitken, the hosts striking twice to win the points on offer.

Back at Easter Road, in front of a crowd of several thousand fans, the reserves ran riot against the Paisley second string and crashed home ten goals for the loss of just two. The Buddies had put out a reasonably strong side including internationalist Gemmell, ex-Hibee John Higgins and first-team regulars Vince Ryan and Tommy Leishman, but the wee Hibs were outstanding on the day and scored through Jock Buchanan (4), Johnny Frye (3), Pat Hughes, Jimmy Gibson and Ken Allison.

Two days after the defeat to St Mirren, Hugh Shaw took the senior side to Tynecastle for the final of the East of Scotland Shield. The Hibees went there as holders, but with three reserves in their ranks they were not good enough on the night and lost 3–0, leaving the trophy in Gorgie.

Concern was growing among the Hibs support that defeat was becoming a little bit too much of a habit for Hibs. With Celtic coming to Easter Road for the next game those fears were compounded by the news that Baker had taken a knock in training and might be doubtful for the game. In his programme notes Hugh Shaw expressed the view that Hibernian had many talented players, capable of much more than their results had indicated and suggested that while he enjoyed watching the lads playing good football just as much as the next man it was time that football was used to get winning results. Nobody who turned up for the game that day was about to argue with those sentiments.

In years yet to come there would be a feeling among football fans that any suggestions of players possibly missing a match because of injury were really attempts by managers and coaches to mislead the opposition. Whether this game provided an early example of that ruse we will never know because when the team was announced Baker had made a 'miraculous' recovery from the training ground injury reported just days before. Not only did Joe 'recover', he stamped his undoubted ability all over the game by securing a hat-trick while Celtic could only find the net twice. It was a stunning victory, achieved by playing good passing football, only this time the end result was in Hibs' favour.

Also in the match programme for the Celtic game was news of a forthcoming benefit match to be played in recognition of the service given to Hibernian by Lawrie Reilly. Players from all four home countries would make up the opposition in an international select and a big crowd was expected to attend to honour Reilly. That match was, however, put to the back of the minds of the Hibs players as they faced their next challenge in the league, a testing trip to Dens Park to face Dundee. In what was becoming a pattern for this Hibs side, they played very well and yet they lost. Des Fox found the target for Hibs, but the Dark Blues struck twice and Hibs headed home empty handed yet again.

Ken Allison, who had been banging in the goals for the reserves, was lined up to travel with the party to Dundee but injured himself playing in a floodlit challenge match when a young Hibs team defeated Bo'ness United 8–0 at Easter Road just a few days earlier. It really was bad luck for the youngster whose goalscoring in the reserve team had fully merited his intended inclusion for Dens, but surely his chance would come again.

The winter was setting in with a vengeance now as pitches became frosty one week and like a mud bath the next. Those factors, combined with injuries and suspensions, certainly stretched the playing pool and Fox got a few starts in the first team as a result. He certainly played his part in Hibs securing a welcome two points in their next league game which brought Partick Thistle to Easter Road. Indeed, Fox and his colleagues adapted well to a tricky playing surface and rattled in four goals without reply. Thistle keeper John Fairbairn was in good form otherwise the greens may have scored more but they were happy to settle for a double each from Baker and Gibson. The home fans left in buoyant mood having watched their favourites create and take so many chances, but four was a small number of goals in comparison to the number notched up in the next game at Easter Road.

Monday 15 December 1958 had been selected as the date upon which Hibs would face an International Select in Lawrie Reilly's testimonial game. In honour of the Hibs legend, Hugh Shaw played his strongest available eleven and they faced a star-studded side containing players from both sides of the border. The International Select lined up as follows – Farm (Blackpool), Grant (Hibs), McNaught (Raith Rovers), Docherty (Arsenal), McColl (Rangers), Peacock (Celtic), McKenzie (Partick Thistle), Fernie (Middlesbrough), Mudie (Blackpool), Johnstone (Manchester City) and Liddell (Liverpool), but they were caught in a goal blitz from an on-fire Hibs side who ran out 9–3 winners. Ormond, Smith and Baker each got two with singles from Fox, Turnbull and Preston completing the rout. The Select goals came from ex-Famous Fiver Johnstone (2) and Mudie. Around 6,000 fans attended on a very cold night and every one of them stood to applaud the guest of honour when he was introduced before the game. Cold it may have been, but at least the hands would be kept warm applauding all of those goals!

It was back to league duty the following Saturday as Hibs travelled up the A9 to Annfield to play struggling Stirling Albion. Once again the pitch was frosty but Hibs adapted well and easily won the game 3–0 with Baker getting two, his third double in three games, and Smith finding the target for the first time since coming back from his long injury absence. Astonishingly, that was Gordon's 363rd goal in senior football, a quite remarkable total for a winger.

In the crowd at Annfield that day was a scout from Arsenal and it became known that he was keen to take 19-year-old centre half Jackie Plenderleith to Highbury, but thankfully Hibs were not keen to sell their outstanding young talent. That story broke in the Sunday newspapers and that same weekend the *Sunday Post* carried an interview with Mr Cricket, John Arlott, who was asked: 'What is your outstanding memory of Scotland?' to which he replied: 'That wonderful Hibs forward line of Smith, Johnstone, Reilly, Turnbull and Ormond.' Clearly the great man knew his football, but he was, after all, the football correspondent for *The Observer* as well as the voice of English cricket.

The final game of the year brought Kilmarnock to Easter Road on the Saturday between Christmas and New Year and as always seemed to be the case when these two sides met there were goals galore in an end-to-end tussle more akin to a cup tie. When the dust finally settled, Hibs emerged 4–3 winners with Baker getting yet another double and Fox and Turnbull, the latter from the penalty spot, each getting a single. It was another two very welcome points as Hibs eased towards mid-table and thoughts of slipping into the relegation zone disappeared over the festive holidays.

New Year's Day 1959 took Hibs to Tynecastle where they would meet a Hearts side fighting out top spot with Rangers and scoring lots of goals along the way. Few gave Hibs much of a chance, especially as the earlier league meeting at Easter Road had seen Hearts easily win 4–0. When the season ended Hearts would finish second, two points behind winners Rangers, but they would not win those two points in this game as Hibs played magnificently in winning 3–1. Alex Young scored for Hearts, but a double from wily winger Ormond and a cracking solo from Fox ensured it would be the Hibs fans who left the ground singing.

Two days later a bumper holiday crowd of 33,000 flocked down to Easter Road to cheer on the men who had spoiled Hearts' New Year celebrations, but visitors Motherwell were in no mood to join the party and fought out a gritty 2–2 draw, with Baker hitting yet another double to take him clear of Willie Bauld of Hearts at the top of the scoring charts. Joe really was in sparkling form but of course he owed his debt to the brilliant lead-up play of Gordon Smith and Willie Ormond on either wing. Motherwell too had their stars and included in their number the likes of John Martis, a towering centre half, Ian St John, Pat Quinn and Willie Hunter, the latter two going on to play for Hibs later in their careers while St John was an integral part of an exceptionally good Liverpool team.

In the week leading up to the next game the draw was made for the Scottish Cup and it paired Hibs with Raith Rovers at Stark's Park. Ahead of that tie the green and whites had a long trip down to Dumfries to face Queen of the South in the league and it earned them another two points as they easily swept aside their hosts 4–1. For once Baker didn't score a double – he got three and Preston notched the other. This was another good result in the quest to improve the league position and Hugh Shaw was delighted with the form displayed on a hard pitch almost entirely covered with sand.

Ironically, before they could meet in the cup, Hibs and Raith Rovers first had to face each other in a league game at Easter Road. The club were anxious that fans did not see this as a dress rehearsal for the cup tie, but inevitably that was exactly how the majority present viewed it and so they were delighted to watch Hibs win 4–2 on a frosty surface. The goal machine otherwise known as Joe Baker got yet another double. Gibson and Ormond also found the target and had it not been for Charlie Drummond in the Rovers goal, Baker would most certainly have had a hat-trick. Joe was put clear by Gordon Smith and struck a vicious drive towards the top corner then had to look on in disbelief as Drummond leapt high to fingertip the ball around the post. It was great entertainment for the fans and, despite the concerns of the club, taken as an omen as to how the cup tie might go. That win took the December/January tally in the league to seven games without defeat, 13 points and a barrowload of goals.

That win over Raith Rovers had been achieved in midweek and so just a few days later Hibs made the short journey to Falkirk for a league game hoping that the good run of form could be continued. They say all good things come to an end, however, and that's exactly what happened to the league run as Falkirk scraped home 1–0 on a rutted pitch where good football was at a premium. Falkirk keeper Bert Slater was in inspired form and for once Baker didn't get his name on the scoresheet, a rarity in the recent weeks given his form.

The day of the cup tie finally arrived and Hibs took a sizeable support to Kirkcaldy where the sides battled for the entire 90 minutes, asking and giving no quarter, in an attempt to get through safely into the next round. Neither achieved that aim as the sides drew 1–1, Smith getting the Hibs goal which ensured the players would have to go through it all again in the replay at Easter Road.

Foul winter weather in Edinburgh saw that replay postponed twice and before it could be played Hibs had to go through to Glasgow on league duty to face Clyde at Shawfield. In a quite miserable performance, Hibs were totally eclipsed by a much hungrier Clyde outfit and went down 4–1 to their hosts, only Ormond's goal offering any consolation.

The defeat in Glasgow was hardly ideal preparation for the cup replay two days later, but Hibs managed to shake off that disappointment and in another gutsy game with plenty of action the Hibees got home 2–1 thanks to a Turnbull penalty and a strike from the edge of the penalty area by Fox. Unfortunately, Baker fell awkwardly in a challenge and had to leave the field injured, much to the obvious dismay of all at Easter Road.

That cup win took Hibs through to the second round and due to the need for a replay it would be Hibs' next match, with Falkirk the opponents at Easter Road. Despite intensive treatment Baker remained unfit and could not play, his number nine jersey being handed to Fox with Aitken being drafted in at inside right. Hibs had revenge on their minds as well as progression to round three as just a couple of weeks earlier the Bairns had halted Hibs' good league run in the match at Brockville. Of course the sides had also clashed in the League Cup, and so this tie would be the fifth meeting since August. Going into the game each side could claim two wins apiece. Once again it was a cup tie full of effort and commitment which at the end of the day saw Hibs progress to round three thanks to a 3–1 win. Replacement centre forward Fox, Aitken and Ormond from the tightest of angles all managed to beat Bert Slater in the Falkirk goal, setting up a home tie with Partick Thistle in the process. Man of the match by a country mile was Jackie Plenderleith, who was commanding throughout and who did his chances of a Scotland call-up no harm at all.

The games were coming thick and fast now and the following midweek brought Aberdeen to Easter Road on league business. Joe Baker was absent again, taking a bit longer than he had hoped to recover from the injury sustained against Raith Rovers. Both Plenderleith and Aitken also missed out, their places going to John Paterson and John Baxter. Aberdeen were a well organised outfit who liked to close the play down when the opposition had the ball and they carried that off to good effect for almost the entire 90 minutes. Only a flash of genius from Jimmy Gibson opened them up when he skipped past two challenges inside the box and rattled a low drive under the diving John 'Tubby' Ogston. It wasn't the best of games from a spectator's point of view, but the two points were very welcome nonetheless.

Three days later Hibs visited Broomfield where they faced an Airdrie side not short on skill. They also had a bite to their play which attracted somewhat unfair accusations in the media of the Diamonds being overly physical. They had some big lads in their side certainly, but were quite capable of playing a passing game and that was the side of Airdrie in most evidence as they took both points in a seven-goal thriller. Ormond was back on the wing but Baker didn't make it and Des Fox played at centre. Gibson, Aitken and Turnbull found the net, but slack defending saw Lawrie Leslie beaten four times, though he was blameless on all four occasions and had a couple of very notable saves either side of half-time. Hibs had trailed 4–1 at one point but struck two goals fairly late into the match and many observers felt they were unlucky not to secure a point. In the crowd that day was a certain Mrs Ormond, mother of Hibs' Willie and Airdrie's Gibby – no indication was gained as to which side she was supporting!

On the Monday evening after the Airdrie game, Hibs entertained West Calder United in a floodlit friendly and fielded a predominantly young side, including recent signing Hugh Herschell, a lad from Kilwinning in Ayrshire, John Hardie in goals, and Malcolm Bogie at outside left. In an entertaining game the hosts came out on top, winning 2–0 with goals from Jock Buchanan and Jimmy McDonald.

The Scottish Cup third round presented Hibs with their next challenge as they faced Partick Thistle at Easter Road on 28 February 1959. Although Baker was back in training he was not yet ready to play and Fox again led the line. Leslie was victim to a flu bug and so Jackie Wren stepped in to replace him and played his part in a 4–1 victory for the home side. Ormond and Aitken each scored twice, but it was the twinkling feet of Smith on his customary right-wing beat that had the fans cheering throughout. Gordon was outstanding that day and looked to have left all of his injury worries behind him as he prodded and probed at the Thistle defence.

Playing at left half that day was Tommy Preston and the match programme for the game held an amusing article about a 'job' Tommy had secured for the coming close season. Apparently, Shelley Paterson, sister of centre half John, had, in her capacity as an agent to models, persuaded Tommy to appear as a mannequin in a made-to-measure suit at the Ideal Home Exhibition at the City's Waverley Market. Apparently John was considered too 'bandy legged', but Tommy was thought perfect for the role. Needless to say his team-mates ribbed him mercilessly, suggesting he would be very good at standing around doing nothing!

Having been involved in cup duty on the Saturday, Hibs' next outing in the league was that following midweek when title challenging Rangers rolled into town. The Glasgow side were packed with big-name players – the likes of Bobby Shearer, Eric Caldow, Ian McMillan, Davy Wilson and Jim Scott's big brother Alex – while Hibs were weakened by the continuing absence of both Leslie and Baker. The Gers tested Hibs throughout the 90 minutes but hard work, stout defending and good forward play ensured the points would be shared in a thrilling 2–2 draw. Fox and Preston were on target for Hibs and but for the woodwork, young Des would have had two and perhaps won the game for Hibs as he struck the bar in the dying seconds of the game. Given Hibs' indifferent league form over the season so far, a 2–2 draw with the mighty Rangers was very encouraging for the home fans.

That same week the Scottish Cup draw was made and paired Hibs with Third Lanark at Cathkin Park. Coincidentally, the tie was scheduled to take place a week after the Hibees were due to visit the same venue on league business. Thirds had been having a similar kind of season to Hibs in that their form was a bit up and down and both occupied mid-table places in the league.

Also that week, Joe Baker found out that he had not been selected for the Under-23 team to face France, but there was little surprise at the news, given Joe's already lengthy absence from the Hibs first team with a jarred knee.

Around this time came the sad news that former Hibernian stalwart Paddy Callaghan had died at his home in Edinburgh. Into his eighties, Paddy starred for Hibs in the Scottish Cup-winning team of 1902, a side which also won the league title in 1902/03, and played alongside the great Harry Rennie and Bobby Atherton.

The next league game for Hibs took them through to Glasgow for that meeting with Third Lanark and once again a point was gained in a 2–2 draw, with Fox and Aitken on target. It is true to say that Hibs were missing Baker but equally true to say that Fox was doing a pretty good job of trying to fill the centre's boots as he once again found the target. Also missing from that game was Gordon Smith, the latest flu victim at Easter Road, and his place was taken by Johnny Frye, who had the pleasure of laying on Aitken's goal with a fine deep cross from the right wing.

In the following midweek, Baker made his long-awaited return in a reserve game at Easter Road against Clyde. News that Joe was playing spread quickly and a decent crowd turned out to see his return but left disappointed as the second string went down 3-1, although it was Baker who struck the Hibs goal.

Having come through that reserve game unscathed, Joe took his place in the starting line-up at Cathkin when Hibs returned to Glasgow for their Scottish Cup tie against Third Lanark. For the Hibs fans it must have been agonising to watch as the green and whites dominated the game, making chance after chance but taking only one, while their hosts scored twice to end the dream for yet another season. Ormond netted for Hibs, but the loss of Plenderleith early in the game to injury clearly upset the balance of the defence and Lawrie Leslie didn't stand a chance with either of the goals conceded. Hugh Shaw was as disappointed as the next man and felt his side were at least worth a replay. Few would have disagreed, but it's goals that count. The manager later said it was back to 'auld claithes and parritch' for the rest of the season, his way of suggesting there would be no need to look out the best gear for a Hampden final or to arrange any celebratory meals.

Poor Jackie Plenderleith not only missed out on the remainder of that cup tie but also lost the chance to represent the Scottish League in a game set for the following midweek. The injury came about when he was struck on the ankle in trying to block a shot and at first it was feared it might be broken, but a later X-ray showed no breaks or fractures, although there was heavy bruising and the lad was in considerable pain. One player who did wear his country's colours was Willie Ormond, who had a fine game on the wing in that Scottish League side who faced England. Such was Willie's level of performance that star English full back Alex Parker of Everton was moved to compliment the Hibs man on giving him such a difficult 90 minutes.

The starting eleven for a visit by Dunfermline saw Grant, Paterson, Nicol and 19-year-old debutant Malcolm Bogie drafted in and all played their part in an excellent 3–1 win, the Hibs goals coming from a Fox penalty, Fraser and Aitken. Once again Baker was absent and once again Fox deputised and scored, albeit from the penalty spot but in fairness he led the line well throughout. Bogie, although a right winger, played in Ormond's left-wing position and acquitted himself well, the former Balgreen Rover earning special mention from manager Shaw.

A letter arrived at Easter Road that week, posted in Gibraltar by Johnny McLeod, who was stationed there for his National Service. He told of playing in an Army team against their Moroccan counterparts in

Casablanca. The game apparently attracted a huge crowd of over 50,000 and Johnny described the home fans as 'absolute fanatics who lived for their football'. Little could he, or anyone else for that matter, know that some 50 years later Hibs would have two Moroccans on their books.

Hibs' next game brought St Mirren to Easter Road and saw Gerry Baker, Joe's brother and himself a future Hibs player, lead the line for a Buddies side which defended deep, hit on the break and scored the only goal of the game to secure the two points on offer. The Saints were a decent outfit and arrived at Easter Road as Scottish Cup semi-finalists and so it was no surprise that they offered up tough opposition. Our own Baker boy didn't play, as was the case with Ormond, Smith, Turnbull and Plenderleith. Malcolm Bogie retained the number eleven jersey and played well enough, but Hibs just couldn't break down a Saints defence brilliantly marshalled by Jackie McGugan.

That same day the reserves travelled to Paisley and won 2–1 with a double from Christie securing the points at the start of a hectic eight days for the second string. On the Monday following they faced Hearts in a 'wee' derby at Easter Road and won 2–1 with Jock Buchanan getting both goals. Two days later they beat Stirling Albion 2–0, again at Easter Road, with McDonald and Baker, returning again from injury, finding the target. Their fourth game in eight days brought Celtic to Easter Road, but neither side could find the net in a 0–0 draw. While the reserves were fighting out that draw the first team travelled to Parkhead and lost 3–0 in a pretty one-sided affair that only ever looked like being a home win.

Only a few more games remained until the season ended and Hugh Shaw, safe in the knowledge that relegation was not an issue, decided to give a few youngsters their first-team chance, starting with a home game against high-flying Dundee. Critics may have suggested it was ill advised, especially after Dundee won the game 2–1 with future Hibee Alan Cousin among the scorers, but there can be little doubt that if reserve players are to improve they must be given a chance to do so at that higher level. Incidentally, Dundee scored all three goals that day as Jimmy Gabriel put through his own goal. Gabriel was a wonderful player and went on to star for the likes of Everton and Southampton, managing the former after his playing career ended. He was part of an excellent Dundee outfit that also boasted goalkeeper Bill Brown, who went on to play for both Tottenham Hotspur and Scotland.

The following Saturday Hibs travelled to Glasgow and fought out a 2–2 draw with Partick Thistle at Firhill. Manager Hugh Shaw put out a very young side but the lads held their own with a Donlevy own goal and a Fox header gaining a point at a tricky venue. Meanwhile the reserves were continuing their run of playing two or more fixtures in a week, and although they went down 3–1 at Dundee, with Jock Buchanan getting the goal, they bounced back to beat Partick Thistle 4–3. Frye grabbed all four goals at Easter Road before they visited Motherwell and again triumphed 4–3, Buchanan getting a hat-trick and Aitken the other.

For some players at Easter Road the season nearing its end was a blessing in disguise as it would give them a couple of months to recover properly. There was a long list of such players, including Tommy Preston, who had been out for a month but was glad to hear he would not need a cartilage operation; Des Anderson, who although away doing his National Service, did need a cartilage operation; Jimmy Kane, a long-term absentee with a particularly nasty leg break that had kept him out of action for the whole season; Eddie Turnbull with a troublesome ankle knock and Lawrie Leslie with, of all things, tennis elbow! Let's not forget either the absence of Joe Baker, whose jarred knee had kept him out for a number of games and which still troubled him even though he managed a few appearances in the closing weeks of the season, or Gordon Smith's ankle problem that flared up on a number of occasions during that same period.

A team who had spent their season worrying about relegation were next to visit Easter Road but, those fears finally having been put away, Stirling Albion played in that relaxed way only a side knowing the pressure is finally off can play. Once again Baker was missing and no one else seemed capable of filling his shooting boots that day as Albion, with the quaintly named Jimmy Hailstones at left back, won the match 1–0 and the two points. That was Hibs' last league game of the season and there would be only one more game for the first team to play as Hearts arrived at Easter Road on Saturday 25 April 1959 to contest the final of the East of Scotland Shield. The Gorgie men arrived as League Cup holders and runners-up in the league championship, but Hibs were unimpressed by those credentials as they won the game 2–0 with goals from Ormond and Baker.

If that win over Hearts could be considered a fine way to end a season the reserves were providing their own version in their last three games. Stirling Albion at Annfield were first to topple as Buchanan and Allison found the net in a 2–1 win. Next it was off to Pittodrie and a 1–1 draw, marred by ankle ligament damage to Buchanan. John Fraser got the Hibs goal in a side which had young John Proudfoot in goal and, back from National Service, Johnny McLeod at outside left. The curtain came down for the reserves at Kirkcaldy when the wee greens won 3–1 with goals from Aitken, Baxter and Fraser.

It had been a long and difficult season, but plans were already afoot for the new campaign. Hearts would be off to Australia for a pre-season tour and Hibs had the luxury of choosing from three options: Central and South America, a combination of France/Switzerland/Austria and Germany or the one they finally opted for, Spain.

The first match on the tour saw Hibs face the might of Barcelona and take a sixth-minute lead through Ormond, giving the 30,000 home crowd some food for thought. Next, Baker eluded his marker, but his fierce shot came back off the post, and then play switched to the other end where Segarra equalised before the interval. As the sides lined up for the second-half it became apparent that the hosts had made no fewer than seven substitutions, one of whom, Villaverde, saw his shot hit Grant and fly past Leslie to make it 2–1. In 68 minutes it was 3–1 when Martinez scored with a header and then there was the sight of some of the subs being replaced by those players they had replaced earlier! Hibs were tired now and confused as to who should be marking who and as a result they conceded two more goals to Martinez and Hermes to make the final score 5–1.

Just 24 hours later the tourists faced second division Tarassa, a club based about ten miles from Barcelona. The hosts had a number of players guesting for them from Barcelona's other senior club, Espanol, including leading Spanish striker Aguerra, who opened the scoring after a quarter of an hour. The tight and bumpy pitch didn't really suit Hibs but they plugged away, earning applause from the 7,000 fans watching on. A second goal, scored by Coll, had Hibs on their heels for a spell, but Baker managed to pull a goal back only to see Tarassa score a late third through Chelo. It was reported after the game that Real Madrid had a scout watching the action and that he had been hugely impressed with Joe Baker.

A scheduled game against Murcia was postponed due to a torrential downpour and so Hibs played their third and final tour game against Real Gijon in front of 35,000 fans. Such was the play of the men from Easter Road that the home fans offered up warm applause on a number of occasions in appreciation of their efforts. Alvare put Gijon ahead with a headed goal, but Jim Scott soon equalised after beating two defenders and striking the ball home from ten yards. A strong penalty claim, when Baker tumbled, met with a negative response from the referee and little more than a minute later Alvare scored again for the hosts. That proved to be the last goal in a game in which Baker once again impressed, the Madrid scout again watching on.

Chapter Fourteen

1959/60

JOHNSTONE RETURNS

The season opened with a match played for the Allison Cup which brought together an Edinburgh Select to face English giants Newcastle. The Select won a thrilling match 4–3, Hibs youngster Jim Scott bagging the goal of the game and earning himself a man of the match award into the bargain. His prize for the achievement was in the form of savings certificates presented by Mrs John Park, wife of the president of the SFA. No bottles of whisky/champagne, etc, in those days but a nice glow in heading home knowing that the vast majority of the 26,237 spectators in attendance would be experiencing the very same thing.

Pre-season friendlies were something of a rarity and most fans got their first chance to see their heroes, as well as any new signings, when the club held what it called an 'open trial match' which saw the first team take on the reserves at Easter Road. Around 5,000 turned up on a bright and sunny afternoon to watch the firsts beat the seconds 7–2, Baker nabbing four, Scott two and McLeod the other. Scorers for the reserves were Buchanan and Aitken. Making a first appearance was new signing Graham Pate, who turned out at inside left for the reserves, while Tommy Slavin played for the first time in a long while after being dogged by injury. Young Willie Wilson kept goal for the second team and the widely held view by all present was that he was faultless in conceding seven and surely had a bright future ahead of him.

Out of action before a ball had even been kicked in earnest was Tommy Preston, who went over on an ankle in training and damaged his Achilles tendon. Also out was keeper Lawrie Leslie, whose ongoing elbow problem flared up again, while full back Allan Robertson was out with a badly strained groin. On the positive side Jimmy Kane had recovered from a nasty leg break and Des Anderson from a cartilage operation.

As always the competitive season opened with the League Cup section matches and it promised to be a tough task to qualify, with Rangers, Motherwell and Dundee in the group. The opening day brought league champions Rangers to Easter Road and that attracted a crowd in excess of 45,000. Sadly, Hibs were lacklustre against a very powerful Glasgow outfit and crashed 6–1 to their visitors. With Baker well marshalled by Davis and Telfer in the heart of the Rangers defence, only Ormond managed to beat keeper George Niven while poor Jackie Wren in the Hibs goal looked to have finished the game with a sore back.

In the following midweek Hibs and Dundee shared no fewer than 15 goals between them at first- and second-team level. Tuesday 11 August brought Dundee's reserves to Easter Road and in a thrilling first-half they rocketed into a 4–1 lead only to scrape a point at the end of the game thanks to John Fraser missing a penalty in the last minute. By that time Hibs had drawn level, but on reflection a draw was probably a fair result as both teams entertained a decent home crowd. Scorers for Hibs were McLeod with two and for Fraser and Buchanan, one apiece.

Twenty-four hours later the first team turned out at Dens Park, where Willie Wilson took over in goal, Hughes replaced Nicol in defence and Aitken took over the number ten jersey from Davie Gibson. After their mauling by Rangers this was a much improved performance and only a last-minute goal from the home side denied Hibs a share of the spoils in a 4–3 defeat. Ormond was again on target, as were Baxter and Baker. Hibs had led 2–0 at half-time only to collapse in the second 45 when both McClelland and Baker were struggling with knocks.

A good Motherwell side presented the next challenge for Hibs, who were already as good as out of the competition. In his programme notes manager Hugh Shaw asked the fans to set aside the two defeats and look upon the positives as he firmly believed that Hibs would improve with the going and make a significant effort in the league race. That improvement was still to come as Hibs went down 3–1 at home, only Fox beating Hastie Weir in the 'Well goal. All the attention after the game went, quite rightly, to Ian St John of Motherwell, who cracked home a hat-trick inside an incredible two and a half minutes, beating the previous record holder, Celtic's Jimmy McGrory, who scored three in three minutes, bizarrely against Motherwell.

Watching from the stand was Hibs' latest signing, Joe Davin, a 17-year-old schoolboy from Dumbarton were had been courted by a number of clubs but chose Hibs as he knew that the Edinburgh side were always willing to give young players an early chance of first-team football if form merited it. Davin had been capped as a youth international and had played alongside two other Hibs kids, Jim Easton and Duncan Falconer.

With the League Cup group games now half completed, attention turned to league football and Hibs welcomed Aberdeen to Easter Road for their opening fixture. With a few Edinburgh lads in their side the Dons were a decent outfit and laid claim to being the only British side to have an Indian-born player on their books. Defender A. Mascarenhas had been signed from Bombay State, but he would not feature in this game which Hibs won 2–1 thanks to a glorious double by Baker, who beat John 'Tubby' Ogston twice with sharp volleys from Ormond crosses. After losing their first three competitive games this was a welcome outcome for the Hibees and a fine start to their long league campaign.

The following weekend saw Rangers providing the opposition and having hammered Hibs 6–1 in Leith they went to town again on their own turf and notched a very worthy 5–1 win, only Aitken's consolation goal giving the few visiting fans anything to cheer about.

Meanwhile, at Easter Road a quite astonishing result was developing. Leading Rangers 1–0, the reserves lost the services of Pat Hughes, who had to leave the field with a nasty head cut which required four stitches. As only 20 minutes had elapsed it would have been expected that Rangers would make their extra man advantage count, but nothing could be further from the truth and with only ten men for 70 minutes of the game the reserves crushed Rangers 7–0. The ever improving Johnny McLeod scored four, while John Fraser, Johnny Frye and Jimmy McDonald weighed in with a goal each. McLeod must surely have been knocking on the first-team door by now, but he was no doubt aware that the present incumbent of the jersey he so dearly wanted was none other than Willie Ormond.

With no points from the four games played so far in their League Cup group, Hibs hoped to improve on that situation when Dundee visited Easter Road on Wednesday 26 August, but once again the home fans would leave the stadium disappointed as the Dark Blues took the points in a 3–1 win. Ormond was on target for the home side but a strong Dundee, with future Hibee Alan Cousin at inside right, were more clinical in their finishing as Cowie, Hill and Robertson all beat young Willie Wilson in the home goal.

The League Cup group stages came to an official end at Fir Park, Motherwell, on Saturday 29 August though in truth Hibs' League Cup campaign had ended a whole lot earlier. It was to be wooden spoon time for the green and whites as the home side prevailed 4–2, although the Hibs goals scored by Baker and Aitken were both crackers.

The following midweek the reserves kicked off their Second XI Cup campaign with a narrow 3–2 win over Airdrie at Easter Road. Jimmy McDonald, Jock Buchanan and Andy Aitken bagged the goals, but star of the show was outside left Johnny McLeod who tormented the visiting defence throughout 90 exciting minutes.

A training knock to Ormond opened the door for young McLeod to get his chance in the number eleven jersey and he could not have asked for a tougher baptism as Hibs made the short journey across the city to face Hearts. In a typical derby match, with both sides going all out for a win, the fans in attendance were treated to four great goals and, thankfully from a Hibs point of view, two of those were scored by Baker. Hibs had Jim Scott on the right and McLeod on the left and each was credited with an assist for Joe's goals. The point won at Tynecastle meant that Hibs had secured three out of the four available, a far healthier picture than in their League Cup group.

Having conceded 11 goals to Rangers in their two prior meetings, Hibs were entitled to feel somewhat apprehensive when the Ibrox club visited Easter Road in what would be the third league match of the season. Goals galore did not materialise on this occasion, with the net only being found once and unfortunately that was by Rangers. Optimists looked upon that as a sign of improvement while the pessimists saw it as the beginning of a slide in form.

Initial indications were that the pessimists were right as Hibs visited Cathkin Park and lost 5–3 in a very tousy game. Defensive errors were to the fore as poor Willie Wilson was left unguarded all too often in the Hibs goal. At the other end, the forwards were doing their bit as Baker scored twice and McLeod got another, but the slip-ups at the back would prove too costly in the end.

If the pessimists were feeling in an 'I told you so' mood their cause was not helped in the days following the collapse at Cathkin Park. News was sweeping Edinburgh that Famous Five legend Bobby Johnstone had rejoined Hibs. This was just what the optimists ordered as Johnstone was renowned for his play making abilities and brought with him experience of playing at the top level in England where he had won an FA Cup winners' medal with Manchester City.

The Tuesday evening following the Third Lanark game saw the reserves turn out at Easter Road to face Hearts and an astonishing 8,000 fans turned up hoping to see Johnstone play. Sadly, he did not arrive at the ground in time to take part but his absence was forgiven as the home fans saw their side secure a handsome 5–2 win, Fraser and Fox getting two each and Baxter the other. That put the second team in the position of having won their opening four league games and having scored 19 goals in the process, so it is no surprise that they often attracted decent attendances wherever they played. Indeed, prior to the Hearts game, they had visited Ibrox and hammered Rangers 5–1 with goals from Fraser, Ormond, two from Buchanan and one from Gibson.

As Bobby Johnstone was arriving at Easter Road another fans' favourite was leaving as Aitken was transferred to West Bromwich Albion. Andy was a popular player in Leith and left with the best wishes of all connected with the club. They were delighted to hear that in his first two games for the Baggies the Midlands club had beaten both Leeds United and Newcastle United.

Saturday 26 September 1959 saw a huge crowd turn out at Easter Road to witness the return in emerald green and white of Bobby Johnstone in a league match against Kilmarnock. The little inside forward didn't let his adoring public down as he orchestrated a 4–2 win for Hibs, with his promptings leading to goals from Baxter who got two, Baker and McLeod. It really was a masterclass from Johnstone, who looked as though he had never been away and had the crowd roaring their pleasure with his every touch. Young players like Baker and McLeod could surely only get better with his experience on tap for them.

As part of the deal of Johnstone rejoining Hibs it had been agreed that the green and whites would send a side down to the Borders to play Bobby's home-town team of Selkirk, and on the Monday evening following that fine win over Kilmarnock, Bobby watched as a young Hibs side triumphed 4–0. A fiercely proud Borderer, Bobby was delighted to see his two favourite teams meeting and a good night was had by all.

Hibs headed west next as they travelled to face a strong Clyde outfit at Shawfield. Despite dominating for virtually the entire 90 minutes, they still managed to lose the game 2–1, Baker notching the solitary strike for the visitors.

Traditionally, Hibs had staged an annual friendly against a British Army XI and with Jackie Wren in goal for the injured Willie Wilson the Easter Road outfit comfortably won the game 4–0 after Johnstone, McLeod, John Young and an own goal found the target. The performance and result were welcomed by one and all, Hugh Shaw suggesting afterwards that these kinds of display needed to be seen more often when league points were at stake. In fact it could be argued that points were at stake, albeit not league ones, as the British Army XI were a side included in Hibs' Floodlit League group.

After an indifferent start to the league season there was high hope among the spectators that the visit of Motherwell would give the Hibees the chance to collect a couple of valuable points and a measure of revenge for the 3–1 home defeat inflicted by the Steelmen in the earlier League Cup match. Once again the game finished 3–1 and once again it was the visitors that took the spoils as Hibs huffed and puffed, with only a Buchanan strike to show for their efforts. The goalscorer was back in the team following injury but Hibs were still without the services of Pat Hughes and Jim Scott, the latter fracturing a toe in a freak training accident. Despite the absence of some key players the home support was somewhat unforgiving in complaining that manager Shaw was not putting out a winning side.

Another home game followed as Dunfermline crossed the Forth on league business. The big home support arrived in uncertain mood as their favourites had not been playing all that well of late, but by the end of the game they were marvelling at the 11-goal spectacle they had just witnessed. In a rip-roaring 90 minutes both sides attacked at every opportunity and when the final whistle blew it was the Hibees who won the day by seven goals to four. A Baker hat-trick and singles from Preston, Ormond, Baxter and Young ensured that Pars keeper Connachan had a slightly busier day than Wilson in the home goal.

Two days later Hibs welcomed Bolton Wanderers to Easter Road for their latest Floodlit League match and the English club arrived with the current England goalkeeper, Eddie Hopkinson, between the sticks. Various other players had secured league caps as well as full international honours but all this meant nothing to a buoyed up Hibs side who won a very thrilling game 5–2 with Baker (2), McClelland, McLeod and Ormond giving the home crowd reason to cheer.

Things were surely looking up for Hibs now after two good wins, so they next travelled to Airdrie in confident mood. Broomfield was traditionally a difficult place to win with its tight pitch and the home side were known for their robust style of play just to add to that difficulty. On this day, 24 October 1959, those factors seemed to mean little to a rampant Hibs side who crushed their hosts 11–1. Unbelievably, Baker only managed a hat-trick while Preston bagged four, prompting the latter to quip that he was after the number nine jersey! Two from McLeod and single strikes from Ormond and McClelland sealed the fate of the hapless home side and sent the Hibs fans home with huge grins on their faces.

Back at Easter Road, the reserves were serving up their own demolition job in cuffing the Airdrie second eleven 8–0, Buchanan getting a hat-trick and Fraser (2), Falconer, Frye and Gibson completing the rout.

The last day of October brought Celtic to Easter Road and once again the fans got treated to a bit of a goal feast with each side finding the net three times. Two from Baker and one from Johnstone won Hibs a point against the league leaders.

Twenty-one goals in three games had certainly set the Hibs fans in good mood for the next challenge, which brought Middlesbrough to Easter Road in the latest Floodlit League match. The 'Boro arrived with strike sensation Brian Clough leading their line and this certainly added spice to the event as Clough and Baker were vying for the attention of the England selectors. 'Boro had Peter Taylor in goal and both he and Clough would go on in years to come to guide Derby County and Nottingham Forest to many honours. Up front with Clough was Willie Fernie, who had joined Middlesbrough the previous season as a big money buy from Celtic. In a fast, furious, skill-packed game it was honours even as the two sets of players fought out an astonishing 6–6 draw. Baker didn't do his England chances any harm by grabbing a hat-trick, with Johnstone (2) and Ormond the other scorers.

A trip to Love Street presented Hibs with their next challenge in gaining league points and in a closely fought contest the visitors won 3–2. For once Baker was not among the goals as Preston, Johnstone and Baxter found the mark. The reserves completed a double winning weekend in putting the Buddies' second eleven to the sword in a convincing 4–1 win, the goals coming from Frye, Buchanan, Fox and Bogie.

The squad travelled to Ayresome Park in the following midweek, where Middlesbrough would be expecting to go one better than the draw they had achieved at Easter Road. It was not to be for the hosts, however, as Hibs turned in a sparkling display to win the match 4–3 with goals from Preston, Ormond, Baker and McLeod. Present at the game were the England selectors, who had also taken in the earlier encounter at Easter Road. They continued to be impressed by the 'Baker Boy' as they promptly named him in their squad for their forthcoming internationals.

All in all, things were going quite well for the Hibees at this stage and so it was something of a disappointment when in their next league outing against Raith Rovers at Stark's Park they went down 4–2. John Grant was missing due to injury and Preston took a very heavy knock early in the game which hampered his mobility for the remainder, but the general consensus was that even with those setbacks Hibs should have won. It was not to be, however, and the goals from Baker and Preston offered the only consolation to the visitors.

In the week leading up to the next home game, Hibs held their annual general meeting and Harry Swan was re-elected as chairman for the 26th year in succession. In recognition of his sterling work for the club throughout those years he was also elected as a life director, an honour indeed for the hardworking and Hibs-daft Swan. The only 'bad' news reported was a trading loss of £4,000, but the club were happy enough with that situation as the deficit had been caused by the expense of concreting the terracing, a move which had proved very popular with the Hibs support. In effect the board were keeping their promise to plough as much money back into the club as possible 'for the benefit and comfort of supporters'.

With the off-field business taken care of, attention returned to the visit of Dundee and their talented bunch of players, who included Bobby Cox, Jimmy Gabriel, Alan Cousin and Jimmy Bonthrone. Arriving for the game, Hibs fans were informed via the match programme that the Easter Road side were being courted by the Canadian Football Association with a view to touring there in the coming close season. Negotiations were at an early stage, but it was taken as a huge compliment that Hibs were the club approached. Whether anyone from the Canadian Association was in the crowd that day is unknown but if there were, they would surely have been impressed by the fine performance of the men in green and white in defeating Dundee 4–2. It had not started well for Hibs, with two early goals conceded, but once the players got into their stride that old Hibernian fighting spirit came to the fore as Johnstone and Baker each grabbed a double to secure the points.

Hard on the heels of that fine win over Dundee, Hibs had another home game the following weekend against Stirling Albion. In the week building up to that game the Easter Road club had secured the services of a player they had been tracking for some considerable time. Now 24, he might well have signed some four years earlier when Hugh Shaw offered him a contract but the player was only half-way through an eight-year service period in the RAF which took him to such places as Malaya, Hong Kong, Cambodia, Vietnam and Singapore. Once back on Scottish soil however, Shaw was quick to get him to put pen to paper. Although his arrival was pretty low-key, Bobby Kinloch would go on to create his own piece of Hibernian history in the years ahead.

When Hibs and Albion took the field that Saturday it was the home side who showed a greater will to win and the points were secured in a 3–1 win with Baker (2) and Johnstone getting the vital goals. Up at Annfield, the reserves had Bobby Kinloch making his first start, and he got a goal in the 5–2 win. A Jock Buchanan hat-trick and a solo effort from Des Fox meant two points were secured by the high-scoring second string. Astonishingly, the Hibs reserve team were now the highest scoring side in the whole of the UK, with 55 goals scored in 14 league outings. Top scorer with 17 was Jock Buchanan while Des Fox was a distant second with eight. Certainly they were going really well and the addition of Bobby Kinloch, who had impressed greatly at Annfield, simply served to make them an even stronger outfit.

With 1959 nearing its end, the draw for the first round of the Scottish Cup saw Hibs receiving a bye – good news indeed given the club's ongoing lack of success in that tournament. One of the ties which came out in a rather dull first-round draw paired St Mirren with Glasgow University. Not one to make the mouth water you might think, but when the tie did take place a certain Gerry Baker, brother of Joe and himself a future Hibs player, managed to bag TEN goals, a feat almost equalled by his brother Joe in times to come – but more of that later.

The early December weather was kind and Hibs headed to Arbroath for a tricky game at Gayfield. With the wind howling in off the sea, an occupational hazard to any player appearing there, the visitors cruised into a three-goal lead courtesy of yet another Baker hat-trick but then took their foot off the gas in the last 20 minutes and conceded two soft goals to make it a frantic finale. Thankfully, they held out and another two points were in the bag.

Mid-table Ayr United were next up as they visited Easter Road on

Saturday 12 December. Always stuffy in defence, the Ayrshire men proved difficult to break down and in the early part of the game it looked as though Hibs were in for a long afternoon, but they stuck to their task and triumphed in the end with a handsome 5–1 win. Johnstone scored two, one from the penalty spot, and there were singles from Baker, Ormond and McLeod. Over at Somerset Park, Ayr's reserves were the next to face the Hibernian reserves goal machine and once again the wee Hibs routed the opposition in a 7–2 victory. Fraser and Fox got two apiece with singles from Kinloch, Buchanan and Scott.

On the Monday evening following the Ayr United game, a young Hibs team took on a Scottish Amateur Select side at Easter Road. Just what the amateur side got out of the game is open to conjecture as they were soundly thrashed 13–4. Fraser (4), McDonald (4), Scott (2) – (both penalties), trialist Jimmy Robertson (2) and Bogie all found the net guarded by J. Hendry of Edinburgh University.

Anyone who had taken in the last two games at Easter Road, watching the Hibees score 18 goals, and who then elected to travel to Firhill the following Saturday, must have thought all their birthdays and Christ-mases had come at once because a rampant Hibernian totally demolished Partick Thistle 10–2. From the off Hibs attacked the Thistle defence and the goals seemed to be flying in from all directions. In his match report after the game, Stewart Brown of the *Edinburgh Evening Dispatch* said, *'Who can stop these Easter Road gluttons? From the first minute to the last Partick were petrified by this pounding smooth side which hadn't one failure.'* As you might expect the goals were shared around and when the dust settled it would be Baker (2), Ormond (2), McLeod (3), Preston (2) and a Wright own goal that would be recorded in the record books. Given that Hibs also had two goals disallowed the Partick team and defence might have suffered even more, but to hit ten – away from home – was a feat worthy of the praise heaped upon them by the sporting press.

Boxing Day took Hibs on the long trek north to Pittodrie and once again the fans were treated to a ten-goal display, but sadly on this occasion Aberdeen got six of them. On any other occasion Johnstone's double, one from the spot, and goals from Ormond and Preston would have been enough to secure the points, but the loss of six at the other end meant a losing end to the decade.

New Year's Day 1960 fell on a Friday and brought Hearts to Easter Road. In his programme notes Hugh Shaw pointed out that Hibs had a bogey to lay as they had not defeated their oldest rivals at home since 1952. Hopes were high among the Hibs support: despite the reversal at Pittodrie, their favourites were going into the game in good form. After 90 agonising minutes the bogey remained. The Gorgie men were in sparkling form against a lacklustre Hibs and easily won the game by five goals to one, only Johnstone's goal giving the Easter Road faithful anything to cheer about. It was a devastating blow to all connected with the club as once again bragging rights were the order of the day for the Hearts support. One small crumb of comfort came the way of the disconsolate Hibs support with the news that the reserves had gone to Tynecastle and secured a handsome 6–2 win, thanks to goals from Fox (3), Fraser, Buchanan and a Scott penalty.

With New Year's Day falling on the Friday, Hibs were in action just 24 hours later, and they must have travelled to Ibrox in some trepidation following their mauling by Hearts. As it turned out they played a whole lot better in securing a 1–1 draw. Baker struck the goal which put Hibs ahead and eventually earned them a point. Back at Easter Road there was another goalfest as the wee team overcame Rangers by six goals to four.

Third Lanark and their newly appointed manager, former Rangers and Scotland stalwart George Young, were next to arrive at Easter Road. Two defeats and a draw in the last three games meant that it was vital Hibs get back to winning ways and that's exactly what they did in cruising to an easy 6–0 win. A Baker hat-trick and singles from Preston, Young and McLeod could have been doubled but for the woodwork and some heroics from George Ramage in the Thirds goal. As ever the reserves ran riot again and hammered Third Lanark 9–0 at Cathkin, meaning that the wee Hibs remained top scorers in the whole of the UK with a staggering 93 goals in 21 league games.

Rugby Park had always proved a testing venue for Hibs and their record at that venue was not improved when they went down rather tamely to a 3–1 defeat in mid-January. Baker scored for Hibs, but the defence had an off day and the points stayed in Ayrshire. Making his debut that day at Kilmarnock was 18-year-old Duncan Falconer, who played at right half and who would go on to give sterling service to Hibernian.

During the following week Hibs were delighted to welcome Jackie Plenderleith and Bobby Nicol back to the fold after their time in the Army had finally come to an end. Their return was well timed as Hibs faced a tough schedule of fixtures with league, cup and floodlit ties ahead of them. The first such tie was a league fixture against Clyde at Easter Road and little did the fans in attendance know as the teams kicked off at 3pm that they would be witnessing a ten-goal thriller with chances galore being made and taken by both sides. The result was a draw with five goals apiece after yet another Baker hat-trick and a double from the mercurial Johnstone were cancelled out by some pretty awful defensive lapses.

Having received a bye in the first round of the Scottish Cup, Hibs had a free Saturday on 30 January 1960 but rather than lie idle the club decided to invite Manchester City north for a friendly and the game finished at 1–1, Johnstone netting for the Hibees.

Into February now and Hibs were at Fir Park, Motherwell, to face a side very much in form. After 90 pulsating minutes which kept the crowd entertained throughout, Hibs took the points with a fine 4–3 win after Baker, McLeod, Ormond and Preston all caused the home net to bulge. Back to winning ways for the reserves, too, as they trounced their Motherwell counterparts 6–2 at Easter Road, thanks to goals from Fox, who got two – his first being the 100th league goal of the campaign – Gibson, a Scott penalty and a brace from the irrepressible Buchanan.

Scottish Cup day arrived on 13 February and would have brought Dundee to Easter Road looking to be the latest side to end the dreams of the green and white faithful, but the weather took a hand in proceedings and the game was postponed. In fact that match would be postponed no fewer than seven times due to the weather and would eventually be played at the end of the month. Prior to that, East End Park managed to pass a late inspection and Hibs made the short journey to Fife, returning with a point after securing a 2–2 draw with goals from Baker and Baxter.

On the last day of February, that Scottish Cup tie was finally played and Hibs triumphed 3–0 with goals from McLeod (2) and Johnstone. The prize for progressing into round three was an away tie against East Stirling at Firs Park, and indeed due to the postponements of that Dundee game it would be at Firs Park that Hibs next took to the field. A pretty one-sided affair was settled by two goals from Baker and one from Fox with the Falkirk club unable to respond.

Postponements caused by February's bad spell of weather had Hibs in action again on the Monday night and in a tense and closely fought encounter at Parkhead the hosts scraped home with a narrow 1–0 win.

The fourth-round Scottish Cup draw had not done Hibs any favours as it paired them with Rangers at Ibrox, although ahead of that tie Hugh Shaw was quick to tell anyone who would listen that his side actually had a decent record against the Glasgow side in the cup. A Johnstone penalty in the first two minutes set Hibs up nicely, but defensive lapses at crucial times were very costly and despite McLeod hitting a second for Hibs, Rangers scored three. And so ended another attempt at winning that all too elusive trophy. On the same day, the reserves went to Love Street and defeated a very strong St Mirren side 2–1 as McDonald and an own-goal by McGugan sealed the points.

They say you can never predict anything in football with any real degree of confidence as it is a sport which continually throws up the unexpected, and that's what it did the following Wednesday at Easter Road when no fewer than eight of the St Mirren players who had appeared in that 2–1 reserve defeat turned out for the first team and played their part in securing a shock 3–1 win over a Hibs side seemingly still hung over from their Scottish Cup exit. It was dismal stuff from Hibs on the night with only a Johnstone goal to cheer. Baker missed the game due to injury and unfortunately Buchanan was unable to carry his goal-scoring exploits into the first team with him.

It was turning into a dismal March for Hibs, and things got even worse when Raith Rovers arrived at Easter Road on Saturday the 19th, leaving with both points after finding the net three times without reply. Once again Hibs were poor on the day and, in truth, the better team won. Thankfully, the reserves continued to sparkle and were becoming genuine contenders for the Reserve League title, doing their chances no harm whatsoever with a crushing 6–1 win at Stark's Park.

Just two days after that drubbing from Raith Rovers, Hibs welcomed Manchester United to Easter Road for a floodlit challenge match. Home fans turned up full of trepidation as their favourites were somewhat off colour and they would be faced by the likes of Harry Gregg, Bill Foulkes, Maurice Setters, Wilf McGuiness, Johnny Giles, Dennis Viollet and Bobby Charlton in a star-studded United line-up. On the night it was mostly one-way traffic and the visitors thoroughly deserved their 4–0 win as Hibs rarely troubled Gregg in the United goal. Still, it was a great experience for youngsters like Pat Hughes, Duncan Falconer, Johnny McLeod and Joe Baker to test their skills against such a quality outfit and there is little doubt that despite the score the home fans enjoyed having the opportunity to watch such a classy team as Manchester United.

The following weekend it was back to league football and a visit to Dens Park to face a Dundee side bent on revenge for their earlier Scottish Cup defeat. In a free-flowing, high-scoring game the hosts won 6–3, the Hibernian goals coming from Fraser, Johnstone and Fraser. Disappointing as that result was there was always the form of the reserve side to enthuse about and the colts did the home fans proud in disposing of Dundee in a 5–1 win. Kinloch, Scott, Bogie and another two goals by Buchanan gave the impressively large home support something to cheer about.

On the Monday evening following that great win over Dundee, Hibs entertained Raith Rovers in the Second XI Cup fourth-round replay, the first game having finished at 0–0. There would be goals this time, however, and it needed extra time to provide us with a winning side as the wee Hibs won through by four goals to three. Gibson (2), in-form Malcolm Bogie and an own-goal from the unfortunate McNaught saw the home side through and kept alive the hope of a league and cup double for the colts.

That same evening the big team was down in Leicester playing a floodlit challenge match, and thanks to a cracking strike by Johnstone a 1–0 victory was secured. At least it stopped an horrific run, but it would remain to be seen whether the league position could be improved with the season in its last few games.

Just 24 hours after winning in Leicester, Hibs were back on the field to face Airdrie at Easter Road. The last time the teams met Hibs had demolished the Lanarkshire side 11–1, but obviously the travelling to and from Leicester had taken its toll as the green and whites could only scrap out a 3–3 draw. Baker found the net once more but was outdone on the day by Johnstone, who got two, one from the penalty spot after Baker had been fouled when about to shoot into an empty net.

Saturday 2 April 1960 saw Hibs visit Annfield to take on Stirling Albion and it was to be a good afternoon for the green and whites as they got back to winning ways by a 3–2 margin. Goals from Baxter (2) and Johnstone secured the two points for a leg-weary Hibs, who trooped off at the end looking quite exhausted by their recent efforts.

With the league title firmly in their sights it was expected that the wee Hibs would easily dispose of Stirling Albion at Easter Road, but, as I said earlier, nothing can be considered a certainty in football and defying all the odds the visitors trotted out a well earned 5–0 win. Two days later Hibs' form returned and just in time to secure them a place in the final of the Second XI Cup following a narrow 1–0 win over St Mirren. The winning goal came from the boot of Jim Scott, who calmly converted a penalty in a tense and very closely fought match.

At this time Hibs announced their tour plans for the close season, which involved playing Portsmouth at Fratton Park before taking in the English FA Cup final at Wembley and thereafter moving on to Holland, Germany, Italy and Switzerland. Their planned itinerary saw them facing Sparta Rotterdam, Bayern Munich, Fiorentina, Lazio and Grasshoppers Zurich, a testing schedule for sure.

Ahead of all of that there were still some league fixtures to fulfil and those started with a visit from Arbroath on 16 April. In a very one-sided game the Hibees easily triumphed 5–0 with two goals from Baker, two from McLeod and one from Ormond.

Two days after demolishing Arbroath, Hibs faced Hearts in the final of the East of Scotland Shield at Tynecastle and came away with the trophy after recording a very impressive and fully merited 3–2 win, with two goals from Johnstone, including a penalty, and one from Ormond. Beating Hearts in any competition is always special but beating them on their own patch – and for a trophy, too – just added to the enjoyment of a large and noisy Hibs support.

In an unusual step for the time, the Ayr United v Hibs game was moved to a Friday to avoid competing with the Scottish Grand National, which was being run on the Saturday at Ayr Racecourse. The game was played in the evening and was only possible because there was enough daylight to complete it, Ayr not yet having installed any floodlights. On the night the home side were just a little too strong for Hibs and deserved their 2–1 win, with McLeod getting the Hibs goal.

On 30 April Hibs played their final league match of the season and fought out a fairly entertaining 2–2 draw with Partick Thistle. Baker and Nicol got the home goals while Ewing and Paterson counted for the Jags. Prior to leaving for their close season tour, Hibs were forced to change their itinerary and would now visit Germany and Yugoslavia after their friendly in Portsmouth.

With Joe Baker away on international duty, other Hibs forwards would have a chance to show what they could do during the tour matches and in the first of those it was Davie Gibson who caught the eye with two cracking goals against Portsmouth at Fratton Park. Jock Buchanan also found the net, but so too did Pompey's Cutler, Harris and Howells in an entertaining 3–3 draw.

Six days later Hibs faced Bayern Munich in Germany where a sizeable crowd gave Jock Buchanan a standing ovation at the end of the match following his fine hat-trick which saw the visitors edge a close game 3–2. Jock's first goal came early, but Huber soon equalised and then Wagen-bauer shot the hosts ahead before the break. Midway through the second-half McLeod hit the post and Buchanan netted the rebound before getting his third around five minutes later.

It was on to Yugoslavia next and a game against Dinamo Zagreb. The visitors were under the cosh for most of the game but still managed an impressive 1–1 draw in quite tropical conditions. Indeed, Johnstone had put Hibs ahead with about 15 minutes left to play, but the hosts got a deserved equaliser when Blaic scored in the last minute.

Still in Yugoslavia, Hibs next met first division side Rejika; Bobby Kinloch had a quite outstanding game, a cross by Fraser allowing him to open the scoring. He then turned provider to set up Johnstone for a second. Twenty minutes from the end Lukasic pulled one back, but before the end McLeod netted following a great through ball from Kinloch.

A successful tour concluded, the party had a few more days to relax before returning home to Scotland.

Chapter Fifteen

1960/61

EUROPEAN SEMI-FINALISTS AGAIN

As the Hibs players gathered for pre-season training they were able to welcome back Tommy Preston, who had trained through the summer in an effort to recover from a second cartilage operation, and to congratulate John Baxter on his appointment as club captain. As was the norm in those days, Hibs held a public trial match and this drew a fair crowd to Easter Road as the reserves were beaten by a strong first team. Noted among those who showed promise in the second string were Holy Cross schoolboy George Brough, centre half Jim Easton and inside left Kenny Knox. Goalkeeper Willie Wilson played for the reserves and did a good job, though he couldn't stop young Joe Baker bagging four goals.

The League Cup section matches kicked off the season and Hibs had a tough group with Kilmarnock, Dunfermline and Airdrie providing the opposition. They got off to a poor start in falling 4–2 at Rugby Park thanks to a hat-trick from Bertie Black and a single from Andy Kerr. Goals from Baker and a Johnstone penalty did little to ease the pain for Hugh Shaw's men.

A midweek visit by Dunfermline followed, and the Hibs support got its first chance to see the newly installed half-time scoreboard which had been made bigger and would now have two showings to keep the fans bang up to date with scores both north and south of the border. Electronic scoreboards were, of course, still in the future and the Easter Road structure was huge, standing in the top corner of what was known then as the Dunbar End and which is now the site of the South Stand. The guys who manned it had to climb in via a ladder and display each score against a letter of the alphabet which corresponded to the fixtures listed in the programme.

Also on display for the first time was a newly designed club programme which cost thruppence (1.5p) and which boasted a front cover showing a fine aerial view of Easter Road. It's interesting to read these old programmes, and one of the most obvious things to strike the reader is the language used. For example, Hibs had upgraded the dressing rooms in the close season, but the programme described them as 'stripping boxes', which conjures up an altogether different picture. Having been inside those 'stripping boxes', I shudder to think what they were like *before* being upgraded.

The Pars side which faced Hibs that night included keeper Eddie Connachan, a young Cammy Fraser, ex-Hibee Tommy McDonald and ex-Hearts legend Jimmy Wardhaugh, but they were somewhat over-whelmed by the home side, who won 3–0 thanks to goals from McLeod and Kinloch, together with an own-goal by left back John Sweeney, who was helpless in knocking a Baker shot past his own keeper.

Another home game followed, against Airdrie, and once again there was ex-Hibs representation, the Diamonds having Lawrie Leslie in goal and John McNeill at left half. Poor Lawrie must have wished he'd stayed at home as Hibs hammered in six, with strike sensation Joe Baker getting four and Johnstone and Baxter grabbing one apiece. An interested spectator in the stands that day was one Wilf Taylor, not a household name down Easter Road way, but a man who would have a very positive bearing on the playing future of Joe Baker. Taylor was in fact an England selector and cannot have failed to be impressed by Joe's performance.

On the Tuesday of that week a visitor arrived at Easter Road carrying a large picture of Hibs' 1902 Scottish Cup-winning team. James Hogg was a right back with the club at that time but missed the final due to a cartilage injury, though he was still awarded a medal having played in all the rounds up to the final. Needless to say, he was given a very warm welcome by all at the stadium.

Although the League Cup was still in full swing, the league campaign commenced on Wednesday 24 August and Hibs opened with a visit to newly promoted Dundee United at Tannadice. The Tangerines were in fine form as they recorded a 3–1 win against a disappointing Hibs, for whom Ormond scored a consolation goal. Not the best of starts in the league race and Hugh Shaw was quick in stressing to his players the need for greater effort and consistency.

On Saturday 27 August Willie Waddell brought his Kilmarnock side to Easter Road for a League Cup fixture. They went into that game leading the group with maximum points while Hibs sat second, two points adrift. By the end of the 90 minutes the positions were unchanged as goals from Baker and Fox were cancelled out by Black and a John Young own-goal for the visitors.

Hibs had qualified for the Inter Cities Fairs Cup and were eagerly awaiting news of the draw as they prepared to meet Dunfermline the following midweek. Eventually news filtered through that Hibs had been drawn to play the Swiss club Lausanne, with the first leg scheduled to be in Switzerland. Those fans who made the short trip to East End Park would have been wondering what the foray into Europe might bring as they watched a poor Hibs performance end in a 3–1 defeat and certain elimination from the later stages of the League Cup. The Pars scored through Ron Mailer (2) and George Peebles. Hibs' only consolation was a cracking strike from McLeod.

With a league match against Hearts looming it was disappointment once more for lacklustre Hibs as they finished a dismal League Cup campaign by going down tamely to Airdrie at Broomfield in another 3–1 reversal. Given that Hibs had hammered them 6–1 just a couple of weeks earlier it was quite a shock to see how easily Airdrie disposed of the green and whites on this occasion. Kinloch's goal was scant consolation as George Rankin, Jim Storrie and John Craven counted for the Diamonds. The only real plus from the game was that Jim Easton made his first-team debut and despite the result had a decent game.

Hearts came to Easter Road as reigning league champions and in recognition of that feat the match programme had a full-page picture of their victorious squad – which, if nothing else, proves that in the 1960s there was mutual respect even for derby matches. The previous season Hibs had earned a creditable draw at Tynecastle but had crashed 5–1 at Easter Road, and this time it wasn't a lot better as the Maroons ran out worthy 4–1 winners. Preston's solitary strike was more than cancelled out by Bowman, Murray, Young and Blackwood. It has to be said that our nearest neighbours were pretty awesome in those days and as well as being the current title holders they had also won the League Cup the previous season.

With the disappointment of that derby defeat still fresh in the mind, Hibs next travelled to Kilmarnock, this time for a league match, but once again they were to lose both points as Killie triumphed 3–2. That man Bertie Black scored again and his strike was added to by Kerr and Wentzel while Baker and McLeod found the target for Hibs. Consolation from the game came in the shape of a wonderful penalty save by keeper Willie Muirhead and a solid performance from John Young in defence after his return following an injury.

With Raith Rovers due up as the next opponents, Hibs would have to buck up their ideas after a poor start to their league campaign. Also, there was the small matter of a European tie on the near horizon. Whether the thought of that tie was in the minds of the players or not only they could say, but a truly dismal home performance brought a 1–0 defeat, Andy Matthew grabbing the points with a fine goal.

Seven days later things had gone from bad to worse as Hibs lost yet again, this time to Partick Thistle at Firhill. The hero for the Jags was Davie McParland, who scored a hat-trick. Hibs had to be content with a penalty strike from Kinloch. The pressure was now beginning to build on manager Hugh Shaw as the Hibees toiled to play anything like the kind of football the players were more than capable of, and there were very few happy faces in the crowd the following midweek when a 2–2 draw was all Hibs could manage against Second Division Cowdenbeath in the Penman Cup first round at Easter Road. A strong team had been selected, but goals from Fraser and McLeod provided scant consolation for the paying punters.

The following Saturday Hibs travelled to Muirton Park and lost tamely to St Johnstone by a score of 2–0 as a once reliable defence continued to lose sloppy goals and the forwards failed to take what few chances were being created. It was perhaps as well that due to circumstances outwith their control Lausanne scratched from the Inter Cities Fairs Cup and Hibs went through on a bye to the next round. The Swiss team apparently had players away on international duty and so felt unable to field a strong enough team. Had they looked at the league table in Scotland they may have run the risk of playing, even with a weakened side.

On Monday 10 October 1960 Hibs made the long trip south to face Swansea City in what was billed as a 'Floodlit Match' and gained themselves a 4–4 draw. The defence, it seemed, was still struggling but at least the forwards had found their shooting boots as Baker, Ormond and Eric Stevenson found the net, while a player rejoicing in the name of Nurse put the ball through his own goal. No doubt there were a few jokes made about a Nurse being required because Hibs were so out of sorts.

Back home in Edinburgh, Hibs prepared for the visit of Celtic to Easter Road, knowing that they would need to be at their best to stop the rot of six straight league defeats. It was not to be, as Hibs were trounced 6–0 in a very one-sided game with Bobby Carroll (2), Stevie Chalmers (2), Willie Fernie and Bertie Auld doing the damage. By this time the home support were losing their patience and loud booing was the order of the day as the players trooped off the park, their heads bowed.

With the Lausanne game cancelled, Hibs invited English First Division cracks Middlesbrough to Easter Road for one of those 'Floodlit' matches and suffered yet another defeat as the visitors ran out 4–2 winners. Scorers for Hibs on the night were Stevenson and Kinloch, while McLean, Henderson, Harris and a talented young striker by the name of Brian Clough were on target for the visitors. In his programme notes for the game, manager Hugh Shaw lamented the shocking result against Celtic and prayed for a return to fitness of those recognised first-team players who were on the sidelines. He offered his apologies to the fans and promised that things would get better very soon.

Three days later, the players had the chance to prove him right as they visited Airdrie at Broomfield. Back in August, in the League Cup, Hibs had thrashed Airdrie 6–1 in the home tie but contrived to lose the return

3–1, and it was lose again this time around as the home side triumphed by the odd goal in seven. Preston bagged two and Baker the other, but Sharkey (2), Caven and Duncan ensured that Hibs' miserable run continued.

Bizarrely, Joe Baker had been showing fine form when selected to represent England at both U23 and full team level but he had little chance to shine for Hibs around this time as goalscoring opportunities were at a premium.

Finally, on 29 October 1960, Hibs recorded their first league win of the season in beating St Mirren 4–3 at Easter Road. It had been a long time coming and though the match was tense from start to finish the home support went away happy having watched Kinloch grab a fine hat-trick and Ormond a single. The visitors' scorers were ex-Hibs player John Frye, Miller and Gerry Baker. It was only two points but it was a start and at least the sequence of losing league games was broken.

With the draw for the second round of the Inter Cities Fairs Cup pending, Hibs travelled north to face Dundee at Dens Park hoping they could gather another two much needed points. Gather them they did as they defeated the Dark Blues 1–0 in a very close game. Kinloch was again the scorer, but special mention to young Jim Easton who, along with Pat Hughes at the back, managed to keep Alan Gilzean quiet – no mean feat as the Dundee man was a hugely talented striker.

The following midweek brought the draw for the Inter Cities Fairs Cup and, boy, did Hibs strike it big when they were pulled out of the hat with the holders, Barcelona. With that draw in mind, Hugh Shaw immediately arranged for Hibs to meet the German side Bayern Munich who were in the UK touring. Imagine that scenario nowadays!

While there is no doubt the Hibs fans could hardly wait for a sight of Barcelona and the Hibs players most likely felt the same, there was the small matter of building on back-to-back league wins to consider when Ayr United visited Easter Road. At last Hibs seemed to have found some form and the Ayrshire side were beaten 3–1 in a game which was more one-sided than the scoreline suggests and in which Fraser stood out clearly as man of the match. Baker, Preston and Buchanan struck for Hibs while Fulton hit a consolation for the visitors.

Now that the corner appeared to have been turned league-wise, Hibs sent a largely reserve side to Central Park, Cowdenbeath, for the Penman Cup first-round replay and lost 1–0 on the night.

Aberdeen offered the next opposition in the league when they visited Easter Road in mid-November and left with a point in a cracking 2–2 draw. Kinloch got both Hibs goals, his second a beautiful diving header, taking his recent tally to six in four games. Brownlee bagged a brace for the Dons.

The following midweek saw Bayern Munich entertained in a 'Floodlit Match' and soundly beaten 3–0 in a fine Hibs performance, Baker, McLeod and Preston getting the goals. Sadly, Joe was injured and would miss the next match, but on the night it was a treat for the fans to watch Hibs beating such high-class opposition. It was also a good exercise for the players ahead of the Barcelona clash.

The next game brought Hibs back down to earth with an enormous bump as they were thrashed four goals to one by Motherwell at Fir Park. True, they had no Baker in the team but they never really got going against the Steelmen, who were both pacy and determined in their approach. A Pat Quinn hat-trick and a single from Weir placed the strike from Buchanan very firmly in the consolation goal bracket.

A week later Hibs were back at Easter Road where they faced and defeated a stubborn Dunfermline by a 2–1 scoreline. Kinloch and Buchanan struck the decisive goals, but special mention must be made of defenders John Fraser and Jim Easton, who were immense throughout. Dunfermline lost defender Jim Stevenson, who broke his leg in unfortunate circumstances, and so Alex Smith's goal was of little consolation to the Fifers. Smith, of course, went on to manage successfully in the Scottish League, most notably with Aberdeen.

On the following Monday the draw was made for the Scottish Cup and Hibs pulled a tough tie away to Clyde – though most fans were of the view that given the ongoing lack of success in that tournament it was pretty pointless worrying about who the opponents might be. That week saw the players training hard for the visit of Rangers and the tie the following midweek against Barcelona. Sadly, Hibs went down 2–1 to the Gers, despite Ronnie Simpson pulling off a tremendous penalty save, while Sammy Baird netted for Hibs from the spot at the other end. Rangers were just too strong over the piece and took the points with goals from Wilson and Brand.

At last the big day had arrived – Spanish champions and European and Inter Cities Fairs Cup holders Barcelona would grace the Easter Road turf on Wednesday 14 December 1960 – or would they? You can't legislate for the weather in Scotland and the match was postponed when a thick fog enveloped Easter Road. The effect of this postponement was that Hibs would now travel to Spain for what would have been the second leg and the Spanish would return to Leith at a later date to conclude the tie.

Meantime Hibs resumed league business with a tricky trip to Shawfield. Kinloch was out injured, but Baker was back in the fold and among the scorers, McLeod and Baird getting the others. Clyde countered through Colrain (2) and Steel. The 3–3 draw was a fair result on the day.

With Third Lanark due to visit Easter Road on Christmas Eve 1960, it was a subdued Hibs support which received the news that the postponed

Barcelona game would not now be played until the following February, due to the many commitments of the Spanish side. Whatever doldrums the fans were in were soon dispersed as Hibs and Third Lanark dished up a 12-goal Christmas cracker of a match, the home side winning 8–4. Top man Baker notched no fewer than five goals while Baxter, sporting six stitches in a head wound but still insisting on playing out the game, nabbed two with Scott getting the other. Thirds counted through Goodfellow (2), Hilley and Gray. It was certainly a contrasting day for both goalkeepers, what with Jocky Robertson losing eight and Ronnie Simpson saving two penalties.

Eight goals seemed like good preparation for any game, but would it breed enough confidence to cope with the might of Barcelona? We were about to find out as Hibs flew out to Spain on the Monday following their win over Thirds. Only 13 players travelled and they would have only one night in the Spanish city before facing their hosts at the world famous Camp Nou Stadium.

Tuesday 27 December 1960 proved to be a day which would live long in the memories of Hibernian fans as their heroes took a 4–4 draw with the giants of Spanish football. Indeed, Hibs had led 2–0 and then later 4–2 with only six minutes left, but their hosts grabbed a late double to keep themselves in the tie. The Hibs goalscoring heroes that night were Baker (2), McLeod and Preston, but the whole team gave a marvellous performance of pacy, attacking football which had the Scottish newspapers lavishing praise upon the men in green.

'Hibs struck a glorious blow for Scottish prestige in putting on a dazzling exhibition and the first hour was unbelievable. It was like the Hibernian team of the 1948 era' proclaimed the Scottish Daily Mail.

Not to be outdone, the Daily Record enthused: 'Eleven Hibs heroes gave Scottish football its greatest ever boost and the Easter Road miracle men were close to bringing off the football story of the century. Hibs were magnificent, every man of them.'

It truly was a wonderful Christmas that year!

Back in Scotland, the players had to set aside the euphoria of their great result so as to concentrate on improving their poor league position and they did just that on the last day of the year by defeating Dundee United 2–0 at Easter Road. Scott and Baxter scored the important goals in a stuffy match with little to warm the fans on a cold afternoon.

Two days later Hibs faced Hearts at Tynecastle and continued their good run of form by winning 2–1 in front of around 43,000 fans. It was not a game for the football purist, but every player on the field at least gave their all and on the balance of play the better team won. Baxter, who started the game wearing a skullcap to protect his recent head wound, was outstanding as were goalscorers Scott and McLeod. But the man of the match award justifiably went to Hibs' keeper Ronnie Simpson, who produced three magnificent saves in open play and then saved a penalty from Ian Crawford. Remarkably, that was Simpson's sixth penalty save of the season. The two points were very welcome as was the satisfying feeling of avenging the earlier defeat by Hearts at Easter Road.

Kilmarnock offered the next challenge to Hibs' recovery in league form and when they came to Easter Road on 7 January they were quite simply swept aside by a team playing free-flowing, attacking football. McLeod (2), a McClelland rocket shot from just inside the penalty area and a quite wonderful solo effort from Baker put Hibs on easy street in a hugely merited 4–0 victory.

After the exertions of their festive period glut of fixtures the Hibs players enjoyed a 'normal' week leading up to their tricky away fixture at Stark's Park. Raith Rovers were competing well in the league and it took a couple of pieces of Baker magic to win the points when the young number nine scored twice in a three-minute spell, knocking all of the fight out of the home side in the process. That took Joe to 18 for the season, and there would be a lot more to come.

I mentioned earlier how much the use of language has changed in a relatively short period of time and the official programme for the visit of Partick Thistle the following Saturday offered a fine example of this. Under the heading *'Dance was Gay Affair'* there appeared a story that the club had held its annual dinner dance at the North British Hotel, where players and officials alike had enjoyed *'the usual gay affair'*. Somehow I don't see that headline being dusted down for use anytime soon! Star of the evening was keeper Ronnie Simpson, described by his team-mates as Easter Road's answer to debonair dancer and actor Fred Astaire.

As to the game itself, Partick offered up their usual stuffy resistance in gaining a creditable 1–1 draw, Scott striking for Hibs and Closs for the Jags. Interestingly, a young lad named Joe McBride played at centre forward for Thistle that day. Joe would go on, in time, to make his mark at Easter Road where he became a fans' favourite almost from the day he arrived.

It was Scottish Cup time again and Hibs travelled west to face Clyde at Shawfield, knowing they would have to be at their best to progress into the next round. In a sometimes bruising affair the Bully Wee were unlucky to lose their goalkeeper to injury after just 35 minutes, and goals from McLeod and Baker sealed a victory for the visitors. Once again, Simpson was outstanding, saving twice in the early minutes and performing well throughout. McLeod was continuing a good run of form that had seen him star for the Scottish League the previous midweek and which had many commentators calling for him to be capped at full international level.

February 1961 should have started for Hibs with a visit from St Johnstone, but snow made the Easter Road pitch unplayable until the following midweek. When the teams finally met on the Wednesday evening the Hibees never quite hit the form expected of them but still had enough in the locker to run out 3–1 winners, thanks to goals from Baxter, Baird and Ormond. Saints struck through a penalty from Carr, the first to beat Simpson from the spot that season.

A few days later Hibs were at home in the second round of the Scottish Cup, their opponents being Peebles Rovers. The Rovers had disposed of Gala Fairydean in the previous round and arrived in Leith with two former Hibs players in their number – Renwick Sanderson, a striker who had notched a quite remarkable 520 goals in his career to date and nine hat-tricks this season alone, and Walter McWilliams at inside left. It was McWilliams who found the net for the visitors but Hibs went on to score no fewer than 15 goals that afternoon. Baker got an incredible triple hat-trick, Ormond (2), Baxter (2), McLeod and Baird got the others. That same day, in order to get as many players as possible match fit in view of the forthcoming game against Barcelona, a young Hibs team travelled to Stirling and went down 3–2 to Albion, Eric Stevenson and Tommy McDonald scoring for the green and whites.

The weekend before the return Inter Cities Fairs Cup tie, Hibs visited Parkhead and rather disappointingly went down 2–0 to an in-form Celtic. Hibs were hampered early on by an injury to Grant, who tore a muscle, but in truth they were always second best to a hungry home side. Not the best of preparations for such an important game, and poor John Grant would be a definite absentee just to make life that little bit more difficult for Hibs.

If Tuesday 27 December 1960 was a proud date in the history of Hibernian Football Club then Wednesday 22 February 1961 surpassed even that as mighty Barcelona were defeated 3–2, meaning that Hibs would progress on a 7–6 aggregate. In a quite stormy affair, which at one point had referee Herr Malka of Germany seeking police protection from the angry Barcelona players, Baker and Preston had scored for Hibs while the Paraguayan centre forward Eulogio Martinez and Hungarian star Sandor Kocsis had countered for Barcelona, leaving the sides level as the game entered its last few minutes. At this point, Herr Malka awarded a penalty kick to Hibs and the incensed Barcelona players chased the official around the pitch. Some minutes passed while Herr Malka attempted to restore order and meanwhile Bobby Kinloch stood patiently waiting to take the kick. Finally, with order restored, Kinloch coolly slammed the ball home to send the Hibs fans into raptures and the Barcelona players into a rage. As the final whistle approached Herr Malka positioned himself near the players' tunnel, blew for time and then sprinted towards his dressing room. Against all the odds the greens had reached the semi-finals with what was a magnificent result and once again the Scottish press sang the praises of Hibernian's heroes.

'Hibs were more than worthy winners and the deplorable incidents late in the game should not be allowed to push into the background what was a truly wonderful display by Hibs. There was no greater star than Joe Baker who outshone by far every one of the high priced Barcelona forwards', reported the *Scottish Daily Express.*

'Hibs can once again take their stance in world football' – *The Scottish Daily Mail*

'Floodlight the Castle, fire a 21 gun salute for Hibs' never say die heroes who gave Scottish football its greatest boost in years' – *The Evening Dispatch*

'A magnificently achieved victory in which every Easter Road man gave wholeheartedly of his best' – *The Daily Record*

The Hibee heroes that night were Ronnie Simpson, John Fraser, Joe McClelland, John Baxter, Jim Easton, Sammy Baird, Johnny McLeod, Tommy Preston, Joe Baker, Bobby Kinloch and Willie Ormond.

It was back to domestic duties the following weekend and a Scottish Cup third-round tie against Hamilton at Douglas Park. The Second Division team were no match for the conquerors of Barcelona and a Kinloch double plus single strikes from McLeod and Baker saw the Hibees into round four.

After just a couple of days' rest Hibs were in action again on the Monday night when Airdrie came to Easter Road on league business and went home with a point after securing a 3–3 draw against a weary-looking Hibs. Once again Kinloch scored a brace, one from the penalty spot, and Baker got the other. Storrie, Caven and Duncan bagged goals for the Diamonds.

The Scottish Cup draw paired Hibs with Celtic at Parkhead, but before that tie could be played the Easter Road men travelled to Paisley, where St Mirren edged them out by a 2–1 scoreline at Love Street. Bryceland and McFadzean scored for the Buddies while Baker struck for Hibs.

The Scottish Cup had eluded Hibs for decades and the green and whites hoped to rectify that by going to Glasgow and knocking Celtic out in the fourth round. A 1–1 draw, thanks to goals by Chalmers for the Celts and the in-form Kinloch for Hibs, ensured a replay the following midweek. Astonishingly, it would be Celtic's first visit to Easter Road on cup duty for

54 years and it took an extra-time goal from John Clark to ensure their passage into the semi-final for a showdown with Airdrie. It was a pulsating cup tie, and the general consensus was that Hibs were unlucky to lose out, but the fans were used to hard luck tales in that particular competition.

At least Hibs were still in Europe and a plum tie against crack Italian side Roma awaited, but the business of climbing the league came first as the green and whites travelled through to Somerset Park and defeated Ayr United 1–0, thanks to a McLeod strike.

The following Monday, Dundee came to Easter Road looking to leapfrog Hibs in the table but in a tight game the home side, with young Joe Davin in the number four jersey, secured both points thanks to a Baker effort and some heroic goalkeeping by Simpson. The Dens Park outfit had some promising players, and some would go on to make a name for themselves in the game in the years ahead. Ian Ure at centre half secured a big-money transfer to Arsenal, where he starred for many years; Alan Cousin would go on to play for Hibs; Alan Gilzean made his name with Spurs and Bobby Seith would go on to manage Hearts, a job he held in January 1973 when the greens would humble their near neighbours in a devastating display of football resulting in a 7–0 win at Tynecastle.

Next up for Hibs was the long journey north to meet Aberdeen at Pittodrie, where they would face an Aberdeen side just one point behind them in the league. Hibs went into the game in sixth place and the Dons in eighth, but in a somewhat one-sided affair it was the visitors who took both points with an impressive 4–1 win. In fact Hibs scored all of their goals before half-time, Baker (2), Scott and McLeod being the marksmen. Easing off in the second-half allowed Aberdeen a glimmer of hope, but Simpson was again in fine form and the home team's only consolation came from a good goal by Coutts.

The East of Scotland Shield brought a welcome diversion from the pressures of league football when Hearts came to Easter Road on Wednesday 29 March 1961. With Hearts struggling in the league and the last four meetings in this competition going in favour of Hibs, the visitors certainly had it all to do. In a quite thrilling game Hibs raced into a four-goal lead and then eased off, allowing Hearts to strike two back in reply. The first Hibs goal was a 25-yard belter from Baxter and then Baker brilliantly dribbled past three defenders before slotting the second. Stevenson bagged number three. Then Baker lobbed the ball over Marshall in the Hearts goal, ran round him and walked it into the net for number four. Joe also missed a penalty, otherwise Hibs may have gone nap on the night. As it was, Bauld and Crawford gave the scoreline a more respectable look for the visitors. Interestingly the Hibs legend and former Famous Five member Gordon Smith played at outside right for Hearts that night.

The weekend brought league duty back to the fore with a visit from Motherwell, who were tucked nicely into third place behind Rangers and Kilmarnock but a huge 11 points behind the Ibrox outfit. In the 'Well team that day were Willie Hunter and Pat Quinn, both of whom would join Hibs later in their careers, and Morris Stevenson, a former Easter Road player. In a fast-flowing end-to-end game a brace from Baker earned both points in a 2–1 win and enhanced Hibs' chances of European football the following season.

Hibs had two more league games to play before Roma arrived for the first leg of the Inter Cities Fairs Cup semi-final and the first of those ended in a disappointing 4–2 defeat away to Dunfermline. Goals from Baker and Baxter were not enough on the night and it was a disappointed Hibs support which travelled home from Fife that evening. Another away match followed and in a close affair at Ibrox the Hibees were decidedly unlucky to lose 1–0 having failed to capitalise on the few chances they created.

At last the glamour of European football arrived again in Edinburgh. Having disposed of the Spanish League leaders, could Hibs now beat one of the top teams from Italy? In a pulsating match played in front of a very noisy home crowd the final score was 2–2, Baker and McLeod scoring for the Hibees. With the winners of the other semi-final being either Birmingham City or Inter Milan, there was the possibility of an all-British or all-Italian final, but it would surely be a monumental task for Hibs to qualify now.

Prior to the second leg, Hibs had their final home game of the season against lowly Clyde and duly disposed of them 4–0 with the goals shared by Scott, Stevenson, Baker and Baxter. Thankfully, Hibs had found their shooting boots and took their goalscoring form to Rome, where they performed heroically in a 3–3 draw with Roma. In later years, such a result would have taken Hibs into the final on the away goals rule, but in this year's tournament it meant a deciding game would have to be played. The venue was decided on the toss of a coin, but there are stories in Hibs folklore which suggest that Hibs were prepared to give up the chance of a game in Edinburgh for a financial reward. Whatever the method of deciding the venue, it proved to be Rome.

A weary Hibs party returned to Edinburgh knowing there would be just one league game left to play, against Third Lanark at Cathkin Park. Whether the rigours of their journey caused heavy legs or whether Hibs were just poor on the day we will never know, but the home side dished out a 6–1 thrashing, only McLeod gaining any satisfaction from the tie, courtesy of his goal.

That win by Third Lanark ensured they would finish third in the league behind champions Rangers and runners-up Kilmarnock. Hibs meanwhile finished eighth while Clyde and Ayr United were relegated. The Hibs reserve side managed a very creditable fourth-place finish in their league, which offered encouragement that some good youngsters were pressing for promotion to the first team in the season to come.

Of course Hibs' season was not yet over as they had to return to Rome for that cup decider. Without having played in a month, the under-prepared Hibs team were trounced 6–0 on 27 May 1961, bringing to a close a season full of mixed fortunes. A historic win over Barcelona, a semi-final place in a European tournament again and a nine-goal display by Joe Baker were all highlights. Scottish Cup defeat by Celtic and an atrocious start to the league campaign were best forgotten.

In terms of goals scored, Baker notched an astonishing 48 in all competitions, with Kinloch bagging 18 and McLeod 17. Baker had 52 starts, making his goals haul all the more remarkable, while McLeod topped the appearances chart with 54 in all competitions. Overall, the first team scored 128 goals in all competitions and conceded 112.

Chapter Sixteen

1961/62

BAKER OUT, BAKER IN

In the summer months of 1961 Hibs fans were, as ever, looking forward eagerly to the new season which brought not only the league race and the chance to play for two domestic cup trophies but also the opportunity to once again savour the delights of European football. Could the greens go one better than last season and reach a European final? Surely they must have been in with a shout as they had a good squad of players, and if the defence could do its job they were always going to get goals with the Baker boy leading the line.

Imagine the shock, then, of learning that Joe Baker, scorer of no fewer than 48 goals in season 1960/61, had been transferred to Italian side Torino. The fans were both angry and upset that their goalscoring hero had been allowed to leave. In an effort to appease them, manager Hugh Shaw wrote in the first home programme of the season that Joe, along with Johnny McLeod, who left for Arsenal, had wanted to leave and despite the best efforts of the club to keep them both players were now away from Easter Road. In later years we would learn from Joe himself that he had no desire to leave Hibs and that he was not only told that his request for a wage rise of £5.00 per week was being turned down but that the club had also accepted an offer for him from Torino for his transfer.

As ever, the season started with the League Cup being played on a sectional basis and Hibs were drawn in a group alongside St Johnstone, Celtic and Partick Thistle. The opening game for Hibs took them to Muirton Park, Perth, where they fought out a 1–1 draw with St Johnstone, John Baxter striking the Hibs goal with Gardiner scoring for the home side. On the left wing that day was new signing Ally McLeod, who had joined the club in the close season from Blackburn Rovers, having previously played for Third Lanark and St Mirren. Ally would go on to leave an indelible mark on the history of the game in Scotland as he managed Ayr United, Aberdeen and, of course, the national side which qualified for the 1978 World Cup finals in Argentina.

The following midweek Partick Thistle came to Easter Road and proved to be very stubborn in defence as the Hibees found wave after wave of attacks being repelled. Eventually they were worn down with Eric Stevenson's double winning the points, although Alex Wright struck for the Jags. The match programme that day informed the fans that Hibs had been drawn to meet Portuguese cracks Belenenses of Lisbon in the Inter Cities Fairs Cup, with the first game at Easter Road. The competition had 28 teams involved and these were divided into four sections, Hibs sharing a section with Belenenses, Birmingham City, Basle of Switzerland, Red Star Belgrade of Yugoslavia, Hanover of Germany and Espanol of Spain. Interestingly, Hearts were also in this tournament and their first-round opponents would be Union St Gilloise of Belgium.

The weekend brought Celtic to Easter Road. The visitors were a point behind Hibs in the group, having beaten Partick Thistle but losing to St Johnstone. In a game which could have gone either way it looked as though the visitors might triumph after scoring through Hughes and Chalmers, but Hibs were dogged in their determination not to lose and Tommy Preston's double earned a point. An interested spectator in the directors' box was none other than Joe Baker.

Preston's first goal in that game was a superb left-foot strike and the second came from a header after Stevenson had set him up. Hibs fans found out in the match programme that the centre stand would be all-ticket for the forthcoming Belenenses tie with briefs costing 7s 6d (32.5p), while entry to the wing stands would be 5s (25p), the enclosure 4s (20p) and the terracing 3s (15p). Prior to attending the game, fans were invited to try the hospitality provided in Lawrie Reilly's Bar in Mitchell Street, the Safari Lounge (Station Bar), Cadzow Place, or The Olde Football Arms, which stood on the corner of Thorntree Street and Easter Road. Younger fans and teetotallers were invited to call in 'for a quick snack' at The Tiffin in Easter Road.

Although only half-way through the section matches in the League Cup the league now commenced and Hibs had the 'pleasure' of travelling through to Glasgow on Wednesday 23 August and opening their campaign at Ibrox. They started really well but, after losing the first goal, dropped out of the game and suffered a 3–0 defeat, Brand getting a double, one a penalty, and Wilson the other.

Back at Easter Road on the Saturday Hibs welcomed St Johnstone in the League Cup and comprehensively defeated them 4–1. Davie Gibson, Bobby Kinloch, Stevenson and McLeod were on target while the Saints countered through Gardiner. It was a good performance by the Hibees and things were beginning to gel nicely with the European tie looming. On the downside, poor Jim Easton was carried off after clashing heads with Gardiner and later needed six stitches in a head wound.

Ahead of that tie Hibs had two further League Cup ties to play, the first involving a trip to Firhill where Partick Thistle handed out a 2–1 defeat in a dull affair of a game where McLeod's goal was cancelled out with interest by Ewing and Williamson. A feature of that game was the outstanding display of Ronnie Simpson in goals. The other tie also had Hibs in Glasgow; this time at Parkhead where once again they went down 2–1 after Divers struck a double which made Gibson's goal merely a consolation.

Those back-to-back defeats were hardly the best preparation for the match on Monday 4 September 1961 when Belenenses provided Hibs with a stern test of their resolve. The visitors had a decent pedigree having in previous years defeated the likes of Barcelona, Stade Reims, Newcastle, St Etienne, Valencia and Seville, and so Hibs would have to be at their very best. In what turned out to be another of those magical European nights under the floodlights at Easter Road both sides gave their all in a fast, exciting game which flowed from end-to-end and finished up as a 3–3 draw. The visitors had stunned the home support with goals from Matateu (2) and Yauca, but in a brilliant fightback John Fraser bagged a brace and Sammy Baird was as cool as a cucumber in slotting home a late penalty to ensure a share of the spoils.

With that first leg tie out of the way it was back to league business for Hibs the following Saturday as Raith Rovers visited Easter Road. Hibs had suffered a spate of injuries to key players and the fact that schoolboy signing Tony McGlynn was named at inside left highlighted the lack of any depth in the playing pool. To his credit, McGlynn did not allow the occasion to overwhelm him and indeed he opened the scoring for Hibs, who went on to win the game 3–2 after Fraser and Stevenson also found the target. The Rovers scored through McNamee and ex-Hibee Des Fox, but it was never really that close a game.

A week later it was derby day in Edinburgh and Hibs were still struggling with players out injured. Pat Hughes, another youngster drafted in of late, continued in the right-back berth while Brian Marjoribanks found himself at centre forward. Again the youngsters did well, Marjoribanks striking a cracking first-half equaliser but although McLeod also found the net for Hibs it was not enough on the day as Hearts scored four through Hamilton (2), Ross and an own goal from the unlucky Jim Easton.

Hibs' last game before the return Inter Cities tie in Portugal brought Kilmarnock to Easter Road in what would be a stern test for the hosts. Under Willie Waddell, Killie had become a real force in Scottish football. In what proved to be a cracking 90 minutes Hibs came out on top 3–2 thanks to goals from Stevenson, McLeod and John Baxter, the visitors striking via Mason and McInally. It was the perfect preparation for Hibs before they jetted out the following Monday to Lisbon. Anyone reading the programme at the Killie game would have seen that win, lose or draw in Portugal, Hibs were guaranteed to face another top continental side in the weeks ahead as Joe Baker's Torino had agreed to play a friendly at Easter Road in mid-October.

Although things could have been going better on the home front, Hibs still managed to produce one of the best performances seen of them in a long while when they took on Belenenses at a packed Restello Stadium and defeated them 3–1. Hibs opened the scoring through Baxter and as the Portuguese outfit got more and more frustrated the game became more physical. The Hibs players showed remarkable restraint at times and stuck to the task of playing football, allowing Baxter to score a second and Stevenson a third. Matateu had scored for the home side, but Hibs ran out 6–4 winners on aggregate and progressed to the next round.

Back home in Edinburgh, Hibs fans were enjoying the thought of another European adventure in the offing and they were joined by Hearts fans, who had witnessed their heroes easily dispose of their Belgian opponents in a 5–1 aggregate win. These were happy days indeed for the Edinburgh sides, with both making good progress in European competition.

It was back to earth with a bump on the Saturday for Hibs as they met Dundee United at Tannadice. In a frighteningly one-sided game, United pulverised the Hibs defence and ran out worthy 4–0 winners with goals from Carlyle (2), Irvine and Mochan. A week later saw Falkirk visit Easter Road for another game with four goals scored, only this time it was two for each side. Jekyll and Hyde Hibs looked devastating at times and scored two very fine goals through Jim Scott and Sammy Baird only to then become anxious in their play and concede a double to ex-Hibs and Famous Five legend Willie Ormond.

League points, or rather the lack of them, were beginning to cause some concern and so when another vital point was dropped the following Saturday, when Hibs drew 2–2 with Airdrie, there were rumblings among the support that something had to change for the better. Manager Hugh Shaw was quick to point out in his programme notes that 'quick improvement' was required and offered a brilliant piece of insight in suggesting that points were being lost 'because we are not scoring as many goals as we are conceding'. The two conceded against Airdrie came when Storrie easily sidestepped his marker. Hibs countered through a Brown own goal and Sammy Baird. Poor John Grant collided with Ronnie Simpson in trying to halt an Airdrie attack and ended up with two fractured ribs which didn't help the Hibs cause at all.

On the Monday following the Airdrie game, Joe Baker's Torino arrived at Easter Road to play in the friendly arranged as part of the deal which took the Baker Boy to Italy. The visitors were sitting second-top of their league and included several internationals in their line-up including, of course, Baker and one Denis Law, so it was a highly creditable outcome when Hibs defeated them 2–0 with goals from Fraser and Baxter. Best for Hibs on the night were Simpson, who made several vital saves, Easton, who kept Joe Baker on a tight leash, and Stevenson, who tormented the Italian defence throughout the game.

These friendlies were all well and good, providing entertainment and the opportunity to see players from other countries, but they did nothing to help Hibs gain much needed league points and when Partick Thistle next hammered the Hibees 4–1, alarm bells were ringing loudly down Easter Road way. With Baird and Baxter suffering a form slump, the Jags broke through at will and but for Simpson the defeat could have been much heavier. As it was, McParland, Duffy, Smith and Williamson all found the net with only McLeod scoring for Hibs. While it was true that Hibs had injury problems and couldn't always play their strongest team they were not the only club in that position and yet seemed to be toiling more than most. That fact was underlined when the next home game ended in a 3–1 defeat by Third Lanark. The visitors were lying fifth, but it was more the manner of the defeat which was worrying as Hibs created very few chances and scored only thanks to a Kinloch penalty.

The league form was hardly ideal preparation for an Inter Cities Fairs Cup tie in Belgrade. Although Hibs gave a decent account of themselves on the night they still crashed 4–0 and had Easton sent off five minutes from the end, referee Herr Seipert of Austria the culprit in spoiling the young centre half's spotless disciplinary record. Amazingly, for a defender, Easton had not even had a booking in his career before that night and the fact that he was kicked and punched by a Red Star player following the tackle which led to his dismissal was shamefully ignored by the referee. Needless to say, the offending Belgrade player went unpunished. It should be pointed out that Hibs' trip to reach the venue was a nightmare, taking 30 hours when ten was the expected duration. Fog, flight delays and a 4.30am start on the day of the match didn't help, but it would need a miracle for Hibs to claw back this tie in the second leg.

Struggling Aberdeen were Hibs' next opponents and the game at Easter Road would go some way to determining which club might continue its struggle at the wrong end of the league. After a gruelling 90 minutes there was no winner as the sides shared the points in a 1–1 draw, with McLeod on target for Hibs and Callaghan striking for the Dons. It was poor fare and the supporters were getting mightily fed up with watching a Hibs side struggling so badly, week in and week out.

Seven days later Hibs were trounced 5–1 at Fir Park, Motherwell, a result which proved to be the final nail in the coffin for manager Hugh Shaw, who then parted company with the club. Hibs were dismal that day and though Preston scored a peach of a goal they were never at the races as Delaney (3), McPhee and Quinn rifled five past poor Ronnie Simpson. In fact, had it not been for Simpson the score could well have been seven or eight, but he had a series of magnificent saves during a torrid encounter.

The following midweek, managerless Hibs entertained Red Star Belgrade in their return Inter Cities tie and slumped to an uninspired 1–0 defeat, meaning they'd lost 5–0 on aggregate. Belgrade were a decent outfit but the Hibs fans expected so much more from their team which had, after all, beaten the mighty Barcelona just a few months before. Edinburgh's interest in European competition took another blow when Hearts lost, also on a 5–0 aggregate, to Inter Milan. A new Hibs manager with a proven track record was needed and fast, not to mention some new blood in the team.

It would be the new blood which arrived first as a story swept through Edinburgh that Hibs had signed Baker. The story was totally accurate, but rather than the return of the idolised Joe it would be his brother Gerry who had been snapped up from Manchester City. In a way, Gerry lived in the shadow of his brother, certainly as far as the Hibs fans were concerned, but that was more than a little unfair because Gerry was a fine footballer in his own right. On Chelsea's books as a schoolboy, he returned north and signed for Motherwell before moving on to St Mirren, where he enjoyed goal scoring success before heading south again to join Manchester City. Brother Joe won many headlines for scoring nine goals in one game when Hibs defeated Peebles Rovers in a Scottish Cup tie, but Gerry actually went one better in that same competition, netting ten against Glasgow University.

With the 'new boy' in the side and making his debut, Hibs travelled to Muirton Park, Perth, on Saturday 18 November 1961 and took both points in a fine 2–0 win over St Johnstone, with Baker having a hand in the goals scored by Stevenson and Fraser. Hibs had to play with just ten men for a while when Kinloch was knocked out just before the half-time whistle. He was able to resume after treatment and Hibs were worthy winners on the day.

The joy of victory was short-lived as Hibs crashed at home again just seven days later when Dundee took the points in a deserved 3–1 win. Stevenson struck for Hibs while Gilzean, Penman and a certain Gordon Smith struck for the visitors. The irony of that Smith goal was there for all to see as the man cruelly discarded by Hibs came back to Easter Road at 37 years of age and ran the show. Although in opposition colours, Smith was applauded both on to and off the park by a Hibs support which had been so dismayed to see him go a few years earlier.

As the search for a manager continued, Hibs were still struggling to find consistency but had a good day in Paisley when they defeated St Mirren 3–2 at the start of December. Fraser, Gibson and Baker secured the points, although the Buddies fought to the end with goals from Kerrigan, who would later join Hearts, and a Clunie penalty running Hibs close.

The first round of the Scottish Cup was pending and ahead of that fixture, which would involve a tricky tie away to Partick Thistle, Hibs finally unveiled their new manager. There were more than a few stunned expressions from both within the game and on the terraces when Walter Galbraith was appointed. A Douglas Fairbanks look-alike, Galbraith was plucked from the relative obscurity of Tranmere Rovers and had previously managed both Accrington Stanley and Bradford. His was not a household name in his country of birth, though he had played professionally in Scotland with Clyde. In all truth, very few Hibs fans had even heard of him. Time would tell whether Galbraith was up to the task and his first job was to try and steer Hibs into the next round of the cup. Just 90 seconds prevented Galbraith from getting off to a winning start as despite losing a first-minute goal to Ewing, Hibs struck twice through Baker and it was very late in the game when Duffy equalised to force a replay.

Three days after the cup tie, Hibs were back in Glasgow and facing Celtic at Parkhead. In what was universally accepted as the game of the season, the sides shared seven goals, Hibs twice leading through Duncan Falconer and Eric Stevenson only for Celtic to score three. Hibs were not beaten yet and Falconer scored to level, but minutes later Divers hammered home his third and Celtic's fourth to win the points. Celtic's other goal was scored by Hughes, but the general consensus of the press was that Hibs were extremely unlucky to lose on the day – some things never change.

Hibs' next scheduled match was the cup replay against Partick Thistle at Easter Road, but a thick fog lay over the ground for most of the afternoon and evening so postponement was the only real option. That meant that manager Walter Galbraith's home debut was against Dunfermline, who arrived as Scottish Cup holders and with good recent league form. Unfortunately for Galbraith, it was not a winning start and the hosts went down 2–1, young Duncan Falconer striking for Hibs while Dickson and ex-Hibee Tommy McDonald counted for the Pars.

Another attempt to replay the cup tie followed, but this time heavy snow caused further postponement in what was turning out to be quite a saga in determining whether Hibs or Partick Thistle would go through to meet Stirling Albion in the second round. By coincidence, Stirling Albion provided Hibs' last competitive match of 1961 when the green and whites travelled to Annfield and returned with both points in a hard-fought game which saw Falconer again on the mark. There was snow on the park, but the referee declared the surface playable and instructed the lines be cleared. Unfortunately, Easton suffered a quite nasty injury in damaging ankle ligaments and he would be sorely missed in the weeks ahead.

Snow was once again in evidence on New Year's Day 1962 and the Edinburgh derby scheduled for Easter Road was postponed as a result. Twenty-four hours later, however, Hibs were back in action at Stark's Park, which had a sprinkling of snow and a few icy patches but passed inspection. This time victory over Raith Rovers was achieved without injury to any players, while Stevenson and Gibson mastered the conditions sufficiently to find the target. Although not ideal conditions for the taller, heavier players in the team, both Preston and Young gave particularly impressive performances.

The hectic holiday fixture list brought Rangers to Easter Road just four days later, but there was little by way of sparkle in this game as the sides fought out a 0–0 draw. Bright spots included the fact that it was the third game in a row without conceding a goal, and Rangers had been scoring freely until that day, but Hibs fans had been raised on watching attacking football, a commodity short on display under the new manager so far. While trying hard to focus on the play there must have been a temptation to read the match programme during the duller periods and in doing so you would have been invited to take any train, any day, to Glasgow for just 10/6 (52.5p) or perhaps 9/- (45p) to Motherwell – though quite why you'd want to only British Rail might know!

At long last the cup replay with Partick Thistle got the go-ahead on Wednesday 10 January 1962, but it would end in disappointment as the recently improved defensive record took a knock with the loss of three goals to a Joe McBride penalty and further goals from Ewing and Smith. Fraser scored two beauties for Hibs, but the cup dream was over once again, extending the barren spell to 60 years. To be fair, Thistle were a good outfit and in league terms were second behind Dundee, while Hibs were well off the pace in tenth, having scored just 29 goals for the loss of 43. For once, league form followed the teams into this cup tie and when Falconer was carried off injured any hope of progression in the tournament went with him.

Three days later those defensive frailties reared their ugly head again as Hibs shipped four goals to Kilmarnock at Rugby Park. An own-goal and a Baker strike were not enough as Kerr (2), Yard and McIlroy beat Simpson in the Hibs goal. Strangely, Hibs could and should have won the game and had Gibson's penalty found the net early in the second-half things might have turned out quite differently as the Hibees played very well on the day.

The rearranged New Year's Day derby was next up and it was painful to watch as Hibs, without a home win since September 1961, continued

that appalling run in going down heavily to Hearts by 4–1. This win gave
Hearts their sixth consecutive derby victory at Easter Road and the fans
were far from happy at the outcome. A mini fightback, prompted by a
Gibson goal when the Hearts were 2–0 up, was thwarted by another two
for the Gorgie men, who counted through 17-year-old schoolboy forward
Alan Gordon, Wallace and Bauld. Of the Hearts scorers, Gordon would
one day become a Turnbull's Tornado, Wallace a European Cup winner
with Celtic and Bauld a Hearts legend, so if there's consolation in defeat
at least it was to a very good Hearts team.

An early opportunity to win back the fans' favour came just a few days
later when Dundee United visited Easter Road on league business and the
opportunity was taken as Hibs triumphed 3–2 with a bright performance
of attacking football. With Easton and his replacement, John Young,
both out injured, the number five jersey was handed to young Pat Hughes
and he had a solid game at the back as Hibs scored with a Baker double
and a single from Stevenson. United countered through Irvine and
Carlyle, but Hibs' superiority for long periods in the game was not
reflected in the closeness of the final score.

With the Scottish Cup just a dream again, Hibs filled their blank
Saturday by inviting Bolton Wanderers to play a friendly at Easter Road,
continuing a long-running tradition of friendlies between the two sides. In
a keenly contested match Hibs ran out 2–0 winners thanks to a smart
double from Baker. The win seemed to have a positive effect on morale as
a week later the Hibees travelled to Brockville and destroyed Falkirk 4–1
with a breathtaking display of attacking football. This was more like the
Hibs we all know and love, with Falconer (2), Baker and Kinloch on
target for Hibs while the Bairns took consolation from a Sammy Reid
strike. The goal from Kinloch was a thing of beauty as he met a dropping
ball on the full volley and crashed it past Willie Whigham in the Falkirk
goal. Playing for Falkirk that day were John Lambie and Willie Ormond,
both men with strong Hibs connections over the years.

Three wins in a row was a bit of a treat for the Hibs fans who travelled
to Broomfield Park the following Saturday hoping for a fourth, but they
should have known better as a pacy, physical Airdrie punished them with
a 4–2 defeat. The game had started so well for a confident-looking Hibs
side, but soon the Diamonds were knocking their opponents off their
stride and when the final whistle blew McLeod and Stevenson's goals
counted for nothing thanks to strikes from Duncan (2 pens), Newlands
and Murray for Airdrie.

Next up there was a chance to avenge that Scottish Cup defeat by
Partick Thistle and the men in green and white took full home advantage
in beating the Jags 3–0 with goals from Falconer, Fraser and Baker. It was
a bitter sweet result with most Hibs fans wishing the cup tie had favoured

Hibs so decisively but it started a mini run of good form which resulted in an improvement in league standing.

Scottish Cup day on 17 February 1962 saw Hibs at Cappielow to face Second Division Morton in a friendly. In a keenly contested game it ended with honours even, Jim Scott grabbing both goals in a 2–2 draw.

A week later Third Lanark provided the first opportunity to begin a winning run in the league and thanks to goals from Baker and Falconer a 2–1 win was secured at Cathkin. The Thirds scorer was Gray and it was interesting to note that their left back that day was Joe Davis, who would go on to be a huge favourite at Easter Road in the years ahead.

March 1962 began with a tough away trip to Pittodrie, where Baker and Fraser secured a 2–1 win and two very welcome league points in a keenly-fought contest. It was a great game of football and only the most diehard Dons fan could have thought the result anything but an accurate reflection on the game.

Seven days later Hibs should have been meeting Motherwell at Easter Road, but the Steelmen were playing in the quarter-finals of the Scottish Cup and so Everton, early fallers in the FA Cup, were invited north for a friendly. In a decent game the sides finished even with one goal apiece, Stevenson counting for Hibs and Derek Temple for the Toffees. Prior to that game kicking off the fans were treated to another game, this time a trial match between two groups of players hoping to turn out for Scotland at youth level. A reading of the names in the match programme revealed a few who would go on to bigger and better things. E(rnie) McGarr played in goal for the 'A' team and later starred with Aberdeen. R (Bobby) Watson played at wing half and would later be a star player for Airdrie and Motherwell, while one P. Cormack of Tynecastle Boys' Club would enjoy a long and successful career at Hibs, Liverpool and Nottingham Forest.

In the midweek following the friendly with Everton, Hibs entertained Motherwell to fulfil the fixture postponed due to the latter's Scottish Cup commitments, but despite enjoying lengthy passages of possession Hibs lost the game 2–1 with Falconer getting the goal which kept him right up there alongside Stevenson and Baker in the race to finish as top scorer at the club. The Motherwell scorers were Delaney and Morris Stevenson, while Ronnie Simpson saved a penalty from future Hibs signing, Pat Quinn.

When St Johnstone arrived at Easter Road the following Saturday they were desperate for points so as to avoid becoming involved in the relegation battle, but Hibs were not in charitable mood and easily won the game 3–1 thanks to goals from Baker, Fraser and Falconer. In the Saints line-up that day were Alex Ferguson and Bobby Kemp, who later signed for Hearts.

Two days later, on Monday 19 March, Hibs made the short journey over to Dunfermline and were soundly thrashed 4–0 in a quite dismal display which was hard to watch and even harder to understand. These players had shown decent form of late, but in a horror show of a game you'd have been forgiven for thinking the guys had never met before. Not to take anything away from the hosts, they played very well and shared their goals among Miller, a Cunningham penalty, Melrose and Paton.

At the end of that week the Hibees travelled to Dens Park and although the performance improved somewhat they still lost, this time 1–0, Waddell getting the goal for the Dark Blues. The end of March came with a defeat on the last day by Hearts at Tynecastle in the final of the East of Scotland Shield. Although it was not as prestigious a competition as it once had been, both sides fielded strong line-ups and Stevenson's goal did little to appease the Hibs fans in the crowd as Hearts scored three times through Paton (2) and Wallace.

Just three games remained for the season and all would be at home, the first coming against St Mirren. It was both wet and windy at Easter Road on Wednesday 4 April, but Hibs mastered the conditions better than their opponents and won the game more convincingly than the 2–1 scoreline might suggest. A start in the number nine jersey for young Brian Marjoribanks proved to be a dream come true for the youngster as he bagged both Hibs goals in a fine display. Saints' Icelandic winger Therolf Beck snatched a consolation for the visitors.

Celtic were the next outfit to visit and the battle of the greens ended up a 1–1 draw with Falconer's goal being cancelled out by Divers. It was a close game, but had a definite end-of-season air about it, even though the visitors had a Scottish Cup semi-final against St Mirren in the offing.

A long and sometimes entertaining domestic season came to an end with a visit from the doomed-to-relegation Stirling Albion. Hibs won the game 3–1 with goals from Baker, Falconer and Stevenson, thereby ensuring an eighth-place finish in a league won by Dundee.

The domestic season may well have been over, but the players could not relax quite yet as the club had agreed to a five-match tour of Czechoslovakia and took a squad of 15 players with them. At the last moment manager Walter Galbraith took ill and could not travel, meaning the squad would be managed by trainer Eddie Turnbull.

Spartak Pilsen provided the first opposition and it took a long and bumpy coach ride from the team hotel to reach the compact little stadium which was their home. Goals from Falconer, a right-foot rocket from McLeod and a tap-in for McLeod's second resulted in a 3–2 win and a good start to the tour. Brno was the venue for the next match, which involved a short flight in a scary thunderstorm before the Hibees could line up against Spartak Kralovo Pole. By the time the game took place the sun had broken through and it was blisteringly hot as Hibs secured a 2–2 draw, both goals coming from Fraser.

After a day's rest Hibs flew from Brno to Ostrava for a game against local side Vitkovic, and a bizarre event that would prove to be. Kick-off was 20 minutes late because a cycling race was passing through the stadium. With Hibs leading 2–0 thanks to a brace from Baker, the match was abandoned after 67 minutes when, as a Czech player lay in the centre circle getting treatment for an injury, a squad of Swiss mechanics rushed on to the pitch to erect a steel platform to hold an electrical timing apparatus as the cycling race neared its climax!

Another flight, this time to Prague, ensured a few days of rest for the weary players before a bus trip to Usti, where the home side did well to contain the visitors until the 58th minute when Falconer pounced on a loose ball in the box to fire Hibs ahead. The 70th minute brought a goal for Baker, his 200th in first-class football, and with it a 2–0 win and the satisfying knowledge that Hibs were the first foreign team to beat Usti at home for more than six years.

The day before coming home Hibs played their final tour game against Spartak Sokolovo and got off to a cracking start when Baker pounced on a goalkeeping error inside the first 60 seconds. With half-time seven minutes away Hibs scored again, this time through a left-foot drive from Fraser. A second-half fightback by the home team secured a 2–2 draw but could not prevent Hibs from going through their tour undefeated.

In terms of goals scored it would be a second consecutive season for a Baker to lead the way. This time, of course, it was not Joe but his brother Gerry who notched 18 in all games. Behind him young Duncan Falconer grabbed an impressive 14 with Eric Stevenson finishing on 12.

Chapter Seventeen

1962/63

RELEGATION WORRIES AND EUROPEAN NIGHTS

A new season generally brings changes at any football club and Hibs were no exceptions as they welcomed Morris Stevenson from Motherwell, Doug Logan from Queen's Park and John Blair from Bradford, together with a couple of new apprentices named Jimmy O'Rourke and Bobby Duncan, while young Duncan Falconer joined the professional staff for the first time. Stevenson had been in great demand, with Sparta Rotterdam offering a trial as did Nottingham Forest, but the Elphinstone-born lad preferred to remain closer to home.

Having toured Czechoslovakia in May, Hibs decided against any real pre-season warm-up matches and instead headed north where they trained, relaxed and played a few five-a-side games against local outfits. Manager Walter Galbraith therefore took his players into the first game of the League Cup qualifying section against the current holders Rangers on Saturday 11 August 1962 not having played a 90-minute match. The programme for that game was the much coveted handbook edition, which contained full records of the previous season's appearances, goalscorers, etc, and cost twice the normal price at 6d (2.5p in current terms) while providing plenty of reading for stats enthusiasts.

The programme contained the usual batch of adverts extolling the pleasures of popping into the Albion Bar for a pint both before and after the game, while those who enjoyed the 'gramophone records' played prior to the start of the game and at the interval could purchase those records at Bandparts of Union Place. I'm fairly certain I wasn't the only young fan who bought his favourite single on the way back from a game. More importantly, the programme also contained the news that Hibs had drawn IFC Boldklub Copenhagen in the first round of the Fairs Cup, with the prospect of facing Utrecht of Holland if they managed to progress.

The game against Rangers failed to provide the winning start Galbraith had hoped for. The Ibrox side dominated a game in which they ran out worthy 4–1 winners. Injuries had weakened Hibs, for whom Morris Stevenson made a scoring debut at inside left, but there could be no excuses as the visitors played very well and scored through Brand, who got two including one from the penalty spot, Henderson and Wilson.

The following Wednesday Hibs travelled to Paisley to meet St Mirren at Love Street and fought out a thrilling 3–3 draw. Johnny Byrne and Eric Stevenson had Hibs ahead at one point, but at the end of the day they needed a late strike from Baker, against his former club, to secure a point. Byrne had been brought north from Tranmere Rovers not long after Walter Galbraith had arrived from the same place, but injury had kept him out and this match would provide him with his Hibs debut, as it did for Doug Logan. One low point in the game was an injury to John Fraser, who pulled a muscle and looked as if he might be out for several games.

The other club in Hibs' League Cup section were Third Lanark and it was they who next visited Easter Road. The hosts struggled to find any consistency and even when Thirds were reduced to ten men in the second-half Hibs struggled to take command of the game. Incredibly, Fraser had recovered from the injury sustained at Love Street and he scored twice, while a McCormack own-goal gave Hibs a 3–2 win, Edinburgh-born Davie Grant bagging two for the visitors.

With three of the six scheduled League Cup ties now completed, Hibs had won, drawn and lost a game, but before they faced Rangers in the return tie at Ibrox they travelled to Shawfield to open the league campaign by facing Clyde. Defensive frailties were very prominent in this game and the Bully Wee ran out worthy 3–1 winners, having scored through Thomson, McLean and McLaughlin, while Hibs countered through young Duncan Falconer, who later badly injured his knee and had to be carried off. At first there were concerns that the striker had damaged cartilage in his knee, but later tests carried out at hospital confirmed it was only badly twisted. Even so, he would be missed as he took some time to recover.

Ibrox is a daunting place to visit at the best of times and when Hibs travelled there on Saturday 25 August it was to face the League Cup section leaders. In a tense match Hibs changed their system somewhat and defended magnificently in holding the Light Blues to a 0–0 draw. It wasn't glamorous, but it was effective and it kept Hibs in with a chance of qualifying for the later stages of the tournament.

In the following midweek Hibs welcomed St Mirren to Easter Road, still on League Cup duty, and won the game more comfortably than the 2–0 scoreline might indicate. Leading through a Fraser goal, Hibs had to wait until the dying moments of the game before making sure of the two points with a Morris Stevenson goal. The match programme for that game informed Hibs fans that the dates had been set for the Fairs Cup meeting with IFC Boldklub Copenhagen and that Hibs would be at home first, on 3 October, with the return in Denmark on 23 October. Interestingly, the Danes would be a select side, drawn from eight clubs in the Copenhagen area, a system they had operated for almost 60 years and which seemed to work as they had lost only 5–4 to Portuguese cracks Benfica earlier in the year.

The League Cup section drew to a close on 1 September when Hibs travelled west to meet Third Lanark. Victory for Hibs, coupled with defeat for Rangers at the hands of St Mirren, would see the green and whites into the latter stages. The first part of that double was achieved in some style as Hibs dominated their hosts from start to finish with a Baker hat-trick and a single strike from Morris Stevenson ensuring a 4–1 win, Bryce scoring for Thirds. Sadly, St Mirren could not provide the second part of the equation, and so Rangers qualified from the group in finishing just one point ahead of Hibs.

With the League Cup out of the way, Hibs recommenced their league championship campaign with a home derby against Hearts and it proved to be an unmitigated disaster for the defence as the Gorgie men hammered four goals past Ronnie Simpson while their own keeper, Gordon Marshall, had a trouble free game. Paton's hat-trick was added to by Cumming and the Hibs fans went home a pretty sickened bunch that night. Defeat is always difficult to take, but a heavy defeat by our oldest rivals is extremely painful and manager Galbraith came in for some fierce criticism during and after the game.

In the week leading up to the next match, which would see Hibs travel to Fir Park, Galbraith decided that he would bring a new player to the club by returning to his old Cheshire stomping ground and 'snapping up' a local lad, Harvey McCreadie. No doubt Galbraith was pleased to secure the lad's signature which, he said in his programme notes at the next home match, was being eagerly sought by clubs in the Manchester area. This didn't excite the Hibs support much. The 'Manchester area' of course includes both City and United and the way the notes are penned in the programme it's as if the bold Walter was trying to convince us that those very clubs had been pipped by him. The 'Manchester area' also includes a host of other clubs considerably less famous than City and United and the more likely truth is that it would be one of those clubs Galbraith had pipped!

In any event, McCreadie made his first-team debut against Motherwell and by all accounts had a reasonable game as Hibs took a point in a 2–2 draw, with Baker and Byrne on target. Lindsay and Roberts countered for 'Well and Hibs were unlucky not to take both points when Baker hit the bar in the last minute.

With the first tie against Copenhagen looming, Hibs next faced

Rangers at Easter Road, hoping for a much improved performance after the 1–4 reversal in the earlier League Cup tie. Rangers didn't score four this time, however: they notched up five, with Hibs getting only one in return through that man McCreadie. The Glasgow club cruised to victory with Millar (2), Wilson (2) and Jim Baxter beating Simpson in the Hibs goal. With just four league games played, Hibs were struggling at the foot of the table with only one point and having scored just four goals but having conceded 14. Disgruntlement among the home support was evident.

Some respite from the league campaign came in the shape of the first-round, first-leg Fairs Cup tie against Copenhagen and Hibs performed majestically on the night in winning handsomely by four goals to nil. Three goals in seven minutes rocked the Danes and eventually Byrne, Baker, Morris Stevenson and an own goal gave Hibs a great lead to take into the second leg and the result was all the more impressive when you consider that the visitors had four full and five under-23 internationals in their ranks.

This was surely the kind of performance and result that would boost morale and lead to better domestic performances, or at least you could be forgiven for thinking so, but just a few days later Hibs travelled to Tannadice and were hammered 5–0, with Carlyle (2), Gillespie, Pattie and Irvine finding the target. Hibs were a shambles defensively and had no threat going forward, with service to Scott and McCreadie virtually non-existent. Once again the Hibs support was in a hostile mood with Walter Galbraith getting pelters from those who had made the trip to Tayside. Things were not much better at reserve level either and those who watched the second string were less than impressed, although there were some encouraging signs in the play of the likes of Peter Cormack, Jimmy O'Rourke, Malcolm Bogie, Willie Wilson and Bobby Duncan, who was playing as a striker but who would later be a first-class right back in the top team.

Fellow strugglers Raith Rovers were the next side to face Hibs and the Easter Road crowd was less than impressed with its heroes as the hosts stumbled to a scrappy 1–0 win thanks to an Eric Stevenson penalty. Still, it was two precious points and the reserves emulated their senior counterparts by winning 1–0 in Kirkcaldy with a goal from Harvey McCreadie. For some obscure reason chairman Harry Swan was at the reserve game, but took ill and was treated at Kirkcaldy Royal Infirmary before being allowed home. It may seem an unkind thing to say, but perhaps he chose the reserve game to avoid listening to the growing discontent on the terraces at Easter Road.

A second home game followed the win over Raith when reigning league champions Dundee came to Edinburgh hoping to find Hibs an easy nut to crack. It was not to be, however, as the Hibees found some form and seemed well worth the point gained from a 2–2 draw. Byrne and Baker found the target for Hibs while Dundee scored through Penman and Cousin.

Back in August, Hibs had fought out a thrilling 3–3 League Cup draw with St Mirren at Love Street, and when they travelled to the same venue on league business on 20 October another cracking game ensued with the honours once again even as the game finished 2–2. It was a great fighting performance by the Hibees, who lost Eric Stevenson to a broken leg in the first-half, but rolled up their sleeves and scored two fine goals through Byrne and Easton. White scored twice for St Mirren but ten-man Hibs finished the stronger side.

The unfortunate Stevenson was in plaster and would miss the return game against IFC Boldklub Copenhagen. Despite his absence, Hibs turned in a great display in winning the match 3–2 and the tie 7–2 on aggregate, qualifying to face Utrecht in the second round. Two goals from Morris Stevenson and a single from Byrne were replied to by Dyrmose and Christensen. The Danes had in fact taken the lead and for a little while they dominated the game but Byrne's equaliser seemed to knock the stuffing out of them and Hibs actually led 3–1 in the second-half before the Danes struck again.

The final game in October saw Queen of the South visit Easter Road, but Hibs had found some form now and ran out convincing 3–0 winners with goals from Byrne, McCreadie and Morris Stevenson. It is interesting to note that playing in goal for Queen of the South that day was George Farm, ex-Hibs of course and now combining playing with managing at Palmerston Park. Farm was joined by two other former Hibees that day in Johnny Frye and John Rugg, a giant of a centre half who had been a provisional signing at Easter Road but never made the first team.

They say winning is habit forming and Hibs were certainly in the habit when they visited Cathkin Park to face a Third Lanark side twice beaten in the League Cup section and struggling at the wrong end of the league. Grant scored for Thirds, but Morris Stevenson (2), McCreadie and Scott ensured a fine 4–1 win for the Hibees.

The winning habit came to an end at Pittodrie, where Hibs dominated the first-half but couldn't score and then conceded three in the second period, with Cummings (2) and Smith the scorers. Still, things had picked up in recent weeks and manager Galbraith was slowly winning back favour with the fans as Hibs climbed the league and remained in the Fairs Cup. A huge help to the manager was the fact that the club had managed to persuade Barcelona to come to Easter Road to play a friendly and that was the next but one game in the schedule!

Ahead of the friendly, Hibs met Kilmarnock at Easter Road. The

Ayrshire club were flying high in the league and they continued to do so as they beat the visitors 2–0 with goals from Mason and Kerr.

Barcelona! The Spanish side were enjoying a whistle-stop tour of Europe which would see them meet a Berlin select, Racing Club of Paris and of course Hibs. It was a cold Wednesday evening in November when the players ran out on to the Easter Road turf and a cracking game ensued. Although only a friendly, this was a prestigious game and the fact that it was played under the floodlights added to the magic of the occasion for the sizeable crowd, which was royally entertained as the visitors put in a great display in winning the game 3–1. Jim Scott scored for Hibs and no doubt he enjoyed telling the tale of his goal against Barcelona for years to come.

Three days later Hibs were struggling again when they visited Airdrie at Broomfield and went down 2–1. It was a tough, physical game: Easton suffered a broken leg while Baker, Scott and Byrne all had to go off at some point for treatment, leaving Hibs playing with ten men and occasionally only nine for periods. Debuting Peter Cormack, drafted in at outside left following Eric Stevenson's leg break and an ankle injury to Ally McLeod, scored the goal for Hibs while McColl scored twice for the Diamonds.

The defeat at Broomfield and a mounting injury list were hardly the best preparation for a Hibs side travelling to Holland to face Utrecht in the first leg of their Fairs Cup tie and so the 1–0 victory secured there was all the more creditable. Duncan Falconer, fit again, struck the goal and despite the best efforts of their hosts no equaliser was forthcoming, which set Hibs up nicely for the return leg in Edinburgh.

Ahead of that game it was back to league business and a visit from Celtic, with the Glasgow side in good form and challenging at the top of the table. A goal from top scorer Morris Stevenson and some heroic goalkeeping from Ronnie Simpson ensured a point in a 1–1 draw, Murdoch scoring for the visitors. In the press reports following that game, praise was rightly heaped upon Simpson, who pulled off a string of superb saves with one from Divers being described as 'beyond belief'. It may have been beyond belief to that reporter, but Hibs fans had watched Simpson do that kind of thing week in and week out and they knew just what a great keeper he was.

The match programme for the Celtic game offered the intriguing information that should Hibs defeat Utrecht in the Fairs Cup they would go on to meet either Dunfermline or Valencia in the quarter-finals. Two Scottish clubs facing each other in the quarter-final of a European competition sounded like the stuff of fairytales, but of course for that to have even a chance of happening Hibs would have to finish the job against Utrecht, their next but one fixture.

In preparation for the Utrecht encounter, Hibs welcomed Partick Thistle to Easter Road in a league game which brought two mid-table sides together. Manager Galbraith could be considered unlucky to have watched his side dominate the first-half only to see Falconer carried off with concussion and then Thistle snatch a goal just before the interval, when Duffy jabbed the ball home from close range. With Falconer back on the park but looking decidedly groggy, Hibs went in search of the equaliser but couldn't break down a resolute Thistle rearguard and when Duffy scored a second near the end the points were lost.

Utrecht provided the opposition at Easter Road on Wednesday 12 December, vowing to make Hibs work hard for a second victory and subsequent qualification for the quarter-finals where either Valencia or Dunfermline awaited. With a big and noisy crowd behind them, Hibs attacked from the off, knowing that a goal would mean the visitors required to score three to progress. A magnificent run down the right wing by Baker ended with the striker firing an unstoppable shot past Van Zoghel in the Utrecht goal, much to the delight of the players and the home support. A little later 16-year-old schoolboy Jimmy O'Rourke, making his first-team debut, struck the crossbar with a fierce drive and then Morris Stevenson doubled the Hibs lead before Guertsen pulled one back for the visitors. The 2–1 win gave Hibs a 3–1 aggregate victory as the news came in that Valencia had thumped Dunfermline 4–0 in Spain, making them favourites to meet Hibs at the next stage.

By coincidence, Dunfermline and Hibs met three days later at East End Park in a league match and the Fifers showed no signs of a Spanish hangover as they triumphed 3–2. Byrne and O'Rourke scored for Hibs but Dunfermline, with their own 16-year-old on the right wing, scored three as Smith (2) and Cunningham found the target. Little did we know that those two 16-year-olds would end up playing together at Easter Road in the years ahead, the young Par being none other than Alex Edwards.

Four days later the entire Hibs first team, management and board attended the Dunfermline v Valencia second-leg Fairs Cup tie and watched on in admiration as the Fifers recorded a stunning 6–2 win, meaning the tie was level at 6–6. This was before the away goals rule was established and it meant an extra game had to be played, which Valencia narrowly won 1–0, so Hibs now knew who their next opponents would be.

The normal glut of fixtures over the Christmas and New Year period was severely curtailed as Scotland found itself in the grip of a fierce winter. In fact, following the visit to East End Park on 15 December 1962, Hibs played only two more competitive matches between then and 6 March 1963. The first of those games came two days before the New

Year and it was a bit of a disaster for Hibs, with lowly Clyde grabbing a 2–1 win at Easter Road. Pat Hughes put through his own goal and Harry Hood added a second for the Bully Wee while Hibs could only counter with a McLeod penalty.

The other pre-March game involved facing Brechin City at Glebe Park in the Scottish Cup and on a frosty pitch Hibs easily saw off the minnows by 2–0, with Fraser and Morris Stevenson on target, setting up a third-round tie with a Dundee outfit still going strong in the European Cup.

One plus point from the lengthy cold snap and subsequent postponements of numerous games was that the injury list shortened and even long-term victims Easton and Eric Stevenson were nearing fitness when Hibs hosted Dunfermline in a friendly in early March. It was a keenly contested game as both sides strove to regain match fitness after their enforced layoff and a 2–2 draw was about the right result, with McCreadie and Morris Stevenson on target for Hibs while Smith and Dickson scored for the Pars. Prior to kick-off both sides had agreed to allow 'replacements' during the game so that as many players as possible could get a run out. This early evidence of substitutions saw Hibs make four changes and Dunfermline six.

The following Saturday league business resumed and Hibs fought out a disappointing 1–1 draw with Third Lanark. Fraser scored for Hibs and Grant for Third Lanark, but there were obvious signs that both teams had suffered from a lack of competitive football. With just a friendly and one league match since January, Hibs were ill-prepared for meeting Valencia the midweek following the Third Lanark match. On the night, they were simply outplayed and outclassed by the Spanish cracks, who recorded a 5–0 win at the Campa de Mestalla. Waldo (2), Mano, Roberto and Chicao were the men who hammered Hibs, with each goal finely crafted and taken as the visiting defence appeared to be chasing shadows.

Back in Scotland, Hibs played hosts to Aberdeen in a vital league match and lost out 3–2 with Baker and O'Rourke on target for the home side, Charlie Cooke, Cummings and Coutts scoring for the visitors. Hibs were now in a very precarious position league wise and the defeat by the Dons left them in second-bottom spot, eight points ahead of Raith Rovers and five behind Clyde, although the Glasgow outfit had played two more games at that point.

The annual exit from the Scottish Cup came next as Hibs fell to Dundee at Dens Park by the only goal of the game. The visitors defended exceptionally well against a pacy Dundee forward line, but the supply to the Hibs forwards was poor and so another cup disappointment was inevitable. Given that the team were out of the Scottish Cup and all but out of the Fairs Cup, perhaps the players could focus on getting some badly needed league points?

With a backlog of fixtures to catch up on, most teams were playing twice a week and on Saturday 22 March Hibs travelled to Rugby Park to face a Kilmarnock side which was chasing the league title along with Rangers, Celtic and Partick Thistle. Again the Hibees played quite well, but goals from Black and Mason won the points for Killie and Hibs were left to rue missing the few chances they created.

The trip to Brockville in the following midweek brought Hibs up against a Falkirk side desperate to avoid being dragged into the relegation battle and their determination to do so brought the reward of a 3–1 win, Tommy Leishman scoring a rare goal for Hibs while Bain (2) and Adam counted for the home side.

Things were getting pretty serious now and the Hibs supporters were less than impressed with the poor form of the team, making their feelings loudly known as Hibs hosted a struggling Airdrie side and allowed the Diamonds to take both points with a 2–0 win. Murray and Newlands scored for Airdrie. Baker unluckily hit the bar for Hibs, who never really looked like taking anything from the game. A worried home support trooped out at full-time knowing its heroes now faced four consecutive away games against Celtic, Dundee, Rangers and Partick Thistle. Dundee were still going well in the cup while the other three occupied lofty league positions. Things were therefore bleak as a demoralised Hibs got ready to play the second leg of that Fairs Cup tie against Valencia.

Contrary to what might have been expected of the visitors, they did not field a weakened side, safe in the knowledge that Hibs were trailing in the tie by five goals, and so it is to the credit of the Hibernian players that they managed a fine 2–1 win on the night. A big and excited crowd enjoyed a good game of football which saw Preston and Baker score for Hibs and Nunez for Valencia. Of course this meant Hibs would exit the competition 6–2 on aggregate, but they had given a good account of themselves over the piece. Making his Hibs debut that night was 32-year-old centre half Willie Toner from Kilmarnock. Toner was a good defender and had won seven caps for Scotland in a career which saw him arrive at Rugby Park from Sheffield United. His experience would be invaluable in the remaining league matches. In later years, his son Kevin would become a Grade One SFA referee.

European football would certainly not be gracing Easter Road the following season as Hibs began a series of games vital to their continued presence in the First Division, and that series began with a visit to Glasgow, where Celtic narrowly defeated the visitors 2–0 with goals from McKay and Price. Hibs played well that day but the defenders' job was made all the more difficult because the forwards were not scoring. All that changed, however, when Hibs played reigning league champions Dundee at Dens Park and ran out worthy 3–1 winners. The Hibees had gone looking for revenge having been knocked out of the Scottish Cup at the same venue and from the moment Baker opened the scoring there seemed only one likely winner. Baker added two more to secure a fine hat-trick while Penman slotted home a consolation penalty for Dundee.

It was a confident Hibs then that travelled next to Ibrox, but although that man Baker scored again the Gers struck through Wilson (2) and Brand to seal the points. Again Hibs played well and again Willie Toner defended exceptionally, but at the end of the day it was still two points dropped and another game played in which to draw clear of second-bottom spot.

On 13 April Hibs played their fourth consecutive away game in just eight days when they met high-flying Partick Thistle at Firhill. Leading through a Baker goal and looking comfortable with it, Hibs suddenly slumped and lost two quick goals against the run of play. Thankfully, Jim Scott popped in a late equaliser to secure a vital point. Four away games, four points won and all against strong teams was pretty good by any standards and absolutely vital to a Hibs team who would now enjoy a spell in front of their own fans with four further games to follow in rapid succession.

The first of those brought mid-table Motherwell to Easter Road, a side some eight points ahead of Hibs, but by the end of 90 tense minutes the gap was reduced to six as Baker's solo strike kept the points in Leith, the first league win at home since 27 October of the previous year. Special mention must go to Willie Toner, who was a tower of strength in the Hibs defence, inspiring those around him to help keep a clean sheet against Motherwell's busy forwards. With Raith Rovers looking doomed at the foot of the table, Hibs were chasing Clyde, who were three points ahead before this game but with a game more played, and so it was a relieved support which headed home that night knowing the gap had not widened.

Dunfermline provided the next test and Preston had the Hibees a goal up inside two minutes. Try as they might they could not breach the Pars defence again and the visitors secured a point with a second-half equaliser. It was disappointing to gain only a point, but Clyde also drew and so no ground was lost in the battle to avoid finishing second-bottom.

The last but one of four consecutive home games saw Dundee United arrive at Easter Road boasting an impressive defensive record of having conceded just 40 goals in 28 games, a feat only bettered by the top three sides, Rangers, Kilmarnock and Celtic. Despite this, Hibs dominated for long spells and took a deserved lead through Fraser, but the longer the game went without a second goal being scored the more nervous the players got and it was a hammer blow to lose an equaliser very late in the game. Prior to that game kicking off, Hibs trailed Clyde by four points but with a game in hand, so it looked as though the second relegation spot would go to the wire with Raith Rovers already doomed.

With just five league games remaining and only two of them at home, Hibs 'used up' a home match when Falkirk came to town on Saturday 27 April. Well clear of any relegation worries, the Bairns played relaxed attacking football while Hibs were obviously feeling the strain of needing to get a result. At the end of the day the nerves won and Hibs went down 3–0 in front of a worried and very disgruntled home support. The greens now had just four games left, away to Hearts, Queen of the South and Raith Rovers and at home to St Mirren.

Tynecastle had not been a very happy stamping ground for Hibs in recent years and when half-time brought with it a 2–0 deficit that trend seemed set to continue. In a stirring second-half, however, during which Hibs lost Willie Toner with a dislocated shoulder, the men from Easter Road came storming back and eventually drew 3–3, thanks to goals from Scott (2) and Fraser. Late in the game, with the scores tied, the Hearts keeper Gordon Marshall pulled off a wonder save to deny Fraser his second and Hibs' fourth, but at least a vital point was saved as Hibs lived to fight another day and things got even better when the news filtered through that Celtic had defeated Clyde.

St Mirren provided the final home opposition of the day and in a stirring programme note manager Walter Galbraith pleaded for 'rousing support from the terracing this afternoon . . . you can play your part in helping the team'. That encouragement was duly forthcoming and the players responded by winning the game 2–1, Baker and Baxter grabbing the vital goals.

With two away games left, Hibs needed three points to make sure of safety and that was the worst-case scenario based on Clyde winning their one remaining fixture against Rangers at Shawfield. The game in hand for Hibs involved a potentially tricky trip to Palmerston Park to face Queen of the South. A tight pitch and a noisy support would cause problems, but a large number of Hibs fans made the journey and the noise they themselves made more than cancelled out that of the home support. An early goal settled the nerves and at the end of the game Baker (2), Scott and Eric Stevenson had scored to give the visitors an emphatic 4–0 win.

And so we came to the last game of the season, with Hibs visiting already-relegated Raith Rovers and Clyde entertaining Rangers. A huge Hibs support made the trip over the Forth and they were well rewarded as the Hibees ran riot and secured a second consecutive 4–0 win, with Baxter (2), Fraser and Baker the marksmen. It was celebrations all around Stark's Park as Hibs had avoided relegation and, to add to the relief, it became known that Clyde had failed to beat Rangers.

When the euphoria/relief subsided it was sobering to realise that in 34 league games Hibs had won just eight, with nine drawn and 17 lost. Only 47 goals had been scored with 67 conceded and the final tally of 25 points was just two away from a relegation place. Better things were hoped for next season, but new faces were required and Walter Galbraith had to improve his own record if he was to continue as manager.

Unsurprisingly, Gerry Baker finished top scorer with 22 in all games while Joe McClelland made the most appearances with 44, one more than Ronnie Simpson.

Chapter Eighteen

1963/64

MARTIN'S THE MAN

There were some new faces around Easter Road as season 1963/64 drew near, with changes both on and off the park which would have a significant impact on the club. Chairman Harry Swan decided to step down from that role but retained his position as a board member, his chairmanship going to William P. Harrower, an Edinburgh businessman and lifelong Hibs supporter. Harrower was a successful bookmaker with more than 50 shops in and around the capital, had been a season-ticket holder for many years and it was hoped his acute business brain would assist the club in growing in stature.

Another new face that season was that of trainer Tom McNiven, who joined the club from Third Lanark at the age of just 29. 'Tam' was an instant hit with the playing staff and went on to give Hibs many valuable years of service.

On the playing front, Hibs snapped up Tranent-born Neil Martin from Queen of the South and this was to prove a master stroke by manager Walter Galbraith, who had been having a tough time keeping the disgruntled support off his back. Martin had been banging the goals in on a regular basis at Palmerston, with 32 the previous season alone, and he brought that form with him when he signed for the Hibees. Ironically, Neil had thought of giving up the game as he still had his home in Tranent, his wife living there, while he also had a place in Dumfries. The inconvenience and expense were getting to him and rather than go part-time with Queens he had actually considered leaving the game altogether – until he got the call from Walter Galbraith.

Signed up on professional forms also were two very promising young-sters, Peter Cormack and Jimmy Stevenson each signing on the dotted line having reached their 17th birthdays. Stevenson had been one of three of that name, with Eric and Morris the others, but Morris moved on in the close season. Meanwhile the Simpson count was doubled when Ronnie was joined by Billy, a young centre half signed from Edina Hibs.

Captaining Hibs for the opening games was longest servant John

Grant, who had joined the club as a youngster in 1949 and who was widely respected by both his team-mates and the home support. His first task as captain was to lead the side to a creditable 1–1 draw with St Mirren at Love Street in the first tie of the League Cup, where Hibs shared a section with the Buddies, Dundee United and Aberdeen. In a game dominated by the visitors, Neil Martin, who had to leave the field injured with just 20 minutes left, opened his account for the Hibees, but a late equaliser from Kerrigan meant the spoils were shared.

The following midweek brought Dundee United to Easter Road and in an exciting game the home side triumphed 3–2, a result which took them to the top of their League Cup section. The first-half was a pretty dour affair but the second more than made up for it, with two of the Hibs goals coming in a thrilling four-minute spell, and the game was poised on a knife edge until the final whistle. Martin, Baker and O'Rourke struck for Hibs with Mitchell getting two for the Arabs, the second from a penalty. As an aside, it was amusing to watch 'new boy' McNiven on the Hibs bench, as he seemed to kick every ball and even threw himself forwards in mimicking a diving header by Neil Martin.

Having started well in the League Cup section, Hibs looked to continue that trend when they entertained a very talented Aberdeen side that next weekend. Baker injured himself in training in the lead-up to the game and so the number nine shirt was handed to the versatile John Fraser, who more normally would be in defence or midfield. Unsurprisingly, Fraser did not let anyone down and had a hand in the first goal, scored by O'Rourke after the young inside right took a pass from the centre and dribbled his way past several defenders before coolly slotting the ball past the diving 'Tubby' Ogston. Outside left Eric Stevenson added a second and though Hume pulled one back it looked a home win all the way until a bizarre incident occurred late in the game. Hibs were breaking out of defence when a referee's whistle was blown loud and clear, causing the home side's rearguard, which had been outstanding all afternoon, to stop playing. At this point, Billy Little stole in to gather the ball and shoot home past the bemused Simpson. It was only when the referee pointed to the centre circle that the Hibs defenders realised the whistle had been blown by someone in the crowd. There was little point in protesting and the game finished at 2–2.

Up at Pittodrie on the same day, a piece of Hibernian history was in the making when the second team defeated the Dons 3–0 in an impressive display of open, attacking football. Trainer Jimmy McColl was delighted with his charges and none more so than the scorer of the second goal, one Patrick Gordon Stanton, his first ever for the club.

With the first three League Cup ties played and Hibs sitting a point clear of Aberdeen at the top of the group, it was time for the league championship campaign to commence as Third Lanark visited Easter Road on Wednesday 21st August. The visitors were now managed by a former Easter Road favourite in Ally McLeod, the ex-Hibee starting out on a managerial road that would, at a future point, take him all the way to Argentina. The midweek start to league campaigns had been in place for a few seasons now and to find an opening day win by Hibs you had to go all the way back to 1959/60, when a brace from Joe Baker won the points against Aberdeen.

This was to be one campaign, however, that did kick off with a win as Hibs easily brushed aside their visitors in an emphatic 3–0 victory. All three goals were peaches, with the third just shading it over the other two. The first came from Eric Stevenson who bulleted home a left-foot piledriver from the edge of the box, the ball zipping past keeper Mitchell before hitting the underside of the bar on the way in. The second came when Scott's perfect cross was met by the inrushing O'Rourke and the youngster's header flashed past Mitchell almost before the keeper had a chance to move. The icing on the cake came when Baxter, who never seemed to know how to score ordinary goals, went on a 60-yard run before belting the ball home from about 25 yards.

It was back to League Cup business next for Hibs as they welcomed St Mirren to Easter Road. For the second time in four days the home fans were treated to an emphatic 3–0 win with a double from Baker and a single from Martin securing Hibs' lead in the group. Once again the defence looked rock solid with Baxter in particular catching the eye while Eric Stevenson, who had a hand in all three goals, gave Buddies right back Cameron Murray a game he would want to forget.

The League Cup section was all but won the following midweek when Hibs travelled to Tannadice and handed the home side a 4–2 defeat in a game thought by many pundits to be the best they had seen in a long while. Both teams attacked from the start and had the usual quota of half chances hit the target it may well have finished 7–9, such was the goal-mouth action during the 90 minutes. As it was a Briggs penalty and Rooney header were not enough for United as Hibs, who lost 16-year-old Jimmy O'Rourke to injury, struck through Eric Stevenson 2 (1 pen), Baker and Martin. Could it be that Hibs would reach the last eight for the first time in a long while?

The last game in the group would take the Hibees to Pittodrie, where Aberdeen would have to win by a hatful to deny the Easter Road men, but the visitors kept it tight and refused to concede any goals, while Martin and Baker were on target at the other end in a comfortable 2–0 win. The last eight/quarter-final place had been achieved in some style, but a tricky home and away tie against Dundee would soon follow.

Prior to the first leg of that tie, Hibs had to go to Tynecastle to face

Hearts in the league. In a tough-tackling, no-holds-barred game which was finely balanced until the final few minutes Hibs lost their first game of the season in going down 4–2. At 3–2 there was still a chance of rescuing a draw, but Hearts defended well under mounting pressure and then sealed the points with a late strike. Scorers for the home side were Wallace (2), Ferguson and Davidson. The Hibs goals came from a Baker double before the centre was forced to leave the field for a good five minutes with an ankle injury.

The Wednesday following took Hibs to Dens Park for that first-leg quarter-final tie against a very talented and powerful Dundee. Once again the reporters present described it as a wonderful game of flowing football, while the fans of both sides cheered their heroes to a 3–3 draw. Penman, Gilzean and Waddell found the net for the Dark Blues, Eric Stevenson (2) and Baker striking for Hibs. 'Stevie' was in fine form in notching his double, the first from a fierce drive and the second a header, while Baker thought he'd also notched a double, but the second was ruled offside. There was a laugh for the fans at one point as Baker, who was off the park behind the Dundee goal getting treatment from Tam McNiven, leapt to his feet shouting 'Goal!' when he thought Stevie had scored. In fact the ball hit the side-netting. If Baker looked embarrassed, McNiven looked stunned: the injured ankle he had been treating had suddenly leapt from his hands and into the air.

With the second leg a week away, Hibs first had to host Falkirk on league business and whether they had one eye on the Dundee game or not we will never know, but they had to fight hard in the end to secure a point in a 2–2 draw. Eric Stevenson notched another brace, both from the spot and both earned when Scott was hauled down in the box by Rae. The game marked the first-team debut of Bobby Duncan, who was handed the number eight shirt when Martin had to withdraw with a throat infection. Duncan played well enough, as did Scott, Stevenson and Byrne, who had to have stitches inserted in an eye wound but still managed to finish the game.

Wednesday 18 September saw Dundee arrive at Easter Road for the second leg of the League Cup quarter-final and it was one of those magical floodlit nights when the home support roared their heroes to victory thanks to goals from Martin and Baker. The defence was out-standing and Ronnie Simpson never looked like being beaten as Hibs advanced to a semi-final tie against Morton at neutral Ibrox. Over 50,000 fans had watched this two-legged affair and it is safe to say they had been thoroughly entertained by two very good footballing sides.

With their tails up and confidence seemingly high, Hibs next travelled to Glasgow to meet Rangers but had a horrible 90 minutes and were soundly thrashed 5–0. Trailing 1–0 at half-time, there was a brief spell early in the second-half when it looked as though Hibs might make some headway. Uncharacteristically, they looked hesitant in defence and never seemed to win enough second ball. The noisy home crowd of 50,000 were roaring their team forward and Brand's first-half goal was soon added to by McLean, Forrest, Brand again and an unfortunate own-goal by Jim Easton. It was a blessing when the final whistle sounded and a disconsolate Hibs side trudged off the park.

The heavy defeat at Ibrox signalled the start of a poor run of form for Hibs, who failed to find the net against an in-form Kilmarnock at Easter Road and went on to lose both the game, thanks to a Murray double, and two league points in the process. Seven days later a visit to Fir Park brought more disappointment and a 4–3 defeat, future Hibee Joe McBride grabbing a hat-trick and Weir the other, with Baker, Martin and Pat Stanton replying for Hibs, his first for the senior eleven.

This was hardly the best preparation for a cup semi-final, but Hibs had just two days to recover as they faced Morton at Ibrox on Monday 7 October. Pat Stanton retained his place but it was a case of very mixed fortunes for Martin, who struck the Hibs goal but then had the misfortune to break his wrist, an injury that would keep him out of action for some weeks. After Morton had equalised, the 46,000 fans did their best to lift their respective favourites, but both sides had chances to win and spurned them, meaning a replay would be required the following Monday.

Of significance during that week was the fact that Hibs looked south in signing a new player – former Motherwell man Pat Quinn, who was enticed north from Blackpool. Quinn had been one of 'Ancell's Babes' in a first-class Motherwell side and had been capped by Scotland, so his capture was viewed very positively by the Hibs support. Sadly for Quinn, his debut was not one for the scrapbook as Hibs crossed the River Forth to face Dunfermline at East End Park. Boss of Dunfermline that night was Jock Stein, while teenager Alex Edwards played outside right and opened the scoring before Kerray and Lunn made it three, whereas Hibs hardly had a shot at goal throughout the whole 90 minutes despite some excellent probing passes from their new boy.

With another poor performance weighing on their minds, the Hibs players travelled back through to Ibrox on the Monday following to meet Second Division Morton. It was a dour struggle from start to finish and once again Hibs failed to hit the target, eventually losing to an Allan McGraw penalty, the Morton man slotting the ball past Simpson and knocking out the team he would later join.

Deflated, demoralised and disappointed probably sums up well the feelings of all connected with Hibs at this point. The promising start to the season, with fine play winning a semi-final place in the League Cup, seemed but a memory as form slumped dramatically in the league. Things got worse when in their next league outing the Hibees crashed 0–4 to Dundee at Easter Road, the Dens men gaining revenge aplenty for their earlier League Cup defeat. Though it may not have been a game the home fans would wish to readily recall, the same could not be said for the travelling fans or for Dundee number ten Alan Gilzean, who scored all four of his side's goals, the last from the penalty spot when he pounced on Ronnie Simpson's initial save to score at the second attempt. Four goals in one game is a magnificent achievement, but Gilzean was himself a magnificent player, as he went on to prove with Tottenham Hotspur and Scotland.

With the defence leaking goals all too readily, Walter Galbraith once again entered the transfer market, beating off a host of clubs in securing the services of Northern Ireland international John Parke from Linfield. The Irishman was to prove an excellent signing as he replaced the injured Joe McClelland in the number three jersey and made a significant impact in a team struggling to find form.

Parke's debut was a winning one as Hibs disposed of St Johnstone in some style with a convincing 4–1 win at Easter Road. The Saints were truly put to the sword as Hibs suddenly rediscovered goalscoring form with Falconer, Baker, Eric Stevenson and Grant on target while the visitors took some consolation from a McIntyre penalty, that seeming to be the only way they would beat Simpson in the home goal.

With that fine win under their belts, the Hibees travelled to Firhill the following Saturday and despite a quite sparkling performance managed to lose the game 2–1. It was a bizarre outcome to a game Hibs could and should have won as Simpson put in another stunning display between the posts, but the forwards missed chances galore. Peter Cormack's fine strike was merely a consolation as Hainey and Yard both struck wonder goals beyond the unlucky Simpson.

Another away game followed with Hibs travelling down to Dumfries to take on Queen of the South at Palmerston Park. Neil Martin returned from injury and made his mark against his former club with two cracking first-half goals, taking his tally for the season to ten. Hibs seemed to have everything under control, but Queens put in a stirring second-half display to secure the points by scoring three goals of their own through Gardiner, Murphy (pen) and Coates. It was a disappointment to see Hibs fold under pressure and even though both Fraser and Falconer were injured during the contest those injuries did not excuse the form slump in the second-half.

The league form and position were poor and the home support was not impressed with manager Galbraith's seeming inability to get the tactics right, but they still turned out in sizeable numbers for the next match which brought Celtic to Easter Road. In his programme notes for that game, Galbraith suggested results were not indicative of performance, claiming the team were showing good form but had been unlucky at both Firhill and Palmerston. The fans, though, had heard it all before and their patience was wearing mighty thin. The same match programme gave the sad news of the death of David Wyper, a long-serving and very valuable scout who had brought a lot of promising young players to Easter Road, including Lawrie Reilly. Davy was 70 when he died and Hibs would miss his services.

In the game itself, Hibs gave a debut to Willie Hamilton. They had captured him from Hearts and the 24-year-old, who hailed from Airdrie and had been with Sheffield United and Middlesbrough as a youngster, lived up to his famous name and scored a cracking goal to secure a 1–1 draw, with Bobby Murdoch striking for the Celts. It was a decent performance from Hibs, but you were left with the feeling, and not for the first time, that but for the form of Ronnie Simpson in goals it may well have proved a quite different outcome.

Heavy rain had fallen incessantly in Paisley for a good 48 hours before Hibs arrived there to meet St Mirren on 23 November 1963 and so the pitch was like a bog as both teams fought to put together more than a couple of passes before losing possession. In a tousy first-half, Fraser was carried off on a stretcher after he suffered a badly gashed knee which required four stitches. With Fraser still off getting treatment, Hamilton took a sore one in the lower back and he too had to leave the field of play, which meant Hibs were down to nine men on a pitch which sapped the strength with every minute that passed. Bravely, Hamilton returned to boost Hibs back up to ten, and it is to their credit that the visitors managed to salvage a point in a 1–1 draw, Quinn scoring his first for the club and Carroll counting for the Buddies. When down to nine men, Neil Martin showed true versatility by first moving to right half and then right back, putting in a fantastic 90 minutes on the treacherous surface. Interestingly, Hibs had travelled to Paisley the season before, lost Eric Stevenson with a broken leg and Jim Easton with an injured shoulder and yet still managed a 1–1 draw – déjà vu, as they say.

Two successive draws had at least brought the losing streak to an end and so when Aberdeen visited Easter Road the following Saturday the home fans were looking to step that up to a victory, though that was a tall order against an in-form side. With Fraser and Hamilton out injured, Hibs brought 17-year-old Billy Simpson in at right back and Neil Martin resumed a striking role with Quinn at inside right. It was a great game, with both sides creating good chances and both goalkeepers pulling off vital saves. Ronnie Simpson was continuing his great run of form and Aberdeen keeper John 'Tubby' Ogston was emulating the Hibs man until

Baxter stepped up to lash a thunderbolt into the top corner, giving Hibs a vital lead in a close game. The Dons, with a youthful Charlie Cooke in their ranks, pushed more men forward looking to equalise, but the Hibs defence dealt with that pressure and eventually the Hibees took the points when Eric Stevenson slotted home a penalty kick after Ally Shewan had upended him in the box.

A busy December started with Hibs going through to Broomfield to face Airdrie in a game which produced goals galore as the Diamonds struck five to Hibs' three. It was end-to-end exciting stuff, but if it had been asked before the game whether Simpson could lose five goals in one game the questioner might have been considered mad. Though Ronnie stopped it from being more than five, he also had a bit of an off day along with his fellow defenders. The home side scored through Hastings (2), a Rowan penalty, Hannah and an own-goal from Tommy Leishman. Hibs countered through a Martin double, one of those from the penalty spot, and Eric Stevenson. Entertaining stuff to watch but not so good for the nerves as Hibs continued to flounder in the bottom half of the league, their cause not being helped when John Parke took a sore one to the knee, later diagnosed as a cartilage tear which would require an operation.

Another away trip followed, this time to Falkirk to meet struggling East Stirling at Firs Park on a boggy pitch and with the rain falling in sheets. Jim Easton took a first-half knock which forced Hibs to shuffle the pack and put their injured centre half to outside left. As if that were not bad enough for the big defender, he suffered a broken leg with 14 minutes left to play and would be out of action for some months, joining long-term absentees John Parke and Jimmy O'Rourke. In the game itself Martin bagged a fine brace of goals, one from the penalty spot, before himself being injured, but thankfully he managed to see out the whole game as Hibs were already down to ten men. The other Hibs scorer was Quinn while McNab scored for the home side.

Injury-hit Hibs next faced Dundee United at Easter Road, the home side retaining Simpson at right back and recalling McClelland to the number three shirt while Leishman played at right half. United were able to expose frailties in the home defence and won the game 3–2 with goals from Irvine (2) and Briggs (penalty), while Martin and Hamilton countered for the hosts.

December ended for Hibs with a visit to Cathkin Park to face Third Lanark. On a positive note, long-time absentee Jimmy O'Rourke was able to make his return to the first team, but little else positive can be said as Hibs put in a dismal performance in going down 1–0 thanks to a McMorran effort. The continuing bad form in the league was becoming increasingly worrying as Hibs occupied a spot too close to the relegation battle for comfort and the fans made their displeasure known, with manager Galbraith the main target.

The first game of the New Year brought Hearts to Easter Road and a bumper crowd was in attendance to watch a keenly contested derby in which both goalkeepers excelled. In the home goal, Simpson made a couple of breathtaking saves to deny Gordon and Traynor, while Hearts' Cruickshank emulated that feat by saving brilliantly from O'Rourke and Stevenson. With both sides pressing at every opportunity it seemed likely that despite the superb form of the goalkeepers, goals would come. They duly did, with Martin converting a penalty after Stevenson was tripped by Shevlane in the box. At the other end Wallace steered a low cross past Simpson. A share of the spoils was a fair outcome, with both sets of fans heading home and talking about what might have been.

Just 24 hours later Hibs were at Brockville facing a resurgent Falkirk and the short trip was worthwhile for the visiting fans who watched their side play very well in a 4–1 win. For once Martin was not on the scoresheet, but he did weigh in with a couple of assists as Eric Stevenson (2), O'Rourke and Grant found the target. Falkirk's consolation came from the spot as Hugh beat Simpson low to his left. It was a very welcome and much needed two points for Hibs as they fought to climb from their lowly league position.

Another 48 hours passed and Hibs were playing again, this time at Easter Road against high-flying Rangers. Alex Cameron, who had been handed the number five shirt against Falkirk, retained his place as injuries continued to cause Walter Galbraith selection problems. The big defender played quite well, although he ended on the losing side as Rangers took the points with a solitary strike from Jimmy Millar. Also playing for Hibs that day, their 28th appearance of the season, were the only two ever presents, Ronnie Simpson and Eric Stevenson.

The Scottish Cup provided the next fixture challenge, but once again the draw had not been kind to the Hibees, who faced a very difficult tie at Pittodrie. In an attacking sense Hibs played well and scored two good goals through Hamilton and O'Rourke, but defensively the visitors had a nightmare with slack marking bringing about their downfall as the Dons hit five through Kerrigan (2), Winchester (2) and Hume.

A week later Hibs made another long and fruitless journey which saw them go down 2–1 at Rugby Park. It was a cruel blow on a day when the Hibees dominated large parts of the game but which saw them lose a goal in injury time to Murray. Earlier, King had converted a penalty for Killie while Hamilton had scored for Hibs. The unfortunate Neil Martin broke his nose during the match but very bravely decided to play on rather than leave his side short-handed. There were now just eleven league matches left to play, six of those at home, and Hibs really needed to up their game if they were to steer clear of relegation.

Out of the cup, Hibs undertook to play a friendly match away to Grimsby the following weekend and it would prove to be a day of mixed fortunes against the Mariners. On the plus side, John Parke returned from injury, having fully recovered in record time from his cartilage operation, but Falconer was carried off early in the game and ten-man Hibs lost 3–0 with Young (2) and McLean grabbing the goals.

In the week leading up to a visit from Motherwell to Easter Road, Hibs secured the services of a goalkeeper from Inverurie Loco. Twenty-year-old Jack Reilly had played trials with both Arsenal and Liverpool and so Hibs were very fortunate to secure his signature. A policeman, Reilly would resign from the force and go on to play first-team football at Easter Road in the years ahead. Also announced that week was Hibs' intention to travel to France after the Dunfermline game on 8 February 1964. There they would represent Scotland at the Cannes Sports Festival and would play just one game, against Cannes.

Motherwell arrived in good form and looking to add to the misery of the suffering Hibs support, but they went home with their tails between their legs as Neil Martin inspired the greens to a worthy 3–1 win. A rare start for Tony McGlynn was rewarded with a goal from the forward while Martin himself and O'Rourke completed the scoring and Carlyle countered for the visitors. Shortly after the game Walter Galbraith revealed that Hibs had secured the services of Cowdenbeath centre forward Stan Vincent, and the lucky man arrived in time to qualify for that trip to Cannes.

The journey to France brought its reward with a 3–2 win as Neil Martin (2) and debutant Stan Vincent found the target. Moyano and a Grant own-goal made it look as though Cannes pushed Hibs closer than was actually the case. That game was played on the Tuesday evening and the following day Hibs returned to the UK, basing themselves in London. With Dundee busy on Scottish Cup duty, the Hibees had fixed up a friendly at Loftus Road against Queen's Park Rangers. The English outfit were several steps up in class from Cannes and Hibs toiled for the entire 90 minutes as they went down 5–1, Martin striking the Hibs consolation goal.

Back home in Scotland, Hibs made the journey to Tayside to face a very strong Dundee and were hardly in the game as the Dark Blues romped home comfortably in a 3–0 win. Cameron (2) and Penman were on target and but for Ronnie Simpson the scoreline would have been a sight more embarrassing. At the game that day was Pat Birnie, a Hibs fan employed by Railway Hotels. Pat deserves special mention in a time when going to away games was certainly not the norm. He had missed just two games that season, away to Kilmarnock and Cannes, while he had even journeyed to Grimsby and London to watch his beloved Hibees!

Next, Hibs arrived in Perth to face St Johnstone. With Pat Quinn installed as captain for the day the little number eight dominated the game and led his side to an impressive 4–0 win, Martin and Scott each bagging a brace. It was a great performance from a Hibs side that had 17-year-old Davy Hogg at outside right while Tommy Preston returned after a 16-week absence and occupied the number six jersey to great effect. Worthy of note here also was the faultless performance at centre half by utility player Duncan Falconer, who looked as though he had played for years in what was an unfamiliar position to him.

Seven days later Hibs entertained Partick Thistle at Easter Road and took both points with a hard-fought 2–1 win in front of a sizeable but clearly frustrated crowd. Hibs won, but the style of play was not worthy of praise and the fans were not slow to vent their frustrations. Jim Scott got his second consecutive double while Fleming pulled one back for the Jags, but the Hibees were hanging on in the end and although the points were gratefully received, the pressure on the club to take some positive action was mounting.

Saturday 7 March 1964 brought Queen of the South to Easter Road for a game which would prove to be Walter Galbraith's last in charge. Ironically, the Hibees played very well in winning 5–2, with Martin in stunning form as he struck four, one from the spot, while Scott got the other. A John Parke own-goal and a late strike from Coates put a slightly better complexion on things for the visitors, who had ex-Hibee Jackie Plenderleith at centre half. The main topic of conversation after the game was the fact that the Summer Cup draw had been made and Hibs had been paired with Hearts, Dunfermline and Falkirk.

But just four days later, that conversation switched to the news of Walter Galbraith's departure. The manager offered his resignation and it was accepted by the board, which immediately announced that no rush appointment would be made as the right man was sought out to fill the vacancy.

Galbraith may have moved on, but the fixtures kept coming and although the relegation fears had been eased of late there remained a need to pick up points, if only to cheer up the fans. Managerless Hibs could hardly have asked for a more difficult tie to follow Galbraith's resignation, when they travelled to Parkhead to face a rampant Celtic. In what turned into a horror show the Hibees were thumped 5–0, Murdoch (2 – 1 pen), Chalmers (2) and Divers all beating Ronnie Simpson who, despite the scoreline, did not have a bad game between the sticks.

The East of Scotland Shield was still a prized competition in the Sixties and holders Hibs met Hearts at Easter Road on 21 March. Both sides fielded strong line-ups, though Hibs included three 17-year-olds in their number – Jimmy Stevenson, Peter Cormack and Jimmy O'Rourke. On the night the Hibees were too strong for their city neighbours and won 2–0 thanks to a Cormack penalty and a superb strike from Vincent. It was a great week for Davy Hogg, who went on to play for the Scotland Amateur side against England on the Friday night. That same midweek Neil Martin turned out for the Scottish League against the English League at Sunderland and nobody was the least bit surprised that he scored a real beauty in a 2–2 draw.

With the search for a manager continuing, Hibs welcomed St Mirren to Easter Road, and in a tough encounter they ground out a 1–0 win with Vincent getting the points-winning goal. Effectively, that removed the pressure from Hibs as results elsewhere virtually guaranteed Hibs First Division football for the following season. One player who would not be around to see out the season was Duncan Falconer, who emigrated to Australia the following midweek, although Hibs retained his registration just in case the big defender failed to settle in his new home.

Next on the agenda was a visit to Pittodrie, where Aberdeen had been finding some good form, and that pattern continued as they swept Hibs aside with a 3–1 win. The Dons scored through Lister, Kerrigan and Winchester while almost inevitably, Martin counted for Hibs.

After several weeks of having a vacancy in the manager's chair, the Hibs board finally moved to appoint a successor to Walter Galbraith by enticing Jock Stein away from Dunfermline. It was an ambitious and well received appointment: Stein was recognised as a manager who could restore pride to Hibernian. A centre half with Albion Rovers, Llanelly and Celtic, his playing career was cut short by a serious knee injury, but he immediately moved into coaching with the Parkhead side before taking up his post with the Pars, where he enjoyed a Scottish Cup win in 1961. Just 41 years old, Stein would be an instant success with his new charges.

Airdrie were the unlucky visitors to Easter Road as the terraces were packed for the home 'debut' of Jock Stein. The fans were not disappointed as the Hibees won a lot more easily than the 2–1 scoreline suggests. Scott and Martin scored for Hibs while the Diamonds got their consolation through Murray. Willie Wilson made a rare appearance in goal as Ronnie Simpson's 46-game ever-present record came to an end due to an injury to his wrist. That same weekend Hibs received and rejected an invitation to play some games in Austria in the coming pre-season. Much as the club would have liked to accept, the dates clashed with those set aside for the Summer Cup.

Another East of Scotland Shield tie was next for Hibs, but this time they had to relinquish their hold on the trophy as they went down 3–0 at Tynecastle with White (2) and Wallace on target for the Gorgie men.

Hibs now had a ten-day break, but it would not prove to be a time to wind down for the players as manager Stein worked them hard in training. Having spent some time studying training methods at the invitation of Inter Milan coach Helenio Herrera, Stein introduced an Italian style to the daily sessions at Easter Road and significantly these involved a lot more use of the ball rather than focusing on simply running, as had been the case previously.

Some bad news came at this time also as John Parke was diagnosed as needing another cartilage operation, his second of the season, effectively ensuring he would not play again before the Summer Cup ties. On a brighter note, however, Jimmy Stevenson and Jimmy O'Rourke returned from Holland with enhanced reputations after helping Scotland to finish fourth in the European Youth Tournament.

In their final home league game of the season, Hibs trounced relegated East Stirling 5–2 with a hat-trick from Vincent and a double from Martin. The visitors scored through a Coburn double but the fans were happy and enjoyed the debut at centre half of new signing John McNamee from Celtic. It was an historic day for the visitors as this would be their last game before merging with Clydebank Juniors for the following season and playing under their new name of ES Clydebank.

The curtain came down on Hibs' league campaign with a visit to Tannadice on Friday 24 April 1964, the game having been brought forward from the Saturday to avoid clashing with the Scottish Cup final. Baxter was sent off, but ten-man Hibs still managed a draw thanks to McNamee opening his account while United scored through Young. The draw meant that after struggling for most of the season Hibs actually managed to finish tenth, with Rangers taking the title, some 25 points better off than the Hibees.

Though the league season was over, the Summer Cup would ensure more football for Hibs. The first game took place at Tynecastle and once again it was the home side who triumphed in winning a close and entertaining game 3–2. White (2) and a Hamilton penalty were too much for Hibs to overcome although O'Rourke scored a cracker and Vincent also found the net.

Hibs next faced Jock Stein's former employers Dunfermline, with the Pars having won their opening Summer Cup tie 5–2 against Falkirk. It was a great cup tie and the 1–1 scoreline was probably a fair reflection on how the game went. Martin scored for Hibs from the spot while Tommy Leishman deflected the ball past Wilson in the Hibs goal to earn the Pars a point.

In the match programme for the Dunfermline game, Jock Stein revealed which players would be retained for the coming season and these were: John Baxter, Peter Cormack, Bobby Duncan, Jim Easton, Duncan Falconer, John Fraser, John Grant, George Gartshore, Davy Hogg, Tommy Leishman, Neil Martin, John McNamee, Jimmy O'Rourke, John Parke, Pat Quinn, Jack Reilly, Jim Scott, Billy Simpson, Eric Stevenson, Pat Stanton, Jimmy Stevenson, Willie Wilson, Stan Vincent, George McNeill and Bernard Cullerton. Available for transfer were Ronnie Simpson and Willie Hamilton, while eight players were released – John Grant, Joe McClelland, Tommy Preston, Sandy Keay, Jim Docherty, Pat Hughes, Alex Cameron and Tony McGlynn. One or two surprises there, with the long-standing Grant, McClelland and Preston allowed to leave.

Three days after drawing at home to Dunfermline, Hibs travelled to Brockville, but could not find good form and lost 4–2, with O'Donnell, Houston, Redpath and Fulton on target for the Bairns and Martin and Vincent for the visitors. Of course their cause was not helped in any way by the fact that debutant goalkeeper Jack Reilly dislocated a finger and had to leave the field, meaning that Tommy Leishman had to take over in goals as Hibs finished the match with ten men. This result seemed likely to end Hibs' participation in the tournament, but they still had to play out their remaining fixtures starting with a visit to Easter Road by Hearts. In a dreary game, only Vincent and the home support had much to cheer as the little striker scored the only goal of the game against the section leaders.

The return match with Dunfermline brought an identical result to that of the game at Easter Road – a 1–1 draw. Melrose scored for the Pars while Leishman scored at the right end this time and Wilson had a wonderful game in goals, making a number of impressive stops, including a double penalty save. Astonishingly, Hibs had a chance to finish second in the group if they could beat Falkirk and Dunfermline drew with Hearts. Hibs did their bit by drubbing Falkirk 4–0 at Easter Road with that man Martin scoring a hat-trick, one of those from the spot, and Vincent getting the other. That result meant Hibs and Dunfermline finished in joint-second place and so a play-off was required to determine which side would face Kilmarnock home and away in the semi-final.

Meeting for the third time in 17 days, Hibs and Dunfermline served up a treat of a game in the Summer Cup play-off at Tynecastle, the Hibees winning 3–1 thanks to a double from Scott and another strike by Vincent. Paton scored for the Pars, but Hibs never looked like losing even though they were without top scorer Martin. He was playing for Scotland under-23s in France, where the Scots defeated their hosts, helped by an opening goal from the Hibee, who smashed home a glorious right-foot volley.

The first leg of the Summer Cup semi-final took Hibs to Rugby Park and in a thrilling game the home side just edged it 4–3 with a Hamilton penalty, a McNamee own goal and strikes from McIlroy and McInally.

Hibs countered through Vincent, Martin and Hamilton, while crucially Martin saw his late penalty saved brilliantly by Sandy McLaughlin. But for that save, Hibs would have gone into the second leg on level terms, but it mattered not as three days later they demolished Kilmarnock 3–0 at Easter Road to win the tie 6–4 on aggregate and qualify to meet Aberdeen in the final. The scorers against Killie were Martin, who got two, and Vincent, but special mention must be made of the solid displays of Wilson in goals and McNamee and Stanton at the heart of the defence. The final, as will soon be explained, was delayed and that allowed the players to head off early for a well-earned close season break.

Chapter Nineteen

1964/65

JIMMY AND PAT BREAK THROUGH

Hibs certainly started the 1964/65 season with a bang, travelling to Aberdeen on the first day of August to face the Dons in the first leg of the delayed Summer Cup final. The match had been scheduled for the previous June, but a typhoid outbreak in Aberdeen put paid to any thoughts of the team travelling north until after the close season. The teams had finished ninth and tenth the previous season, Hibs just two points behind their rivals for the silverware, so a close game was anticipated.

Since the arrival of Jock Stein, things down at Easter Road had improved immensely as he immediately made his mark on a mediocre Hibs side by introducing former Celt John McNamee and resurrecting the career of Willie Hamilton. The Pittodrie leg was a close affair, with the home side winning 3–2 despite Hibs giving as good as they got and securing two fine away goals thanks to Jim Scott.

The Dons came to Edinburgh just four days later and this time Hibs triumphed 2–1, with goals from Vincent and Eric Stevenson. Extra time couldn't separate them and the aggregate score of 4–4 meant a replay would be needed, but League Cup activity awaited both sides and so the game was shelved until 2 September, with Aberdeen winning the toss to determine the venue would be Pittodrie.

The League Cup pitched Hibs into a group with Third Lanark, Dunfermline and Airdrie and the Hibees got off to the best possible start with a convincing 3–0 home win over Third Lanark, Martin, Stevenson and a Stanton penalty providing the goals. Playing at left back that day for Thirds was a young Joe Davis, who later went on to join Hibs and became a real stalwart in the defence as well as a deadly marksman from the penalty spot.

League Cup ties were played on successive Saturdays and Wednesdays so the following midweek Hibs travelled to Jock Stein's old stamping ground of Dunfermline. It was not a happy return for the gaffer as he watched his side losing 2–0 to a strong Pars side. As only the team that topped the group would qualify for the later stages, Hibs could not afford a slip-up in their next game, against Airdrie at Easter Road. The defensive frailties which had appeared at East End Park were not in evidence that day as a Scott hat-trick and singles from Hamilton and Martin secured a romping 5–0 win.

The league campaign would now begin and that pushed the remaining League Cup ties to midweek dates. Hibs started the long haul with a trip to Shawfield where they faced newly promoted Clyde and duly gave them a tough introduction to football at this higher level by running out 3–1 winners, thanks to a double from the irrepressible Martin and a cracker from Scott.

Hibs were back in Glasgow the following midweek, when they tra-velled to Cathkin Park where they put a plucky Third Lanark outfit to the sword with goals from Scott and Quinn, thereby making their next fixture in that competition a real crunch game as Dunfermline would be the opposition and Hibs had already lost the first game in Fife. It was not to be, as the Fifers took away a point in a 1–1 draw despite a bullet header from McNamee.

The games were coming thick and fast now with that delayed replay in the Summer Cup on the horizon, but the matter of the last League Cup group tie had to be addressed first, with Hibs visiting Airdrie looking for a win that would only be meaningful if Third Lanark could beat Dunferm-line. Hibs got their win rather easily, Hamilton and a Cormack hat-trick securing a 4–1 win, but Thirds could not overcome the Pars and so the Fifers progressed to the quarter-finals.

The Summer Cup tie was finally played on 2 September 1964, two days before the Forth Road Bridge was officially opened to the public, and so presumably Hibs travelled the long way around to reach Pittodrie. They coasted home 3–1, with the goals from Cormack, Hamilton and Scott very nearly being added to but for an Ogston save from a Stanton penalty and shots against the woodwork by Martin and Cormack. Stein had barely arrived and already there was silverware in the trophy cabinet. Allied to a decent run in the League Cup and a win in the opening league fixture, all was looking rosy down Easter Road way.

Sadly, our near neighbours Heart of Midlothian put a damper on things when they visited Easter Road on league business the Saturday after the Summer Cup win and left with both points thanks to a deserved 5–3 victory. Manager Jock Stein was magnanimous in defeat and accepted that on the day Hearts had punished the Hibs defence for slack play. Unfortunately, Scott's brace and a single from Martin meant nothing.

Stein was a great motivator and soon had his players believing in themselves again as they went to Brockville and returned with both points thanks to a solo effort by Scott. This cheered the travelling fans who returned home in good spirits, possibly to watch the Daleks on *Doctor Who* – the scary robot-like creatures had made their first appearance on BBC TV that summer. An alternative may have been a trip to the pictures to watch Michael Caine in *Zulu* although many argued that *Doctor Who* was more realistic.

Aberdeen came calling next and they were keen to avenge that Summer Cup defeat. Hibs ran out worthy 4–2 winners, thanks to another Scott hat-trick, one of which was a penalty, and a goal from Hamilton. Although Neil Martin hadn't made the scoresheet that day, he was consoled by the fact that he had been selected to play for the Scottish League against the League of Ireland. His previous appearances in the Scotland jersey had brought a goal in each game against the English League and France under-23s.

But for the blip against Hearts, the league campaign had started pretty well and the good form continued as Hibs travelled to Tannadice and defeated Dundee United 1–0, with Scott continuing his purple patch in front of goal. The next game would be a real test for Stein's Hibees as Kilmarnock were due at Easter Road. Killie had a very strong team and the previous season they had finished second in the league behind Rangers, pushing the Ibrox club all the way.

In the Kilmarnock team which arrived on Saturday 3 October 1964 were goalkeeper Bobby Ferguson, a youngster who later played for Scotland on numerous occasions, and Tommy McLean, the diminutive winger who was just 17 and had a glittering career ahead of him as a player. The Ayrshire side were too strong for Hibs on the day and only Martin's strike gave any cheer in a 2–1 defeat.

The following midweek was one which went down in the annals of Hibernian history as Jock Stein had persuaded chairman Willie Harrower that the club could benefit both on and off the park by inviting the mighty Real Madrid to play a friendly at Easter Road. The players would surely gain from facing such star-studded opposition while a guaranteed huge attendance would handsomely cover the Spanish side's appearance fee and also add ever-needed cash to the coffers of Hibernian FC.

Madrid had won the European Cup five times in succession and were giants in the Spanish League, with players such as Ferenc Puskas, Francisco Gento and Jose Santamaria in their ranks. At home in the Bernabeu, over the period from 1956/57 to 1963/64, they had played 109 matches, scoring 366 goals and conceding just 66, but most astonishing of all is that they did not lose a single one of those games.

Thirty-thousand fans flocked to Easter Road and on the night Hibs played brilliantly in beating the Spanish giants 2–0, with goals from Cormack and an own goal via Spanish defender Zoco. That own goal was Hibs' 200th against foreign opposition and well deserved on a night when Jock Stein out-thought his Spanish counterpart and Quinn, Stanton and Hamilton excelled in a team with no failures in its ranks.

The tails were up now among the Hibernian players and the following Saturday they went to Ibrox and thumped reigning champions Rangers 4–2, after a double from 17-year-old Peter Cormack and thrilling strikes from Quinn and Hamilton. Playing a 4–2–4 formation had Rangers guessing, and although they twice took the lead the better team won on the day.

Stein had his team flying now, and a visit to Muirton Park to face St Johnstone saw no drop in the style of play with Hibs playing some fine football in winning 3–1, Cormack, Quinn and Martin securing the points. Morton were next to face the rampant Hibs and left with nothing as Cormack and a Scott penalty snuffed out a stuffy visiting defence in a 2–1 win. In between those two games, a fine servant of the club, centre half Jim Easton, was transferred to Dundee, leaving behind his replacement and good friend John McNamee.

The three-game unbeaten league run was extended to four when Hibs travelled to Motherwell and won 2–0, thanks to Quinn and a Scott penalty. Neil Martin had missed out that day due to injury while Irish international John Parke captained the team from his customary left-back slot. After ten games, Hibs were sitting third behind leaders Killie and second-placed Hearts, the only two clubs to have beaten them so far, with Celtic only fifth and Rangers even lower.

Manager Jackie Cox brought his talented St Mirren team to Easter Road knowing that the Hibees were in great form and looking for a fifth win on the trot. In the Buddies' line-up that day was Archie Gemmell, who later played in Brian Clough's European Cup-winning side at Nottingham Forest and made many appearances in a Scotland jersey. A goal from midfielder Ross earned the visitors a point as despite much huffing and puffing the home team could manage only one goal through Jim Scott.

During the following week, John Parke was transferred to Sunderland, and one wonders whether Stein giving him the captaincy two weeks earlier against Motherwell had been a way of recognising the superb service the player had given to Hibernian. His replacement was Joe Davis, signed from Third Lanark, who would be Hibs' next opposition at Easter Road. It's not clear who replaced Joe in the Thirds defence, but he must have had a torrid time as the Hibees hammered five goals without reply. A Hamilton double was only bettered by Martin's hat-trick, the big striker clearly in the mood having scored two for Scotland the previous midweek against Spurs in the John White testimonial match at White Hart Lane.

Feeling good after a nap hand against luckless Thirds, Hibs popped

over the recently opened Forth Road Bridge hoping to avenge their
League Cup exit at the hands of Dunfermline, but in a hard-fought game
the strikers left their shooting boots at home while leaving the points in
Fife following a 1–0 defeat.

Dundee were sitting mid-table when they arrived at Easter Road, but
were no soft touch as their form the previous season had won them a
place in Europe in the shape of the Inter Cities Fairs Cup. Manager Bob
Shankly had a fine squad of players at his disposal, including former
Hibee Jim Easton, goalkeeper Ally Donaldson, midfield maestro Andy
Penman and lethal striker Alan Gilzean. In a pulsating end-to-end
encounter the teams finished level at 2–2, with Murray and Penman
scoring for the Dark Blues while Hamilton and Quinn found the net for
Hibs.

Jock Stein was philosophical about it all in the week leading up to the
Airdrie game at Broomfield and felt that Hibs should have had more from
the games against Dunfermline and Dundee because, he felt, they had
certainly played well enough. Ironically, the side spluttered through the
Airdrie game, but won both points thanks to a single goal from Cormack.
The league was fast approaching the half-way stage and Hibs were still
sitting in third place with Hearts and Killie above them as the tough
winter weather began to affect fixtures, leaving the table showing teams
having played an uneven number of matches.

Partick Thistle were languishing near the foot of the table when they
came to Easter Road the week before Christmas 1964 and Hibs were in
no mood to hand out early presents as they triumphed 2–1 with a penalty
from Scott and a goal from Quinn. Boxing Day brought Clyde to Easter
Road and on a boggy pitch the players from both sides served up a seven-
goal thriller, the Hibees coming out on top 4–3 thanks to a double from
Martin and goals from Hamilton and Vincent, who had replaced an
injured Jim Scott in the starting line-up.

The New Year started with the short journey to Tynecastle and high
hopes that Hibs could both avenge that earlier 5–3 defeat and put a dent
in the Gorgie side's title hopes. Both were achieved and in some style, if
not in the narrow 1–0 victory then in the astonishing winning goal struck
by Willie Hamilton from what looked like an impossible angle.

As New Year's Day had fallen on a Friday, there was another game set
to be played the following day, with Falkirk the visitors. Clearly buoyed
by their win across the city, Hibs set about destroying a Falkirk side
which boasted one John Lambie among its number. It was a day for the
strikers as Martin scored an astonishing four goals while Vincent chipped
in with a couple to secure the points in a thrilling 6–0 victory.

The January weather in Aberdeen was kind enough to allow the game
the following Saturday to survive, and Hibs came back with a point in the

bag thanks to a Hamilton strike in a 1–1 draw. It was the start of a very testing remainder of the month but the five points out of six possible was a good platform as Dundee United arrived at Easter Road. In his programme notes, Jock Stein warned that United would offer stiff opposition and his words rang true as the Arabs departed with both points in a 4–3 win. It was a quite amazing game. United raced into a 4–0 half-time lead, with Dossing (3) and Persson, the Scandinavian contingent at Tannadice, getting the goals. A spirited second-half fightback by Hibs saw Cormack (2) and Quinn (pen) almost rescue a point, but it was not to be.

The next two games would measure the championship aspirations of Stein's side as they were against league leaders Kilmarnock and reigning champions Rangers. The Killie game fell victim to the weather and so Hibs' next outing was against Rangers at Easter Road. The Ibrox outfit were smarting over the 4–2 win by Hibs earlier in the season and arrived looking for revenge, but for the first time for 62 years Hibs did the double, thanks to Neil Martin and a 1–0 win. Hibs played Rangers off the park that day and were most unfortunate to score only once. The two points kept Hibs in touch with Killie and Hearts at the top of the league.

The following Saturday saw Stein's men facing up to ES Clydebank at home in the Scottish Cup. This was the visitors' first ever Scottish Cup tie, as they had previously been East Stirlingshire until the Steedman brothers bought them out and moved them lock, stock and barrel to Kilbowie Park in Clydebank.

In the ES Clydebank line-up for that cup tie were goalkeeper Johnny Arrol, who later gave sterling service to Dundee, and a speedy number ten by the name of Andy Roxburgh! No doubt both players contributed well to the minnows holding Hibs to 1–1, Martin scoring for Hibs but Jones equalising. Rarely do 'underdogs' get a second bite at the cherry and that proved to be the case in the replay four days later, when Hibs went comfortably through 2–0 with goals from Hamilton and Cormack.

Back to league action and a visit from St Johnstone to Easter Road. Stein was anxious to secure the points as the postponed away tie to Killie had been arranged for the following Tuesday. His players didn't let him down, and the victory was somewhat easier than the 2–0 scoreline suggests. Martin (pen) and Eric Stevenson were the marksmen.

Killie were leading the championship race when Hibs came calling and the game was an absolute classic, with two skilful attacking sides going at each other from the off. The general consensus of the press corps was that the visitors were extremely unlucky in going down by four goals to three. Lady luck deserted Hamilton, Stevenson and Davis, who all hit the woodwork, so the goals from Martin (2) and Quinn were not quite enough on the day.

Another home tie in the Scottish Cup paired Hibs up with fellow First Division outfit Partick Thistle and the Jags suffered badly at the hands of a thrilling Hibs performance, going down 5–1 thanks to a double from the fit again Jim Scott and single strikes from Quinn, Martin and Cormack. Hibs were in the quarter-finals and the draw paired them with Rangers at Easter Road. Before then they had to travel to Cappielow on a freezing cold Saturday late in February and sadly they failed to win the game after a below-par performance by the defence. An early Jorn Sorensen goal was cancelled out by Scott before Joe Caven restored the Morton lead. Sorensen then scored again and although Quinn reduced the leeway, Hibs could not find an equaliser.

Having beaten Rangers home and away in the league there was an optimistic feeling among the support and players that maybe they could make it a hat-trick and that optimism was well founded as the Hibees ended the Ibrox outfit's cup dreams with a brilliant 2–1 victory. Baxter and Hamilton were credited with the goals, but many felt a Joe Davis lob had crossed the line before Rangers keeper Billy Ritchie scooped it out, only for Baxter to head home. With just two minutes left and a replay looking likely, Fraser blasted the ball at goal and Ritchie dived, only for Willie Hamilton to glance the ball off his head and divert it into the net. Three wins in one season over Rangers – heady days indeed.

Hibs fans were to be rocked that week with the announcement that manager Jock Stein was leaving to join Celtic. Just when the side was going so well in both league and cup it transpired that Celtic had made an approach and Stein had told a distraught chairman Willie Harrower that he wanted to move to the club where he had once played. An actual date for the move had not yet been decided, but Hibs were off their mark in looking for a successor. Early favourites were Eddie Turnbull and John Prentice, but Willie Harrower was a very single-minded man and he'd set his heart on luring Bob Shankly away from Dundee. He did so successfully, and the new man arrived with a good recent record, having taken Dundee to league-winning status in 1962 and then into the semi-finals of the European Cup the following season.

Four days into his new job, Shankly put out his team to face Motherwell at Easter Road and was rewarded with a good 2–0 victory, thanks to goals from Martin and Scott. In that same week Willie Hamilton returned to the international scene with a call-up to the Scottish League side scheduled to play their English counterparts at Hampden. It was no more than Hamilton deserved given his sparkling form in a green and white jersey.

The draw for the Scottish Cup semi-final had paired Hibs with Dunfermline, and Tynecastle was selected as the venue, but Hibs still had league business to take care of ahead of that tie, starting with a visit to

Love Street. In a dour game, with defences very much on top, the home side held Hibs to a 0–0 draw and another vital point had slipped away from the Hibees in their fight to remain in the league race.

Another tricky away tie followed, but Hibs fared better this time around by going to Cathkin Park and beating Third Lanark 2–0 with goals from Hamilton and Cormack. Glasgow beckoned again just two days later as Hibs travelled to Parkhead ready to face the charges of their former manager, Jock Stein. In a wonderful display of attacking football, the visitors won 4–2, with Martin scoring a hat-trick and an own-goal from full back Young completing the rout. Shankly was ecstatic and Hibs readied themselves to face Dunfermline for the chance to reach the Scottish Cup final.

Regrettably, it was not to be. A pale shadow of the victorious Parkhead side never really got going in the game and Dunfermline punished them with goals from Melrose and Smith. It was a bitter disappointment for the club and the supporters. There was little consolation in the fact that Hibs entertained the same opponents just four days later in a league match at Easter Road and won more convincingly than the solitary strike from Martin would suggest.

The league campaign was nearing its end, and Hibs were too far adrift to win the title, which would go to a last-day decider when Killie beat Hearts 2–0 to clinch it. Still, the Hibees were determined to make the best of the remaining matches, but travelled to Dens Park in early April and lost 2–1 in a tight game, which saw Vincent hit the visitors' goal.

Celtic came next and they arrived at Easter Road looking for revenge after Hibs had given them a hiding on their own patch just a couple of weeks earlier. Jock Stein was able to field seven of the side which went on to win the European Cup in 1967 and they were in devastating form as they crushed Hibs 4–0. Later that season, Stein would lead his side to Scottish Cup victory over Dunfermline.

The Summer Cup draw was made and matched Hibs, the holders, with Hearts, Dunfermline and Falkirk, but two more league ties awaited ahead of that competition starting. In the first of those, Hibs hosted relegation-doomed Airdrie at Easter Road and hammered the Diamonds 5–1, with goals from Hamilton (2), Scott, Martin and Cormack.

And so the final league game of the season had arrived and Hibs travelled to Firhill to play Partick. They were well and truly stung as the Jags triumphed 4–2. The Hibs goals were struck by Martin and Hamilton, but in truth the better team won on the day.

The final league table that season was very tight at the top, with Killie winning it on goal average – the preferred method in those days rather than the goal difference we use in the modern game. Goal average was arrived at by dividing the number of goals scored by the number of goals conceded. Killie had a goal average of 1.88, while Hearts finished with 1.84. Had the current rules applied, Hearts would have won the title with a goal difference of 41 as against just 29 for Killie.

During the following week, Hibs sent a side down to the Borders to face a Hawick side proudly opening their new stadium, Albert Park. A mix of first team and reserves proved too strong for the hosts as Martin (4), Scott (2), Cormack and Vincent rattled in eight goals, but the biggest cheer of the night was reserved for ex-Hibee Tommy McDonald, who got the only goal for Hawick.

Hibs had kicked the season off on 1 August the previous year, but it wasn't over yet as they began their defence of the Summer Cup with a home tie against oldest rivals and league runners-up Hearts. A superb 3–0 home win saw Hibs dump their neighbours and get off to a great start in what was a very difficult group. The goals came from Martin (2) and Scott, although it took the Hibees an hour to finally break down a stuffy Hearts defence.

Over the bridge next, to East End Park. This was not a happy hunting ground for the men from Leith – it had been six seasons since they had tasted victory over Dunfermline. Hoodoos are there to be broken, and two fine solo efforts from the mercurial Willie Hamilton allowed that to happen as Hibs triumphed 2–1. Group-topping Hibs then hosted Falkirk at Easter Road and the Bairns gave a good account of themselves, despite going down 3–2, thanks to goals from Cormack (pen), Scott and Baxter.

Things were certainly going well for the Hibees as they went to Tynecastle and left with a point in a 2–2 draw, Cormack and Martin getting the goals in a tight, even game. Dunfermline then arrived looking for revenge and duly got it in the shape of a 2–1 win at Easter Road, Martin scoring for Hibs, his 33rd of the season.

To qualify for the semi-final, Hibs had to win at Brockville and hope the result between Hearts and Dunfermline worked out in their favour. The first part was achieved thanks to goals from Cormack (pen), Eric Stevenson and O'Rourke, the youngster earning his chance after scoring 25 goals in that season's reserve league. Thankfully for Hibs, things went their way and they qualified to meet Motherwell in a two-leg semi-final, with the first game at Easter Road.

Things looked promising for another trip to the final when the Hibees went on to beat Motherwell 2–0 at Easter Road, thanks to a couple of cracking goals from Cormack and Stevenson, but four days later the Steelmen had reversed that score at the end of the regulation 90 minutes and the game went into extra time. The wheels came off the bus for Hibs at this stage and despite two goals from Cormack (pen) and Quinn, the hosts scored four more to win 6–4 and end the Hibs defence of the trophy.

An incident-packed season finally drew to a close and Hibs had finished fourth in the league, just four points behind winners Kilmarnock, and had reached the semi-final of the Scottish Cup. The manager had changed during the season also, with Jock Stein departing for Celtic and Bob Shankly arriving from Dundee. Real Madrid had come a-calling and had left suffering a 2–0 defeat and Jimmy O'Rourke had broken into the first team alongside his lifelong friend, Pat Stanton. There was also the small matter that Hibs would once again be playing in Europe, a stage upon which they had excelled in the past.

It was to be a very short close season for Hibs as they departed on a 20-day trip to North America, which involved nine games against opposition in both Canada and the USA. Most of June 1965 was taken up with either playing, training or travelling but it was a worthwhile trip in that it allowed the players to bond as a group.

First up, and probably the most difficult game of the tour, was a meeting with Nottingham Forest and in a close-fought encounter Hibs won 2–1, with goals from Baxter and Quinn. A game against British Columbia All Stars was very one-sided, with Hibs just failing to reach double figures, their nine goals coming from Martin (4), Cormack (2), Hamilton, Eric Stevenson and Davis. Calgary Kickers tried their best, but lost 7–1. Martin got a hat-trick as did Cormack, while Jim Scott grabbed the other.

Concordia All Stars fared little better in going down 15–1, with the prolific Neil Martin getting five, Quinn three, Hamilton, Cormack and Scott two each and a single from O'Rourke. The tour was as much a holiday for the players as anything else and they were enjoying the relaxed nature of the challenge games. Manitoba next offered up their All Stars and this time it finished 11–0, with Cormack and Scott each getting a hat-trick, two from Hamilton and singles from Quinn, Derek Whiteford and Eric Stevenson. Toronto Italia put up a better fight and lost only 4–0, the goals coming from Cormack, Scott, Martin and Eric Stevenson.

In Ottawa, where Hibs defeated the local All Stars 15–0, it was announced before the game that a beautiful silver salver would be presented to the game's outstanding personality. Hearing of this, Willie Hamilton decided to stake his claim, scoring seven of the goals and setting up a few others to boot. The salver was duly presented, but to Willie's dismay it would not fit into his kit bag and so he solved the problem by simply folding it in half! His team-mates, including the remaining goalscorers, Jimmy Stevenson (2), Cormack (2), Baxter, Quinn, Scott and Billy Simpson, could only look on in amusement.

Montreal Italia came next and a 3–0 win was recorded, courtesy of Hamilton, Jimmy Stevenson and O'Rourke, while it was across the border for the final game against New Jersey All Stars and a 6–1 win, thanks to Scott (2), Hamilton, Eric Stevenson, Quinn and Jimmy Stevenson.

At the end of the trip, fellow tourists Nottingham Forest returned home to England to face a domestic season in which they would go on to finish only 18th – missing relegation by just three points but also with the knowledge that the World Cup was being held in their country and that as hosts their national side would participate. Hibs, on the other hand, returned knowing that Scotland would not be involved in that tournament but that domestically they had everything to play for in challenging for a league championship won the previous season by Kilmarnock – by only a few points over Hibs and on goal average over city rivals Hearts.

Chapter Twenty

1965/66

SHANKLY SHAPES HIS SIDE

With Bob Shankly about to commence his first full season in the hot seat, Hibs would find themselves involved in four competitions, starting off with the Scottish League Cup, which began in its group format and matched the green and whites with Falkirk, St Mirren and Morton – all in the same First Division as the Easter Road outfit. The competition opened on 14 August, Hibs visiting Brockville, and despite playing some attractive football the visitors seemed still in the holiday mood as they went down 3–1, with Jim Scott scoring.

In this tight group it was important that no more points were dropped if Hibs were to progress to the later stages and so when St Mirren came calling the following Wednesday it was a relief to all concerned that Hibs carved out a 1–0 victory against all the odds, having lost goalkeeper Willie Wilson to a head injury after just 17 minutes of the first-half. There were no substitutes allowed in those days, and Wilson's departure meant that Peter Cormack had to take over in goal for the remaining 73 minutes. Cormack, ably assisted by defenders Billy Simpson, Joe Davis, John McNamee and captain John Baxter, kept the Buddies at bay, while a superb lay-off from Pat Stanton allowed Eric Stevenson to shoot the only goal of the game. Very bravely, Wilson came out for the second-half and played on the right wing rather than have his side carry on with just ten men. Amazingly, he almost added to Hibs' lead with a shot that whistled past a post.

The sun was shining on that Wednesday evening and it was just as well because the majority of the home crowd were standing on open terracing, but that situation would soon change as Hibs forged ahead with their plans to build a covered enclosure at the Albion Road (Famous Five Stand) end of the ground. In years to come, that enclosure would become a favourite gathering place for the Hibernian 'choir', but often not exclusively for 45 minutes of each game – the absence of segregation meant that many fans chose to stand behind the goal Hibs were attacking and then to move to the other end at half-time.

A visit to Cappielow on the Saturday saw Hibs thumping Morton 4–2. The goals were shared by Scott, Martin, McNamee and Baxter, who had the misfortune to also 'score' one of Morton's goals. With Willie Wilson still suffering from that head knock, Jack Reilly took over between the sticks and proved an able deputy with a number of good saves.

Although slap-bang in the middle of the League Cup qualifying group, the actual league campaign now kicked off, and in one of those quirks of the fixture calendar, Hibs found themselves back at Cappielow on the opening day of the new league season. Fielding the same starting team, Hibs improved their performance at both ends of the park by winning 5–1 this time around and once again the goals were shared with Martin (2), Scott, Quinn and Cormack on target. The Morton goal was scored by Allan McGraw, who went on to score a barrowload that season and earn himself a transfer to Easter Road.

Back to the League Cup again and a chance to avenge the opening tie defeat by Falkirk was duly taken when Quinn (pen), Martin and McNamee scored in a 3–1 win at Easter Road. The Bairns arrived that day in the charge of manager Sammy Kean, who had both played for and been trainer of Hibs in the past. In their line-up on the park, they included John Lambie and Johnny Graham, both of whom would in time end up at Hibs, and 'Big' Doug Baillie, captain, centre half and one-time Rangers player who would, in later years, carve out a career for himself as a football journalist with the *Sunday Post*.

A number of items in the match programme for that Falkirk game seem worthy of being highlighted. Firstly, the Hibs reserves were leading their own League Cup group, with Colin Grant and Stan Vincent most notable among the goalscorers, while Thomson Allan was doing his stuff between the sticks following Jack Reilly's enforced promotion to the first eleven. Also announced in that programme was the fact that Hibs had signed two promising youngsters on to their groundstaff, and they were named as John Murphy from Tynecastle Athletic and John Blackley from Gairdoch Juniors. Finally, supporters were advised that Hibs, having drawn Valencia of Spain in the Inter Cities Fairs Cup, would be making the home tie, due on September 8, all-ticket in respect of the Centre Stand. Briefs would cost 15/- (75p) and could be purchased during office hours.

A tricky visit to Love Street followed as Hibs continued their march through the League Cup section and this time they managed to finish the game with their keeper still in goals as they triumphed 3–0 with goals from Scott (2) and Cormack. That double not only took Jim Scott to the top of the Hibs scoring chart, it also helped ensure qualification for the quarter-final stages, where Alloa awaited.

The final League Cup group tie at home to Morton was a formality, but Hibs kept their run going with a fine 3–0 win when Cormack, Stevenson and Martin all scored in a pretty one-sided game. Of note that day was the fact that wearing number two for Morton was one John Madsen, who would later join Hibs and become a commanding centre half in the Easter Road defence, while wearing number 11 was a very young Joe Harper, who also ended up at Hibs, albeit via Aberdeen and Everton.

With qualification for the later stages of the League Cup secured, Bob Shankly might have been tempted to give some of his promising reserves a run in the Morton game, but he decided instead to leave a winning team alone as the following midweek Valencia arrived. The Spaniards were rightly reckoned to provide formidable opposition for the Easter Road men, but on yet another of those glorious European nights under the floodlights, Hibs secured a worthy and deserved 2–0 victory thanks to goals from Scott after just five minutes and McNamee, the latter netting his headed effort on the stroke of full-time. Valencia had packed their defence, and even when Hibs broke through they found keeper Zamora in sparkling form to deny them a bigger advantage ahead of the second leg in Spain.

There was to be no resting on their laurels for the Hibees: just three days later they faced reigning league champions Kilmarnock at Easter Road in a league fixture. In a quite fantastic advert for the Scottish game, two highly skilled and highly entertaining teams fought out a 3–3 draw, the goals from Cormack, Scott and Martin taking Hibs to the top of the First Division ahead of the first derby of the season, which would take place at Tynecastle the following Saturday.

Ahead of that tie, Hibs had to travel to Recreation Park, where they secured a comfortable 2–0 win over Alloa in the first leg of the League Cup quarter-final, with Martin and Quinn getting the goals against the plucky Second Division outfit. This seemed to guarantee a semi-final place, although the return leg still had to be faced before qualification was guaranteed. The likely opponents, should Hibs go through, were a Celtic team rejuvenated under the guidance of Jock Stein but Shankly would not have been thinking of the possibilities of that tie just yet as a derby match beckoned.

Bearing in mind that Hearts had only just lost the championship on the last day of the previous season, a stern test was anticipated by the Hibs camp, but after just ten minutes Shankly was delighted to see his team leading 4–0 in Gorgie, thanks to doubles from both Jimmy O'Rourke and Eric Stevenson. O'Rourke had been a replacement for the injured Neil Martin and he simply continued his reserve team scoring ways in blasting that double past Jim Cruickshank in the Hearts goal. It was a stunning victory and Hibs were simply flying at this stage, with the fans eagerly anticipating each game.

Alloa were next to fall to the Hibernian goal scoring machine and they did so in quite spectacular fashion as the green and whites crushed them

11–2 at Easter Road, thanks to Martin (4), Scott (4), Quinn, Joe Davis (pen) and Stevenson. It was around this time when Eric Stevenson began the routine he followed each time Hibs won a penalty. Basically, while the penalty was being taken by one of his team-mates, Stevie would go to the half-way line and crouch down with his back to the taker, relying on the crowd's reaction to make him aware of the outcome.

When Falkirk arrived at Easter Road the following Saturday on league business, they did so knowing they would be facing a team which had scored 42 goals in all competitions to date and it was only 25 September! By the time they had left again that total had increased to 47, thanks to a 5–1 thumping of the Bairns with goals from Martin (4) and Scott. Only one more game remained to be played before the eagerly anticipated League Cup semi-final with Celtic and that saw Hibs travelling to Shawfield to face Clyde where defenders McNamee and Baxter took time off from trying to stop the opposition from scoring to bag a goal each in a 2–1 win.

Ibrox was the chosen neutral venue for the Celtic game and 46,000 fans packed into the ground. A Neil Martin double had put Hibs 2–1 ahead, but with the Edinburgh side's fans praying for the final whistle a momentary lapse in concentration in defence in the 90th minute cost them dear when Bobby Lennox scored, and so extra time was needed. Neither team could score again, meaning a replay at the same venue was required. Prior to that, a very busy schedule would see Hibs taking on Motherwell in the league at Easter Road and then out to Spain for the return game against Valencia.

Hibs still led the league going into the Motherwell game, but the Fir Park side offered tough opposition and took a point home in a 2–2 draw. Hibs had led through Martin, but a double by 'Well, via Thomson and Delaney, looked as if it might earn the visitors the points until Davis cracked an equaliser from the penalty spot. In a somewhat controversial ending to the game, Jim Scott thought he'd struck the winner, but referee Mr Smail from Selkirk insisted he had blown for full-time before the ball beat Peter McCloy in the Motherwell goal.

At last the return game with Valencia had come around, some five weeks after Hibs had beaten them 2–0 in the first leg at Easter Road. The Hibees travelled to Spain knowing a very difficult game awaited them as Valencia were going strongly in La Liga, but Shankly was quietly confident his troops would not let him down. No Scottish team had ever won on Spanish soil. That, unfortunately, was still the case at the end of 90 eventful minutes in the Mestalla Stadium in front of 65,000 fans as the home side came out victorious by two goals to nil. Hibs gave a superb account of themselves, with Wilson, Stanton and McNamee the pick of the bunch, but a typical 'banana bend' free kick from Waldo after 14 minutes and a Sanchez Lage penalty against the run of play just 16 minutes from the end determined that a third game would be required to separate the teams. In those days, extra time and penalties had not yet been introduced, and Hibs lost the toss to decide where that game would be played.

A weary Hibs side arrived back in Edinburgh to face a home league game with Rangers, the side who had replaced them at the top of the league on goal average, and there they stayed thanks to a 2–1 victory – Willoughby hitting a double for the visitors while Stevenson countered for Hibs. This was a very strong Rangers side, despite the loss of Jim Baxter to Sunderland, including such stalwarts as John Greig, Billy Ritchie in goals, Ron McKinnon, Jim Forrest, Willie Henderson and Willie Johnston. They had worked their way to the top of the league by handing out a six-goal thumping to Kilmarnock the previous week.

Two days after meeting one of the Glasgow giants, Hibs travelled through to meet the other in the replay of the League Cup semi-final and suffered a 4–0 reversal, going down to goals from McBride, Hughes, Lennox and Murdoch. It was to say the least a major disappointment and Shankly was distraught after the game but refused to offer any excuses, concentrating instead on rightly praising a fine performance by Jock Stein's side, who had now earned the right to meet Rangers in the final.

Hibs got the show back on the road the following Saturday when they went to Love Street and defeated St Mirren 2–0, with goals from newly appointed penalty king Joe Davis and 19-year-old Jimmy Stevenson, who'd been promoted from the high scoring reserves for the day. All of the games Hibs were playing in such a short space of time were taking their toll. Players were suffering injuries which either kept them out of the side or meant they were playing at less than 100 per cent fit, and so it was ideal for Shankly that his reserves were doing so well. Playing regularly in the second string in those days were players such as Thomson Allan, Bobby Duncan, Colin Grant and Jimmy O'Rourke, all of whom would go on to make their mark in the first team in the seasons ahead.

A second successive away game took Hibs to Glasgow to face Partick Thistle and the Jags came out on top in a thrilling match by 3–2 after the visitors had stormed into a 2–0 lead with goals from Quinn and Cormack. Defensive lapses allowed Thistle back into the game, with goals from Gibb and future Scotland manager Andy Roxburgh, who grabbed a double. This result meant Hibs dropped to sixth in a table led by Rangers with Celtic and Dunfermline in hot pursuit.

On Wednesday 3 November 1965 the Hibs v Valencia epic was finally decided, almost two full months after the first leg had been played at Easter Road, and it was the hosts who triumphed in front of their own fans on a soaking wet Spanish evening. The scoreline read 3–0, but the fact that the home fans gave the Hibees a standing ovation at the end of the 90 minutes perhaps shows that the game was much closer than the result would suggest. Hibs had hit both bar and post through McNamee and Scott respectively, but Zamora was not to be beaten on the night and Shankly sportingly agreed that the Spanish deserved to go through. In the newspapers sold in Valencia the following day, Hibs were paid glowing tributes and named as the best foreign team ever to have played there! High praise indeed, but the European adventure was over and Hibs needed to get back to winning ways in the league.

When Hamilton Academical arrived at Easter Road on Saturday 6 November they were to be the first visiting team to play at an Easter Road boasting a new covered enclosure! The 'shed', or 'cave' as it became affectionately known, had been erected behind the goal at the now Famous Five Stand end of the ground and Hibs celebrated the formal opening of it in style by thumping Accies 11–1. The goals came from Eric Stevenson (3), O'Rourke (2), Scott (2), Cormack, Davy Hogg, Davis and an own-goal, with Anderson getting the Accies consolation. Stevie's hat-trick was his first for the club and took him on to ten goals for the season.

Members past and present of the Hibernian Supporters' Association in Sunnyside will be interested to read that the following Monday their clubrooms were opened at the then address of 172 Easter Road Lane. Hibs' chairman William P. Harrower formally opened the clubrooms a couple of weeks later at a dinner dance organised to celebrate the affair.

From 12 goals in one game to seven in the next there was certainly no shortage of goalmouth action whenever Hibs were playing. On this occasion, however, only three of those seven were scored by Hibs as they went down 4–3 to Dundee at Dens Park, goals from O'Rourke, Eric Stevenson and Stanton failing to make Bob Shankly's return to his old stamping ground a happy one. Hibs were excellent value for money going forward, but were prone to defensive lapses, and on this occasion it had cost them dear with another two points dropped.

In an effort to overcome the defensive shortcomings, Shankly signed Alan Cousin from Dundee and the big fella made a winning debut appearance as Hibs travelled to Annfield and defeated a plucky Stirling Albion 2–1. Cousin, who replaced the suspended McNamee, made good use of the ball throughout and was involved in the passing move which saw Cormack score the opener. A Davis penalty secured the points.

Dunfermline provided the Easter Road opposition the following Saturday. The Pars were third-placed behind Rangers and Celtic and on the back of a seven-game unbeaten run, including a six-goal romp at Shaw-field the previous Saturday. That run had produced 35 goals, a fantastic average of five per game, and so Hibs would have to be at their best to stop the goal scoring machine. There had been an early winter snowfall the night before the game and conditions were tricky underfoot, but both teams served up decent football and the end result of 1–1 was a fair reflection of the game. The Pars scored through Ferguson while Hibs' O'Rourke netted his sixth of the season with a finely placed header beyond keeper Eric Martin, who had replaced Jim Herriot in the Dunfermline goal following the latter's transfer to Birmingham City.

The Scottish weather worsened and the scheduled home fixture against Dundee United suffered a late postponement and would not actually take place until the following April, which was probably a bigger blow to Jimmy O'Rourke than most as he looked set to claim the number ten jersey vacated by Neil Martin, who had been transferred to Sunderland. It was nearing half-way in the league race with Rangers leading on 24 points, Celtic next on 21 and Hibs lying fifth with 17. Four Hibs men were ever-presents until that point – Joe Davis, Pat Stanton, Jim Scott and Eric Stevenson.

Failings in front of goal cost Hibs dear in their next match against Celtic at Parkhead. The popular post-match consensus was that Hibs had been the better team but were punished for failing to take the chances which came their way, while Hughes and McBride did their jobs in securing a 2–0 win for the home side. Although postponements had hit the first team, the reserves were still managing to play, and one or two names were jumping out from the various match reports. Centre forward Stan Vincent struck his tenth goal of the season to beat Reserve League leaders Celtic while at the same time keeper Thomson Allan managed a fourth successive shut-out.

As Christmas fast approached, St Johnstone turned up at Easter Road hoping Hibs would be in a giving mood. They were, but sadly for the Saints it was a 3–0 thumping that was given, with Cormack, Cousin and O'Rourke getting the goals. The reserves were also going well and a new name had begun to appear regularly among the scorers – Colin Stein.

On Christmas Day 1965 Hibs travelled to Pittodrie where they faced an Aberdeen team which had not lost in its previous ten games. Courtesy of goals from Cormack, Scott and McNamee, that run was ended as Hibs took the points in a 3–1 win and moved on to 21 points from 16 games, just six behind leaders Celtic. McNamee's goal could have been added to in that game but for a goal-line clearance by Ally Shewan, but the one that did count was his fifth of the season, a valuable contribution by the big defender.

Having given up their Christmas Day the players now had to forfeit New Year's Day also, with the pitch at Easter Road being fit for play and of course Hearts providing the opposition. The Gorgie side were not doing so well in this league campaign, but they arrived looking to avenge the 4–0 drubbing Hibs had given them back in September at Tynecastle. Storming into a two-goal lead thanks to a brace from Cormack, Hibs looked good value for the points, but the defensive lapses that had blighted earlier results came back with a vengeance and Hearts scored three times without reply, via Wallace, Kerrigan and a very unfortunate own-goal from McNamee. 'What must Hibs do to beat Hearts?' would have been the question on the lips of the home fans as they trooped out after the game. That comeback extended the Gorgie men's run to 13 seasons without losing at Easter Road, which no doubt spoiled as many New Year parties as it enhanced.

So 1966 had not started well for Hibs and two days later Kilmarnock compounded the misery by winning a tight game 1–0 at Rugby Park. The Hibees played well below their best and lost Jimmy O'Rourke during the game after the youngster took a sore one on the shin. Two straight defeats did not help the league position and Shankly, anxious to reverse that trend, shook the team up a little for the visit of Morton the following Saturday.

Spotted playing left back or left half for Armadale Thistle, Colin Stein was snapped up by Hibs and pushed straight into the reserve team, where he turned out as a striker and bagged 11 goals in 12 games, earning him the chance to make his debut for the first eleven that turned out against Morton on Saturday 8 January 1966. Although not among the goals his fine play contributed to a good 4–1 victory which saw O'Rourke and Cormack each grab a double.

With the Scottish Cup looming, Shankly was anxious to try and get some consistency going among his players, but his cause was not helped at Brockville the following weekend when the Bairns did what others had done before in overhauling a Hibs lead to win the game 3–2. The Hibs goals were the first of many which Colin Stein would score in his career, but the youngster would have been disappointed that the points were lost when there for the taking. Scoring two for the Bairns that day was future Hibs signing Johnny Graham.

Foul weather in the Edinburgh area meant that Hibs would not play again until the end of January and many wished the bleak winter had claimed that away game to Motherwell. A miserable performance from the green and whites saw them trounced 4–0, which hardly bred confidence in the Hibs fans, who now knew that their heroes would begin the latest quest for Scottish Cup glory by playing Third Lanark at Easter Road the following Saturday.

The form being displayed by Hibs had prompted Shankly to hit out in his programme notes as he suggested the 0–4 reversal at Fir Park happened because Hibs had turned in their worst performance since he took over. Calling upon his charges to shake off the lethargy and get back on the road by achieving a comprehensive home win over Third Lanark, who had been relegated the previous season, Shankly must have been a little relieved to see his men struggle to secure a narrow 4–3 win to take them through. While Cousin, Scott, O'Rourke and a penalty from Davis gave the home fans entertainment, Hibs also contrived to lose three bad goals in front of that same nervous home support.

Meanwhile, over at Tynecastle, Hearts were disposing of Clyde to set up an Edinburgh derby in the next round, which would take place in Gorgie just two weeks later. In the interim, Hibs had the small matter of playing a league game at Ibrox and a first-half knee injury to keeper Willie Wilson hardly helped as the visitors went down 2–0 to the league leaders.

And so to Tynecastle, in the hope that maybe, just maybe, this would be the year Hibs would end their Scottish Cup winning drought. Alas, it was not to be as Hearts recorded a 2–1 victory despite a sterling effort from the visitors in the dying stages to force a replay. John McNamee struck the solitary goal for the unfortunate Hibees.

Despite a poor first-half showing in the next league game against Partick Thistle at Easter Road a much changed Hibs side, with youngsters Thomson Allan, Colin Stein, Bobby Duncan and Colin Grant prominent, defeated a stuffy Jags outfit 2–0, Cormack and Stein being the scorers. His third goal in senior football would be one to remember for Stein as he weaved in from the left, defenders strewn in his wake, before thrashing a fine left-foot shot past keeper George Niven. A flu bug had given the youngsters their chance, with Eric Stevenson and Jim Scott particularly badly affected, and the kids certainly made the best of the opportunity.

Going into the next fixture, which brought St Mirren to Easter Road on a cold March Wednesday evening, Hibs were sitting in seventh place, some 14 points behind leaders Rangers, while the Buddies were fighting for their lives at the wrong end of the table, just two points off a relegation spot. As anticipated by manager Shankly in his programme notes, the visitors put up a real fight and some argued they were unlucky not to take a point from the clash, but the truth is that Hibs spurned a number of good scoring opportunities so the 3–2 victory was merited. Grant, Stein and Cormack claimed the goals for Hibs, with Adamson and Robertson countering for the Buddies.

Earlier in the season Hibs had struck 11 goals against Hamilton, but the return match at Douglas Park was an altogether tamer affair, with a paltry attendance of just under 1,000 fans witnessing the visitors scrape home 2–1 after going a goal behind. Grant and an own-goal won the points and really the most significant factors were that the win extended the unbeaten run to three games, while Grant's strike, his second in senior football, was Hibs' 100th of the season.

The March weather was being kind and Hibs had Easter Road playable for the visit of Dundee on league business on 12 March. The Dark Blues were well known to manager Bob Shankly, who had been responsible for signing most of them, but his 'inside knowledge' failed to pay off in the shape of a victory as Sammy Wilson, an addition to the squad after Shankly's departure, won the Taysiders a point. The Hibs goal came from ex-Dundee stalwart Alan Cousin, playing in a midfield role that day.

Struggling Stirling Albion were the next team to face a Hibs team which had dropped only one point in its previous four games, and although they put up a decent show, particularly in a defensive sense, Cormack settled things with the only goal of the game. On the international front, 21-year-old Pat Stanton was selected to play for the Scottish League against their English counterparts at St James' Park, Newcastle, and turned in a fine performance, surprising no one at Easter Road, where everyone knew just how good a player he was.

Back in January, the Hibs v Clyde game had fallen victim to the weather and was now finally about to be played, some two months later. The Shawfield outfit had been having a bit of an up and down season and although in 11th place on the day of that game, the Bully Wee were now a mere five points ahead of second-bottom St Johnstone in the fight to avoid joining Hamilton in the relegation positions. Hamilton, remember, had conceded 11 goals at Easter Road and with 26 games played they had amassed just three points and conceded 98 goals in the process, so it was obviously not just Hibs that had given them a pasting!

The Glasgow side arrived straight off the back of an impressive 6–1 victory over title-chasing Dunfermline and so it was imperative that Hibs stay tight at the back while creating chances for the forwards. Manager Shankly had the team prepared well and goals from O'Rourke, Stein and a Davis penalty secured a 3–1 win, with top scorer Joe Gilroy netting for the visitors.

Qualification for the following season's Inter Cities Fairs Cup was still a possibility at this time, but a difficult run-in to the end of the season awaited a Hibs team blighted by injuries and suspensions. On the visit to Dunfermline, Hibs twice came back from a goal behind and looked good for a share of the spoils before a late and suspiciously offside-looking winner from Paton who, along with Ferguson, had scored the others for the Pars. Yet another successful strike from the spot by Joe Davis and a stunning individual goal from Eric Stevenson were not quite enough on the day.

Dundee United were among the clubs challenging Hibs for a place in Europe and did their chances of qualifying no harm whatsoever when they won a thrilling nine-goal encounter against the green and whites at Tannadice. In a game littered with penalty kicks, Hibs fought back from 3–1 down to level at 3–3, only to lose a fourth that looked well offside and a fifth from a twice-taken penalty when keeper Thomson Allan saved the first attempt but was adjudged by referee Webster to have moved. United's goals came from Gillespie (2), Dossing (2) and Mitchell (pen). Hibs countered through Davis (2, 1 pen), Cormack and Stanton.

Successive odd-goal defeats in the games against Dunfermline and Dundee United effectively put paid to all hopes of European qualification by the time champions-elect Celtic visited Easter Road on 16 April and in what proved to be the club's only goalless draw of the season, a point was secured thanks to a good defensive display. Bearing in mind that Celtic had arrived having scored 101 goals in 31 games that wasn't a bad return. Leading the way in the Parkhead scoring charts with an incredible 41 in all competitions was Joe McBride, who would go on to play for Hibs in later years.

Just 11 days after that high-scoring meeting at Tannadice, Dundee United visited Easter Road to fulfil the fixture scheduled for earlier that season but cancelled due to bad weather. Once again goals were flying in from all directions and when the dust had settled at 4.40pm there was to be a share of the points in a 3-3 draw. Stein, Stevenson and a Smith own-goal counted for Hibs while Gillespie (2) and Briggs struck for United. That goal from Briggs must have been particularly sore for Shankly to take as the United full back was his son-in-law.

Just four more fixtures remained before Hibs could shut up shop and settle back to watch the 1966 World Cup finals. The first of those took the Hibees to Muirton Park, Perth, with Shankly looking for his troops to do the double over St Johnstone. That feat was duly achieved when goals from Stein, Scott and Stevenson earned a 3–1 victory, a Richmond penalty giving the Saints their goal in the first minute of the game. The highlight of the game, however, was the performance of young Colin Stein, who not only scored one but also laid on the other two. Shankly described Jim Scott's goal, after brilliant lead-up play by Stein, as one of the best he had ever witnessed.

The final league match of the season saw Eddie Turnbull bring his blossoming Aberdeen side to Easter Road and leave again with both points in the bag, thanks to a solitary strike by the veteran Harry Melrose. Despite this win the Dons finished only eighth, two points behind Hibernian.

It had been a mixed bag of a league season in terms of results. Home draws had cost dearly, as had odd-goal defeats, but performances such as those put up against Valencia augured well for the future. So too did the achievements of the reserves, with Allan, Stein and Grant among those breaking into the first team while others such as Bobby Duncan would also have their day. Top league goalscorers were Cormack (15), O'Rourke (10), Eric Stevenson (10) and Davis (8).

The month of May 1966 saw a double meeting take place with Hearts as the 1965 and 1966 East of Scotland Shield finals were contested on the 4th at Easter Road and the 7th at Tynecastle. Hearts went into the first game as holders and retained that right in defeating Hibs 3–1, Davis getting the Hibs goal from the spot. At Tynecastle, the Gorgie side completed a double in winning 4–2 and this time it was Stein and Scott who found the target.

Chapter Twenty-One

1966/67

A TIME OF MOURNING

Preparation for this new season took the form of a couple of friendly matches against English opposition, the first of which brought Nottingham Forest to Easter Road, the visitors buoyed by the fact that they had finished fifth in their league the previous season. They also boasted their new signing from Arsenal – a lad by the name of Joe Baker. In an entertaining game the visitors took the lead twice through Baker, but Hibs fought back on each occasion and went on to win the game 3–2, with goals from Stein, McGraw and a Davis penalty.

Facing a tough opening League Cup tie against Rangers due the following Saturday, Hibs completed their preparations with a visit to Hull City and crashed 3–1 to the Tigers – a Davis penalty the only strike for the visitors. Shankly's team played well enough at Boothferry Park but couldn't convert chances into goals. A similar situation unfolded at Ibrox in that League Cup match when a goal from George McLean just five minutes from time secured the points for a Rangers side who had two new signings – Alex Smith from Dunfermline and Dave Smith from Aberdeen.

Wednesday 17 August brought Kilmarnock to Easter Road in the second group match and they arrived with a pretty impressive record of results against Hibs in Edinburgh, the home side having to look all the way back to 1961/62 for evidence of a win. It was a tight game, with both sides having chances and both goalkeepers in fine form, but eventually a double from McGraw cancelled out Queen's strike for the visitors in a 2–1 win.

The day before Hibs next played – against Stirling Albion at Annfield – all connected with Hibernian FC were plunged into mourning following the death of club director and former chairman Harry Swan at the age of 70, after a period of illness lasting many weeks. Swan became a director in 1931 and was made club chairman in 1933, a position he held for 30 years, after which he handed over those reins to William P. Harrower and was made a life director of the club in recognition of the fine service given to Hibernian. During his chairmanship, Hibs won three league titles and were pioneers of the game in Europe as well as being first to install floodlights.

Football goes on, however, and Hibs faced a Stirling Albion side who were coming off the back of losing eight goals to Rangers. Whether the mood of the players was affected following the death of Harry Swan can only be a matter of speculation, but the Hibees did not play their normal standard of game. Although Albion caused them some problems, the result was right in the end as Cormack and Scott each grabbed a double in a 4–2 win.

With the qualifying group at the half-way stage, Hibs were sitting second, a point behind a Rangers team who were yet to concede a goal when they arrived at Easter Road the following Saturday. That soon changed as Hibs showed tremendous depth of fighting spirit in dumping the Glasgow outfit in a 3–2 win. Big John McNamee played a blinder in scoring one and setting up another for Scott, while McGraw also found the target. This result allowed Hibs to leapfrog their visitors into pole position with the tricky visit to Rugby Park due up next.

Manager Bob Shankly was a relatively mild-mannered individual who kept his thoughts largely to himself, but as subsequent programme notes would show he was anything but quiet in his views on the refereeing decisions by Mr Crawley of Glasgow at Rugby Park as ten-man Hibs lost 3–0. On a night when the gods were not looking favourably on Hibernian, McNamee was sent off in very controversial circumstances after just 35 minutes and then Scott was hauled down well inside the Killie area, only for the referee to award a free kick outside the box. Meanwhile, the home side were awarded two penalties. Both were saved by Thomson Allan, but sadly for Hibs, Queen followed up to score that second effort. Brian McIlroy chipped in with a double, and the final score of 3–0 to the home side made it very difficult for Hibs now to qualify.

Effectively, Hibs had to beat Stirling Albion at home in the final group match and then hope that Killie and Rangers would draw at Rugby Park. The Albion hurdle was overcome with a good 3–0 win, thanks to a double from McNamee and a solitary strike from Scott, but as the home fans celebrated the win, news filtered through that Rangers had beaten Killie 1–0 in Ayrshire to go through to the quarter-finals.

With the cup competition out of the way, Hibs started their long league campaign in fine style with a convincing 3–1 home win over neighbours Hearts, thanks to an early penalty conversion by Davis and further strikes from both Scott and Derby debutant Allan McGraw.

Astonishingly, this was Hibs' first home league win against Hearts in 14 years, but it was achieved in some style and Kerrigan's goal was very much a consolation for the visitors. Potentially, Hearts could have fielded three players who would one day end up wearing the green and white of

Hibernian, but only Chris Shevlane took part, while the other two, Roy Barry and Alan Gordon, sat out through injury.

Dunfermline provided the next challenge at East End Park and a Hibs victory there was also long overdue as supporters had to look all the way back to November 1958 for the last one. In a quite astonishing game, Hibs took first a 4–0 and then 5–2 lead before eventually winning 6–5 with almost the last kick of the ball. The Hibs heroes were McGraw (2), Scott (2), Cormack and Stevenson, while the Pars struck through Delaney (2), Hunter, Robertson and Ferguson. Although Jim Scott struck the all-important sixth goal, full credit must be awarded to McGraw for his part in the matter. Having been fouled on the stand touchline, he quickly got to his feet and took a smart free kick, releasing Scott to score.

Two games in and Hibs shared top spot equally with Celtic and Dundee when Partick Thistle arrived at Easter Road. Shankly had explained in his programme notes that while all present considered the Dunfermline game to be a real classic he would agree, but he had been working hard the following week to eradicate the mistakes which allowed five goals against. It clearly worked as a hapless Thistle went back to Glasgow having been soundly thrashed 7–0 by a rampant Hibs, two goals each from Cormack, Stein and Scott plus a single for Eric Stevenson raising the tally to a remarkable 16 in three matches. In the Thistle team that day was a young and very highly rated Arthur Duncan, who later gave many years of valuable service to Hibs when they beat several interested clubs down south for his signature.

The match programme for that Thistle game held a number of interesting adverts, some of which were for companies and services all too familiar at the time, but which seem now to have dropped off the face of the earth. The most interesting of all was perhaps one which ran the headline *Why not come into a secure industry?* – placed by the National Coal Board. How times change!

After the disappointment of not qualifying for the League Cup quarter-finals this was a most encouraging start to the championship and the good form continued through to the next game, which saw Hibs pip Motherwell 2–1 at Fir Park, with goals from Stein and McGraw countering a lone strike by Campbell for the Steelmen. As Celtic also won that weekend the two were now neck and neck at the top of the table, with the champions next up at Easter Road.

In the week leading up to that clash with Jock Stein's men, Hibs lost the services of John McNamee and Stan Vincent, the former being suspended by the SFA for 28 days and the latter joining Falkirk on a transfer. McNamee's absence would be a blow to Hibs while many felt sorry for Vincent. Although he had scored regularly in the reserves, his first-team opportunities had been limited by the excellent form of players such as Stein, Cormack and Scott.

Hibs had committed to playing a benefit match against Stirling Albion on the Tuesday before the Celtic game and this allowed Shankly to try a few things out in a 2–1 win, McGraw getting both goals. The match had been arranged to honour long-serving full back John McGuiness and a decent crowd boosted funds for the player.

With both sides in free-scoring mood leading up to the game, it would have been no surprise to the rest of Scottish football that they served up an eight-goal thriller, the visitors winning 5–3 in front of an incredible 43,256 spectators. Anyone not at the game might, upon hearing that McBride had scored four of the five Celtic goals, think it was a bit of a one-man show, but nothing could be further from the truth as the visitors looked strong in every position and, like their hosts, attempted to play good passing football at every opportunity. Celtic's other goal was scored by Chalmers, and the Hibs marksmen were McGraw, Davis (pen) and Cormack.

Having played well but lost against Celtic, the Hibees proceeded to do exactly the same in their next fixture at Rugby Park. A combination of poor finishing and defending, together with a stunning performance by Bobby Ferguson in the home goal, led to a 2–1 defeat, with Stein on target for Hibs. The team seemed to be missing the presence and influence of the suspended McNamee in the centre of defence as the goals at Kilmarnock were given away very easily.

When Dundee United visited Easter Road on 22 October they did so with their now customary sprinkling of Scandinavians in the team. Orjan Persson, Lennart Wing and Finn Dossing were all regular starters in manager Jerry Kerr's line-up, but it was Norwegian Finn Seamann who got among the goals in a 2–2 draw, Mitchell getting the other, while penalty king Joe Davis scored yet again from the spot and Cormack got the other for Hibs.

After a run of four wins out of four at the start of the campaign Hibs were now beginning to struggle. Things did not improve at Pittodrie, when Cormack's goal was merely a consolation as the Dons hit two through Winchester and Watt. It was not a happy first-team comeback for goalkeeper Willie Wilson, who was back between the sticks for the first time in eight months, but Hibs only had themselves to blame as they led but then made two sloppy defensive mistakes and travelled home pointless as a result.

The return from suspension of John McNamee was the talking point among the fans as they trooped down to Easter Road on the first Saturday of November 1966 and their journey was rewarded with a fine 3–1 home win against Falkirk, a Stein double and a Davis strike – not from the spot for a change – winning the points. Sadly, that was to prove only a brief respite from poor play as Hibs next went to Shawfield and crashed 5–1 to Clyde, when O'Rourke's goal was the only good thing achieved in 90 horrendous minutes of play.

A trip to Dens Park followed and although the performance was much better the outcome was the same – defeated 2–1, Davis hitting the Hibs goal from the spot. While November 1966 had started well for the green and whites, things soon turned sour and there was yet another loss when Rangers came to Easter Road and won 2–1, O'Rourke netting for the home side. Manager Bob Shankly was seething and vowed that December would see his side get back on track in the chase for a Fairs Cup place.

The month of December could not have started better for Hibs as they welcomed Stirling Albion to Easter Road and handed them a 6–0 thrashing, thanks to goals from Stevenson (2), O'Rourke, Cormack, McNamee and Davis. The Davis goal was a little different from the norm – he followed up a penalty save from goalkeeper Murray to crash the ball home from a few yards. That was actually Joe's second penalty in the game after he had uncharacteristically missed an earlier one.

It was St Mirren's turn to miss a penalty in the next game as Hibs travelled to Love Street, where the Buddies were starting their first game under new manager Alex Wright. That penalty miss cost them dear as a Cormack double and a successful penalty strike by Davis led to a 3–1 victory, Hamilton scoring for the home side.

On the road again the following Saturday, Hibs arrived in Ayr to face United at Somerset Park on a thoroughly miserable day when there was a howling gale and driving rain to contend with for the entire 90 minutes. The home side dug in well, but an early strike from Stevenson and a late one from O'Rourke sealed the win and boosted the chances of that European spot so keenly wanted by Shankly.

On Christmas Eve, Bobby Brown brought his St Johnstone side to Easter Road on the back of a pretty indifferent run of form, although their most recent tussle had earned a draw with Rangers and they could not be taken lightly. In what manager Shankly later described as one of the worst Hibs performances he had ever witnessed, Hibs went down heavily by 5–2, the Saints' goals coming from ex-Partick Thistle and Airdrie striker Gordon Whitelaw (3), full back Coburn and outside left Alex McDonald, who later went on to make a name for himself as a player with Rangers and as a manager with Hearts. Stevenson and O'Rourke scored the Hibs goals.

Hibs clearly needed to up their game. The wins over Stirling Albion, St Mirren and Ayr were all very well, but those three teams actually occupied the bottom three places in the league. St Johnstone were mid-table, as were Hibs' next opponents, Airdrie, who went down by a single

Davis penalty goal at an icy and very cold Broomfield. This game held further significance in that it marked the debut of Danish defender John Madsen, signed from Greenock Morton the day after John McNamee had been transferred from Hibs to Newcastle United.

It would be a busy start to 1967 for Hibs with no fewer than three games in six days, two of those away from home, always assuming the weather did not disrupt the fixture list. In fact, early January was relatively mild and so Hibs started their busy schedule with a January 2nd visit to Tynecastle, where they fought out a 0–0 draw, Davis missing a penalty which might have won the points. It was difficult to be critical of Joe as he was normally so very reliable in such situations, while a top-quality display from Cruickshank in the Hearts goal defied all other efforts from the visitors.

As the fans flocked down to Easter Road the following day – yes, two games in two days – there was a lot of talk as to whether Dunfermline, the visitors, would be involved in another thriller of the 11-goal variety fought out between the sides at East End Park the previous September, but it was not to be on this occasion. Although the goals were fewer in number it was still a highly entertaining match, and Dunfermline manager Willie Cunningham conceded that but for his goalkeeper, Bent Martin, being in such wonderful form the 2–0 Hibs win might have been a much wider margin. As it was, the keeper was helpless to keep out a couple of cracking efforts by Cormack and McGraw.

When Hibs travelled next to Firhill it was in the knowledge that although they had managed a 7–0 demolition of Partick Thistle earlier in the season they'd not won for some time when visiting the Glasgow side. Thankfully, their good form continued as goals from Stevenson (2), Davis (pen) and McGraw saw the Hibs cruise home 4–1, the Jags goal also being scored by a man in green, the unfortunate Alan Cousin firing past his own keeper. The fourth Hibs goal in that game, Stevenson's second, was Hibs' 50th of the season and only leaders Celtic boasted a superior number.

The good start to January continued with a hard-fought 2–1 home win over a strong Motherwell, Cormack and Davis (pen) countering a strike from the 'Well outside right Lindsay. Once again a top goalkeeping display stopped Hibs from scoring more as Peter McCloy pulled off several top-notch saves. The form of Eric Stevenson on the left wing was a joy to behold unless your name was George McNeill, who occupied that spot in the reserve team and was scoring goals for fun but could not dislodge Stevie from the first team. McNeill, who had lightning speed and once won the Powderhall Sprint, never did break into the first team and eventually departed the scene.

The cup draw paired Hibs with Brechin City at Easter Road, affording manager Shankly the opportunity to consider that his side might go the whole of January without defeat, but first they had the monumental task of visiting leaders Celtic at Parkhead. The Edinburgh men put up a great show but missed several early chances before eventually losing 2–0 and proving yet again that if you don't take your chances against the big Glasgow clubs you pay the price. Wallace and Chalmers inflicted the damage, with a goal each in front of more than 41,000 fans, and the travelling support was left to journey home wondering what might have happened had the early chances been taken. The absence of Colin Stein, out with a pulled muscle, did not help but there were no excuses from Shankly as he bowed to defeat by a better team on the day.

When Brechin arrived at Easter Road for a third-round clash it was being suggested by many that the outcome was a foregone conclusion. After all, they were a Second Division part-time outfit. But the cup is a great leveller and it's credit to the men from Glebe Park, and especially goalkeeper Sandy Henderson who among other things saved a Davis penalty, that Hibs won only 2–0, goals from Cormack and O'Rourke taking them through to a fourth-round clash against Berwick Rangers at Easter Road. Although the Hibs game slipped almost unnoticed into the pages of football history, the date – Saturday 28 January 1967 – did not, as the mighty Glasgow Rangers travelled to lowly Berwick, where the home side stunned the whole of Scotland by winning 1–0, Sammy Reid writing his name into the history books as the man who struck the winner. In goal for Berwick that day was Jock Wallace, whose future, ironically, took him to a highly successful managerial career at Ibrox.

League business stood between Hibs and their game against the giant-killers from Berwick, and February started with a cracking 3–1 home win over Kilmarnock, who were flying high in the league alongside Hibs and were separated from them only on goal average in the race for a European spot. The victory was all the sweeter as it was achieved without top scorer Peter Cormack, out with a throat infection. Goals from Scott (2, one a pen) and Stein secured the two points despite a counter from Morrison. This was the game in which Joe Davis decided to relinquish his role as penalty taker, as he had missed a few of late. Jim Scott took over.

John Madsen had settled really well into the centre of the Hibs defence and the big Dane had his best game to date when up against countryman Finn Dossing at Tannadice. Although Dossing scored for United he was kept very quiet otherwise as Hibs banged home three goals of their own, through O'Rourke, Cormack and Jim Scott (pen), to brush the Tangerines aside.

Cup fever hit the capital the following week as black and gold scarves appeared in significant numbers among an impressive crowd of 29,911 to see if Berwick could add another top-division scalp to that of Rangers. In a game which Hibs dominated throughout, only a Scott goal separated the teams at the end and Berwick travelled home happy that they had shown the people of Edinburgh that football outside the top league could be played to a decent standard.

An undefeated January had been made impossible following defeat at Parkhead, but Hibs had the chance to survive February without loss if they could overcome Aberdeen at Easter Road. Going into the game the Dons were sitting third on 32 points. Hibs were fourth on 30 points, and as the cup draw had paired them together at Easter Road this was the ideal rehearsal for both sides. In a rip-roaring game only a stunning strike from Cormack separated the teams as Hibs shut the points gap with their rivals and homed in on the much desired European place.

That February saw a couple of other quite significant occurrences at Easter Road. Firstly, Pat Stanton and Peter Cormack were named in the Scotland under-23 side scheduled to play England at St James' Park, Newcastle, and on the signing front the Easter Road club secured the full-time services of Peter Marinello, while calling up Willie McEwan from Uphall Saints. Both would go on to play for the first team, Marinello eventually departing south in a big-money transfer to Arsenal.

Hibs extended their unbeaten run to six games with their first fixture of March 1967 by beating Falkirk 2–0 at Brockville, thereby securing a double over the Bairns. It wasn't a great game and Hibs seemed to have one eye on the forthcoming cup clash with Aberdeen, but goals from O'Rourke and Stein settled the issue. Peter Cormack missed the game after damaging a thigh muscle in helping the under-23s defeat England 3–1, but the pain would no doubt have been compensated for by his scoring of one of those three goals.

Quarter-final day in the cup saw Aberdeen return to Easter Road vowing to do better than suffer another defeat similar to that of two weeks earlier. They were in those days a dour side when playing away from home and were very difficult to break down, so the pattern of play was quite predictable as they packed their defence in an attempt to stop the home side from scoring. Thanks to Eric Stevenson they failed in that mission as he slammed a cracking left-foot shot high into the net guarded by Bobby Clark. The Dons were then forced to up the pace and come at Hibs more, but the home defence coped really well until the dying moments when Jimmy Smith punished a moment of slackness to grab an equaliser that meant a replay at Pittodrie. It was a cruel blow to Shankly's side, who really deserved victory on the day.

Ahead of the cup replay, Hibs entertained Dundee at Easter Road knowing that the Fairs Cup spot they desired could only be won by increasing the points on the board in the league. Hibs started the day fifth behind Aberdeen and Clyde with Dundee in sixth. Hearts, incidentally, occupied a mediocre 11th place, well out of contention for a European spot. Dundee arrived without club legend and prolific goalscorer Andy Penman, but in their starting eleven were George Stewart and Jocky Scott, who would both go on to join Hibs in one capacity or another in future years. Centre forward Sammy Wilson scored for the visitors, but goals from Stevenson and Stanton gave Hibs both points.

The following Wednesday Hibs headed north for the replay with Aberdeen in the knowledge that should they get through they would meet Dundee United in the semi-final at neutral Dens Park. It was not to be, as the Dons turned on a display of attacking football and crushed Hibs 3–0 with goals from Winchester, Storrie and Munro. The cup dream was over for another year and so concentration turned to the league, the target being European qualification, but a very difficult tie at Ibrox meant better form would require to be shown.

Rangers were chasing Celtic hard in the title race and in no mood to give up that pursuit as they won a hard-fought game 1–0, thanks to a second-half goal from Alex Smith. Shankly adopted Aberdeen-like tactics in packing his defence for a tough away game, but it backfired and two vital points were dropped.

Clyde were next to arrive at Easter Road. Along with Hibs, Kilmarnock and Aberdeen they formed the pack behind the leading two of Celtic and Rangers. Harry Hood and Kenny Knox formed the Clyde spearhead, but it was inside left Ian Stewart who struck the goal to earn a 1–1 draw, McGraw heading home for a Hibs side that had suddenly found scoring goals to be a problem. The Shawfield men had an outstanding season and went on to finish in a European qualification spot, but were barred from playing in the competition because UEFA rules determined that each city could have only one club in their competition – a very sad situation for the Bully Wee.

At the bottom end of the division, both Falkirk and Stirling Albion looked doomed to relegation, but that did not stop the latter from securing only their second win of the season in defeating Hibs 1–0 at a muddy Annfield on 1 April. Hibs certainly looked the April fools as they missed chance after chance before a very late strike from Davy Grant sent the home supporters away with huge grins on their faces.

That European spot was beginning to look as though it might slip from their grasp as Hibs prepared for the visit of a St Mirren side languishing near the foot of the table. In an attempt to rediscover the scoring touch, manager Shankly shuffled the pack a little by introducing O'Rourke and Grant at the expense of Quinn and Scott, the latter dropping to a bench which in those days contained only one allowed substitute.

The changes had little effect as Hibs struggled to a 1–1 draw. Peter Kane scored early for the Buddies, while Hibs had to rely on Davis striking their goal from the penalty spot after Cormack had missed an earlier award and was reluctant to take the second. That result meant Hibs dropped to sixth place, with Kilmarnock, Clyde and Aberdeen ahead in the race for third place. The players that day may have been unhappy with the outcome, but one particular Hibs man found reason to smile as he had drawn rank outsider Foinavon in the Grand National and following a massive pile-up towards the end of the race that horse came sailing through from the back and went on to win at odds of 150/1.

Saturday 15 April 1967 is a day which will long be remembered in Scottish footballing folklore, as this was the day when Scotland became world champions! Well, perhaps not literally, but it was the day upon which World Cup holders England played their first game after having won that trophy on their own soil and Scotland were the ones invited along to take part in the celebrations. It would seem, however, that no one told Messrs Jim Baxter and Co. that this was meant to be England's day, and in a display of football of which later Scotland teams could only dream the visitors won 3–2. It wasn't just the victory that was celebrated north of the border but also the manner in which that victory was achieved, as Scotland at times toyed with their hosts and could so easily have won more convincingly.

Back in Edinburgh on that day, Hibs were entertaining an Ayr United side who were propping up the rest of the table with only eight points secured from 29 games and 74 goals conceded to date. Given the current form of Shankly's men there seemed little prospect of that goals-against column suffering much damage, but in fact the Hibees found their form again and hammered the hapless Ayrshire outfit 4–1 in a very one-sided game. Reinstated as penalty taker, Joe Davis struck two from the spot. Stein and McGraw chipped in with one each and former Killie stalwart Bertie Black struck for the visitors.

Ayr boss Ally McLeod, who would go on to make his very own unforgettable mark in Scottish football when he guided the national side to the World Cup finals, was quoted after the game as saying he felt Hibs, a team for which he had once starred, were a great footballing side who could become a major force in the game. He always was a sweet talker was Ally!

That victory over Ayr resulted in Hibs doing the double over the Somerset Park side, but the next opponents would not offer that oppor- tunity as Hibs headed to Muirton Park set upon avenging the shock 5–2 drubbing handed out by St Johnstone when they had visited Edinburgh back in December 1966. A double from McGraw secured a 2–1 win, with Whitelaw scoring for Saints. That was McGraw's third double of the season and took his tally to 15 overall, one behind top scorer Peter Cormack and level with full back Joe Davis.

The final game of the season offered Hibs the chance to finish in third place if they could overcome an Airdrie side they'd scraped past at Broomfield on the last day of 1966. Both Clyde and Aberdeen would have to lose in their games against Stirling Albion and Celtic respectively. Things did not go to plan at all as Airdrie won 2–0, while Clyde beat Stirling Albion and Aberdeen drew with Celtic. This had the effect of putting Clyde third, Aberdeen fourth on goal average and Hibs fifth, but as pointed out earlier Clyde were barred from competing in Europe because of the one club per city rule, and so Hibs qualified for the following season's Inter Cities Fairs Cup.

A disappointing ending to the season in terms of goals scored, games won and standard of football, and yet still a creditable finishing position in a league won by Celtic, who finished three points ahead of Rangers.

INDEX